Praise for *Banning the Bomb, Smashing the Patriarchy*

"This is a fascinating and much-needed dive into the ICAN movement and the history of anti-nuclear protest from the 1960s and 1970s to the present day. A key strength to this story is the centrality of the author to the events reported, offering readers a pleasing participant observation angle to the events." —**Kate Hudson**, general secretary for Campaign for Nuclear Disarmament and activist

"Written from the perspective of an activist who is intimately involved in the process of shifting the discourse of nuclear weapons from deterrence and national security to humanitarian considerations, this book is an excellent case study on how interests, identities, and norms can change—how these are socially constructed. The material from the author's interviews with diplomats and activists provide essential strategies for effective campaigning." —**Kristen P. Williams**, Clark University

"Likely to be a crucial source of feminist-inflected inspiration for activists working for global change, this book is also a must-read for scholars of the global nuclear order, international norm change, and transnational advocacy networks. At its heart is a forensic dissection of the Humanitarian Initiative and the negotiations resulting in the UN Treaty on the Prohibition of Nuclear Weapons. Ray Acheson tells a gripping story of why and how diplomats from non-nuclear states and anti-nuclear campaigners together achieved the seemingly impossible. Fighting back against the gendered, racialized, and colonial underpinnings of mainstream 'nuclearism' and 'nuclearspeak,' the power plays of nuclear states, and the stalled Nuclear Non-Proliferation Treaty negotiations, these dissident actors refocused attention on the devastating social and ecological impact of the stockpiling, use, and testing of nuclear weapons and reimagined the role of international law as a catalyst for change. Acheson sheds particular light on the role of the Nobel Prize–winning ICAN network in this process, illuminating its internal tensions as well as its impact. An engaging mix of scholarly erudition and insider knowledge, this book is also a powerful demonstration of the importance of an intersectional feminist approach to the struggle for a safer and more just world." —**Catherine Eschle**, senior lecturer in politics, University of Strathclyde, Glasgow

"In 2017, the vast majority of countries in the world negotiated and adopted the Treaty on the Prohibition of Nuclear Weapons in the face of stubborn recalcitrance on the part of the countries that possess these means of mass terrorism. Acheson provides a unique and detailed view of this effort to prohibit the most destructive of weapons. We learn here of power politics and decisions made by the high and mighty behind closed doors, of creative struggles and building coalitions of the not-so-powerful, of personalities and personal risks. Written from the dual perspective of an analyst who is among the best informed about the state of nuclear disarmament diplomacy, and from that of a committed activist, this book provides an understanding of why nuclear weapons exist, who they benefit, and how we can fight against their influence and change this risky state of affairs. Reading this, you will understand why abolishing nuclear weapons is, and has to be, part of the larger struggle for a peaceful, anti-capitalist, anti-racist, anti-colonial, and feminist future. In the face of the multiple ecological and social crises that we are confronting, such a future is the only one that offers any hope of justice and sustainability." —**M. V. Ramana**, professor and Simons Chair in Disarmament, Global and Human Security, School of Public Policy and Global Affairs, University of British Columbia

"Acheson, renowned feminist peace activist and winner of the Nuclear Free Future Award for 2020, exposes the deeply entrenched systems of exterminist thought and practice that have sustained nuclear weapons for more than seventy years and tells a compelling story of a new generation of transnational activists, diplomats, and academics working together to challenge and change the foundational narratives of the nuclear age about what is necessary, credible, and possible. In her vivid account of how the first global treaty banning nuclear weapons was achieved, she highlights key lessons and challenges about building a movement and a campaign informed by feminist, queer, Indigenous, antiracist, and post-colonial perspectives, on the importance of grounding politics in the real life worlds of people, and shares insights on how a radical feminist democratic politics can inform the many struggles for justice around the world." —**Zia Mian**, School of Public and International Affairs, Princeton University

"With an articulate and reasoned voice, Acheson deconstructs and debunks the dominant narrative of nuclear weapons as mandatory tools for national and international security and demonstrates the extreme and immediate humanitarian and environmental dangers of nuclear weapons across the globe. Set within the larger antinuclear movement since 1945, *Banning the Bomb, Smashing the Patriarchy* illuminates the magnificent efforts by activists, diplomats, and nuclear survivors to create an enormous international coalition, reframe the narrative of nuclear weapons, defy powerful nuclear-armed states, and establish an international treaty to prohibit nuclear weapons from the world. This book is essential reading for anyone who strives to find new ways to redefine power, confront the complex and seemingly impenetrable political and economic authority of some nations, and create social and political change for our own and future generations." —**Susan Southard**, author of *Nagasaki: Life After Nuclear War*

"Nuclear weapons are finally illegal! Acheson shines a ray of light and hope as she guides us through the talk, tensions, and collective efforts that have delivered our best chance to get rid of our worst weapons. This is an important record of a critical time and a timely call for us to redefine the limits of what is possible." —**Dave Sweeney**, leader of the Australian Conservation Foundation's Nuclear Free Campaign

"In *Banning the Bomb, Smashing the Patriarchy*, Acheson provides a detailed account of how a global ban on nuclear weapons was achieved. From inception to ratification, Acheson takes the reader on a journey showing the struggles, commitment, and dedication it took to make the impossible possible. Acheson's work provides much-needed hope for the future and tells the story of when millions around the world decided to speak with one voice in saying: No More Hiroshimas." —**Vincent Intondi**, author of *African Americans Against the Bomb*

"Acheson's fascinating book on how the nuclear ban treaty was won is essential reading for everyone. Bringing years of rigorous reporting on the UN and disarmament labyrinths, she explains and unpacks this exciting story with feminist understanding, wisdom, and subversive wit. Beautifully written and accessible, this is a brilliant achievement of academic analysis and feminist-humanitarian activism." —**Rebecca Johnson**, Acronym Institute for Disarmament Diplomacy

"*Banning the Bomb, Smashing the Patriarchy* is courageous and inspiring. Acheson beautifully articulates the complex background and evolution of the anti-nuclear movement. The success of the Treaty on the Prohibition of Nuclear Weapons is due to the laser-focus placed on the humanitarian perspective on nuclear weapons. As a second generation *Hibakusha*, I had an epiphany reading this book and it clarified my role in this far-reaching, collaborative social movement. I shed tears several times in appreciation for the many people who fought so hard for decades." —**Mitchie Takeuchi**, producer of *The Vow from Hiroshima*

"Acheson tells a profoundly important and timely story of movements and resistance, of protest and vision, of diplomats and activists who have committed to banning the bomb. This book will make you understand the urgent need to prohibit and eliminate nuclear weapons." —**Katrina vanden Heuvel**, editorial director and publisher, *The Nation*

"A comprehensive and engaging account of the history and efficacy of the fight to eliminate nuclear weapons. Acheson uses this careful case study to illuminate the nuanced and powerful process of collective action for social change. An inspiring read!" —**Deva Woodly**, associate professor of politics, The New School

"This timely book by Ray Acheson is an imperative read for all who are deeply concerned about the survival of life on earth. Summarizing the many attempts by wonderful people and organizations over the past seventy-five years to induce nuclear disarmament, a startlingly new initiative to ban nuclear weapons at the United Nations is about to reach fruition and Ray has been one of the leaders." —**Helen Caldicott**, founding president of Physicians for Social Responsibility; author of *Missile Envy*

"This vitally important book tells the story behind the Treaty on the Prohibition of Nuclear Weapons, one of the most significant international agreements of this still young century. Ray Acheson, an insider to the process, captures in rich personal detail the motivations, emotions, political obstacles, strategic maneuvering, and successes and failures of the activism and negotiations that brought the Treaty to reality. It's a story of relevance to all those who believe it's still possible to change the trajectory of human civilization in a positive direction and who want to see how it can be done in practice." —**Thomas Homer-Dixon**, author of *Commanding Hope* and *The Upside of Down*

"An urgent and inspiring case study on the power of grassroots organizing to shake up violent institutions at the highest level. Ray Acheson puts you in the front row of a tenacious network of abolitionists transforming the dangerous stalemate of disarmament diplomacy into genuine action. The road to nuclear disarmament has been blocked for decades. This fascinating and well-timed record of how that road was opened is essential reading for anyone who wants to live in a world free of nuclear weapons." —**Scott Ludlam**, former senator and deputy leader of the Australian Greens

"Seventy-five years after the first international effort to outlaw nuclear weapons, the United Nations has finally banned them. Ray Acheson tells the remarkable story of the activists and diplomats behind that achievement. And she reveals how sexism, racism, militarism, and colonialism have long been inextricably linked to the nuclear threat. We cannot eliminate one of these crimes against humanity, Acheson makes clear, without changing the mindset and the power structure responsible for them all." —**Eric Schlosser**, author of *Command and Control* and *Fast Food Nation*

BANNING THE BOMB, SMASHING THE PATRIARCHY

BANNING THE BOMB, SMASHING THE PATRIARCHY

RAY ACHESON

ROWMAN & LITTLEFIELD
Lanham • Boulder • New York • London

Published by Rowman & Littlefield
An imprint of The Rowman & Littlefield Publishing Group, Inc.
4501 Forbes Boulevard, Suite 200, Lanham, Maryland 20706
www.rowman.com

6 Tinworth Street, London SE11 5AL, United Kingdom

British Library Cataloguing in Publication Information Available

Library of Congress Cataloging-in-Publication Data

Names: Acheson, Ray, 1982- author.
Title: Banning the bomb, smashing the patriarchy / Ray Acheson.
Description: Lanham, Maryland : Rowman & Littlefield Publishing Group,
    2021. | Includes bibliographical references and index. | Summary: "After
    decades of campaigning work for nuclear abolition by activists, survivors,
    and diplomats, in 2017 the United Nations adopted the Treaty on the
    Prohibition of Nuclear Weapons. This book covers the story of their
    collective action-a story of courage and hope, as well as lessons learned,
    that will inform and inspire others working for social justice"—Provided
    by publisher.
Identifiers: LCCN 2020055336 (print) | LCCN 2020055337 (ebook) |
    ISBN 9781786614896 (cloth) | ISBN 9781786614919 (epub)
Subjects: LCSH: Treaty on the Prohibition of Nuclear Weapons (2017 July 7)
    | Nuclear arms control—Citizen participation.
Classification: LCC KZ5652 2017 .A333 2021 (print) | LCC KZ5652 2017
    (ebook) | DDC 341.7/34--dc23
LC record available at https://lccn.loc.gov/2020055336
LC ebook record available at https://lccn.loc.gov/2020055337

For the survivors and victims of nuclear weapons, past and present,

and for
Raf Wright Wilkinson
Amaya Jay Mahajan
Olivia Niamh Odat-Mulligan
Freyja Vallí Áslaugardóttir Robinson,
the next generation of activists

CONTENTS

ACKNOWLEDGMENTS

Like banning nuclear weapons, this book is a collective endeavor. As Nick Estes says, "All knowledge is produced through relationships."[1] Throughout my years as an activist I have learned so much from so many people, some of which is reflected in these pages. It would be impossible to acknowledge everyone, so I will focus on those that helped with this book specifically. Even that is a feat.

I have immense gratitude to those who encouraged me to undertake this project and who helped keep my spirits up even when I felt it perhaps wasn't going in the right direction or when I realized I had written several different books and tried to mash them together. Tim Wright, Dimity Hawkins, Catia Confortini, and Zia Mian were relentless with encouragement and moral support as well as reviewing drafts and giving feedback at various stages of this project. Thank you for always letting me bounce ideas off you and for not asking me too many times if I was finished yet. Thanks also go to my parents and brother for generally assuming it was normal that I would write a book and asking me all the time if I was finished yet.

So many people from different fields of work and experience were involved in the effort to ban the bomb. Limiting my framing just to those who were involved in the particular efforts described in this book, I still cannot acknowledge them all. So, instead I will just give a huge thanks to those who offered their generous insights and time for the creation of this book, in interviews, e-mails, or chats over coffee or at karaoke. They include Maratee Andamo, John Borrie, Loreta Castro, Maritza Chan, Simon Collard-Wexler, Michiel Combrink, Clare Conboy, Sharon Dolev, Katy Donnelly, George-Wilhelm Gallhofer, Vanessa Griffen, Leo Hoffman-Axthelm, Daniel Högsta, Michael Hurley,

Thomas Hajnozci, María Antonieta Jáquez Huacuja, Erin Hunt, Cesar Jaramillo, Alexander Kmentt, Fernando Luque, Tom Markram, Thea Katrin Mjelstad, Celine Nahory, Linnet Ngayu, Helena Nolan, Jackie O'Halloran, Joy Onyesoh, Zahid Rastram, Shorna-Kay Richards, Nick Ritchie, Gem Romuld, Larissa Schneider Calza, Michael Spies, Willem Staes, Carlos Umaña, Elayne Whyte Gómez, Cristian Wittmann, Reto Wollenmann, and Tim Wright, as well as others who did not wish to be named. Your work to ban nuclear weapons, and the reflections about your experiences that you shared with me, made this book what it is. Also, a special thanks to Helena Nolan for sending me hilarious videos about how to write a book.[2]

It turns out that once a book is written, it is time for it to be rewritten. Thank you to everyone who read certain chapters, or certain drafts, or many drafts, providing insights or suggesting edits, including Matthew Bolton, Cynthia Enloe, Alicia Godsberg, Dimity Hawkins, Nela Porobić Isaković, Madeleine Rees, Megan Mackenzie, Ashish Mahajan, Zia Mian, Allison Pytlak, MV Ramana, Emily Welty, and Tim Wright. Thanks also to those who didn't really read the book but nevertheless provided advice and support along the way including Laila Alodaat, Amy Brown, Maria Butler, Blaise Dupuy, Gem Romuld, Felicity Ruby, Kathleen Sullivan, and Jacqui True. (Gem did take the first manuscript on a 900km nuclear-ban-awareness-raising bicycle ride from Melbourne to Canberra but did not end up having time to read it. That must have been quite annoying for her.)

The first draft of this book was written in Australia while on a short sabbatical from work (thank you, WILPF). Much of this work took place on unceded Yuin land, which in early 2020 came under grave threat of fire; and many surrounding communities, land, and animals suffered immeasurably. I am grateful for my time in this special part of the world and am thankful that Gulaga protected so many of her neighbors from the fires.

Being in Australia gave me a chance to talk to several of the folks who started ICAN, meet many incredible activists who have spent their lives opposing radioactive violence in all its manifestations, and to live with some of my favorite people for varying periods of time. Thank you to Felicity Ruby, Gem Romuld and the Wonoona Ryders, and Jono Wilkinson and Tim Wright for the housing, and also to Dimity, Cath,

Zach, Gem, Alex, and the Friends of the Earth crew for many high jinks. Also, thanks to Scott Ludlam and Dave Sweeney for talking me out of the original title for this book. I wonder what you think of this one; I didn't ask your opinions this time. I'm not sure I really did the first time, either.

Many other people contributed in some way to this book, including through conversations, writings, and actions over time. As noted in the beginning, I can't possibly thank all of you, but I do want to mention in particular the survivors of nuclear weapon use and testing and their families and communities still struggling with those impacts. I have had the honor to learn from some of you over many years and profoundly appreciate your dedication to ending the nuclear age. Among others, thank you to Abacca Anjain-Maddison, Sue Coleman-Haseldine, Karina, Rose, and Yami Lester, and Setsuko Thurlow for your perseverance, hope, and inspiration, and for the generous time you have spent with ICAN activists from around the world.

In addition to the time I spent talking to people to craft this book, reading through endless documents was also a major part of the effort. I'm grateful to everyone who thinks and writes about nuclear weapons, but I just want to give a special shout-out to the University of Michigan for its excellent provision of the verbatim records of the Eighteen-Nation Committee on Disarmament—an indispensable resource for research on disarmament negotiations. And, of course, high fives to everyone who has ever worked at the Reaching Critical Will program of WILPF, for collecting, scanning, and posting online statements on disarmament for the past twenty years. Even though I was at these meetings, I could not have written this book as it is without this unbelievable archive.

Thanks, of course, also go to the team at Rowman & Littlefield, especially Catia Confortini, Shweta Singh, and Tiina Vaittinen for editing and Dhara Snowden, Rebecca Anastasi, and Brianna Westervelt for guiding me through this process and producing this book. It's been incredibly fortunate for me to learn from you about shaping this story in a coherent way and to have seasoned academics help guide an activist's attempt to weave history, empirical study, theory, analysis, ethnography, and personal commentary into something legible and useful.

This book, like the Treaty on the Prohibition of Nuclear Weapons or the International Campaign to Abolish Nuclear Weapons, is not a perfect thing. But like the treaty and the campaign, it is an honest

xviii   *Acknowledgments*

attempt to give something useful to the world. It is my hope that this book provides insights and hope to activists, diplomats, academics, and others who want to work together with other people to make stuff happen. At the end of the day, that is really the best we can do. Sometimes it works, a lot of the time it doesn't work, and sometimes it feels like we fail spectacularly. But we never really fail if we try. Doing the work, against the odds, in defiance of the naysayers, despite our own shortcomings; striving to improve ourselves and the world around us—this, in my opinion, is what makes life worth living.

FOREWORD

Setsuko Thurlow

I am a member of the family of *hibakusha*—those of us who, by some miraculous chance, survived the atomic bombings of Hiroshima and Nagasaki. I was just thirteen years old when the United States dropped the first atomic bomb, on my city, Hiroshima. I still vividly remember that day. At 8:15 a.m., I saw a blinding bluish-white flash from the window. I remember having the sensation of floating in the air.

That bright summer morning turned to dark twilight with smoke and debris rising in the mushroom cloud. I saw a mass of grotesque, ghostly figures—bleeding, burned, blackened, and swollen, with skin and flesh hanging from their bones. My beloved Hiroshima disappeared from the face of the earth, with about three hundred thousand men, women, and children indiscriminately killed instantly by *one* atomic bomb, and over time by the continuing effects of the radiation—still claiming the lives of survivors more than seven decades later.

Since that fateful day I have committed my life to bringing an end to the nuclear age. For seventy-five years, we *hibakusha* have worked for the total abolition of nuclear weapons. We have stood in solidarity with those harmed by the production and testing of these horrific weapons around the world—people whose lands and seas were irradiated, whose bodies were experimented upon, whose cultures were forever disrupted.

Each person who has died from nuclear weapons' use and development had a name. Each person was loved by someone.

We *hibakusha* are not victims. We have refused to wait for an immediate fiery end or the slow poisoning of our world. We have refused to sit idly in terror as the so-called great powers took us past nuclear dusk and brought us recklessly close to nuclear midnight. We rose up. We shared our stories of survival. We said: humanity and nuclear weapons cannot coexist.

The story told in this book is part of a collective effort to end nuclear weapons. It tells the story of activists around the world working with governments to refocus energy and attention on the humanitarian impacts of nuclear weapons. To remind the world what nuclear weapons do to our bodies, to the land and water. To outlaw these weapons, once and for all, as weapons of genocide and massive, indiscriminate harm; as weapons that threaten the lives of future generations.

On 7 July 2017, I was overwhelmed with joy when a great majority of the world's countries voted to adopt the Treaty on the Prohibition of Nuclear Weapons. Having witnessed humanity at its worst, I witnessed, that day, humanity at its best. I believe that this moment marked the beginning of the end of nuclear weapons.

Hibakusha were involved in the crafting of the treaty, in the work with diplomats and other government officials to turn our dreams into a reality. Our work for this treaty is in memory of all those we loved. Our work is to prevent the ultimate evil of nuclear violence.

The story told in this book is about people coming together, across the divide of diplomacy and activism, to achieve something of lasting importance. Our experiences, hopefully, offer lessons to those wanting to make positive change in the world; and at the same time, we in the antinuclear movement continue to learn from others who work for human rights, social justice, and ecological protection.

I am immensely grateful to Ray Acheson, for her scholarship, leadership, and activism. In recounting what we have achieved and how we achieved it, Ray provides courage and inspiration to change makers across the world who confront the many challenges that face us in our time.

For we are, as this book demonstrates, all part of the global movement for peace and nonviolence. This goes beyond the atomic bomb— our movement is about justice, equality, and care for all. The principles of feminism and antiracism expressed in this telling of the story to ban the bomb provide touchstones for what is necessary to guide us out of the dark night of nuclear terror.

As I said in Oslo in 2017 when accepting the Nobel Peace Prize on behalf of the International Campaign to Abolish Nuclear Weapons, "No matter what obstacles we face, we will keep moving and keep pushing and keep sharing this light with others. This is our passion and commitment for our one precious world to survive."

PREFACE

S ince the final manuscript of this book was submitted to print, incredible achievements have been made in advancing the legal and normative force of the UN Treaty on the Prohibition of Nuclear Weapons (TPNW).

On 24 October 2020, just over three years after it opened for signature, the Treaty reached the fifty national ratifications needed to become international law, setting the TPNW up to enter into force ninety days later: on 22 January 2021.[1]

This milestone was reached on United Nations Day, which marks the seventy-fifth anniversary of the UN Charter. The very first resolution of the UN General Assembly called for the elimination of nuclear weapons, making it particularly serendipitous that UN Day would see the ratification of a global agreement that prohibits these weapons. The year 2020 was also the seventy-fifth anniversary of the first nuclear weapon test explosion in New Mexico and the horrific atomic bombings of Hiroshima and Nagasaki, all conducted by the United States.

Securing these fifty ratifications, in the midst of a global pandemic, is a historic moment for nuclear abolition. The adoption of the TPNW and the achievement of its entry into force shows us what happens when those committed to multilateralism and transnational activism work together to change the world. As a result of these efforts, nuclear weapons will be unlawful to possess, develop, deploy, test, use, or even threaten to use for TPNW states parties. The treaty puts nuclear weapons on the same legal footing as biological and chemical weapons and as landmines and cluster munitions, and advances and reinforces international customary law and norms against nuclear weapons. Although much work remains to achieve the elimination of nuclear weapons, their prohibition is crucial.

The majority of the world's countries support the TPNW. One hundred and twenty-two states voted for its adoption in 2017; since then, governments from around the world, particularly Latin America and the Caribbean, Southeast Asia, the Pacific, and Africa, have signed and ratified the treaty. Some critics say that the treaty is irrelevant because none of the countries that have joined so far possess nuclear bombs. But that doesn't matter right now. Over time, as described in this book, the treaty will have a normative impact on the behavior of other countries, regardless of whether they join, and on financial institutions and other national and local actors. The changes that the nuclear ban brings to law, politics, and economics will lead us to nuclear disarmament.

Already, more than sixteen hundred elected officials in countries that have not yet joined the TPNW have pledged to work to get their governments on board.[2] Cities and towns around the world have adopted resolutions encouraging their governments to join the treaty, including capitals in nuclear-armed states such as Paris and Washington, D.C.[3] Financial institutions have started divesting from nuclear weapons-producing companies, including within countries that have not yet joined the treaty. Public support is also already behind the ban. Public opinion polls show that 79 percent of Australians, 79 percent of Swedes, 78 percent of Norwegians, 75 percent of Japanese, 84 percent of Finns, 70 percent of Italians, 68 of Germans, 67 percent of French, and 65 percent of U.S. citizens support their government joining the TPNW.[4]

The nuclear-armed states know this—which is why they are panicking. As the Associated Press reported in October 2020, the U.S. government sent a letter to countries that ratified the treaty informing them that they have made a "strategic error" and "should withdraw" their instruments of ratification or accession.[5] This is yet another indication that nuclear-weapon possessors and supporters know full well that the TPNW threatens their unlawful policies and practices.

This is what social movements do. They challenge the narratives and behavior of those deemed to be in positions of power, shaking the establishment from the ground up. We can see this all around us, in every aspect of our societies. The hope for nuclear abolition and the resilience of the antinuclear movement lies in the efforts of all activists

for social justice. Everyone who is demanding disarmament and abolition of police forces and prisons; calling for a redirection of military
spending toward collective care; envisioning a more equitable, just,
and peaceful world order—all of their efforts are complementary to the
efforts for nuclear abolition. Whether deliberate or not, our work for
peace, social and economic justice, decolonization, and environmental
protection is entangled. The world we seek to build—a world of solidarity, health, and well-being across peoples and our shared planet—is not
compatible with a world with nuclear weapons viciously safeguarded by
our so-called leaders.

As past social movements have taught us, change doesn't happen
in an instant—it is iterative, contested, and must be constantly defended
and built upon. The work must continue. "Nuclear abolitionists everywhere can be incredibly encouraged and empowered by this new legal
status" of the TPNW, said Hiroshima survivor Setsuko Thurlow at an
event marking the final few ratifications for the treaty. We have a long
path to achieve the elimination of nuclear weapons, she noted, but
"with the Treaty on the Prohibition of Nuclear Weapons, we can be
certain that that beautiful day will dawn."

INTRODUCTION

Nuclear weapons have a history and a legacy of anguish, pain, and suffering. From the horror experienced by people in Hiroshima and Nagasaki in 1945, to the torment of Indigenous populations whose lands and waters nuclear weapons were tested upon in the ensuing decades, to the fear of the entire world held in the grip of possible nuclear annihilation, nuclear weapons have scarred our global community. Every minute since July 1945, when the United States tested its first nuclear weapon in New Mexico, we have been living under the threat of massive nuclear violence. Nuclear weapons are designed to incinerate cities, to burn and irradiate human bodies, to destroy everything we have built and that we love. Nuclear weapons are perhaps the ultimate symbol of the extreme edge of human power and hubris—the ability to devastate the entire planet.

The potential use of nuclear weapons is never far away. Although U.S. presidential threats of unleashing "fire and fury like the world has never seen"[1] have put the specter of nuclear war back in the headlines, it was never off the table. U.S. nuclear policy doctrines, as well as those of the other eight nuclear-armed states—China, France, India, Israel, North Korea, Pakistan, Russia, and the United Kingdom—all envision the possible use of nuclear weapons.[2] Attempts to convince or cajole those that possess nuclear weapons to work seriously for disarmament have been unsuccessful. Although the United States and Russia dismantled thousands of warheads after the Cold War, they and the other nuclear-armed states have continued to invest billions since that period in "modernizing" and extending the lives of their nuclear arsenals.[3] These countries have broken disarmament commitments they made to each other and to the rest of the world.[4] The situation has been untenable for

1

years, but those without nuclear weapons felt largely unable to change it—until recently.

From about 2010 to 2017, a new initiative emerged. Activism and advocacy, combined with diplomatic action on the international stage, achieved a renewed discourse on the humanitarian impacts of nuclear weapons, and then a legal ban on the bomb. On 7 July 2017 at the United Nations, 122 governments voted for adoption of the Treaty on the Prohibition of Nuclear Weapons, which outlaws the development, testing, production, manufacture, acquisition, possession, stockpiling, stationing, deployment, transfer, use, or threat of use of nuclear weapons, or assisting with any of these prohibited activities. You cannot do anything with nuclear weapons under this treaty—except get rid of them. The International Campaign to Abolish Nuclear Weapons (ICAN), the coalition of activist groups that helped achieve this treaty, was awarded the Nobel Peace Prize in December that year.[5]

You might not have heard about the ban, though media did cover it at the time—albeit sparsely, and with skepticism. The skepticism was greatly encouraged by the countries that possess nuclear weapons. Those countries did not participate in the negotiations. Nor did the countries that claim security from U.S. nuclear weapons—countries that rely on the fantasy of "nuclear deterrence" for their perceived protection (those of the North Atlantic Treaty Organization, as well as Australia, Japan, and South Korea).

Meanwhile, the governments supporting the ban were largely those of the global south. Most of the countries in Africa, Latin America and the Caribbean, the Pacific, and Southeast Asia participated actively in this initiative. A cross-regional "core group" of countries, consisting of Austria, Brazil, Ireland, Mexico, Nigeria, and South Africa, together with a number of others such as Costa Rica, Jamaica, New Zealand, and Thailand, drove the process forward despite the opposition to it. They were compelled to do so by a simple logic, one that seems lost to policy makers in nuclear-armed states: nuclear weapons have catastrophic humanitarian and environmental consequences and must never be used again. The only way to ensure that they are never used again is to eliminate them.

These countries were not driven just by logic, however. Each had, to varying degrees, norms related to multilateralism and to humanitarian disarmament embedded in their national or governmental identities. Most of these countries had led in other disarmament processes, had been strong advocates for the treaties banning landmines and cluster munitions, and had strongly opposed nuclear weapons throughout the atomic age. A few did not have such a history but did have a number of dedicated people operating within their government systems that inspired deeper engagement and even leadership when it came to the nuclear ban.

THIS STORY

The story of banning the bomb belongs to these diplomats, along with activists who brought a legacy of protest and a vision for an alternative future to the international table. This is, ultimately, a story of resistance and of movement building. It is a story of activists from around the world working with diplomats in nuclear weapon-free countries to say, "¡Ya basta!," enough is enough, to the nuclear-armed governments. But this movement did not just reject what the nuclear-armed were offering. It consciously, creatively, and collectively sought to build something new—to generate and promote ideas, arguments, and frameworks that would disrupt mainstream myths and narratives, institute new international norms and laws, and ultimately put in place key mechanisms for the abolition of nuclear weapons.

This is a story about human processes as much as political processes. It is a story about how individual people came together, across borders, occupations, experiences, and identities, to challenge power. In order to do so, they had to work within international and domestic institutions and processes, and in some cases, had to resist and overcome inertia, working to achieve change from without and within, and to adapt these institutions to ensure their resilience against pressure. This meant building up trust among the individuals involved, diplomats and activists alike. It meant building a sense of capacity among those who had to convince others to help change policies and positions and building a sense of hope that these efforts were not futile—that collectively we could have an impact against the interests of some of the most militarily and economically intimidating governments in the world. This is a story of changing discourses and ideas, changing conceptions of what is credible, possible, and from where power or change can be derived.

This particular version of this story is written by an activist within one of the partner organizations of ICAN. I represented my organization, the Women's International League for Peace and Freedom (WILPF), on ICAN's International Steering Group. WILPF is an antiwar feminist peace organization, founded in 1915 during World War I by women from around the world. ICAN's international steering group is the policy-making body of the campaign. It is made up of a group of ten activist organizations, and it works closely with ICAN's staff team to lead the campaign, which in turn is made up of hundreds of other activist groups. Representing WILPF in this body gave me the opportunity to promote an intersectional feminist vision of both process and product—to bring theories and experiences of feminist and queer activists to the work of ICAN. I had been an antinuclear activist for more than a decade by the time I joined ICAN's leadership, and this new position gave me the chance to explore and struggle with questions of movement building, diversity, and critical theories of process and change.

This book is intended to offer a firsthand account of how the treaty banning nuclear weapons came to be. This is not necessarily the only story that can be told about this process. It is not a definitive historical account of antinuclear activism; it is not even a definitive account of ICAN. Many people were involved in the process to ban the bomb, and none of us has a completely comprehensive view of it all. It is, however, a story from a feminist, antimilitarist disarmament advocate who worked on this particular project with others over many years—activists, diplomats, academics, and others at the United Nations and in capitals around the world.

Despite the admirable work of many people, this is a story told without individual attribution. This is in large part because the diplomats who were part of this process cannot, for internal governmental purposes, be identified. Although not attributing responsibility to individual diplomats is in many ways a shame—as they should be recognized for their commitment and passion to solving the problem of nuclear weapons—it also is an opportunity to write a story about collective action rather than individual achievements. Without being able to attribute responsibility or credit to individual diplomats, it seemed unjust to do it for activists. Therefore, no individuals are identified in this story, except where this book quotes from work they have published in the public domain.

This is a story about all of these people, from different experiences, countries, and stations, working together to make a change against all odds. It is an example of what international or transnational activism can achieve. This campaign took resources—human and financial—and so I certainly do not mean to suggest that this is a simple or unprivileged undertaking. But it does offer a glimpse of how activists can build a campaign in coordination with governmental allies who give a damn, and how such a campaign can gain traction over time with relentless work that mostly does not offer much in the way of publicity or recognition.

This story is one of passion and creativity. In this work, we faced many challenges—some internal to ICAN as an activist collective, some in relation to the broader antinuclear movement, and some with the powerful governments that we confronted through our actions. ICAN was not a perfect campaign, nor is it a monolith of thought and perspective. We struggled with each other, with issues of diversity, class, access, power, and ego, with some of the age-old challenges of organizing and activism. These struggles are described in this book—but so are the joys, victories, and camaraderie that come with any good activist campaign. We didn't always know what we were doing; sometimes we did the wrong thing—as individuals or as a collective—but at the end of the day we built something together, not just among ourselves but with a cadre of diplomats, government officials, and others who were just as keen as we were to change the world. This story, hopefully, should demonstrate how, as a group of people, we worked to reinvigorate a social movement, and how it may be possible to shake things up, disrupt the status quo, and make meaningful change in a world that can feel oppressive and overwhelming in its slavishness to the militaristic capitalist order.

It is a story of disrupting dominant narratives about nuclear weapons and positing alternatives in return. This process draws on the experiences of survivors of nuclear weapon use, testing, and development, using their lived reality, rather than myths of "deterrence doctrine" and "strategic security," as the basis for action. It's a story that learns from those who have fought against privilege and patriarchy—feminist, queer,

Indigenous, antiracist, and environmental activists—in order to strategically and effectively undermine traditional frameworks of security and power and offer a picture of another world in which humanitarian principles and human rights are the guiding norms for government policies, rather than violence and domination. It's a story about experiencing and, for the most part, overcoming fierce pushback from those who want to maintain the status quo, including political pressure and economic threats.

Ultimately, the Treaty on the Prohibition of Nuclear Weapons is a feat of collective action by people who came together to do something that had not been tried before. Like anything that people create, it has its imperfections. It has not solved all problems related to nuclear weapons: as of 2020, nearly fourteen thousand still exist in the arsenals of nine governments.[6] Tensions and threats among those countries are on the rise. Billions of dollars a year are being spent to "modernize" and extend the lifetimes of these weapons for future generations.[7] Yet despite the investments, risks, and threats associated with nuclear weapons, the nuclear ban treaty—and the campaign to achieve it—gives a glimpse of what is possible in this world, including that it is possible to do something all of the "great powers" are trying to prevent you from doing. Resistance may take time to have an effect, but it makes a difference.

SHAPE OF THE STORY

Chapter 1 of this book provides context to the problem of nuclear weapons, dissecting the traditional security, deterrence-based narrative about nuclear weapons through the lens of alternative perspectives about the role of the bomb in international relations. It looks closely at the opposition to nuclear disarmament, examining the racist, patriarchal, and capitalist critiques of banning nuclear weapons that the nuclear-armed states and some of their supporters have employed. It exposes the ways in which those who claim security from nuclear weapons have framed their arguments, and how challenging these perspectives also works in support of broader movements for social justice.

Chapter 2 includes a brief overview of global activism against the bomb, international efforts for nuclear disarmament, and the ways in which those governments possessing nuclear weapons have managed to hold onto these immensely destructive weapons for the past seventy years. It gives history as well as analysis of these efforts and zooms in on the post-Cold War era, looking at what happened to the antinuclear movement and what challenges we faced at the beginning of the ban process.

Chapter 3 explains how diplomats and activists began agitating for particular change in 2010. It sets out the strategy of shifting the nuclear weapon discourse from one of deterrence and abstract security policy to one that focuses on the humanitarian consequences of nuclear weapons—a process that came to be known as the "humanitarian initiative." This chapter describes some of the diplomatic processes that nonnuclear-armed states tried to enact for nuclear disarmament and how these led certain governments to begin a series of international conferences looking at humanitarian impacts of nuclear weapons and certain activists to begin articulating the case for a treaty banning nuclear weapons.

Chapter 4 turns to the human and institutional processes that enabled the growth of a collective movement to ban nuclear weapons. It explores how ICAN activists worked to build interest and capacity with government officials and other partners to build capacity and willingness for the humanitarian initiative and to ban nuclear weapons.

Chapter 5 examines how activists revitalized and built a transnational network of campaigners working to challenge the status quo, confront power, build alternative narratives around nuclear weapons, engage a new generation of activists and diplomats, and learn from those who had come before—from those who participated in the processes to ban landmines and cluster munitions. This chapter discusses some of the struggles ICAN faced and highlights some of its key successes.

Chapter 6 explores how diplomats and activists brought the theory of the nuclear ban treaty into the UN. It shows the importance of the humanitarian initiative in making an intellectual and political case for banning the bomb. It also reveals some of the ways in which the nuclear-armed and their allies started to push back against this effort.

Chapter 7 outlines the growing momentum for a nuclear ban treaty at international diplomatic meetings. It exposes some of the pressure tactics that nuclear-armed states and their proxies used to prevent the development of a ban on nuclear weapons. Dipping back into the weeds of UN processes, it examines moments when their hostile opposition to the nuclear ban actually fostered more support for this treaty—the arrogance, racism, and patriarchy of those supporting nuclear weapons drew increasing numbers of governments toward the ban rather than pushed them away from it.

Chapter 8 walks through the actual treaty negotiations, outlining some of the challenges and successes with the process and the substance of these negotiations. It highlights contributions from activists, survivors, and others who brought key perspectives to the negotiations and discusses key points of the treaty's text.

Chapter 9 describes the process of the negotiations, looking at how deliberations were structured, who was engaged, the key challenges, the dynamics of gender and regional diversity, and how all of the various actors managed their relationships.

The conclusion then sets out where we go from here. It reviews where humanitarian initiatives and the negotiation of the nuclear ban treaty have taken us, and where we need to take it next. It discusses the relationship of this process to other contemporary movements for social justice and offers hope for social change amid what might sometimes feel like a hopeless situation.

My hope is that this book is useful to anyone—activist, diplomat, academic, or anyone in the general public—who cares about the world and wants to work with others to change it for the better. I hope it offers some inspiration about the power of collective action against a seemingly dominant force and the importance of relentless activism even when it seems like nothing you can do will make a difference. The thing about this work, I believe, is that even if you cannot "win," even if you believe your goal to be entirely elusive, you are required to try. Life is in the struggle, argued philosopher Albert Camus.[8] It is our duty to work for a better world, whether or not we are sure we can achieve it. Sometimes, we even surprise ourselves.

1

"TERMINALLY UNSERIOUS"

Ideologies and Oppressions of Nuclear Weapons

Banning the bomb was not an idea born in the twenty-first century. It is rooted in activist and diplomatic efforts since 1945 to confront the handful of governments that have invested billions of dollars in these objects of mass destruction and in the mythologies that are used to justify their existence. To understand how and why those of us working on this project sought a treaty prohibiting nuclear weapons, it is important to understand the systems of thought and practice that have sustained nuclear weapons for more than seventy years.

We have all been subjected to the power of entrenched narratives on this subject, as if discourses about "nuclear deterrence" and "strategic stability" provide the only reasonable way to think about nuclear weapons. Abolishing the bomb requires us to consider alternatives to what we have been force-fed for decades. This means approaching issues not from traditional international relations theory but by invoking and learning from feminist, queer, Indigenous, antiracist, and postcolonial perspectives, in order to expand our understanding of the realities of nuclear weapons and the possibilities for eliminating them. It means bringing the lessons of practice and process from these sites of struggle to bear on nuclear weapon policy and process in order to challenge what is normative and credible and generate a sense of capacity among those who genuinely want to achieve nuclear disarmament.

This chapter offers an explanation of why nuclear weapons have persisted for so long and the frameworks of thought and resistance that can be useful for mounting a successful challenge to these weapons. It sets up some of the analysis that will be used throughout this book to describe and explain both the substance (the why) and the process (the how) of banning nuclear weapons. And it seeks to make the case that those supporting and defending the continued existence and possession of nuclear weapons are the ones suffering from a serious lack of credibility and rationality, not those of us who want to eliminate this weapon of mass destruction.

WHAT ARE NUCLEAR WEAPONS, AND WHY DO SOME GOVERNMENTS WANT THEM?

Nuclear weapons are material objects. They are composed of radioactive materials such as uranium or plutonium. They are explosive devices that use fission or fusion reactions to unleash destructive force. They are designed and built to kill people through blast, fire, and radiation. They can only be used to slaughter civilians indiscriminately, to destroy entire cities, to disrupt economies and societies, and—if multiple such weapons are used—to exacerbate climate change and cause global famine. If enough were used at one time, they would obliterate the planet.

But nuclear weapons are not treated in the mainstream, "credible" discourse as weapons of massive violence. Instead, they are treated, especially by those governments that possess them, as objects that deter conflict, preserve peace, and ensure security and stability. According to this discourse, nuclear weapons are meant not to be used but to act as a "deterrent" to other countries that might seek to wage a war or use a nuclear weapon. In the 1960s, Thomas Schelling argued that military strategy should be based on the ability to coerce, intimidate, and deter.[1] From this developed the doctrine of mutually assured destruction (MAD): the supposition that if each party's nuclear forces are sufficient to destroy the other's, then neither would dare to use nuclear weapons.[2] "War is Peace. Freedom is Slavery. Ignorance is Strength." So goes the slogan of The Party in George Orwell's novel *Nineteen Eighty-Four*.[3] "Nuclear weapons prevent war." So goes the "realist" discourse in academia and international politics. Kenneth Waltz famously argued in favor of the spread of nuclear weapons, saying, "more may be better."[4] As feminist scholar Carol Cohn found in the 1980s, "defense intellectuals" built their careers formulating systems to explain "the necessity of having nuclear destructive capability" and "why it is not safe to live without nuclear weapons."[5] They insist on talking about nuclear weapons in the abstract, as magical tools that keep us safe and maintain stability in the world. Cohn describes the "elaborate use of abstraction and euphemism" that refused to "touch the realities of nuclear holocaust that lay behind the words," including terms such as clean bombs, damage limitation weapons, and surgically clean strikes.[6] From the perspective of those deploying this language and constructing theories of nuclear strategy and deterrence, nuclear disarmament is not realistic or rational—it would undermine "strategic stability," put the world at risk of war with conventional weapons, and undermine the national security of the countries "giving up" the bomb.

All of the nuclear-armed states share this perspective and discourse. They do not see nuclear weapons as inherently unacceptable, as the UK government has said openly, arguing that nuclear weapons "have helped to guarantee our security, and that of all allies, for decades."[7] The United Kingdom does not even refer to its nuclear weapons as weapons at all—they call them their "nuclear deterrents." France does this, too, and argues, "Since it may only be used in extreme circumstances of self-defense, the French deterrent does not violate international law in any way."[8] The United States claims to protect many countries with its nuclear weapons—those that are members of the North Atlantic Treaty Organization, as well as Australia, Japan, and South Korea. India and Pakistan claim they need nuclear weapons to prevent each other from attacking. North Korea says it has acquired nuclear weapons to prevent invasion and occupation by the United States.

These governments all claim nuclear weapons are necessary for their national security. They argue that complete nuclear disarmament is not possible or rational. The United Kingdom, for example, says, "We do not yet have the right political and security conditions for those without nuclear weapons to feel no need to acquire them, nor for those who do have them to no longer feel the need to keep them. Nor is it possible to identify a timeframe for those conditions."[9] The U.S. government even has an official tagline for this position: Creating the Environment for Nuclear Disarmament. It demands a focus on "the underlying security concerns that led to their [nuclear weapons'] production in the first place"—as if nuclear weapons were created by some higher being and bestowed upon certain chosen governments, rather than having been created by the United States first and foremost to incinerate civilians during World War II. In advocating for the creation of this "environment," the U.S. government has asserted that every commitment it has made since the dawn of the atomic age is "from a different time and a different security environment than we currently face" and thus "to make progress we need to look forward, not backwards—we must not fixate on historical language that is out of date and out of step with the current prevailing security environment."[10]

Although the U.S. government posits this approach as new and innovative, this is, in fact, an age-old argument. In 1956, then-UN Secretary-General Dag Hammarskjöld had to refute this type of rhetoric. "On the one hand . . . disarmament is not likely to come about in an efficient, effective way short of further improvement in the international situation," he acknowledged. "On the other hand, I do not think any single policy move will contribute more to an improvement in the international atmosphere than an agreement on even the most modest step in the direction of disarmament."[11] Yet nuclear-armed states continue to rely on this premise to delay disarmament indefinitely. The United States' focus on creating an "environment" conducive to nuclear disarmament is not about what the United States can do for nuclear disarmament but what the rest of the world can do for the United States in order to make it, as the most heavily militarized country in the world, feel "safer."

The U.S. government is not alone in staking out this position. Russia has said that those calling for immediate progress on nuclear disarmament are "radical dreamers" who have "shot off to some other planet or outer space."[12] Officials of all of the nuclear-armed states have said, in various ways, that those desiring disarmament do not understand how to protect their people, that their security interests do not matter, or do not exist at all. Initiatives toward nuclear abolition are illegitimate, naive, or, my personal favorite, "terminally unserious."[13]

But who, really, is terminally unserious about nuclear weapons? Those who believe we can live with the atomic bomb forever without incident, or those who see their continued possession and proliferation as a catastrophe waiting to happen—and as a catastrophe that has *already* happened?

WHY DO OTHERS REJECT NUCLEAR WEAPONS?

The majority of states, international organizations, and activist groups have articulated clearly that nuclear weapons do not provide security and that the consequences of their use are wholly unacceptable. They argue that the theory of nuclear deterrence is dangerous. Asserting that nuclear weapons are good for some is the same as arguing that they are good for all, as an Irish ambassador once said.[14] They either provide security, or they don't. Their consequences are either acceptable or unacceptable. It is illogical to claim that nuclear weapons are legitimate tools of security for some states but not for others.

Claims about the necessity of "creating the conditions for nuclear disarmament" ensure that actual disarmament is perpetually punted down the road to some unknown, possibly unattainable future state of affairs in which the world is at "peace" and security is guaranteed through some other imagined means. The majority of governments consider the prohibition and elimination of nuclear weapons to be a key step in the pursuit of peace, global justice, and security for all. Most countries have already put this approach into practice. Some have even relinquished nuclear weapons, recognizing the insecurity they would bring to their own countries and to the world. Sweden, for example, has explained that it discontinued its nuclear weapons research and development program in the 1960s because it believed that nuclear abolition was the safest option both for its people and for the rest of the world.[15]

So why is there such a stark difference in the way governments and people view nuclear weapons? Why is nuclear deterrence theory treated as undeniable truth by mainstream international relations and political science scholars, particularly in the Western academy? Is this theory actually valid, or is it providing an intellectual cover for something much deeper and darker?

Some who espouse the theory cite the lack of use of nuclear weapons as an act of war since 1945 as evidence of the validity of nuclear deterrence. Others claim that nuclear weapons "ended" the Second World War.[16] However, many counterarguments can be used to damage the credibility of the theory. First, evidence exists of hundreds of near-uses of nuclear weapons.[17] Second, scholars and politicians have pointed to a range of developments and factors that contributed to both the end of the Second World War and to the lack of a direct war between the United States and Soviet Union.[18] The fact that so few countries have sought to obtain nuclear weapons is also a persuasive argument against the idea that nuclear deterrence provides an ultimate security guarantee: instead, it shows that most of the world's governments see nuclear deterrence as a toxic theory that puts all of us at risk.

Even inside the nuclear-armed states, opinions about the rationality of nuclear deterrence plans and policies vary widely. U.S. whistleblower Daniel Ellsberg's latest book, *The Doomsday Machine: Confessions of a Nuclear War Planner*, provides an inside view of what he calls the "institutionalized madness"[19] of the possession of nuclear weapons and preparations for their use. Compiling evidence from his time as an analyst with the Research and Development Corporation and a consultant to the Department of Defense and the White House, Ellsberg catalogs a number of shocking policies and practices that have held the world at the brink of annihilation throughout the atomic age.

The Doomsday Machine, as Ellsberg calls the nuclear weapon complex, is "a very expensive system of men, machines, electronics, communications, institutions, plans, training, discipline, practices, and doctrine." This system, he explains, could "with unknowable but possibly high probability bring about the global destruction of civilization and of nearly all human life on earth."[20] He describes the seven decades of U.S. nuclear war planning as "immoral," "insane," and "a chronicle of human madness."[21] (Note that the quotation of these terms here is not meant to perpetuate a stigma on mental health but to convey Ellsberg's argument, in his own words, that his experience and perception of the nuclear war system is of a system not based in rationality or sound judgment. It is also interesting to see these terms applied to the male-dominated sphere of nuclear war planning, as these are terms that often have gendered connotations—as will be explored later, concepts of irrationality, hysteria, and disconnection from reality are typically deployed against women to prove their incapacity or irrelevancy for political life.) Any social system, Ellsberg writes, that creates and maintains the apparatus and system to destroy the world "*is in its core aspects mad.*"[22]

It is profound to have someone so intimately familiar with the U.S. nuclear machine staking these claims against the policies and practices that he helped shape and maintain. But Ellsberg is certainly not the first to observe the problems inherent in existing nuclear weapon plans and policies. In 1976, for example, Swedish diplomat Alva Myrdal published a blistering review of the state of nuclear disarmament efforts thus far. Among her conclusions was the assertion that the nuclear arms race "is intellectually unreasonable and morally unsound."[23] The buildup of nuclear arsenals and the nuclear establishment, she argued, "has gone, and is going, right against what would be rational from the point of view of the interests of every nation. . . . It is beyond all reason."[24] Suggesting that "there are forces which irrationally drive the governments forward as participants in the international arms race,"[25] she argued that their lack of concern or attention to nuclear danger

> is the result not only of our opportunistic inclination to turn our attention away from disagreeable thoughts, but also of a reckless and systematic propaganda by the vested interests and their obedient servants among politicians, governments, military and foreign policy bureaucracies, and even captive scientists. The mass media serve as megaphones for this propaganda while blacking out our knowledge of facts and rational reasoning.[26]

Yet, there is a risk in arguing that those who design and implement the tools and policies for nuclear war are mad, that they have a psychological affliction. As Ellsberg carefully articulates, "The creation, maintenance, and political threat-use of these monstrous machines has been directed and accomplished by humans pretty much the way we think of them: more or less ordinary people, neither better nor worse than the rest of us, *not* monsters in either a clinical or mythic sense."[27]

Ellsberg was not, of course, the first to make these arguments. Already in 1987, Carol Cohn's "close encounter with nuclear strategic analysis" in the United States led to illuminating (and amusing) articles in *Signs* and the *Bulletin of the Atomic Scientists* about the discourse of those in charge of nuclear war planning.[28] Writing about her experience as a college teacher attending a workshop on nuclear weapons, doctrines, and arms control taught by "distinguished defense intellectuals," Cohn examines the language employed by those discussing nuclear war strategy and the indoctrination of these "likeable and admirable men" who casually and regularly "blew up the world while standing and chatting over the coffee pot."[29]

Although Cohn's work was based on shorter-term participant observation, anthropologist Hugh Gusterson spent years conducting an ethnographic study at one of the main U.S. nuclear weapon laboratories, investigating how nuclear weapon scientists justify and even moralize their work. He found that through ritualized secrecy, institutional bonding, and disciplined emotions, those who design and build nuclear weapons become invested in the goals of their projects as necessary for national and international security. They do not wish harm upon the world, but they are socialized within the lab to conceive of the world, of power, and of security in a very particular way that enables the capacity of mass destruction to seem like a logical and even necessary choice.[30]

Arguably, a trajectory, a road, leads throughout history to nuclear war. Building the capacity for mass destruction—and the willingness to use it—did not materialize out of thin air. Ellsberg, for example, argues that most immediately, nuclear weapon policies grew out of the justifications for bombing cities and civilians during World War II. The willingness, and even desire, to incinerate civilians and destroy civilian infrastructure as part of the war campaign resulted in the practices of firebombing and blanketing wide areas with explosive violence. This approach characterized the latter part of the war, with major civilian centers being deliberately targeted by allied forces long before Hiroshima and Nagasaki were met with the "fire and fury" of Fat Man and Little Boy. It is a disturbing story of how practices previously held abhorrent become normalized in the course of conflict—how what was once held as anathema to "civilized engagement" becomes entrenched in doctrine and strategy. This is how, according to Ellsberg's account, nuclear war policies became what they are today: plans to destroy the world.

IDEOLOGIES OF THE BOMB, OR THE ROOTS OF OUR DISCONTENT

Yet the theory of nuclear deterrence continues to dominate academic and international discourse. Meanwhile, advocates for nuclear disarmament are treated as irrational—as naive peaceniks who do not understand the mechanisms and dynamics of international security. The development of "nukespeak"—"the wide use of abstractions, technical jargon, acronyms, metaphors, playful euphemisms, meaning-laden weapons names and titles, and the wide use of the passive voice"[31]—is part of how those supporting nuclear weapons continue to dominate and direct the discourse about nuclear weapons. It makes the bombs more acceptable, producing and shaping "a set of discursive truths about what is possible or rendered unlikely by nuclear weapons and strategy." As a language of control, "nukespeak suppresses contingencies and contradictions, contains dangers, and normalizes the possession and potential uses of nuclear weapons, in effect obscuring human agency and accountability in nuclear policy and inhibiting ethical reflections on nuclear weapons development and possession," explains scholar Shampa Biswas.[32]

When anyone—from government officials creating policy or scientists developing weapons or activists raising the alarm—has spoken out against the nuclear war machine, mainstream media, academia, or politicians have suppressed their views. Ellsberg accurately describes the practices employed by those controlling the dominant narrative around nuclear weapons to maintain an "objective," dispassionate discourse and to dismiss those who want to talk about nuclear weapons for what they really are as "emotional rather than rational," as "nonexpert," and as "irresponsible."

All of this—the nuclearism that fetishizes nuclear weapons as objects of pride and power; the nukespeak that delineates how nuclear weapons can be spoken about and who can speak about them—is not just "madness." The bloated military budgets, irrational arms races, and escalating dangers of nuclear war are rooted in specific approaches to the "global world order"—in particular, capitalist, racist, and sexist approaches. I'll explore these three challenges briefly here, but much more can be said and will be explored throughout the book.

The Political Economy of Nuclear Weapons

In *The Power Elite*, C. Wright Mills locates the rise of military spending in the ascendancy of the military elite in the higher circles of the political elite. He argues that with the advent of advanced weapon technologies during World War II, especially nuclear weapons, the political elite came to define international reality in predominantly military terms. The military is thus needed to advise the strategic direction of governments through a time of perpetual war. This lens of permanent war and aggression ensured that the "needs" of the military—soldiers, weapons, and technology—would be provided for not only politically, but also economically. Thus, national budgets, especially in the United States but also in other economically powerful countries, came to reflect the militaristic interpretation of the nature of international relations.[33] The U.S. economy, in particular, became both "a permanent-war economy and a private-corporation economy."[34] Further, these structures of political and economic power and their effects also have gendered consequences, as will be explored below.

The problem with capitalism, as Karl Marx has taught us, is that the system must keep reproducing itself in order to survive, leading to ever more extraction and exploitation of people and planet. Capital cannot lie idle, or it will result in devaluation of capital represented by commodities on the market; a breakdown of the credit system; paralysis of the function of money as a means of payment; stagnation and disruption in the reproduction process; and an actual decline in reproduction of the capitalist system.[35] Further, stagnation in production "places the employed workers in conditions where they have to accept a fall in wages, even beneath the average."[36] Enter military spending as a clever way for the state to "prop up an atrophying system."[37] Militarism has provided capitalist societies "the answer to the 'on what' question: On what could the government spend enough to keep the system from sinking into the mire of stagnation? On arms, more arms, and ever more arms."[38]

In the United States, for example, the government gives military production companies contracts to produce a specific commodity—such as nuclear weapons. It awards contracts that cover the cost of production as well as a fee for production efforts, which varies depending on the amount of risk the contractor will incur due to technical uncertainty.[39] The government determines the cost of production of a particular weapon system by using historical costing—looking at what similar weapons cost in the past. Critics of the government's procurement program argue that this means any "fraud, waste, and fat" that were tolerated in the previous weapon system's cost now become the baseline for the new system. "This makes every generation of weapon more and more unaffordable as the waste and fraud from generations before is rolled over to the new weapon. The result is that the bloated costs are expanded exponentially and we have fewer and fewer weapons for more and more money."[40] Meanwhile, the fee awarded on top of the production costs goes directly to the contractor. Any "fat" in the historical costing, plus the fee, amounts to the capital accumulated by the contractor.

Thus weapons production is a relatively low-risk venture for corporate profits. The key objective of weapons spending is not the minimization of costs for any particular weapon system or military good, "but rather the maintenance and enlargement of the entire military-industrial empire."[41] Cost overruns are the norm. Indeed, one of the capitalist states' functions is to "create and continually re[-]create the necessary conditions for the self-expansion of capital."[42] Spending on nuclear weapon programs is apparently considered an excellent way to do this. Estimates from experts suggest that the nuclear-armed states spend from about $2 billion to $35 billion each per year.[43] Current U.S. nuclear weapon expenditure already exceeds the total military expenditure of all but ten countries.[44] The cost of modernization of nuclear forces in Russia, the United Kingdom, and United States is budgeted to run into billions—and in the United States' case, one *trillion*—dollars.[45] Who is profiting from all of this? Corporations such as BAE Systems, Bechtel, Boeing, General Dynamics, Lockheed Martin, Northrop Grumman, Raytheon, among others, build nuclear weapons, their delivery systems, and related infrastructure such as nuclear weapon laboratories. Most of these companies also produce other goods and are open to public investment. Some 325 financial institutions around the world are investing hundreds of billions in the companies that generate and sustain nuclear arsenals.[46]

In addition to the weapon-producing corporations, the political economy of nuclear weapons includes the intellectual bastions of nuclearism, including the think tanks, academic centers, lobbyists, and other institutional agents heavily vested in preserving high levels of nuclear weapons spending.[47] There is much profit to be made in this field and thus a need to justify the expense.

One economic justification nuclear-armed states often use is employment rates. In the United Kingdom and the United States, the argument that it will "create jobs" is frequently used to help sell nuclear weapon investments to the public. Workers at the companies that produce nuclear weapons or manage the nuclear weapon complex are enrolled in supporting the nuclear weapon enterprise, through their employment but also through conflation of the community with the nuclear weapon project.[48] But studies have shown that the weapons industry creates fewer jobs per dollar than the average manufacturing industry. One factor is the high level of technical expertise required for defense-related jobs; another is the high cost of this skilled labor. "Much of the new employment generated by a military buildup goes to people who need it least. Professional and technical workers have the lowest unemployment rate of any occupational category in the economy." Therefore, "military spending creates very few jobs for those most in need of work."[49]

The Los Alamos Nuclear Laboratory, for example, home to the Manhattan Project that created nuclear weapons, is still touted as a regional "job creator" and generator of "economic growth" in New Mexico. Yet as local activists point out, neither jobs nor sheer economic growth, which is often concentrated in a relatively few hands, is a reliable measure of broad economic benefit of military-industrial firms. Greg Mello of the Los Alamos Study Group notes that the claim of providing jobs "obscures more than it reveals. Crucial information omitted includes the answer to the question, *jobs for whom?*" Further, he argues that it is possible that any given military facility "could drive away other jobs, perhaps many more than it provides. . . . So even while adding new jobs, it's quite possible Facility X could increase the number and worsen the plight of the poor in the area, or lead the region toward economic decline, even while adding 'jobs.'"[50]

There are also gendered aspects to the "creation of jobs" argument, which leans heavily on jobs in science, technology, engineering, and mathematics (STEM). These occupations still tend to be dominated by men. In recent years, women in the United States earned about 33 percent of PhDs in STEM fields and accounted for less than a third of those employed in scientific research and development around the world.[51] According to statistics the Los Alamos National Laboratory provided, as of July 2019 it employed 68 percent men and 32 percent women.[52] It does not provide a breakdown about who works in which kinds of jobs at the lab, but as Cynthia Enloe has explored, women working in the military industry often work in low-paid and low-skilled jobs.[53] Where women have become leaders in the nuclear weapon or broader military-industrial complex, serious gendered challenges of perspective and credibility continue to undermine efforts for both diversity and equality, as will be explored further below.

Not only does the production of nuclear weapons thus likely foster men's employment over women's and benefit the well-educated wealthy few rather than the general public, but it also further redistributes wealth because most of the money invested in nuclear weapon programs and other aspects of militarism comes from government revenue through taxation. Compare the increases in military spending to decreases in social spending in many countries engaged in weapon production and warfare. Social costs are associated with the development and production of weapons, the major burden of which will always "be borne by the most vulnerable sections of society."[54] Austerity in the United Kingdom, for example, decimated public sector jobs—the employees of which are majority women—as well as social welfare. It is estimated that women have borne the brunt of cuts, approximately 86 percent.[55] These cuts have been implemented at the same time the government decided to renew the Trident missile system, which is projected to cost US$256 billion.[56]

Finding money for modernization of nuclear weapons and other military expenditures directly influences the amount of money available for investments in the public sector. It also can lead to the cuts, when governments seek to save money on social welfare in order to divert it to militarism. Feminists have documented across various sectors and contexts how cuts in the public sector will disproportionately affect women who depend on public resources in support of their reproductive labor. "When public provisioning declines, women are culturally expected to fill the gap, in spite of fewer available resources, more demands on their time and minimal increases in men's caring labour."[57] Thus cuts in public spending, which will affect supportive mechanisms such as child and elderly care, as well as health care, will most likely make it more difficult for women to take those "new jobs" supposedly offered by the military industry, as diminishing access to supporting mechanisms will increase the burden on them of unpaid care work.

Investing in nuclear weapons and militarism more broadly is also a self-reinforcing loop: as a state's citizens have less of a social safety net and less to live on, as conditions of poverty and inequality rise, the general public consumes less goods.[58] This means that the economy needs to produce less goods for the general public, freeing up more capital and labor to produce weapons and even necessitating the arms industry as a "reliable" source of revenue and employment. It further embeds the bomb in a nuclear-armed state's economy.

Marx described the enslavement of labor to capital.[59] Just as the working class is beholden to capital for its life and can only act in the interests of capital, so, too, is the U.S. government seemingly hostage to the monster of its own creation, a military-industrial complex that consumes its capital and produces its tools of destruction. Despite massive deficit and global economic crisis, the nuclear weapon-industrial complex and the governments that invest in it appear hell-bent on maintaining and enhancing their empire, seemingly oblivious to the struggles of the economy or the citizens of their countries, for which they are ostensibly designed to provide "security." Nuclear weapons produce increased global insecurities, which produce increased justification for nuclear weapons, which means more money is spent on them. This cycle is inextricably bound up with political and economic crises. Perceived threats to military power, "national security," and the global economy result in military buildup—never mind that the drain on the capitalist economy over the past decades has been caused at least in part by military buildup.[60] "The possibility of allocating more and more resources for increasingly otiose ends can become a reality. The manufacture of warfare can overtake the society which it theoretically serves," writes Mary Kaldor.[61] Just as Marx argues, the capitalist system becomes a totality and subordinates all elements of society to itself.[62] So, too, nuclear weapons.

As theory and myth, nuclear deterrence has likely been so successful because it provides a solution to the problem of what to do with nuclear weapons. Economies and careers are bound up in sustaining a rationale for the maintenance of nuclear weapons. These weapons are catastrophic to use, so their existence needs to be justified. In short, nuclear deterrence provides an easy answer to an impossible question—that is, how can the money nuclear weapons absorb be accounted for? One way to justify nuclear weapons is to create a theory that we need them in order to never use them. That we need them to prevent war. That by reinvesting in them regularly, making new kinds, building more facilities— we are ensuring security, stability, and safety for all. It inevitably leads to what Robert J. Lifton and Richard Falk describe as nuclearism: "a political and psychological dependence on nuclear weapons to provide an impossible security."[63]

Over time, through relentless political and academic repetition, the value assigned to nuclear weapons as "deterrents" has come to be treated as intrinsic to the weapon itself. This is because they have become what Marx would describe as "fetish objects."[64] Whereas money, in Marx's analysis, is the mature expression of commodity fetishism, nuclear weapons are the mature expression of the fetishism of force. They are the physical embodiment of power, suggests Anne Harrington de Santana, just as money is the physical embodiment of social value, of wealth. "Just as access to wealth in the form of money determines an individual's opportunities and place in a social hierarchy, access to power in the form of nuclear weapons determines a state's opportunities and place in the international order," she writes. "In both cases, the physical form of the fetish object is valuable because it serves as a carrier of social value. In other words, the power of nuclear weapons is not reducible to their explosive capability. Nuclear weapons are powerful because we treat them as powerful."[65]

Nuclear Weapons as Social Objects

This fetishization occurs through a process. Nuclear deterrence is not an inherent quality of nuclear weapons. It is a concept that we ascribe to nuclear weapons. Thus, some academics argue that we need to look at and talk about nuclear weapons as "social objects"—objects that are embedded in a network of relationships, interests, and identities, objects that we infuse with meaning *based on* these relationships, interests, and identities.[66]

Those of us listening to governments talk about nuclear weapons at the United Nations and other international spaces can see this process very clearly. It sometimes feels as if the diplomats representing nuclear-armed or other nuclear-supporting countries believe that if they say the same thing over and again, they can make it true, even if the majority of other governments believe the opposite. The nuclear-armed assert that nuclear weapons make us safe, while most of the rest of the world says they increase insecurity. Back home in the nuclear-armed states, academics and policy makers are churning out rhetoric and war planning that asserts nuclear deterrence as fact and nuclear weapons as the golden ticket to national security.

"What makes nuclear weapons so valuable are the social and political processes through which they have been endowed with certain meanings," explains Shampa Biswas. "The weapons themselves don't provide material protection or security; indeed, the weapons may make one more vulnerable and insecure."[67] Nuclear weapons, even though talked about as if they will never be "used" because they are just for "deterrence," are "nevertheless considered indispensable, and in arms races induced by panics, they are accumulated in ever-increasing numbers to provide a magical sense of impossible omnipotence that can overcome the paralysis."[68]

Preserving "national security" through nuclear deterrence is the main purported motivation for acquiring, possessing, and brandishing nuclear weapons, but, in reality, the nuclear weapon fetish seems to have much more to do with questions of national identity than security. Images of prestige and political power, coupled with domestic political dynamics, play a significant role in embedding nuclear weapons in the politics, economics, and culture of certain countries.[69] The bomb is a "social institution, with wide-ranging cultural, environmental, and psychosocial, as well as geostrategic effects."[70] A decision to deploy and maintain nuclear weapons is generated by an idea of the state as an important player on the world stage and an idea of nuclear weapons as a crucial element of being such a player. In this context, nuclear weapons are assigned particular meanings that must be strengthened and sustained in order to maintain a country's identity. In short, the thinking goes, if we want to be an important world power, we must have nuclear weapons as a representation of our power and as a means of enabling us to act in the world.[71] This kind of national sense of identity reinforces the legitimacy and necessity of continued nuclear possession. Nuclear weapons have become signs of national power; the "preeminent national fetish" designated as not just the "ultimate arbiter of state security," but also as "the one true sign of 'superpower' status."[72]

Nuclear weapons are also given value as they relate to a country's institutional role in the world—for example, the fact that the five countries recognized by the nuclear Non-Proliferation Treaty (NPT) as "nuclear weapon states" are also the five permanent members of the UN

Security Council is no coincidence. States with imperial ambitions and a sense of invulnerable power use nuclear weapons to coerce other states on matters of international relations. These bombs are not "hidden away in silos and subs awaiting a dreaded day of possible use, but instead are one of many tools used by imperial states to maintain global inequalities between states and within states."[73] Interviewing British nuclear policy makers for his research, for example, Nick Ritchie found that "the possession of nuclear weapons imbues a subtle political confidence and has a quiet, implicit, intangible effect on the political decisions of other states, not as a crude, overt means of exercising influence, but as a deeply embedded, unstated form of political authority."[74]

This production and maintenance of identity through nuclear weapons means that many segments of society are invested in the enterprise. It is within this system that even the leaders of nuclear-armed states themselves are trapped. In a letter to U.S. President Kennedy during the Cuban missile crisis in 1963, Soviet Premier Khrushchev eloquently described the "knot of war" that their two countries had tied and urged both sides to "untie the knot." He wrote of the risks of pulling the knot so tight "that even he who tied it will not have the strength to untie it."[75] Although the two nuclear "superpowers" avoided destroying the entire planet that day, Kennedy and Khrushchev failed to achieve what both men stated they wanted: an end to the arms race and the elimination of nuclear weapons.

Similarly, U.S. President Reagan and Soviet Communist Party General Secretary Gorbachev came as close as the leaders of these two countries ever came to agreeing to eliminate their nuclear weapons. At a summit in Reykjavík, Iceland, in October 1986, the two sides put forward various proposals, including the total elimination of their nuclear arsenals. But Reagan, under pressure from the U.S. military-industrial complex, would not agree to limit research on the Strategic Defense Initiative (aka Star Wars), an antiballistic missile system that the United States said was defensive but that the Soviet Union perceived as offensive. Thus, the talks ended without any agreement or any limits on nuclear weapons. It was, by and large, a wasted opportunity that would have changed the course of history.

As Myrdal wrote a decade before this incident, "The leaders have become prisoners of their concession to special interests and of their own propaganda."[76] Rather than saving "succeeding generations from the scourge of war," as was hoped with the founding of the United Nations in 1945, it appears that the "institutional madness" of the nuclear war machine has been passed on to each succeeding generation. A handful of governments have tied their knots of war so tightly that we are still struggling to untie them more than seventy years later.

Nuclear Weapons and the Patriarchy

Based on what I have seen over the past fifteen years working around the United Nations and even longer as an antinuclear activist, I believe—as several feminists have argued previously—that a significant part of why this knot is so hard to untie is patriarchy. In fact, as a feminist disarmament activist, I have come to believe that more than anything else, the association of weapons with power is one of the foremost obstacles to disarmament. And, as feminist scholars have articulated time and again, that this association is gendered.

Patriarchy is a system of power. It is, in the barest sense, a hierarchical social order in which women are subordinate to men. But it is more than that. It is an order that shapes and entrenches gender as a cultural construction and system that endows the hegemonic conception of what is a "man" with the "right" to dominate and rule over others.

Understanding how patriarchy works requires us to understand how gender works. Gender refers to the socially constructed expectations and norms about how we are supposed to perform as women, men, and others, or in relation to sexual orientations; that is, concepts of masculine and feminine and the normative demands of how to behave in order to "properly" represent the bodies we inhabit or are perceived to inhabit. It comes from a particular—and unfortunately, very dominant—understanding of masculinity. This is a masculinity in which ideas such as strength, courage, and protection are equated with violence. It is a masculinity in which the capacity and willingness to use weapons, engage in combat, and kill other human beings is seen as *essential* to being "a real man."[77]

Feminists have long explored the ways in which gender norms, particularly militarized masculinities, drive conflict and violence and the acquisition and proliferation of weapons. These scholars and activists argue that the association of power and strength, coded as masculine traits, with the accumulation and use of weapons, has a negative impact on disarmament and peace.[78] Militarized masculinity harms everyone. It harms those who do not comply with mainstream gender norms— queer-identified people, nonnormative men—and it harms women. It requires oppression of those deemed "weaker" on the basis of gender norms. It also assumes men to be inherently violent and inclined to participate in violent acts—and thus also more expendable.[79] And it makes disarmament seem weak. It makes peace seem utopian. It makes protection without weapons seem absurd.

When it comes to nuclear weapons, several dimensions to the connection between patriarchal power and militarist masculinities contribute to the difficulty in advocating for nuclear disarmament. We can start with the "ubiquitous weight of gender" throughout the entire nuclear weapon discourse and the association of nuclear weapons with masculinity that Carol Cohn described in her groundbreaking work in the 1980s mentioned earlier. Her analysis of the gendered symbolism of nuclear weapons developed through a discourse of "defense intellectuals" provided the foundations for a feminist analysis of nuclear war, nuclear strategy, and nuclear weapons. She described the "sanitized abstraction and sexual imagery," including metaphors that equate military and political power with sexual potency and masculinity—such as "vertical erector launchers, thrust-to-weight ratios, soft lay downs, deep penetration, the comparative advantages of protracted versus spasm attacks," and discussions about how "the Russians are a little harder than we are."[80] She and Sara Ruddick suggested that this type of highly sexualized language serves to "mobilize gendered associations and symbols in creating assent, excitement, support for, and identification with weapons."[81] It is also "a way of minimizing the seriousness of militarist endeavors, of denying their deadly consequences."[82]

In later years Cohn, along with Ruddick and Felicity Ruby, expanded the inquiry into the sense of masculine strength afforded by nuclear weapons, tying this into some of the broader feminist analysis about violent and militarized masculinities discussed above. They listened to a nationalist leader after India's 1998 nuclear weapon tests explain, "We had to prove that we are not eunuchs." They argue that this statement is meant to "elicit admiration for the wrathful manliness of the speaker" and to imply that being willing to employ nuclear weapons is to "have the balls" or to be "man enough" to "defend" your country.[83] This link between masculinity and the power of force persists today. Think of Trump "becoming presidential" by launching missiles at Syria[84] or of Kim Jong-un and his massive parades of missile hardware in a literal showcase of "mine is bigger than yours."[85] Think of Theresa May giving a resolute yes to the question of whether she would be willing to "personally authorize a nuclear strike that could kill 100,000 innocent men, women and children."[86] It is, after all, women leaders as well as men who are conditioned to prove their capacity to lead by a "manly" show of force.

Simply adding women to the situation is not sufficient to achieve nuclear disarmament. And "men" as a category are not specifically or exclusively the problem. Gendered norms, in particular violent or militarized masculinities, are the main problem. The structural imbalance of power among gender identities is also the problem. A recent study published by New America paints a portrait of the nuclear policy field in the United States, dominated as it is by cisgender heterosexual white men who compose a self-described "nuclear priesthood" that espouse normative masculinized perspectives on security and weapons. Seeking a place at the table within this space, women (mostly white, cisgender women) tend to be inclined to try to gain favor with and impress the priesthood, seeing it as an important challenge to fit in and prove that women are "not afraid of nuclear weapons."[87]

As a case in point, the U.S. nuclear weapon team under the Obama administration included women in the roles of secretary of state (Hillary Clinton), undersecretary of state for arms control and international security affairs (Ellen Tauscher), assistant secretary of state for verification, compliance, and implementation (Rose Gottemoeller), special representative of the president for nuclear proliferation (Susan Burk), permanent representative to the United Nations (Susan Rice), and permanent representative to the Conference on Disarmament (Laura Kennedy). Yet the Obama administration pursued the biggest nuclear arms buildup since Reagan and vociferously opposed negotiations of a nuclear weapon ban treaty. Similarly, as of the beginning of 2019, the CEOs of four of the five biggest weapon producers in the United States—Northrop Grumman, Lockheed Martin, General Dynamics, and the military wing of Boeing—are now women.[88] These women are not challenging the patriarchal structures and systems that have created the militarized world order; they are actively maintaining it and profiting from it.

The solution to the dominance of toxic masculinity in disarmament discourse or capitalism in the nuclear-industrial complex is not simply to include women. Liberal feminism is "dedicated to enabling a privileged few to climb the corporate ladder or the ranks of the military," through which it "subscribes to a market-centred view of equality that dovetails with corporate enthusiasm for 'diversity,'" Nancy Fraser, Tithi Bhattacharya, and Cinzia Arruzza have written for a new feminist manifesto. Rather than abolish social hierarchy, liberal feminism "aims to feminize it, ensuring women at the top can attain parity with the men of their own class."[89] As Cynthia Enloe says, "You can militarize anything, including equality."[90]

To actually challenge policies and practices of the elite decision-making class, it is imperative to create space—inside but also outside of existing institutions—where women and others of diverse gender identities, races and ethnicities, backgrounds and experiences—who are willing and able to approach the issue from different perspectives, including feminist and human security perspectives—can be fully engaged. A lesson from feminist, queer, and Indigenous struggles, among others, is that appealing to the establishment for rights or equality or a seat at the table is at best insufficient to achieve change, and at worst serves to reinforce existing injustices by just making problematic institutions or processes appear more palatable or equitable without actually changing anything those institutions do.

In order for true alternative perspectives to be treated as relevant, credible, and expert—to the same extent as the dominant, toxic, militarized masculinity perspectives—we don't just need diverse participation in mainstream institutions. We must consider and create alternative spaces and relationships in order to engage in meaningful processes. Just as Indigenous struggles refuse to center or appeal to whiteness, and queer struggles refuse to center or appeal to the cisgendered or straight community, we need to work with others whose beliefs are outside the dominant, mainstream narrative of nuclear weapons to generate a new sense of what is normative and credible.[91] This is important for the story of the nuclear ban and for nuclear abolition more broadly, because changing what people view as credible and normative about nuclear weapons is vital to achieving change in nuclear weapon policy. We need to not center the dominant frameworks of thought on nuclear weapons—which were created predominantly by white, cisgender, heteronormative men—but to bring a robust critical approach to these frameworks by centering the perspectives, ideas, and frameworks of thought developed by others who have traditionally been excluded from this area.

This issue of credibility is key. The association of weapons and war as a symbol of masculine strength makes it harder to open up discussions about disarmament or collective security. In an extremely gendered way, proponents of abolition are put down as unrealistic and irrational, as "emotional" or "effeminate."[92] The attempt by nuclear-armed and nuclear-supportive states to undermine nuclear disarmament proponents by asserting a monopoly on rationality and legitimacy is deeply patriarchal. As much feminist scholarship explains, social constructions of gender ascribe contrasting characteristics to masculinity and femininity that are seen as mutually exclusive and in which the "masculine" attribution is valued more highly than the "feminine." Descriptors such as strong, rational, serious, and truthful tend to be associated with masculinity, whereas descriptors such as weak, irrational, emotional, and imaginary tend to be associated with femininity.[93] As will be explored further on in this book, one of the tactics representatives of nuclear-armed states used to undermine the credibility of diplomats seeking a ban on nuclear weapons was to assert that they did not really understand international security and to accuse them of being "emotional" about nuclear weapons.

When things like this were said in the conference room, I was reminded of a story Carol Cohn relayed in an article in 1993. She explains that a white male physicist, working on modeling nuclear counterforce attacks, exclaimed to a group of other white male physicists about the cavalier way they were talking about civilian casualties. "*Only* thirty million!" he burst out. "*Only* thirty million human beings killed instantly?" The room went silent. He later confessed to Cohn, "Nobody said a word. They didn't even look at me. It was awful. I felt like a woman."[94] The association of caring about the murder of thirty million people with "being a woman" is all about patriarchal gender norms. It is about seeing that position—and women—as being weak, caring about wrong things; letting your emotions "get the better of you"; focusing on human beings when you should be focused on "strategy." In this perspective, caring about the humanitarian consequences of nuclear weapons is feminine, weak, and not relevant to the job that "real men" have to do to "protect" their countries. Most of the nuclear-armed states, in particular France, asserted this clearly and repeatedly in their opposition to banning nuclear weapons.

"This is a rather dangerous way of thinking," warn Indian feminists writing against their government's decision to develop nuclear weapons. It "suggests that questions about human life and welfare are somehow neither modern nor properly masculine questions, or that men have no capacity and concern for peace and morality."[95] Yes, this is dangerous. It not only suggests that caring about the use of nuclear weapons is spineless and silly, but also makes the pursuit of disarmament seem to be an unrealistic, irrational objective. Disarmament comes to be construed as a utopian vision of a world that cannot exist because, the argument goes, some people will always want to retain or develop the capacity to wield massive, unfathomable levels of violence over others. Therefore, the "rational" actors need to retain the weapons for protection against the irrational others.[96] This approach also perpetuates a social acceptance of human beings intentionally put in harm's way, as objects, viewed within an abstract calculus of casualty figures. It stands in stark contrast to the concepts and laws of human rights and dignity and poses a serious challenge to global justice.

This kind of thinking also insists upon the notion that states, as coherent units, must always be at odds with one another, seeking an "accommodation" of their differences rather than collectively pursuing a world in which mutual interdependence and cooperation could guide behavior through an integrated set of common interests, needs, and obligations. In her study on how and why certain people value nuclear weapons, Catherine Eschle illuminates how "the protector" is coded as masculine and "the protected" as feminine. She describes how, in a discourse that defends nuclear weapons as necessary for security, this plays into the masculine fantasy of "invulnerability, invincibility, and impregnability."[97] She and Claire Duncanson elaborate on how this guides the framework of security from a "realist" perspective, and how gendered this notion is, wherein women are seen as more vulnerable to violence and thus in need of protection from men. The self-named "realist" school of international relations theory set the stage for a masculinized approach to security that accords status to nuclear weapons as both markers of masculine domination (capable of inflicting violence) and masculine protector (capable of deterring violence).[98] In the context of the nuclearization of India and Pakistan, for example, Runa Das explores how both states rely on religious and cultural notions of masculinity and discourses about the need to protect women from each other as elements of their justification for the development of nuclear weapons.[99]

This gendered discourse around nuclear weapons seems to make it more difficult for people to envision, articulate, or accept different security structures that do not rely extensively on weapons and military might to "protect" the "nation" or its people.[100] This has implications for how some of those opposed to nuclear weapons conceptualize their arguments against the bomb. The security framework surrounding nuclear weapons means that arguments in favor of their elimination by those who want to be considered "credible" by the mainstream academic or policy elite rely on demonstrating that a world free of nuclear weapons brings security. This can become problematic, where arguments in favor of nuclear disarmament tend to rely on commitments to design and develop other technologies of violence. These arguments suggest that nuclear weapons are not needed because so-and-so's conventional military is strong enough, or because a country can develop autonomous weapons or supersonic glide vehicles or the latest tool to slaughter human beings, instead of possessing nuclear weapons. Thus, the pursuit of disarmament in these contexts becomes tied to the search for reassurance of security through technical, strategic, and military substitutes for nuclear weapons.[101]

In this context, policy decisions are still based on conceptions of power imbued with mistrust, threat, fear, and violence. Such policies do not allow for other types of international engagement or relationship between citizens and states; they dismiss alternatives as utopian and unrealistic. This dismissal, not surprisingly, is also highly gendered. When those flexing their "masculinity" want to demonstrate or reinforce their power and dominance, they try to make others seem small and marginalized by accusing them of being emotional, overwrought, irrational, or impractical—in short, by trying to "feminize" them based on conventional gender norms. Women and other marginalized people have experienced this technique of dismissal and denigration for as long as gender hierarchies have existed. The denial of reason in someone else is an attempt to take away the ground on which the other stands, projecting illusions about what is real, about what makes sense, or what is rational.[102]

This is more than just an argument or a difference in interpretation. This is an attempt to undermine and discredit the other's perspective in order to maintain power and privilege. Objectification of others and control of reality, known as "gaslighting" in psychological terms, is as integral to patriarchy as it is to nuclear deterrence as a mechanism to maintain the current global hierarchy.[103] When the majority of states, international and activist organizations all say that nuclear weapons threaten us all and must be eliminated, the nuclear-armed states say that nuclear weapons—in our hands—keep us safe, and we must maintain them indefinitely. When it is pointed out that nuclear-armed states haven't complied with their disarmament commitments, the representatives of these countries claim that they have. They argue that they have done all they can and now it is up to rest of the world—*those countries without nuclear weapons*—to create the conditions for any further disarmament efforts.

This situation is extremely destabilizing. The political ramifications are that the majority of states and the world's publics are held hostage to the whim of a handful of governments that claim to know best while playing Russian roulette with our lives and our planet. But it's not just the reason or rationality of those supporting nuclear disarmament that is denied. It is also the lived experience of everyone who has ever suffered from a nuclear explosion, or mining of uranium, or burial of nuclear waste. This experience, perhaps unsurprisingly, is intimately tied to the experience of racism and colonialism.

Nuclear Colonialism and Racism

The history of nuclear testing is a history of racism and colonialism. Mostly, nuclear-armed states have tested outside of their territories, on lands and peoples that the nuclear-armed states had colonized or were simply deemed inferior. When the nuclear-armed have conducted tests on their own territories, it has mostly been as a settler colonial state exploding radioactive bombs on Indigenous lands and communities.

The United States conducted more than 1,050 tests, including at the Nevada Test Site, which is in the traditional land-use area of the Western Shoshone and South Paiute.[104] The Western Shoshone are known as "the most bombed nation on earth": 814 nuclear tests have been done on their land since 1951.[105] The U.S. government also detonated nuclear devices near the Aleutian island of Amchitka in southwest Alaska; Rulison and Rio Blanco, Colorado; Hattiesburg, Mississippi; and Alamogordo and Farmington, New Mexico; as well as in the Pacific at the islands of Bikini Atoll, Eniwetok Atoll, Johnson Island, and Christmas Island.[106]

The Soviet Union conducted about 715 tests, mostly at the Semipalatinsk Test Site in Kazakhstan. The United Kingdom conducted 45 tests in Australia on Indigenous territory, as well as in the Pacific and at the Nevada Test Site in the United States. France conducted 210 tests in Algeria and French Polynesia. China conducted 45 tests at the Lop Nor test site in Xinjiang. India conducted six tests at Pokhran, and Pakistan six at Ros Koh Hills and the Chagai District.

The common thing throughout the majority of nuclear testing, especially that done abroad, is the impact it had on the people living in those locations. "The testing sites chosen were viewed by these nuclear weapons states as 'open' or 'empty' spaces with little vocal resistance," writes Australian scholar and activist Dimity Hawkins. "But these traditional lands were neither empty nor silent":[107]

> The people on whose lands these tests were conducted included islanders who were removed from their villages, stopped from using traditional fishing areas or eating traditional foods due to on-going contamination. Aboriginal people were stopped from traversing ancient travel routes or accessing traditional hunting grounds. Military personnel who were obliged to be in these situations, who had little or no recourse to contest the orders that they were given, were alleged to have been treated in some cases as guinea pigs and in other cases as controlled studies.[108]

"Governments and colonial forces exploded nuclear bombs on our sacred lands—upon which we depend for our lives and livelihoods, and which contain places of critical cultural and spiritual significance—believing they were worthless," said thirty-five Indigenous groups in a statement to the negotiations of the nuclear weapon ban treaty in July 2017. Delivered by Karina Lester, a Yankunytjatjara-Anangu woman from South Australia, the statement explained that Indigenous people "were never asked for, and we never gave, permission to poison our soil, food, rivers and oceans."[109]

If we look just at testing in the Pacific, a clear pattern emerges. Between 1946 and 1996, France, the United Kingdom, and the United States tested more than 315 nuclear weapons on largely remote, rural and First Nations communities across the Pacific. These tests contaminated vast areas in the Marshall Islands (Bikini and Eniwetok islands), Australia (Monte Bello, Emu Field, and Maralinga), French Polynesia (Moruroa and Fangataufa), and the Pacific islands of Kiritimati (Christmas island), Kalama (Malden) Island, and Johnson Atoll.

As a result of the testing, Pacific Islanders suffered displacement followed by malnutrition and near starvation, lost access to traditional food sources, and were exposed to radioactive fallout. They were subjected to medical experiments and have suffered greatly from the health impacts of the testing. In Australia, the six hundred so-called minor trials,[110] as well as the twelve atmospheric nuclear tests, spread contamination of uranium, plutonium, beryllium, and other toxic substances over a wide area in the South Australian desert.[111] A Royal Commission report found a failure at the first of the UK bomb tests in Australia's Monte Bello islands to "consider the distinctive lifestyles of Aboriginal people."[112] The commission notes that the British did inadequate surveys of the numbers of Aboriginal communities—in fact, they recorded that just 715 were people within the immediate 150km area of the test site of the first Monte Bello tests, "excluding full-blooded Aboriginals, for whom no statistics are available."[113]

Hawkins argues that these cases expose three different but incredibly similar stories about the relationship between the testing governments and the people upon whom they tested nuclear weapons. "One could be seen as a breach of the global trust placed in an administering authority," she notes, while "another showed a gung-ho readiness to comply with the wishes of a former colonial master. The last revealed a relentless adherence to perceived colonial privilege alongside collaboration by local political interests."[114]

Further, these tests have had gendered impacts. Studies on women's health in the aftermath of the Hiroshima and Nagasaki bombings, nuclear testing in the Marshall Islands and in Kazakhstan, and the Chernobyl nuclear power disaster provide useful but incomplete analyses of ways in which women are uniquely impacted by radioactive violence. In particular, high rates of stillbirths, miscarriages, congenital birth defects, and reproductive problems (such as changes in menstrual cycles and the subsequent inability to conceive) have been recorded. A possible link between breast cancer in young women and women who were lactating at the time of exposure to nuclear radiation has also been found to exist.[115]

In 2012, Calin Georgescu, the UN special rapporteur on the Implications for Human Rights of the Environmentally Sound Management and Disposal of Hazardous Substances and Wastes, visited the Marshall Islands to assess the impact on human rights of the nuclear testing conducted by the United States from 1946 to 1958.[116] He found that the full effects of radiation on Marshallese women might have been underestimated. Among other things, the bathing and eating habits of women potentially played a role in their higher rates of contamination. The special rapporteur found that women often bathed in contaminated water, which may have been overlooked as a possible means of exposure, as was the fact that women eat different parts of fish than men, such as bones and organ meat, in which certain radioactive isotopes tend to accumulate. The special rapporteur also notes, "Apparently, women were more exposed to radiation levels in coconut and other foods owing to their role in processing foods and weaving fibre to make sitting and sleeping mats, and handling materials used in housing construction, water collection, hygiene and food preparation, as well as in handicrafts."[117]

For more than sixty years, radiation exposure was measured based on the people primarily developing and testing nuclear weapons: adult white men. Nuclear regulators, including the International Committee for Radiological Protection, use what is called "Reference Man" to evaluate exposure. This model is based on adult white men—officially, "between 20 to 30 years of age, weighing 70 kg, is 170 cm in height, and lives in a climate with an average temperature of from 10°C to 20°C. He is a Caucasian and is a Western European or North American in habitat and custom."[118] Only one study from the bombings of Hiroshima and Nagasaki assessed impacts of radiation based on age and sex. Analysts such as Mary Olson, who now leads the Gender and Radiation Project, have found that sex and age are "potent factors influencing the outcome of radiation exposure."[119]

Similarly, the key reference guide for radiation exposure is not adequate for measuring possible exposure among Indigenous populations. In the United States, for example, due to differences in diet, activities, and housing, the radiation exposure of Native Americans is not well represented in the Department of Energy dose reconstructions. It leaves out exposure to radioactive iodine from eating small game, while exposures from drinking milk and eating vegetables have not yet been properly estimated for these communities.[120]

But the humanitarian impacts of nuclear weapon testing and production on the U.S. Indigenous population are well documented. The Diné/Navajo Nation saw cancer rates double from the 1970s to the 1990s due to nuclear weapon testing as well as uranium mining and milling in the southwestern United States. Abandoned uranium mines in the region continue to pollute water supplies.[121] Uranium mining on Lakota lands in South Dakota is believed to have contributed to high levels of sterility, miscarriages, cancer, and other diseases on the Pine Ridge Reservation. Radioactive waste from the Sequoyah Plant in Gore, Oklahoma, was spread on Cherokee lands. The list goes on.[122]

Social costs are also associated with the development of nuclear weapons, the major burden of which will always "be borne by the most vulnerable sections of society," as Indian antinuclear feminists have argued. "While the inevitable cutbacks in social security and welfare will hurt and damage all poor people, the proportion of the poor who are steadfastly denied a fair share of even the scarce resources, will undoubtedly become larger."[123] Nuclear weapons increase the insecurity of the most vulnerable populations of the world. They may never be used in war again, but even still their pursuit wastes massive human and economic resources; involves exploitative conditions for uranium mining and radioactive waste storage; involves land appropriation and destruction for testing; and has produced radioactive waste. "While radiation may not discriminate," Shampa Biswas notes, nuclearism "does discriminate along lines of class, race, and geography, leading to the differential valuation of human bodies involved in nuclear production."[124]

Despite all of this suffering, those who have been subjected to nuclear testing, and to the harms of nuclear weapon development, have not been silent victims. Far from it. Almost immediately after the tests in the Marshall Islands, for example, islanders were voicing concerns about their relocation and the effects of the testing. In 1954, after the devastation of the U.S. government's Castle Bravo test, they presented a petition to the United Nations Trusteeship Council calling for the cessation of all nuclear tests on the islands. Since then, the country's advocacy has continued in a range of forms, including petitions, court cases, and lobbying through regional and international forums.[125] In 1990 the Marshall Islands entered a Compact of Free Association with the United States,[126] but the Marshallese continue to seek effective remedy from the U.S. government in relation to nuclear testing (more on this later).

Reports of fallout across the Pacific led to some of the most sustained protests against nuclear testing in the world, particularly in the early 1970s when the French were still conducting atmospheric nuclear tests. Periodically, regional governments took strong stands against the nuclear testing, such as when Australia, New Zealand, and Fiji took a case to the International Court of Justice in 1973–1974 to force France to end atmospheric testing.[127] Many Pacific nations created sanctions against French products and French airlines, which were picked up around the world. Algerians have also taken action against the French government for its testing there, with a major human rights organization in Algeria contacting the Human Rights Council in 2017 requesting it look into France's conduct of seventeen nuclear tests in the Algerian desert.[128]

African Americans organizing against nuclear weapons in the United States have frequently connected their work to both antiracism initiatives at home and anticolonial initiatives abroad. Coretta Scott King, Dr. Martin Luther King Jr., W. E. B. Du Bois, and other civil rights leaders elaborated on the inseparability of nuclear disarmament and the end of colonial empires; Bayard Rustin traveled to Algeria to help organize protests against French nuclear testing there with the U.S.

civil rights movement.[129] "Black leftists held firm in their belief that the atomic bombings of Hiroshima and Nagasaki were inextricably linked to colonialism and racial equality," writes Vincent Intondi in his study of Black antinuclear activism.[130] They saw that colonialism, institutionalized racism, and segregation "each grew from the same seed and represented a form of violence," said scholar Jacqueline Castledine.[131]

U.S. Indigenous activists have argued the same. "Colonization isn't just the theft and assimilation of our lands and people, today we're fighting against nuclear colonialism which is the theft of our future," remarked Leona Morgan of the Diné/Navajo Nation in Nevada.[132] The Western Shoshone Nation, which has long protested the bombing of its lands at the Nevada Test Site,[133] today continues its resistance against nuclear colonialism by fighting off a nuclear waste disposal site commissioned for Yucca Mountain in southwestern Nevada.[134] Indigenous activists have also commented on the connection between the struggles of water protectors fighting the construction of pipelines and those fighting to keep uranium in the ground. Tom Goldtooth, executive director of the Indigenous Environmental Network, noted:

> Our Native Nations are on the frontlines fighting a colonial energy system that does not recognize treaties and Indigenous rights, our spiritual cosmologies and the protection of water of life. The link here is a world digging up uranium. In the northern plains, there's uranium in coal with dust particles that are radioactive. There's even radioactivity within hydro-fracking waste. Water is being contaminated and it's flowing into the Missouri River. Spirituality is very important as an organizing tool for us, within an industrialized world that has no understanding of the Indigenous natural laws that guide our traditional Indigenous societies. It's a systems change challenge we are dealing with, that will require all people, all cultures to work together.[135]

Yet even with the protests and legal actions taken by survivors of aggressive nuclear testing by the colonial powers, nuclear weapons have had a colonizing impact on certain peoples and governments. "Nuclear weapons pervade our thinking," laments Indian activist and author Arundhati Roy. They "control our behaviour. Administer our societies. . . . They are the ultimate colonizer."[136] The nuclear nonproliferation regime arguably helps produce and maintain this sense of nuclear colonialism. This relates to the inequalities between nuclear-armed and nonnuclear-armed states written into the Non-Proliferation Treaty (NPT)—to be discussed more in the next chapter—but goes beyond it to the very conception of nuclear weapons themselves and of who is qualified—as "rational" actors—to possess them.[137] This order is guided above all else by "deeply and profoundly internalized prejudices about the global distribution of reason and trust."[138]

As Carol Cohn and Sara Ruddick have pointed out, a clear distinction between the Self, which has a right to possess nuclear weapons; and the Other, which is too unpredictable to possess them, does nothing to prevent proliferation and only makes it more difficult to reduce the perceived value of nuclear weapons as a source of power. When governments act as though their "power and security are guaranteed only by a large nuclear arsenal," they "create a context in which nuclear weapons become the ultimate necessity for, and symbol of, state security." And when nuclear-armed states "work hard to ensure that other states don't obtain nuclear weapons," they "create a context in which nuclear weapons become the ultimate arbiter of political power."[139]

The inequitable, racist, colonial nuclear world order is not just a historical fact. It is one of the dominant paradigms present in discourses and practices around nonproliferation and nuclear disarmament today. During the process to ban nuclear weapons, for example, where the global south together with a few European countries led the way, the nuclear-armed states and their nuclear-supportive allies were quick to argue that these pro-ban countries had no relevant security interests that would entitle them to speak out on this subject. So, at the same time as the nuclear "powers" rode roughshod over the security interests of the inhabitants of the countries and Indigenous nations they bombed, leaving contamination of land, water, bodies, and politics for generations to come, they claimed in international discussions that these same people had no grounds upon which to speak on the subject of nuclear weapons. This incredibly blatant racist approach to nuclear weapon discourse and negotiation has everything to with colonial power and nothing to do with the lived reality of people around the world.

SO WHO IS "TERMINALLY UNSERIOUS"?

The denial of lived experience in order to project the "realism" of illogical arguments is patriarchal and racist. It dismisses the very real pain and suffering, often intergenerational, of those who have experienced the consequences of use or testing of nuclear weapons. These experiences are viewed as not relevant to the policies and practices of governments charged with "protecting" civilians. Their denial overrides lived human reality, sweeping it under the carpet so that abstract theories about "deterrence" and "stability" can hold court in policy and even public circles.

"We are dealing with a world infested by" nuclear weapons, as a Brazilian ambassador once put it.[140] In the view of the majority of countries, this state of affairs threatens security rather than preserves it—and goes against the development of cooperation and collaboration among nations. "When we consider the vast progress which humanity has made since 1945, it seems incomprehensible indeed to us that we should tolerate, much less seek to justify, the continued retention of such uniquely destructive and dangerous weapons when we know they could, in an instant, change human life as we know it forever," said a representative of Ireland. "Is this the best blueprint for security that we can devise?"[141]

Yet whatever forum or discussion the representatives of the nuclear-armed states actively participate in, only their voices or those of their closest allies are treated as credible in the mainstream narrative. Their thinking is all that matters. The room is quieter when they speak. When the ambassadors of the United States or Russia take the floor at the United Nations, you can hear a pin drop. When a representative of Equatorial Guinea is speaking, it sounds like a mosh pit on the conference room floor.[142] This might just sound like rude behavior. But it is more than that. It has meaningful implications—about who is listened to, who is respected, who is taken seriously on these issues—whose perspective, voice, and engagement matters.

The truth, according to the nuclear-armed, is whatever they say it is. They say nuclear weapons are about security—but they only have in mind their own narrow version of what that means, lacking imagination or will to understand why the vast majority of governments in the world, and their own citizens, demand nuclear disarmament. The nuclear-armed want our answer to be the same as theirs: that they are justified in their retention of nuclear weapons. They want the world to understand that they *have* to have nuclear weapons, to protect themselves and to keep the rest of us from starting another world war. Like an abusive partner, they want us to understand that their violence is for our own good. They know best, they are in control, and we are at their mercy. If we disagree with their approach, or challenge their analysis about why they do what they do, we are ridiculed, dismissed, ignored; intimidated and berated until we become more accommodating and understanding. This imbalance of power is used relentlessly and in various ways to try to silence those who believe that a different kind of world is possible.

"No one believes more firmly than Comrade Napoleon that all animals are equal," says the character Squealer in George Orwell's *Animal Farm*. "He would be only too happy to let you make your decisions for yourselves. But sometimes you might make the wrong decisions, comrades, and then where should we be?"[143] Realizing that this was the game afoot has been an important part of the process to ban nuclear weapons. After decades of being ridiculed, told they did not understand international security, instructed to sit down and shut up, governments that reject nuclear weapons got organized. Together with activists, the Red Cross, and academics who rejected normative theories about deterrence and stability, diplomats and officials from these countries said enough.

"Disarmament is a common world interest," wrote Alva Myrdal in 1976. It is not against, but for the true national interests of all countries, "not least for the peoples in the lands of the superpowers and their all too silent military and political allies." But these countries' present policies "are headed for disaster," they are "irrational from the national as well as the international point of view. And they are deeply immoral."[144] This is as true now as it was then. It has been the case throughout the atomic age. But despite the immorality and irrationality of the nuclear-armed state policies, their position of privileged power has enabled them to suppress dissent and maintain the course through racist, patriarchal techniques such as gaslighting, deflection, and denial.

At the time of writing her book, Myrdal criticized the nonnuclear-armed world for being "too submissive, restricting our efforts by assuming that we can act only when we can get the superpowers to agree, between themselves and with us." The result of this approach, she argued, "has been either total failure or some incomplete and ineffective treaties under the label of disarmament."[145] She proposed, "The lack of forward drive by the superpowers should not be an alibi for inaction on the part of the non-nuclear-weapons states." They should be prepared

> to circumvent the superpowers and act independently when necessary. . . . When full support is initially missing, the lesser states should be prepared to proceed on their own, always hoping that if their work is good and its results convincing, the superpowers might later join on one issue of arms regulation after another.[146]

Forty years later, this is exactly what the nonnuclear-armed world did. The next chapter provides the backdrop to the efforts to ban nuclear weapons, offering a brief overview of global activism and intergovernmental initiatives from 1945 to 2010. It gives both history and analysis of these efforts and zooms in on the post–Cold War era, looking at what happened to the antinuclear movement and what challenges we faced at the beginning of the ban process to "circumvent the superpowers" as Myrdal suggested.

2

RAGE AGAINST THE BOMB
A Brief History of Antinuclear Efforts

The feminist, Indigenous, queer, antiracist, postcolonial, and anticapitalist analyses of nuclear weapons explored in the previous chapter, which challenge the key myths and motivations of nuclear policy, have been building for decades. Since the dawn of the atomic age, the rich, fierce history of activism and diplomatic action against nuclear weapons has drawn on and been shaped by these alternative perspectives. There have been several key protest moments against nuclear weapons globally, though a complete cataloging is not possible for this publication.[1] Among governments, attempts have been consistent at the international level to get the nuclear-armed states to disarm.

The following is a concise and incomplete overview, intended only to indicate the breadth and depth of the work and the passion waged against nuclear weapons by activists and some governments over the past seventy years. This chapter also tries to illuminate how nuclear-armed states have always played the "game of disarmament" to deflect, deny, and defer their responsibilities to nuclear disarmament while investing more and more money in their nuclear arsenals. It also looks at some of the challenges facing antinuclear activism in the post–Cold War era, which sets the stage for some of the choices and dilemmas activists and diplomats were confronted with in the current era.

EFFORTS AGAINST NUCLEAR
WEAPONS FROM 1945 TO 1989

From 1945 on, scientists, health-care workers, and the public responded in horror to the U.S. bombings of Hiroshima and Nagasaki. John

45

Hersey's account of the bombing of Hiroshima and the experience of six survivors, published by the *New Yorker* in 1946, became a touchtone for much of the public's reaction beyond the narratives of American prowess in making such a device.[2] In the mid-1950s similar outrage and activism emerged from U.S. nuclear testing in the Pacific—in particular, in response to the radioactive contamination of Japanese fishermen on the Lucky Dragon fishing boat who were soused with radiation from the U.S. Castle Bravo thermonuclear weapon test at Bikini Atoll in 1954. Opposition also rose to atmospheric testing in the United States. From 1955 to 1963, activists pressured the nuclear-armed states to agree upon a nuclear weapon test ban. As part of this work, scientists in St. Louis collected baby teeth to monitor the levels of strontium-90 from radioactive fallout.[3] In 1961, about fifty thousand women brought together by Women Strike for Peace marched against the bomb in sixty U.S. cities.[4]

The 1960s was also an active time for international diplomacy for nuclear disarmament. A UN group issued a report on the economic and social consequences of disarmament. It argued that the urgency of disarmament was not only to avoid nuclear war, but also to avoid further divergence of resources from those "tasks of lightening the burdens and enriching the lives of individuals and of society."[5] The United Nations also set up the Eighteen-Nation Committee on Disarmament in 1962, attempting to establish a dialogue between the United States and Soviet Union. This expanded the previous Ten Nation Committee, which consisted entirely of nuclear-armed states and their allies.[6] The new forum included eight nonaligned, nonnuclear-armed countries: Brazil, Burma (Myanmar), Egypt, Ethiopia, India, Mexico, Nigeria, and Sweden.

At the time of the first meeting, the United States had announced its decision to conduct a new series of atmospheric nuclear tests. France refused to participate in the meeting, which, given France's nuclear testing in Algeria, was particularly upsetting to the African members of the committee.[7] The Soviet Union came to the meeting with a draft treaty for "general and complete disarmament"—which went beyond nuclear weapons to look at the stockpiles and production of all weapon systems. The United States introduced a different proposal. The U.S. and Soviet allies on the committee supported their respective proposals, but nonaligned governments took this opportunity—their first chance to actively contribute in such negotiations—to demand that the two nuclear "superpowers" work together and to propose their own solutions. Thus, while the United States and Soviet Union, backed by their allies, argued over each other's proposals, the nonaligned states put forward possible compromises and new suggestions to overcome the impasses on both a prohibition of nuclear testing and for general and complete disarmament. The Cuban missile crisis in 1963 was the breaking point that led to the Partial nuclear Test Ban Treaty and the nuclear Non-Proliferation Treaty (NPT) in the 1960s, noted a diplomat from Latin America interviewed for this book. But, she argued, it was really the Eighteen-Nation Committee, which allowed nonaligned states to actively contribute for the first time and put forward these ideas, that created the space necessary to advance these treaties.

However, by the end of the committee's work in 1969, the nonaligned states were thoroughly frustrated. "Technology is advancing, weapons are being improved day by day and obstacles go on accumulating," lamented the Mexican representative to the committee. "When we see how, time and again, there have been postponements not only of the conclusion of agreements but even of the beginning of negotiations which the parties themselves and the rest of the world consider to be urgent, we are assailed by feeling that an historic opportunity is being almost irretrievably lost."[8] (As someone who has sat through more than a decade of these types of discussions forty years on, I can report that it continues to be frustrating in exactly the same way.)

By 1967, the countries of Latin America and the Caribbean had decided to establish a regional nuclear weapon free zone treaty, prohibiting the possession, stationing, or use of nuclear weapons in their territories. This was their way of showing the nuclear-armed states that they were no longer willing to play by their rules, said one diplomat from the region, describing the zone as a "declaration of freedom." Other regions eventually followed suit, including the South Pacific in 1985; Southeast Asia in 1995; Africa in 1996; and Central Asia in 2006. Other countries, such as Austria, Mongolia, and New Zealand, have independently declared themselves nuclear weapon free.

In the 1970s, the Pacific was alive with antinuclear activism.[9] In 1972, New Zealand and Canadian activists protested French nuclear testing in the Pacific by sailing small vessels into the test zones. French officials assaulted the activists, but the New Zealand government condemned the nuclear tests, and the Australian government approached the International Court of Justice for an injunction against the tests. Throughout Australia, thousands joined protest marches in the major cities; scientists demanded an end to the tests; unions refused to load French ships, service French planes, or carry French mail; and consumers boycotted French products. (When France announced its intention to resume nuclear testing in the 1990s, similar boycotts took place all over the world.) In April 1975, representatives of dozens of antinuclear organizations, meeting in Fiji, launched the Nuclear Free Pacific Movement. In 1979, in the Marshall Islands, about five hundred people staged a nonviolent occupation of eight islands from which they had been forcibly evicted years before by the U.S. military to accommodate U.S. nuclear missile tests.

The United Nations continued to vigorously investigate the economic and social costs of the arms race and bloated military spending throughout the 1970s and 1980s. The extreme sums being spent on nuclear weapons and militarism at large were consistently found to be undermining the principal goals of the United Nations and tearing at the fabric of human society. In keeping with these findings, in the 1980s two principal activist campaigns were the "Nuclear Freeze"—the demand for the U.S. and Soviet governments to stop building nuclear weapons and delivery systems—and protests of missile deployments in Europe.

The immediate objective of the Nuclear Freeze movement, launched in early 1980 in a "Call to Halt the Nuclear Arms Race" written by activist Randall Forsberg, was a bilateral Soviet-U.S. "freeze on testing, production, and further deployment of nuclear weapons."[10] In 1982, freeze resolutions were introduced in nine U.S. states and passed in eight; later, freeze resolutions, though in watered-down form, passed the House and the Senate. The movement culminated in the largest antinuclear march in world history, when one million people marched to Central Park on 12 June 1982.[11] Around the same time, activists were protesting U.S. nuclear weapon testing at the Nevada Test Site, involving hundreds of demonstrations, peace vigils, and walks through the desert organized by antinuclear, religious, and Indigenous groups.[12]

Protests also raged across Europe in these years. In 1981 in the United Kingdom, activists established the Greenham Common Women's Peace Camp to protest the stationing of cruise missiles at the Royal Air Force Greenham Common in Berkshire. In 1983, about seventy thousand protestors formed a 23km human chain from Greenham to Aldermaston (home of the UK's Atomic Weapons Establishment) and the ordinance factory at Burghfield.[13] In October 1981, half a million people took to the streets in several cities in Italy, more than 250,000 people protested in Bonn, 250,000 demonstrated in London, and 100,000 marched in Brussels. In October 1983, nearly three million people across Western Europe protested nuclear missile deployments and demanded an end to the arms race; the largest crowd of almost one million people assembled in The Hague, The Netherlands.[14] Back in the United Kingdom, 400,000 people participated in what was probably the largest demonstration in British history.[15]

Meanwhile in Australia, on Palm Sunday 1982, an estimated 100,000 Australians took to the streets for antinuclear rallies in the country's largest cities. Growing year by year, the rallies drew 350,000 participants in 1985. In Japan, the major atomic bomb survivor organizations, labor federations, women and youth associations, religious groups, and others established the Japanese National Liaison Committee for Nuclear and General Disarmament. Record numbers of people turned out for antinuclear rallies: 200,000 people in Hiroshima in March 1982 and 400,000 in Tokyo that May.[16] In New Zealand, activists and the Labor government ensured a nuclear-free status for the country, prohibiting U.S. nuclear-capable ships from docking. In 1985, the French foreign intelligence service bombed and sank the Greenpeace flagship, the *Rainbow Warrior*, in the port of Auckland while it was on its way to protest a planned French nuclear weapon test in Moruroa, killing a photographer on board.[17]

In the Philippines, activists fought for and achieved a nuclear-free provision in their new constitution and demanded the closure of U.S. military bases where nuclear weapons were stationed. Antinuclear protests grew among student, women's, and religious groups in South Korea in the 1980s. In 1986, the National Council of Churches called for the removal of all nuclear weapons from the Korean peninsula. Protests also emerged in China: "Enraged by the government's nuclear weapons tests at Lop Nur, in Xinjiang province, local Uighur people staged anti-nuclear demonstrations in Beijing and other Chinese cities."[18] The same year, Israeli former nuclear technician Mordechai Vanunu revealed details of Israel's nuclear weapon program to the British press.[19] In 1989, activists in Kazakhstan formed the antinuclear organization Nevada Semipalatinsk, bringing thousands of people to protests that eventually led to the closure of the Soviet nuclear test site at Semipalatinsk in northeast Kazakhstan in 1991.[20]

WHAT ABOUT ANTINUCLEAR ACTIVISM IN THE POST–COLD WAR PERIOD?

Despite this intense, resilient, and inspiring activism around the world and diplomacy at the United Nations over this period, the end of the Cold War did not lead to the end of nuclear weapons. And since 1989, the political and social landscape related to nuclear weapons changed drastically.

For one thing, most of the general public and many activists assumed that the dissolution of the Soviet Union would lead to the dismantlement of the enormous arsenals both sides had built up during the arms race. Even some prominent government and military establishment elite assumed nuclear disarmament would be logical. Former U.S. secretary of defense Robert McNamara cowrote a *Foreign Affairs* article in 1991 describing the vast majority of the world's nuclear weapons as "militarily worthless." He and his coauthors argued, "With the end of the Cold War, it is hard to construct even a semi-plausible military threat to the United States or to Europe west of the Soviet border in the immediate future."[21] But the military-industrial complex, with its political economy bound up in the nuclear weapon enterprise, was not having this. Those in control of the U.S. nuclear weapon program began to actively seek new justifications and roles for these bombs. The post–Cold War era was marked by an ongoing "project of ensuring US global political-military dominance,"[22] with nuclear weapons at the forefront.

Despite the dangers presented by the dominant militarist culture keen on keeping the nuclear weapon enterprise alive, antinuclear activism was a shell of its former self throughout much of the 1990s and 2000s. In part, this was because perceptions of the immediate danger posed by nuclear weapons diminished among the general public. Membership of popular peace and disarmament organizations shrank, and some of these groups adopted other priorities.[23] A more critical examination of the transformation, however, found that another type of shift also took place. A large segment of the antinuclear movement moved away from broad social mobilization and toward advocacy within established institutions, noted social movement theorist and historian David Meyer, who studied this period of antinuclear activism in the United States.[24] This shift was largely motivated by the withdrawal of support for local groups campaigning for the abolition of nuclear weapons by grant-giving foundations. The funding community, particularly in the United States, began to mostly support centralized, narrowly framed approaches, comprising mainly legislative initiatives targeting individual budget line items and specific treaties dealing with nuclear weapons.[25]

Some grassroots groups kept monitoring nuclear weapon laboratories and trying to raise awareness of the increasing sophistication of the nuclear-industrial complex. But as popular resistance faded, more "technostrategic" organizations came to dominate the nuclear discourse, especially in the United States. They tended to push not for abolition of nuclear weapons but for changes in the status and numbers of nuclear forces and a global arms control regime. Meyer explains that these groups tended to limit their goals as they became increasingly dependent upon their relationships with financial supporters and legislators. And although some of the political action generated victories, such as moderate reductions in funding for particular weapon systems, these achievements were not geared toward abolition or challenging the justifications for nuclear weapons.[26]

But antinuclear activism persisted, even without sustained funding. Passionate activists around the world advocated for negotiations among the nuclear-armed states for the elimination of their nuclear arsenals. Many of these groups supported work at the International Court of Justice in 1996, examining whether the use or threat of use of nuclear weapons was legal. The court affirmed the general illegality of the threat or use of nuclear weapons and an unconditional obligation to negotiate for their elimination. But forward momentum on this objective continued to be hog-tied by assertions by the nuclear-armed states that they had a "right" to possess nuclear weapons. Among other things, they cited the nuclear Non-Proliferation Treaty, adopted in 1968, as establishing in fact five "nuclear weapon states" and setting out parameters for the regulation of the atomic bomb.

NPT: THE NUCLEAR POWERS TREATY

The Non-Proliferation Treaty was a response to Ireland's endeavors in the United Nations from 1958 to 1961 to establish an international instrument to prevent the proliferation of nuclear weapons. India and Sweden also put forward joint proposals calling for a package approach that would include nonproliferation and disarmament measures. This call was supported by the nonaligned members of the Disarmament Committee operating in Geneva described above. But when the Soviet Union and United States presented draft nonproliferation treaties to the UN General Assembly in 1965, their texts ensured unrestricted rights to possess, deploy, and develop nuclear weapons for those countries that already had nuclear weapons, while closing the possibility for other countries to acquire nuclear arsenals.[27]

The final version of the NPT, adopted in 1968, aimed at preventing the spread of nuclear weapons, sharing nuclear technology for so-called peaceful purposes, and pursuing multilateral negotiations for nuclear disarmament. The fundamental "bargain" of the NPT was that states without nuclear weapons would not acquire or develop them but could have access to nuclear technology for energy purposes, whereas states with nuclear arsenals would eliminate them. However, the treaty was fundamentally imbalanced. It placed obligations on the nonnuclear-armed states to accept international inspections of their nuclear installations—that is, nuclear reactors for producing energy or medical isotopes. But the nuclear-armed states—written into the treaty as countries that possess nuclear weapons as of 1967 and thus are not subject to international oversight—only agreed to "pursue negotiations in good faith on effective measures relating to the cessation of the nuclear arms race at an early date and to nuclear disarmament." Plenty of caveats and no time lines—and, just to provide more confusion and cover, tacked on to the end: "and a treaty on general and complete disarmament under strict and effective international control."

Although rhetorically ambitious, in reality this language has been used effectively by the nuclear-armed states to perpetually stall on nuclear disarmament. These governments have argued, for example, that nuclear disarmament cannot take place before or outside of a treaty on "general and complete disarmament." They have also argued that reduction in arsenal numbers over the years since the end of the Cold War constitutes their implementation of this obligation—even though they still possess and invest billions of dollars in their earth-destroying arsenals. Some of the nuclear-armed governments have even used the NPT to justify their "right" to possess and to modernize their nuclear weapons. For example, Tony Blair, then-UK prime minister speaking in the House of Commons in 2007, argued that the NPT "makes it absolutely clear that Britain has the right to possess nuclear weapons."[28]

By formally dividing the world into "nuclear weapon states" and "nonnuclear weapon states," the NPT shaped global dynamics for the indefinite future. It set up a "social nuclear hierarchy that mirrors the permanent membership of the United Nations Security Council, reifies nuclear weapons as a currency of power for a privileged few, and contributes to a naturalized conflation of power, influence, and nuclear possession."[29]

Despite this, compliance with the nonproliferation part of the bargain has held strong over the years, with only India, Israel, Pakistan, and North Korea acquiring nuclear weapons since the treaty entered into force.[30] Of these, only North Korea was ever party to the NPT; it withdrew in 2003 when it began its nuclear weapon program. Meanwhile, compliance with the disarmament obligation has been nonexistent.

The NPT states' parties review the treaty's implementation every five years. At the first Review Conference in 1975, the nuclear-armed states already demonstrated their cynical approach to their obligations under the treaty. They had nothing substantive to offer either in preventing proliferation or achieving disarmament. They refused to accept any proposals put forward by other states, and the United States even conducted a nuclear weapon test during the conference. The nuclear-armed states cooked up an outcome document in advance, spoke in a "singular preharmonized manner," and stonewalled any attempt to get them to commit to nuclear disarmament measures.[31] The final declaration congratulated the nuclear-armed states for arms limitation and disarmament agreements.[32] (Such behavior has continued to the present day, as will be shown throughout this book.)

In 1995, states' parties agreed to indefinitely extend the treaty, which was otherwise set to expire. In exchange for this extension in perpetuity, the nuclear-armed states committed to several concrete provisions for achieving nuclear disarmament, and all states' parties agreed to a course of action to achieve a Middle East zone free of weapons of mass destruction. Given what has happened since then, however, a number of governments have expressed serious regret about agreeing to extend the treaty indefinitely without getting a firm commitment on a time line for nuclear disarmament.

By 2000, the commitments made in 1995 were not fulfilled. Nevertheless, coordinated pressure from nonnuclear-armed states, in particular those that formed the cross-regional New Agenda Coalition (Brazil, Egypt, Mexico, Ireland, New Zealand, South Africa, and Sweden), led to agreement on "thirteen practical steps" for nuclear disarmament. This included the first ever "unequivocal" political commitment that bound the five nuclear-armed states' parties to the total elimination of their nuclear arsenals. The international community was hopeful coming out of this meeting. The new commitments provided a reasonable, implementable roadmap for real nuclear disarmament. The fact that the nuclear-armed states had agreed to them, even if they did push back against them during negotiations, gave other governments and civil society a real sense that change was finally afoot.[33] But the promises made in 2000 proved to be nothing more than words.

Five years later, the nuclear-armed states had not made serious efforts to implement any of the practical steps, and the United States had even withdrawn from the Anti-Ballistic Missile Treaty. The 2005 NPT Review Conference was a dismal failure.[34] Canada's ambassador captured the moment well in his closing statement to the meeting, lamenting, "We have let the pursuit of short-term, parochial interests override the collective long-term interest" in sustaining the NPT's authority and integrity. Time that should have been devoted to the development of common ground was "squandered by procedural brinkmanship," he argued, highlighting the intransigence that more than one state exhibited and the hubris of those demanding that the priorities of the many be subordinated to the preferences of the few. "We have been hampered, frankly, by a lack of imagination and will to break with the status quo and adopt new ways of conducting our business."[35]

Only a few months later, that same ambassador led the charge to shake up things in the UN General Assembly's committee devoted to disarmament. Along with Brazil, Kenya, Mexico, New Zealand, and Sweden, Canada introduced a paper on "initiating work on priority disarmament and non-proliferation issues."[36] The paper outlined elements of a draft resolution that would establish four committees at the Conference on Disarmament (CD), including nuclear disarmament.

I don't want to pull us into the weeds of disarmament acronym soup here. But the CD is important if for nothing else as a masterclass in diplomatic failure caused by power politics. The CD—known as the "sole multilateral disarmament negotiating body," has been unable to adopt a program of work since 1996. (This is still true as of this writing.) Its work has been blocked by the nuclear-armed states, all of which hold competing priorities for what they think the conference should work on next. The CD operates by consensus, which in UN disarmament land has come to mean absolute unanimity—which gives every single country a veto. Sixty-five countries are in the CD, which means sixty-five vetoes.

The proposal that Canada and the others tabled was meant to offer a way around the stalemate by establishing work mandates in the UN General Assembly, but it still gave the CD the responsibility for conducting the negotiations. The proposal created great excitement at the General Assembly. The representative of Kenya described it as an attempt to "re-energize disarmament diplomacy" and suggested that it might be the "silver bullet that turns the tide."[37] But less than a week later, the governments putting forward this proposal announced that they would not table their resolution. According to their joint statement, this innovative proposal "would benefit from the opportunity to mature and for all delegations to gain a fuller understanding of what they entail."[38]

That was the cover story. In reality, it was well known that pressure from the United States was the principal factor why the group of states dropped their resolution. The U.S. government circulated a memo to countries' capitals calling the proposal "divisive" and arguing that it would "likely spell the end of the CD."[39] The United States at the time was the main state blocking consensus on a CD program of work, refusing to allow the forum to engage in work on any subject.

FROM "CAN'T" TO "CAN"

The next year, the Australian chapter of the International Physicians for the Prevention of Nuclear War (IPPNW), which had been awarded the 1985 Nobel Peace Prize for its efforts against nuclear weapons, decided to establish a new advocacy campaign: the International Campaign to Abolish Nuclear Weapons (ICAN). The long-term objective of the campaign was "to mobilize an irresistible groundswell of public opinion around the world that will compel leaders to start and conclude negotiations on a comprehensive legal agreement to finally abolish nuclear weapons before they are used again."[40] To do so, the original strategy of the campaign included efforts to diversify the voices calling for nuclear disarmament, educate professionals and the public on the urgency of nuclear abolition, and stigmatize nuclear weapons using "humour, horror, and hope."[41] Due to the initial housing of the campaign within IPPNW, much of the focus was on bringing young medical students to antinuclear activism.[42] However, it was also geared toward increasing the legitimacy of a new treaty prohibiting and eliminating nuclear weapons through work with diplomats and government officials at the international level.

Following the lessons of the International Campaign to Ban Landmines and the International Action Network on Small Arms, ICAN sought to build a larger, coordinated network of organizations and actors with a focused message and demand that governments would perceive as strong and credible. As part of this effort, ICAN sought to ensure that its messaging contained more hope than fear. Fear-generating approaches worked better in other times, the original strategy document argued, suggesting that a necessary precondition for action in the current time was hope and belief that humans can evolve. Although the horror is a necessary effect from the terrifying reality of nuclear weapons, and although this is useful for drawing attention to the issues, the presentation of horror must be coupled with solutions. And with jokes. "The anti-nuclear movement has a chronic humour deficiency," noted the founding ICAN strategy document. "And no wonder, its authors pointed out. "It is entirely unfunny that humanity is killing the planet with militarism, the idea and reality of investing security utility and symbolic power in weaponry and use of military force." These founders of ICAN thus set out to "carry people through the profound experience of understanding nuclear weapons as suicidal, genocidal and ecocidal" by using humor to "emphasize the absurdities of the risks, nomenclature and theories of the radioactive priesthood.[43]

In the early years of ICAN's existence, as was the case with earlier antinuclear activism, most emphasis was placed on demanding that the nuclear-armed states negotiate the total elimination of their nuclear arsenals. However, the campaign also sought to "name and shame" the countries that included U.S. nuclear weapons in their security doctrines. These countries, which include the members of the North Atlantic Treaty Organization (NATO), as well as Australia, Japan, and South Korea, have understandings or written agreements with the United States that the U.S. government would use nuclear weapons on their behalf to prevent or respond to a nuclear attack by another country. These agreements undermine work toward nuclear abolition, as they embroil more states than just those possessing nuclear weapons into defense of the atomic bomb and nuclear deterrence theory. ICAN sought to work with countries that had demonstrated leadership on nuclear disarmament efforts in the past, in particular countries that had no such relationship with nuclear weapons, to take on the nuclear-armed and nuclear-supportive countries.

ICAN officially launched in Australia in 2007 and was introduced to the international community in May that year at a preparatory meeting for the next NPT Review Conference. The campaign was on its way to prove that "rather than being naive and utopian to think that eliminating nuclear weapons is possible, it's naive and utopian to think that security can be achieved through the nuclear nightmare."[44]

THE NUCLEAR KNOT AND THE CHALLENGE
OF ANTINUCLEAR NUCLEARISM

Enter U.S. President Barack Obama. Riding in on a slogan of "Hope and Change," Obama spoke about nuclear disarmament early in his administration. The speech he gave on 5 April 2009 in Prague opened new space to talk about nuclear weapons and to pursue advocacy for disarmament. His rhetoric ignited the imaginations of those who wanted a nuclear weapon free world. All of the other nuclear-armed governments indicated that they shared this goal. Many activists working for nuclear disarmament were enthralled by this seemingly unprecedented opportunity to make real change.

The fact that his remarks were heavily qualified did not seem to matter. The president of the United States had (sort of) said that he wanted to eliminate nuclear weapons. Well, he said he wanted to *seek the peace and security of* a world without them. And that he would keep his own nuclear weapons until they no longer exist. This position is, of course, an incredible catch-22: nuclear weapons will exist until they no longer exist. Of course, as long as certain countries maintain the doctrine and apparatus of nuclear "deterrence," nuclear weapons will continue to exist—and more states may seek to acquire them in order to obtain a counterbalance against the vastly asymmetrical military power wielded by the United States.

Obama's professed goal of eliminating nuclear weapons was and remains subordinate to preserving the nuclear oligopoly between the United States and Russia and to preserving asymmetry in military dominance more globally. Within this context, nuclear disarmament is promoted as a "vision" that can only be reached through the rigorous pursuit of preconditions—the absolute assurance that no state will seek to develop nuclear weapons at any point in the future under any circumstances. In the meantime, the United States claims that as long as nuclear weapons exist, it will need to maintain an "effective deterrent" to any possible nuclear "outbreak." The other nuclear-armed states, as well as the U.S. allies that include U.S. nuclear weapons in their security doctrines, have since echoed this position.

Nevertheless, Obama's speech was a moment of excitement for activists, especially for those who had spent decades of their lives pushing for just this goal. Few stopped to consider what the stated goal actually was, or what path the president had outlined for getting there. The reality was that the policies flowing from this speech, rather than leading toward nuclear disarmament, instead locked-in the buildup of the U.S. nuclear arsenal, reinforced arguments and practices of nuclear deterrence, and focused on ever-stricter nonproliferation measures. The other nuclear-armed states followed suit, using the rhetoric of disarmament to justify their pursuit of more nonproliferation commitments by nonnuclear-armed states and their investments in developing or modernizing their nuclear weapon arsenals.

Critics of this approach termed it "antinuclear nuclearism." As a policy, it de-emphasizes the offensive nature of nuclear weapons. It simultaneously pursues an aggressive diplomatic and military campaign of nonproliferation efforts aimed entirely at other countries. It requires a fig leaf of disarmament efforts by nuclear-armed states—such as minimal reductions in the numbers of weapons in their arsenals—even while they design and build new bombs and missiles.[45]

This approach was given ideological cover by op-eds in 2007 and 2008 in the *Wall Street Journal* calling for a world free of nuclear weapons. The articles were signed by the former secretaries of state George P. Shultz and Henry Kissinger, former secretary of defense William S. Perry, and former Georgia senator and longtime chair of the Armed Services Committee Sam Nunn.[46] They advised steps for the United States and Russia to take to pursue the goal of eliminating nuclear weapons. Within a year, the 2007 op-ed was endorsed by more than two-thirds of living former U.S. secretaries of state, secretaries of defense, and national security advisers. It was also endorsed by a large number of civil society groups that were focused on nuclear weapons and broader peace issues.

But the recommendations by the four hawkish political figures failed to challenge the financial, political, or administrative interests of the nuclear weapon complex—which include politically powerful nuclear weapon laboratories, the corporations that run them, the universities that feed them scientists and engineers, and the politicians within whose territories they are situated. In fact, all four of these men were themselves intertwined with the nuclear weapon industry, sitting on the board of corporations and universities that administered the nuclear complex.[47] "Far from embodying the spirit of nuclear abolitionism with its inherent link to wider anti-militarist and environmentalist goals," warned critics of antinuclear nuclearism, those pressing for this seemingly new disarmament agenda were pursuing "a pragmatic strategy to maintain US military and economic dominance well into the 21st century," used to secure funding for nuclear labs and facilities.[48]

The Obama administration's stated goal of the eventual elimination of nuclear weapons was subordinate to these interests. This meant trading the new nuclear arms-reduction agreement made with Russia in 2010, the New Strategic Arms Reduction Treaty (New START), for multibillion-dollar infrastructure investments in the nuclear weapon complex. New START reduced the legal limit for deployed strategic warheads but did not actually reduce the number of warheads. The treaty does not require the destruction of a single nuclear weapon, and it "actually permits the United States and Russia to deploy almost the same number of strategic warheads that were permitted by the 2002 Moscow Treaty."[49]

Some activists critical of the deal described the New START as a "force protection" treaty rather than a disarmament treaty.[50] This reality was not lost on other governments. The ambassador of Brazil to the United Nations, for example, argued that New START was "based on the idea of equivalence of arsenals and of mutual security," and that its fundamental underpinning was "the persistent need of nuclear weapons to ensure security."[51] Instead of pursuing real arsenal reductions and concrete disarmament steps, the United States and Russia chose to maintain the status quo. Although it was largely seen as positive that the two governments were able to negotiate and reach agreement after strained years under the reign of George W. Bush, their quest for "strategic stability" rendered moot their rhetoric about a "vision" of a nuclear weapon free world.

By 2010, the rhetoric in favor of nuclear disarmament was already fading. In January that year, the four statesmen issued another *Wall Street Journal* op-ed, this one starkly titled "How to Protect Our Nuclear Deterrent." Calling for a substantial increase in funding for the U.S. nuclear weapon labs, they asserted that the United States "must continue to attract, develop and retain the outstanding scientists, engineers, designers and technicians we will need to maintain our nuclear arsenal, whatever its size, for as long as the nation's security requires it."[52] A few days after this op-ed was published, the Obama administration released its 2011 budget request, which included a spending surge to modernize the nuclear arsenal and its infrastructure, as had been promised to the U.S. Senate in exchange for the ratification of New START.[53]

The United States was not alone in its moves to keep its nuclear arsenal thriving. At the same time that the intellectual defense of nuclear weapon modernization was becoming entrenched in the United States, the other nuclear-armed states were seeking their own arsenal "refurbishments" or buildups. Most were also using the same rhetoric of antinuclear nuclearism to justify these investments. The story that these governments employed goes: We want disarmament, but the conditions are not ripe for it, so let's invest billions in upgrading or expanding our arsenals in the meantime. *Nuclear weapons will exist until they no longer exist.*

In 2009, Russian President Medvedev announced the development of new land- and sea-based nuclear missiles in addition to already ongoing modernization plans for its intercontinental ballistic missiles, submarines, and bombers.[54] In February 2010, Russia published its new military doctrine, which assumed "the maintenance of strategic stability and the nuclear deterrence capability at the level of sufficiency." The notion of sufficiency is defined as ability to inflict "predetermined" or "tailored" damage to an aggressor.

Also, in 2009, the United Kingdom released an information paper outlining steps and conditions toward a global ban on nuclear weapons—all of which focused on nonproliferation initiatives rather than reductions to its own arsenal or efforts to pursue multilateral nuclear disarmament.[55] At the same time, plans to renew its Trident nuclear system were well underway. This modernization program has already cost British taxpayers billions of pounds and will cost many billions more to come.[56]

Meanwhile, France was also in the midst of a broad modernization program involving submarines, aircraft, missiles, warheads, and production facilities; and China was investing in work aimed at increasing the "survivability" of its land-based strategic missiles. India's focus was on increasing the diversity, range, and sophistication of its nuclear weapon delivery systems, with the goal of having the complete "triad" (intercontinental ballistic missiles, submarines, and bombers) operational by

2013. Pakistan was rapidly expanding its nuclear arsenal and delivery systems, as well as increasing its capacity to produce plutonium. Israel had underway the construction of new nuclear submarines. North Korea had tested its second nuclear device.[57]

RHETORIC VS. REALITY: A BRIEF HISTORY OF DISARMAMENT DISAPPOINTMENTS

The disconnect between rhetoric and reality, and the use of antinuclear nuclearism as policy, are nothing new. In fact, both were long established in bilateral and multilateral "disarmament" discussions and negotiations.

Former Swedish diplomat Alva Myrdal described in the 1960s the unwavering tendency of the nuclear-armed states toward "talking disarmament while relentlessly building up their own armaments to dazzling levels."[58] She argues that the opportunity to prevent the nuclear arms race was lost by the early 1950s, when the pattern of the "game" between the United States and Soviet Union was set. In the international arena, "both sides would present proposals for disarmament agreement, of often wholesale dimensions, but would be careful to see to it that these would contain conditions which the opposite side could not accept. This is the way disarmament was, and is, continually torpedoed."[59]

Myrdal was not alone in this assessment of how the two nuclear "superpowers" acted. In the Eighteen-Nation Committee on Disarmament established in 1962, other government representatives were critical of the standard approach, which they described as making proposals they knew the other side could not accept. "It is this procedure which has made the problem of disarmament the preferred field for the cold war," warned the delegation of Brazil. "Proposals which are not feasible are put forward by either side in the expectation, not of any real progress in disarmament, but of an immediate political advantage before international public opinion."[60] Nigeria's representative described it as the two countries tackling disarmament from the angle of trying to gain advantage over each other.[61] The Mexican government questioned the effectiveness of continuing discussions where each side simply reiterates its problems with the other side's proposals. "The constant repetition of and defence of conflicting views," warned Padillo Nervo, will "tend to make their respective positions more rigid and inflexible."[62]

When it came to the Partial Test Ban Treaty, the Sea-Bed Treaty, or Strategic Arms Limitation Talks, Myrdal explains, the United States and Soviet Union would each put forward proposals—the Soviet Union's usually so comprehensive that they could easily be negotiated down; the United States' so limited that they could easily be negotiated up, resulting almost inevitably in agreements that reinforced the status quo rather than advanced serious disarmament or limitations to the arms race.

When they could agree, it was at no cost to either side. When the United States and Soviet Union presented their privately negotiated Partial Test Ban Treaty, their preamble contained their commitment to "seeking to achieve the discontinuance of all test explosions of nuclear weapons for all time, determined to continue negotiations to this end."[63] Yet at the same time, U.S. President Kennedy gave U.S. senators "unqualified and unequivocal assurances" that underground testing would be "vigorously and diligently carried forward."[64] He also promised that the United States would maintain its capacity to test in prohibited environments and would resume atmospheric testing if the Soviet Union did.[65]

"The sacrifice involved in a ban on atmospheric testing was not difficult for either side," notes Myrdal. The Partial Test Ban Treaty "probably was never intended as a measure to curtail the development of nuclear weapons. In any case, it has not had a restrictive effect on nuclear-weapons development, not even on the number and yield of tests by those nations who already possess such weapons."[66]

Similarly, the Strategic Arms Limitation Talks (SALT) did not ask questions about the possession, reduction, or elimination of nuclear weapons. Instead, they just haggled over marginal differences in their continued increase. These talks represented the "mutually agreed continuation of the arms race, regulated and institutionalized." This, in turn, confined the United States and Soviet Union "in a cage of their own making"—by institutionalizing the nuclear arms race in SALT agreements, U.S. and USSR freedom of action for disarmament was significantly reduced, argues Myrdal, shackled even more than before to domestic military, industrial, and political interests.[67]

This was made startlingly clear with the debacle in the United States over ratification of the Comprehensive Nuclear-Test-Ban Treaty (CTBT) in the 1990s. Just as with New START, a huge price tag was attached to the U.S. Senate's ratification of the CTBT. The Clinton administration presented this treaty to the Senate for ratification in 1997 along with a "Stockpile Stewardship and Management" program to maintain nuclear weapons research, testing, and production facilities. This program, initially funded at more than $4.5 billion a year, "called for new nuclear weapons facilities of unprecedented sophistication, and for continued nuclear weapons design and production." The Clinton administration deemed this necessary to secure support for the treaty from the nuclear weapons laboratories, the nuclear forces in the military, and their allies in Congress.

Huge debates among activists ensued over the price paid for the CTBT. Some described the Stockpile Stewardship program as a "Faustian bargain."[68] Others put all of their efforts into supporting Senate ratification, arguing that any step forward is a good step. More than a decade later, many activists similarly supported New START. A minority opinion opposed it, arguing that because the treaty was inexorably tied to billions of dollars in funding for the modernization of nuclear weapons without including any disarmament provisions, it would be unconscionable for activists seeking the abolition of nuclear weapons to advocate for ratification. This minority was bitterly informed by the majority that they were "playing into the hands of those who oppose the treaty." In the end, the U.S. Senate did approve ratification of New START, and nuclear weapon budgets in the United States—and elsewhere—have increased by billions of dollars.

ACCESS AND INFLUENCE

This is one example of the challenge facing activists, where anything critical of alleged "positive steps" is seen as undermining progress, even if those steps create serious challenges for ultimately achieving the goals of activist campaigns. This is also in keeping with the finding of social movement theorists that opportunities for resistance and protest are closely tied to institutional politics.[69] David Meyer, who specifically analyzed nuclear disarmament movements in this context, notes that such movements are most likely to succeed when government policy appears hostile and when "institutional routes for political influence appear foreclosed—precisely those times when they are unlikely to get what they want in terms of policy."[70]

Access is not influence. Political institutions may become accessible, but then they can represent a barrier between citizen pressure and public policy. The turn to institutional channels tends to cede ground to ideas and goals that are more moderate and centrist, whereas the center itself is being continuously redefined by more conservative elements.[71] In *The Authority Trap*, Sarah S. Stroup and Wendy H. Wong outline how what are considered "leading" nongovernmental organizations may seem to have both access and authority—"their reports make international newspapers, they partner with powerful states, and corporations take their calls"—in reality, "their authority constrains their choices and activities."[72] This theory argues that activists working outside of the institutions from which they are demanding change are better positioned both to make these demands and to make sure that the demands are far-reaching. Those working "on the inside" need to appear moderate to maintain their relationships with elites within the system. The authority trap Stroup and Wong describe "pressures them to advance incrementalist proposals and prioritize organizational imperatives over larger—potentially unpalatable—demands to change the status quo."[73] In contrast, those operating outside the halls of power can "hold the line"—they can highlight hypocrisy, agitate and challenge the institutions and structures upholding the status quo, and, in effect, widen the debate and push for broader change than can those working on the inside.

In turn, theorists such as Meyer argue, this gives those working on the inside—those sympathetic to the changes being demanded—more leverage than they might otherwise have, by providing them with a "mass base" of support. It also allows those on the inside more space to push the envelope in terms of their asks for policy change—they can point to the more "radical" demands of those outside as evidence that their own positions are quite "reasonable." At the same time, those outside can help redefine what is "reasonable" by making it clear what they really want rather than making compromises; this can pull the debate in their direction, shifting the middle ground.

This is not just the perspective of activists or academics working on the outside. This phenomenon has been noted and described by politicians and others working inside institutions with authority. "The work that gets done on the outside largely sets the boundary conditions for what happens on the inside," explained Scott Ludlam, a former senator for the Australian Greens, after his tenure in office from 2008 to 2017. Consistent with the social movement theory articulated here, he argued that the "driving force" for change comes from outside of institutions.[74] Similarly, some international development NGOs have started to recognize what they have lost by becoming too institutional. "With money and access to the corridors of places from Westminster to the World Trade Organisation," remarked the Institute of Development Studies in an interview with *The Guardian*, these organizations have "failed to take risks and instead simply pacified everyone at the expense of seeking real change." A former director of one of these NGOs agreed: "We've become used to being in business, so we've become less and less courageous."[75]

Unfortunately, by the end of the nuclear freeze movement in the 1980s, Meyer found that the leaders of some of the biggest antinuclear organizations had abandoned their greatest resource—public support—and turned toward elites. "Intending to maintain good relationships with mainstream elite supporters, arms control and disarmament groups readily narrowed their agendas, winnowing out potentially controversial aspects from their programs."[76] By adopting an institutional focus, Meyer argues, antinuclear weapon groups abdicated their role of imagining, articulating, and advocating for a different future in favor of making politicians feel more comfortable.

This meant that no mass protests occurred in opposition to the nuclear-armed states' commitment to nuclear weapon modernization in the post–Cold War period, because the groups previously capable of mobilizing action from their constituents had been effectively hobbled by their own buy-in to institutional access and monetary security. Trying to do any antinuclear activism under Obama was difficult—as noted above, some activists felt anyone critical of his policies or actions was being too aggressive toward "the best president we've ever had for nuclear disarmament." I even once had a high-level Obama official angrily tell me that by criticizing the U.S. nuclear weapon modernization program, I was undermining the president's efforts to achieve nuclear disarmament.

This challenging context of inside-outside strategies for change also shows the problem of taking a piecemeal approach to nuclear disarmament rather a comprehensive one. Over many, many years, antinuclear activists collectively accepted and celebrated treaties negotiated principally by the nuclear-armed states. These treaties have, time and again, done more to reinforce and institutionalize their nuclear weapon programs and policies than to disarm them. We have also worked primarily within forums, such as the Non-Proliferation Treaty and the perpetually stalemated Conference on Disarmament, that privilege the power of the nuclear-armed states and their nuclear-supportive allies over the majority of the world's governments that have already rejected nuclear weapons. Continuing to cajole and appeal to the nuclear-armed states to pursue negotiations to eliminate their nuclear weapons has been necessary but insufficient.

BUILDING ON THE PAST TO MAKE PROGRESS

The concept of necessity and sufficiency from the field of logics is helpful to understanding the thinking around making a change to international advocacy and activism on nuclear weapons. By 2010, a number of disarmament activists, particularly those of us who had been absorbed in the failures of established forums and approaches, felt strongly that we were in need of something new—not as a rejection of what had come before, but as an understanding that current efforts were not working to achieve our goal of nuclear abolition. This was the founding sentiment of the International Campaign to Abolish Nuclear Weapons in 2007 and helped reorient our strategy in 2010.

Many activists and most sympathetic government officials with whom ICAN interacted around that time believed we needed to revive the mass mobilization of the antinuclear movement heyday. Get one million people back in Central Park, and we can do something about nuclear weapons, was the common attitude. This analysis bears interrogation. We did not achieve nuclear disarmament even with one million people in Central Park in 1982, so would that do the trick now? Of course, one could argue that having mass mobilization not just in the United States but around the world as we did in the 1980s likely prevented even more egregious buildups or deployments of nuclear weapons and provided space for political leaders to claw back some of their policies and practices. But would that work in today's context? Nuclear weapons are a key component of broader militarist, political, and economic structures in the states that possess them. This is not just a question of two "nuclear superpowers"—that situation has festered and morphed, and these bombs have become entwined in the political economies and the doctrines of nine nuclear possessors and about thirty other U.S. allies.

This is a lingering question facing antinuclear activists: do these structures need to be fundamentally altered before public opinion can have an effect on nuclear policies, or does changing nuclear policies have an impact on these structures? Similarly, when all of the established forums for making progress in nuclear disarmament are prevented from functioning, can a mass movement create new space within which governments can operate? Would a street protest compel countries to give up their addiction to the consensus-based wasteland of the Conference on Disarmament?

Another issue was and is the preponderance of global challenges, from climate change and environmental devastation to war and displacement, to poverty and economic inequality, to mass incarceration and police brutality. Could we even raise 1980s levels of interest in nuclear weapons in short order without some kind of catastrophic event—which is exactly what we are trying to avoid? How could we best mobilize people around the world who were facing everyday challenges of finding enough food to eat, or contaminated water, when they are being displaced from conflict or from poverty?

In this context, some antinuclear activists felt that connecting nuclear disarmament initiatives to the efforts of other movements that demand and achieve economic and social justice, rather than resurrecting a nuclear disarmament movement itself, might be a more productive way forward. Their perspective was that disarmament will happen when people demand a justice that requires recasting the nuclear-armed states as countries that no longer colonize and exploit others in order to further concentrate the world's wealth and control the future. Nuclear disarmament would be an inevitable result of the success of movements that demand economic and social justice. Or a movement for nuclear disarmament could be connected with broader social and economic justice issues, framing nuclear weapons as a gross demonstration of the nuclear-armed states' skewed priorities. Cuts to social security, education, health care, and public pensions can be clearly seen alongside massive investments in the military, weapons development, and the modernization of nuclear arsenals.

The lines between economic priorities, social justice, and militarism have been drawn before. The disarmament movements of the 1980s had significant strands that connected disarmament to other issues. People engaged in antinuclear weapon movements included those who had participated "in the labor movements of the 1930s, in various civil rights movements of the 1950s and 1960s, in the anti-war, environmental and feminist movements of the 1960s and 1970s, and others as well."[77] The Women's International League for Peace and Freedom—the world's oldest women's peace organization, founded in 1915—has, for example, consistently articulated the links between these issues.

But by the twenty-first century, the activities of the foundations and other elites funding and directing disarmament work made it extremely difficult for movement organizations to mobilize constituents or do effective work. The institutionalization and professionalization of movement organizations have affected people and groups working on a broad range of issues. In many cases, leading nongovernmental organizations "transitioned from being innovative idealists to professionalized bureaucrats."[78] In this sense, networking with other groups could actually be detrimental for building an overall movement, because more often than not they are seeking their own stable sources of funding and recognition, meaning that they cannot necessarily be relied upon to speak unpopular truths or hold the line against the more powerful institutional actors. The institutional structures and democratic governance that make mass action effective have been undermined by the history of co-optation of left movements, the scope of which goes well beyond those focused on nuclear weapons.

With these challenges ahead, activists working to abolish nuclear weapons knew that building or rebuilding a social movement means starting somewhere. The question for ICAN by 2010 was, do we need one million people in Central Park right away, or can we start with one hundred people in a UN conference room and build from there?

THE GAME AND THE RESISTANCE

As activists were struggling with these questions, the nuclear-armed states were gearing up for or already invested in a new arms race. The 2010 NPT Review Conference was a difficult space to create real opportunities for progressive disarmament. The nuclear-armed states were committed to the "game" of disarmament, having perfected their tactics of stalling and stalemating over the past sixty-five years. In preparation for the 2010 conference, for example, each of the five nuclear-armed NPT members (China, France, Russia, United Kingdom, and United States) put forward a different vision of how to pursue nuclear disarmament.

The U.S. delegation reflected mainly on policy changes stemming from President Obama's speech in Prague, described above, rather than discussing possible future steps it would be willing to take. This approach cast the ongoing post-START negotiations with Russia as the first part of a step-by-step process leading to disarmament, rather than an indefinite end point.

France and the United Kingdom called for further U.S./Russian strategic arms reductions, without supporting processes that would in the near term bind or constrain their own nuclear arsenals, other than adhering to treaties they were already part of such as the nuclear test ban treaty. Whereas the French proposal dealt with broader multilateral arms control issues—particularly the issue of missiles—the UK approach placed emphasis on dealing with nuclear proliferation, linking pursuit of disarmament to dealing with proliferation concerns.

Russia, and to a lesser though increasing extent, China, focused on pursuing disarmament measures that would also incidentally improve possible perceived security imbalances with the United States. Russia specifically called for steps to create a stable strategic security environment suitable for disarmament, outlining its familiar initiatives. These include preventing a buildup of conventional capabilities to offset nuclear reductions and ceasing development of space weapons and missile defenses, both priorities for China as well. For its part, China generally stuck to its traditional positions, such as calling on all nuclear-armed states to agree to not be the first to use nuclear weapons against each other and to agree not to use nuclear weapons at all against countries that do not have a nuclear arsenal. China also called for an end to nuclear sharing and nuclear umbrella arrangements, which are the arrangements mentioned earlier that the United States has with NATO, Australia, Japan, and South Korea.

None of these competing priorities or visions are acceptable to the others; thus, they have become the standard menu brought to every disarmament discussion. They ensure that the discussion will go nowhere, and everyone can blame someone else for the stalemate. Adding to this standard approach, by 2010 the nuclear-armed states had started asserting that fulfillment of the NPT's disarmament obligations is everyone else's responsibility. That is, nuclear disarmament is the responsibility of those countries that do not possess nuclear weapons, rather than of the ones that do. France and the United States in particular argued that preventing proliferation is a necessary condition for disarmament. This built on a joint statement by all five nuclear-armed states, which insisted that other countries need to first "create the conditions" that the five deem necessary for disarmament. "All other States must contribute to fulfilling these disarmament goals by creating the necessary security environment, resolving regional tensions, promoting collective security, and making progress in all the areas of disarmament," they proclaimed in their opening remarks to the conference.[79] As discussed in chapter 1, this tactic was not new, but it was making a mark as the main position of all five countries.

Throughout the 2010 NPT Review Conference, France, Russia, the United Kingdom, and the United States engaged in a seemingly coordinated assault against all concrete disarmament steps in various drafts of the outcome document. China, which kept its powder dry in public, was reportedly delivering handwritten notes to the chair of the meeting with many of the same objections. In several cases, these suggested amendments by the nuclear five would have resulted in a document weaker on disarmament than ever before.[80] Overall, the nuclear-armed states treated the art of compromise like a zero-sum game of "winners" and "losers," in which one party demands another change its position to meet theirs, rather than agreeing to meet that party in the middle. Quick to point fingers at each other, opposing delegations did not engage in diplomacy but, rather, in a game of chicken.

As in the past, it was states not possessing nuclear weapons that put forward concrete proposals while eloquently challenging the rhetoric and tactics of the nuclear armed. "A world without nuclear weapons cannot continue to be just a vision," warned the representative of Norway. "It is an objective which we, states parties to the NPT, are committed to achieve."[81] Noting that nuclear weapons "are a legacy of the past and should be seen as irrelevant and counterproductive in future security policies," Norway's ambassador encouraged further discussion on an "additional legal instrument" to achieve and maintain a nuclear weapon free world. This was the call of the vast majority of activists participating in the conference, including ICAN.

As a step toward such an instrument, Switzerland called for the Review Conference to adopt an action plan for nuclear disarmament, moving beyond the thirteen practical steps from 2000 by including a time frame. It suggested that the plan should include a dimension on quantitative disarmament—including new negotiations between Russia and the United States to reduce their arsenals. It also said that the plan should include ending modernization programs, reducing the operational readiness of nuclear weapon systems (ending the practice of having nuclear weapon systems ready to launch in moments), and reducing the role of nuclear weapons in military doctrines. In addition, Switzerland suggested the start of a debate on the legitimacy of the use of nuclear weapons, as well as discussion on a new treaty to ban nuclear weapons.[82]

The Review Conference did decide to develop an action plan on nuclear disarmament—on the condition that plans also be developed for nonproliferation and nuclear energy, which are considered to be the other two "pillars" or streams of work of the NPT. Under the facilitation of the Austrian delegation, the first draft of the disarmament action plan was surprisingly strong. But it came under concerted attack by the nuclear-armed states, in both public and private meetings.[83] In public, the statements by the nuclear-armed gang clearly demonstrated their intentions and expectations: they wanted to receive lavish praise for their nuclear arms reduction measures undertaken since the end of the Cold War—France specifically requested the Review Conference "hail the gestures" they have made—while they simultaneously rejected any commitments to concrete steps leading to actual nuclear disarmament.[84]

It was a spectacle akin to theater of the absurd, painting a clear picture of the nuclear-armed states' "vision" of a nuclear weapon free world as a world in which they retain their nuclear weapons. In this spirit, the French delegation called for the first paragraph of the action plan's principles and objectives to be changed from resolving "to achieve the peace and security of a world without nuclear weapons" to committing to "creating the conditions for a world without nuclear weapons." Despite the fact that the original language was *based on President Obama's Prague speech*, the U.S. delegation welcomed France's suggestion.

The nonnuclear-armed states rejected this nonsense. "The [nuclear-armed states] consider the possession of nuclear weapons essential to maintaining their self-image of their place in the world and not just a military necessity," observed the representative of Singapore, rather astutely. "We need to find ways to convince all states that nuclear weapons reduce rather than increase their security, and do not enhance prestige."[85] Others focused specifically on the gap between the nuclear-armed rhetoric and the reality of their policies and programs. The Irish delegation, for example, pointed out that reductions alone do not tell the whole story and that one can only judge a state's true intentions by surveying the full range of its actions and pronouncements.[86]

Most nonnuclear-armed states expressed frustration with the lack of benchmarks by which to measure the pace at which nuclear-armed states comply with their disarmament obligations, the degree to which they comply, or the sustainability, the verifiability, or the irreversibility of said compliance. But the nuclear-armed states refused to accept any language on the above issues. The French ambassador argued against the imposition of "artificial deadlines" and said that time lines would weaken the NPT regime because, he argued, nothing is gained by imposing deadlines and not meeting them. A critical look at this assertion reveals the double standard: that deadlines or time frames for disarmament cannot be established, or if established, they cannot be expected to be met, because they are "artificial," but deadlines and time frames must be imposed and met for nonproliferation in order to remain "in compliance" with one's treaty obligations.

Although the U.S. and Russian delegations supported France's perspective and also argued against the "imposition" of deadlines, a number of delegations reacted strongly against this, including Indonesia, Mexico, Brazil, Iran, South Africa, the Philippines, Algeria, Cuba, and Canada. A few states, including New Zealand and Mexico, described some of France's proposed amendments as "unacceptable." Indonesia's delegation pointed out that when states gave up the option of pursuing nuclear weapons, they did so with the understanding that nuclear-armed states would do the same at some point. Algeria's delegation noted that time lines simply offer a tool by which to measure progress, which is something uniquely lacking when it comes to the NPT's disarmament obligation. South Africa's representative cautioned that the nonnuclear-armed states are reaching levels of desperation because they have not yet seen concrete action on nuclear disarmament as specified in article VI. The Canadian delegation, in typical bridge-building fashion, called for language that avoids both overly prescriptive time frames and no time frames at all.

After all the fighting and frustration, NPT states parties did manage to agree on an outcome document with a sixty-four-point action plan on nuclear disarmament, nonproliferation, the sharing of nuclear energy technology, and a plan for pursuing a weapons of mass destruction free zone in the Middle East. Twenty-two of these actions related to disarmament, and after the failure of the conference in 2005 to agree on anything, most people felt relief, if not hope.

But something else made it into the outcome document—the full significance of which was not known at the time, but that set us up to ban nuclear weapons seven years later. This was a relatively quiet reference to the catastrophic humanitarian consequences of nuclear weapons and the relevance of international humanitarian law to nuclear weapons. This groundbreaking achievement, and its implications, is the topic of our next chapter.

3

RECLAIMING OUR TIME

Changing Discourse, Changing Minds

In July 2017, U.S. Congresswoman Maxine Waters became an internet sensation when she calmly and repeatedly uttered the phrase "reclaiming my time" to shut down the rambling, sidestepping efforts to silence her of Treasury Secretary Steven Mnuchin. He was testifying before the House Financial Services Committee about the state of the international finance system when Waters, the committee's ranking Democrat, asked why his office had not responded to her letter inquiring about President Trump's financial ties to Russia. As the *Washington Post* reported, "Mnuchin tried to sidestep the question with platitudes and compliments, apparently attempting to run out the clock on her questioning. It didn't work."[1]

This moment "stands out because it resonates far beyond its original context," wrote Christine Emba, the *Post* columnist covering the incident. "Who among us, after all, hasn't lost irreplaceable time to a uselessly meandering meeting, a pointless conversation or a draining social interaction? Waters's phrase rang out as a rejection of that made manifest, delighting all of us who have been spoken over, ignored or had our time wasted by others." Further, Emba pointed out, "for many women and people of color, the phrase 'reclaiming my time' felt particularly poignant, with the idea of reclamation specifically speaking to both the present and the past. Society has been wasting not only their time but also their voices, agency and potential—for years."

This is how some of us felt at the 2010 NPT Review Conference when language about the humanitarian consequences of nuclear weapons was successfully included in the outcome document. A paragraph, unprecedented in nuclear weapon agreements, expressed states' parties "deep concern at the catastrophic humanitarian consequences of any use of nuclear weapons," and reaffirmed "the need for all States to comply with international humanitarian law at all times."

To have such language included in the outcome of a meeting historically and habitually controlled by the nuclear-armed states to reflect and reify their worldview and their interests was rather extraordinary. It was a moment of quiet, subversive victory for those of us who had spent years or even decades working within that sometimes soul-crushing, otherworldly space of nuclear-armed mythologies. For those who have not bought into the "falsely obvious"[2] beliefs of the magic of nuclear deterrence, talking about nuclear weapons in humanitarian terms in an NPT document was like a glimpse of reality disrupting an otherwise steadfast traditional narrative of unreality.

This language didn't come out of the blue. It was based on years of activism and academic research of decades past. The collection of baby teeth in the 1960s proving children across the United States were being affected by nuclear testing in the Nevada desert; scientific studies on "nuclear winter" and the resulting global famine; books such as *On the Beach* depicting how radioactive fallout would spread across the globe—all of these provided information about the dangers of nuclear weapons to humanity and our planet. But this was not the dominant discourse at intergovernmental meetings about nuclear weapons. Those meetings were, as described in the previous chapter, dominated by countries with nuclear weapons talking about "geopolitical stability" and "strategic security." The minutia of those meetings is rarely reported in the media, but the discussions there set the stage for the policies of Moscow and Washington. The idea that nuclear weapons are essential to security is treated as gospel and justifies the massive investment in these weapons.

But, that's the thing about discourse shift. You have to be willing to put out unconventional ideas and carefully, methodically build the case for them, with the cooperation and coordination of others. Mainstream discourse on any subject reflects and reinforces relations of power "by reproducing accepted ways of being and acting in the world and silencing others."[3] Discourse shapes our understandings of what is "appropriate"—it sets the boundaries of what can be said and how it can be said. It determines "truths" that control "how actors, events, and desired outcomes are defined and interpreted, and what information or knowledge is considered 'real,' legitimate, and therefore relevant."[4]

Seyla Benhabib says that to deconstruct a discourse, one needs to show that what appears as a given is not a "natural fact" but a "historically and socially formed reality."[5] Discourse can become solidified or naturalized as social facts and, thus, become resistant to change. But if different interpretations and approaches emerge, the dominant discourse may be able to be splintered. The very act of contesting and challenging dominant narratives helps this splinter, opening up space for change to take shape. New understandings or practices can develop in response to this contestation and splintering. This process can involve rhetorical shifts by powerful players—for example, the language Obama was using in 2009 about the "peace and security of a world without nuclear weapons." But rhetoric from those in power, as we have seen, can easily be accompanied by and even serve to mask opposing policies. We can't rely on those possessing nuclear weapons to lead the way. Time and history have clearly shown that change would have to come from elsewhere.

This chapter looks at the resurgence of a conversation about the humanitarian and environmental impacts of nuclear weapons, which Norway, Switzerland, and others initiated in 2010. To contextualize this advancement, this chapter also explores the history of previous efforts to get international humanitarian law to address nuclear weapons and to delegitimize nuclear deterrence theory. It examines multiple UN-based efforts to advance a new narrative on nuclear weapons and the consequent pushback from nuclear-armed states.

DEVALUING NUCLEAR WEAPONS
AND DEBATING DETERRENCE

In his history of scientific revolutions, Thomas Kuhn argues that each shift in science is hard to come by, due to resistance of scientists to let go of existing theories.[6] Students study the precepts of paradigms to prepare for membership in the community with which they will later practice. Each person whose research is based on these shared paradigms is committed to the same rules and standards. When scientists, as a community, are confronted with information that is inconsistent with the collective understanding of how the world works, these challenges generally are met with broad resistance. Even when confronted with "severe and prolonged anomalies," they are unlikely to renounce the paradigm that has led them into crisis until they have a new theory ready to take its place.[7] They may experience cognitive dissonance, a psychological stress in which they hold thoughts or beliefs they know to be untrue because nothing else fits with their view of the world, until it can be explained in a way that is broadly acceptable to the community.

This kind of shift in nuclear weapon theory arguably took place—and is still taking place—with the development of the humanitarian initiative, which, as one of its diplomatic progenitors says, "emerged as perhaps the most serious challenge to the nuclear deterrence orthodoxy."[8] This initiative began with the introduction of language about the "catastrophic humanitarian consequences of nuclear weapons" in the 2010 NPT Review Conference final document. It then grew through three international conferences on humanitarian impacts, multiple joint statements at various intergovernmental forums, and a concerted effort by a core group of activists, academics, and diplomats to shift the nuclear weapon discourse from abstract security policy to the concrete humanitarian and environmental consequences of nuclear weapons. The humanitarian initiative challenged the acceptability and legitimacy of nuclear weapons and the policy of nuclear deterrence by reinvigorating discussions and studies on the effects and risks of nuclear weapons. Although such analysis in itself is not new, the paradigm shift is reflected in how this information was presented and used: it was intended to pointedly disrupt the nuclear deterrence myth and lay the foundation for a revolt by nonnuclear-armed states to change international law.

The renewed focus on the humanitarian and environmental impacts of nuclear weapons constituted a deliberate effort to devalue, delegitimize, and stigmatize nuclear weapons. The combined diplomatic and activist process of reframing nuclear weapons as weapons of terror and consequence exposed the cognitive dissonance of "nuclear deterrence," illuminating its corrupt self-serving rationale and its influence over international affairs. Those engaged in this work sought to remove the veil of legitimacy and authority of the nuclear-armed states—dismantling their arguments, disrupting their narratives, and ultimately standing up to their projection of power. This directly challenged the mainstream rhetoric around nuclear weapons in a deliberate undertaking of discourse change, designed to create new space for action among the gaps and holes exposed in a morally bankrupt system of thought.

The argument that nuclear weapons were tools of massive violence with horrific humanitarian consequences was not new. But the spaces in which this perspective was articulated and advanced, and the action toward which it was directed, were new. Activists and diplomats developed a new process to propel the humanitarian narrative forward, with the goal of undermining the dominant discourse on nuclear weapons and disrupting the stage upon which these weapons were traditionally discussed. This meant including and amplifying traditionally excluded voices and working to change the notion of who could speak, and what they could say, about nuclear weapons. Nuclear-free countries constructed an entirely new forum to engage with nuclear questions, focusing solely on humanitarian impacts—rather than debating security postures, they elevated the lived experience of those who have suffered and would suffer in the future from nuclear weapons. The ultimate objective was the elimination of nuclear weapons. But, faced with "the creeping permanence of nuclear weapons 70 years into the nuclear age,"[9] this process was going to require a rewriting of the rules—a fundamental disruption of the religion of these weapons.

As outlined earlier, nuclear weapons are assigned values as part of security policies as deterrents, as part of economies as job creators, and as part of national identities in terms of power and pride. Because these values are ascribed through social, political, and economic relationships and are not written in stone or based on natural fact, these values are subject to change. But achieving material changes, such as reducing nuclear arsenals or ending nuclear weapon modernization programs, means that the value ascribed to these weapons needs to be completely dismantled.

Since the end of the Cold War, cosmetic adjustments have been made to the valuing of nuclear weapons. Absolute numbers of nuclear warheads have been reduced, for example. But "deeper forms" of devaluing require more explicit changes to nuclear doctrines, such as rejecting the policy of nuclear deterrence and related practices.[10] Otherwise, the nuclear-armed states will continue to argue that the devaluing they have done fulfills their NPT obligations while they simultaneously reiterate their belief in the importance of nuclear weapons for "national security" and reinvest in their arsenals.

A deliberate attempt to devalue nuclear weapons in international discourse and policy making began in the 1990s. With the end of the Cold War, academic analysts and government officials alike largely agreed that the role of nuclear weapons would be diminished in strategic security doctrines and policies.[11] This process was reflected in language in the NPT Review Conference outcome documents from 1995 and 2000, as well as in statements from a range of governments to the conferences in 2005 and 2010. In parallel to these meetings, a series of international commissions also highlighted the importance and necessity of devaluing nuclear weapons, including the 1996 Canberra Commission, the 1999 Tokyo Forum, the 2006 Blix Commission on Weapons of Mass Destruction, and the 2009 International Commission on Nuclear Non-Proliferation and Disarmament.[12] These commissions, together with the NPT review process discussions and outcomes, "cemented two key concepts in the disarmament narrative aimed at qualitative change in nuclear policy and practice: reducing the role of nuclear weapons and delegitimizing nuclear weapons."[13]

In part, both of these goals require a confrontation with nuclear deterrence. In 2010, the Swiss government commissioned a study by a set of academic experts and practitioners that examined the validity of deterrence theory. It found that belief in nuclear deterrence creates a fear that without nuclear weapons, major conflict will erupt, and that it is mostly this fear that is preventing nuclear disarmament.[14] For example, around this same time the U.S. government proclaimed at the United Nations that countries "acquired nuclear weapons in order to promote what they saw as their national security" and asserted, "If they are to give them up, they must be convinced that doing so will not harm their security and that of their friends and allies."[15]

Overcoming this fear, many academics and diplomats argued, is imperative to achieving nuclear disarmament. "It is clear that any decision to relinquish nuclear weapons will require an acceptance by the policy elite that nuclear weapons are no longer required to meet national security challenges," noted British academic Nick Ritchie. "Such a decision will necessarily require, at least in part, a transformation of identity conceptions from iterations that currently generate a 'national interest' in deploying nuclear weapons to ones that do not."[16]

To this end, he and others built on previous arguments against deterrence to attack the mainstream narrative. They pointed out, for example, that deploying nuclear weapons with the intent of deterring others from acquiring them or launching an attack does not automatically ensure that others will indeed be "deterred" from doing so. Those who possess nuclear weapons tend to implicitly assign to their nuclear weapons an infallible ability to deter and thus refuse to consider the consequences of the failure of deterrence. But, as Ritchie has noted, nuclear deterrence "is unlikely to work if a state or nonstate actor is determined to enact its aggressive intent; if it does not consider a deterrent threat to be credible and thinks it can control unacceptable risks resulting from its actions; if it thinks it can survive an attack and is prepared to absorb a retaliatory strike; or if it thinks it can eliminate the deterrent threat by pre-emptively destroying an opponent's retaliatory strategic forces."[17]

Opponents of deterrence theory also challenge the assertion that nuclear weapons prevented conflict during the Cold War. This claim is based on the assumption that without nuclear weapons the Soviet Union and United States would have engaged in a direct war with each other. But many other factors prevented a war between countries with nuclear weapons since 1945: The devastation of World War II; economic integration and interdependencies among these countries; and satisfaction with an international status quo that allowed countries to maintain a certain level of privilege and power in international relations. There are also "compelling arguments suggesting that the United States and the former Soviet Union avoided world war for several possible reasons, most notably because neither side wanted to go to war," writes David P. Barash. "Indeed, the US and Russia never fought a war prior to the nuclear age. Singling out nuclear weapons as the reason why the Cold War never became hot is somewhat like saying that a junkyard car, without an engine or wheels, never sped off the lot only because no one turned the key."[18]

Yet without knowing the real relevance or effectiveness of the theory of nuclear deterrence, its proponents insist on its validity even in the face of changing relationships, power dynamics, and converging global crises. "We have not faced a moment in which the fundamental drivers of conflict amongst the most powerful states have been present," points out activist-lawyer Andrew Lichterman. Among these, he cites "competition over key resources, intensifying political tension within states over wealth distribution, and general collapse of a prevailing 'normal' order of international economic and political relationships."[19] How will the theory of nuclear deterrence hold up in these circumstances? Can we afford to wait and see? "What we can say is that, as of this morning, those with the power to exterminate life have not done so. But this is not altogether comforting, and history is no more reassuring," says Barash.[20]

With this in mind, it is also necessary to consider that nuclear deterrence does not automatically stabilize relations between nuclear-armed states. For one thing, different governments may interpret threats and credibility differently. For another thing, the practice of nuclear deterrence creates a sense of instability and insecurity for most other countries. As a nuclear-free state, for example, Austria's leaders have expressed concern that it looks as if nuclear deterrence has become an end in itself. There is a "deeply disconcerting perception among non-nuclear weapon states that the United States and Russia (followed by the other nuclear weapon states) are trapped in a highly dangerous Cold War thought-system which renders them incapable of addressing and solving the nuclear weapons issue in a fundamental way, let alone giving up nuclear weapons," warned Ambassador Alexander Kmentt of Austria in 2013. "It is difficult to accept that the concepts of deterrence, mutually assured destruction, and the logic of nuclear strategic stability have simply been transferred into the twenty-first century and that the chance to remove this sword of Damocles from above our heads is not being seized with far more urgency."[21]

The Austrians weren't alone in expressing these concerns. A cross-regional group of countries that had come together to press for nuclear disarmament, made up of Brazil, Egypt, Ireland, Mexico, New Zealand, and South Africa, argued in 2010 that it saw "no justification for the acquisition or the indefinite possession of nuclear weapons and we do not subscribe to the view that nuclear weapons—or the quest to develop them—contribute to international peace and security."[22]

The same year, Norway's deputy minister of foreign affairs likewise argued, "Nuclear weapons are a manifest threat to our common security, and they cannot be seen as a legitimate means of advancing national interests—whether political or military,"[23] while the Turkish government said, "It is our steadfast belief that nuclear weapons or any other weapons of mass destruction cannot provide additional security for any country in this era. On the contrary, the possession of and the pursuit for such weapons undermines regional security and stability."[24] MERCOSUR, a South American trade bloc made up of Argentina, Brazil, Paraguay, and Uruguay,[25] argued that "Nuclear weapons are the heritage of an era and of a mentality that has already been overcome," and that their existence diminishes the security of all states, including those that possess them.[26] The Jamaican government likewise rejected assertions of the importance of nuclear deterrence, arguing that instead of keeping the world safe, nuclear weapons mean that "human survival remains precariously balanced on the brink of destruction." These weapons, Jamaica argued in 2010, "continue to occupy a place of prominence in the defense strategies of possessor states, despite the fact that history has shown us that rather than creating a situation of safety and security, their continued existence breeds a climate of fear, mistrust, and insecurity."[27]

Those who challenge deterrence theory have often pointed out that whatever one may believe about the effectiveness of nuclear deterrence in the past, nuclear weapons can play no conceivable role in confronting today's challenges.[28] The assertion that nuclear weapons have been successful in preventing or ending conflict has also been challenged. In his book *Five Myths about Nuclear Weapons*, Ward Wilson suggests that it was the Soviet Union's late entry into the Pacific theater in World War Two that prompted Japan to surrender, not the United States dropping the atomic bombs on Hiroshima and Nagasaki.[29] Others have pointed out that nuclear weapons have not prevented proxy wars between nuclear-armed states since the dawn of the atomic age.

The dogmatic insistence on nuclear deterrence theory as fact, despite the evidence or counterpoints against it, has "captured—and imprisoned—our moral imagination on the subject."[30] Nobuo Hayashi suggests that changing our thinking on nuclear weapons requires us to focus on their consequences rather than on their asserted value—to ask, as the humanitarian initiative sought to do, are nuclear weapons so destructive and horrific that they ought to be prohibited and eliminated, regardless of their potential utility as deterrents? He used the example of torture to outline how this can help shift our collective and individual thinking. "Most of us now agree that torture is a moral wrong in itself, and that under no circumstances do outcome-based claims ever justify it," he explains. "We reject torture because it robs its victims, who are still fellow human beings, of their very human quality by reducing them to mere instruments for the benefit of the rest of us."[31]

Andrew Lichterman notes, however, the key difference between torture and nuclear weapons. Although most of the world has rejected torture, this is "likely so because torture has existed for a very long time across a vast range of human experience."[32] In contrast, nuclear weapons are a relatively new part of our history, and were created and are maintained within powerful, secretive institutions. Those that possess and deploy nuclear weapons have been the ones to define or articulate the meaning of these weapons.

Language is a big part of the challenge to changing people's perspectives on any given issue. Michel Foucault suggested that systems of thought and knowledge—what he termed "epistemes"—are governed by rules that delineate possibilities, that determine the boundaries of our thought in any given time period or field. Language or statements come to be accepted as knowledge through a process framed by the current episteme, which determines what is acceptable practice.[33] Feminists and queer theorists have also focused on the importance of language for framing our dominant paradigms or beliefs. From Judith Butler's *Gender Trouble*[34] to Carol Cohn's "Sex and Death in the Rational World of Defense Intellectuals,"[35] feminist and queer critics of the dominant narrative have shown how language is used to determine our understanding of how the world works, desensitize us to violence, and justify oppressive behavior.

With both torture and nuclear deterrence, the tactics used to maintain hegemonic control over the narratives defending these practices include the establishment and promotion of "experts claiming privileged access to knowledges too complex and obscure for ordinary folk to understand and to secret 'information,' and if necessary, attacks on the 'patriotism' of any who nonetheless persist in raising questions."[36] *Who* is considered expert is also determined by the episteme, controlled by those with privilege that they wish to defend. Other voices are actively silenced, belittled, or diminished.

Carol Cohn and Sara Ruddick point out that in much "Western" thought, so-called objective knowledge is produced by people who are constrained by institution or identity. In the context of nuclear weapons, some people speak from or for the perspective of those who have used nuclear weapons; others from the point of view of those who have experienced nuclear attack. "Abstract discussion of warfare is both the tool and the privilege of those who can imagine themselves as the (potential) users of weapons," note Cohn and Ruddick. "The victims, if they can speak at all, speak quite differently."[37]

Further, whatever victims or survivors say is purposefully delegitimized by those defending the use of the weapons. As discussed in the first chapter, it is easier to justify the use of nuclear weapons if you are using abstract language than "the descriptive, emotionally resonant language of the victim. . . . Detailed, focal attention to the human impact of weapons' use is not only considered out of bounds in security professionals' discourse; it is also delegitimated by its association with the 'feminine,' with insufficient masculinity."[38] Feminist approaches reject both the attempts to desituate perspectives and to delegitimize certain perspectives on the basis of gendered notions of "emotion" and "rationality." Feminist thought rejects this "cultural division of meaning" and contests both the idea that prioritizing what is considered "military necessity" over everything else is rational and what falls into the assumption of "military necessity" to begin with. This approach questions the label of "realism" for worldviews that prioritize weapons and state power and argues that rather than being an objective reflection of political reality, the cultural thought of mainstream, institutionalized nuclear deterrence theorists only offers a "partial and distorted picture of reality" and is "a major contributor to creating the very circumstances it purports to describe and protect against."[39]

Nuclear deterrence is a theory purported by certain political, military, and academic folks within nuclear-armed and nuclear-supportive states. It is a theory that can be and is constantly disputed, debated, and dismantled. It is a faith-based theory: it "works as a construct in which simply the belief in the power of nuclear weapons to deter is—in fact—the deterrence."[40] Deconstructing theories such as this requires us to consider other perspectives and experiences just as seriously as we do those embedded in institutional careers and systems that defend and justify nuclear weapons. In her groundbreaking study of gender, queer feminist scholar Judith Butler argues that "naturalized knowledge . . . operates as a preemptive and violent circumscription of reality."[41] What is posited to be factual and normal is prescribed by those who maintain a privileged position of dominance and control. Power is not static; it operates in the production of frameworks of thought. In challenging power, Butler suggests that we need to not just critique the effects of institutions, practices, and discourses that the powerful create. We need to ask what possibilities emerge when we challenge the assertions of what is normative, to challenge what is taken in mainstream understandings to be common ground or absolute reality. "No political revolution is possible without a radical shift in one's notion of the possible and the real," says Butler.[42]

Creating this shift does not happen without effort—ideas and logics do not just change on their own. Change requires concerted work by people to frame things differently and to mobilize others to embrace new possibilities. When diplomats from nonnuclear-armed countries joined antinuclear activists, atomic bomb survivors, and representatives of the Red Cross in the humanitarian initiative, they developed a "new normal" of how to work together and of what was possible to imagine and create together. Taking a human-focused approach to nuclear disarmament, and thereby challenging the dominant state-centered approach to international peace and security, was vital in helping people involved to move past the intellectual block of deterrence theory. The purposeful deconstruction of nuclear weapons as weapons of terror and massive violence through the humanitarian initiative was an instrumental step to changing a lot of minds about what was "real" and what was possible. And it opened space for people who had been long ignored to be heard: diplomats from nuclear-free countries, academics challenging hegemonic thinking, survivors of nuclear weapon testing and use.

Changing the voices involved in the debate, and the frames of reference used to approach an issue, is critical to overcoming obstacles in theory and understanding. Opening our minds and the minds of others to new ways of looking at a problem is imperative. For example, one of the best articulations I've read against deterrence comes from Gwen Benaway, an Annishinabe/Mètis trans woman writing about traumatic childhood abuse and what it revealed to her about the concept of "deterrence":

I know a knife can sometimes stop violence from happening through the threat of further violence. There are moments in life where a knife is all you have. A sharp edge can mean the difference between suffering immense harm or walking away alive. Of course, the trouble with a knife is that once you pick it up, you can never put it down without fearing retaliation from the other party. You look for bigger knives and sooner or later, someone's blood is on your hands.[43]

But perspectives like this are never heard in the United Nations and would likely be laughed out of sites of established nuclear weapon scholarship or national security institutions. We cannot just continue to operate within the institutional structures and the systems of thought that the powerful have designed. We have been suffocating in those spaces for seventy years. We must open our minds to alternative thinking in order to make any progress.

Desiring to change the narrative about nuclear weapons and who has the right to determine the meaning of nuclear weapons, activists and diplomats sought to start a conversation grounded in reality instead of abstract concepts like deterrence. This means talking about what nuclear weapons do to bodies. To tissue. To hearts. To brains. To limbs. Skin. Eyeballs. It means talking about what they do to the environment. To the climate. To food production. To infrastructure. To cities and build-ings and roads and bridges. Among other things, those challenging the mainstream discourse on nuclear weapons asked questions such as, how does the threat to kill hundreds of thousands of people with nuclear weapons fit into a national security strategy? Under what circumstances would the use of such weapons, with their genocidal and suicidal impacts, constitute a "rational" contribution to security?

More than simply arguing with deterrence proponents, those rais-ing humanitarian concerns did so in order to "strip any use of nuclear weapons of any political legitimacy and, in doing so, radically under-mine the legitimacy of possessing nuclear weapons at all," in order to "provoke their elimination."[44] Moving away from trying to debate deterrence or reduce the perceived "value" of nuclear weapons, activists and diplomats supporting the humanitarian initiative instead sought to reduce the perceived "legitimacy" of the weapons.

CHALLENGING LEGITIMACY

Being "legitimate" and acting "legitimately" is a social condition.[45] In the case of nuclear weapons, sources of legitimacy include institutions and governance regimes, such as the NPT. The concept of national security is also used to confer legitimacy on the possession of nuclear weapons. The socially understood "necessity" of military power to provide security for society justifies and legitimizes the acquisition of nuclear weapons. In this context, delegitimizing nuclear weapons requires the stigmatization of nuclear violence.

Governments such as Norway and Switzerland, the International Committee of the Red Cross, and activist groups associated with ICAN had long been arguing that nuclear weapons were not legitimate tools of security. The statements put forward by increasing numbers of governments over the years made the case that nuclear weapons are illegitimate because of the catastrophic humanitarian consequences of any use of nuclear weapons, under any circumstances. Many of these governments directly connected the stigmatization of nuclear violence to nuclear disarmament. In 2009, Steffen Kongstad from the Ministry of Foreign Affairs of Norway declared, "There can be no doubt that nuclear weapons are the most inhuman and indiscriminate weapons ever created. Nuclear disarmament and non-proliferation are essential from a humanitarian perspective."[46]

The former foreign minister of Norway, Jonas Gahr Støre, built on this perspective in a speech he gave in 2010, calling for a humanitarian disarmament approach to nuclear weapons. "International efforts to ban or regulate a particular weapon must also address the effects of the weapon, and not just its intended use," he argued. "In this way, the focus has turned to the humanitarian consequences. This, in turn, reflects a new understanding of security, as an issue that directly affects human beings and their communities."[47] The Swiss government explicitly said that it "will continue to insist on the inherently inhumane nature of nuclear weapons" and "continue to promote the debate on the credibility and usefulness of nuclear deterrence," explaining, "We are convinced that focusing on such issues will contribute to de-legitimizing nuclear weapons and help prepare the ground for outlawing them in the long run."[48]

Experienced nongovernmental entities were eager to turn the tide as well. In advance of the 2010 NPT Review Conference, Jakob Kellenberger, then president of the International Committee of the Red Cross (ICRC), made a statement to diplomats in Geneva in which he set out in stark terms the unacceptable humanitarian consequences of nuclear weapons. He demanded action from all states, calling on them "to seize with determination and urgency the unique opportunities now at hand to bring the era of nuclear weapons to an end."[49] This was the first time that an ICRC president had spoken directly to states solely on the issue of nuclear weapons.

This was the background for action at the 2010 NPT Review Conference, where the Norwegian and Swiss delegations waged a low-profile campaign for putting international humanitarian law (IHL), the so-called laws of war, at the center of nuclear weapons discourse. These laws are contained principally within the Geneva Conventions and their Additional Protocols.[50] Among other things, they restrict the "means and methods of warfare" to mitigate human suffering. The use of nuclear weapons would violate several principles of IHL, including those prohibiting indiscriminate attacks or attacks directed at civilians or civilian objects; and the rules of proportionality, protection of the natural environment, and the obligation to take feasible precautions in an attack.[51]

The goal of Switzerland and Norway during the NPT Review Conference was to emphasize that nuclear weapons are immoral, unusable, and illegal under the rules of IHL. "The continued existence of defense policies based on nuclear weapons only serves to prolong this irresponsible gamble with the future of humanity," said Swiss foreign minister Micheline Calmy-Rey in in her opening remarks. "Nuclear weapons have no use, they are immoral and illegal. . . . Nuclear weapons are not just a means of mass destruction, they are a weapon of extermination." She called for the launch of a debate "concerning the legitimacy of the use of nuclear weapons regardless of the legitimacy of the motive of defence that can be invoked."[52]

With pushback support primarily from the Holy See and Mexico, as well as a few activist groups, Norway and Switzerland pushed to include language about humanitarian impacts and IHL in the outcome document of the meeting. Although the nuclear-armed states offered some resistance, it was relatively easy to get it to stick due to the intense fighting going on over other parts of the text. According to one diplomat engaged in this process, the United States privately informed the chair of the Review Conference and other governments that the inclusion of a reference to humanitarian impacts was a red line for its delegation. In response, one of the supporters of including this language reminded the U.S. ambassador that President Obama had just won a Nobel Peace Prize in part for his alleged support for nuclear disarmament.

To some extent, the inclusion of language about IHL and humanitarian consequences in the outcome document was surprising. The nuclear-armed states had consistently rejected the application of IHL to nuclear weapons throughout the atomic age. As early as September 1945, the ICRC questioned "whether the latest developments of the technique of warfare leave any possibility for international law to cover a firm and sound order of society."[53] It did indeed prove difficult—mostly because nuclear-armed states objected to any reference to nuclear weapons in IHL provisions or documents.

The *Draft Rules for the limitation of the dangers incurred by the civilian population in time of war* presented by the ICRC in 1956 were rejected precisely because they addressed the question of nuclear weapons, explained Yves Sandoz, director for international law and policy at the ICRC. "As a result, and although the international situation made such rules increasingly necessary, the ICRC decided to avoid the problem of nuclear weapons altogether when it drafted the Additional Protocols to the Geneva Conventions, adopted by consensus in 1977."[54] The Diplomatic Conference on the Reaffirmation and Development of IHL Applicable in Armed Conflicts, which drafted these protocols, acknowledged that nuclear weapons were the most destructive weapons. Writing on this conference, former Swedish diplomat Alva Myrdal argued that nuclear weapons, "being the cruelest megamurder arms of all, should naturally fall under a general prohibition of area bombardment or attacks against civilians or indiscriminate methods of warfare."[55] She expressed dismay at the failure of the conference to properly address this issue. Apparently, most participants accepted that the protocols should be restricted only to conventional weapons, because they believed that nuclear weapons had a "special function in that they act as deterrents preventing the outbreak of a major armed conflict between certain nuclear powers."[56] The law, participants felt, could not resolve a problem of so-called strategic balance.

In 1996, in response to a request from the UN General Assembly, the International Court of Justice issued an advisory opinion on the legality of the threat or use of nuclear weapons.[57] The opinion affirmed the general illegality of the threat or use of nuclear weapons and an unconditional obligation to negotiate for their elimination. It also emphasized that IHL applies to all weapons without exception. However, the opinion was qualified by the statement that "the Court cannot conclude definitively whether the threat or use of nuclear weapons would be lawful or unlawful in an extreme circumstance of self-defence, in which the very survival of a State would be at stake."[58] The court declined to directly address the legality of the policy of nuclear deterrence or the possession of nuclear weapons.

In response, the ICRC said that on the basis of scientific evidence submitted for consideration during the court's proceedings, the ICRC "finds it difficult to envisage how a use of nuclear weapons could be compatible with the rules of international humanitarian law."[59] Legal experts with the activist group the Lawyers Committee on Nuclear Policy argued that the threat or use of nuclear weapons, even in a circumstance of "extreme self-defense," remains subject to the requirements of IHL.[60] The organization noted that the court made it clear that a "fundamental" and "intransgressible" rule that military forces "must never make civilians the object of attack and must consequently never use weapons that are incapable of distinguishing between civilian and military targets."[61] The Lawyers Committee also pointed out that the judges' statements on the opinion "show that while the extreme circumstance/survival of the state provision was intensely controversial, support for general or categorical illegality was broad and deep."[62] Three judges objected to the opinion not definitively holding threat or use of nuclear weapons to be illegal in every circumstance.

With all of the evidence gathered from 1945 to 1996—including the direct impacts on victims in Hiroshima and Nagasaki, the horrific effects of blast and fallout on survivors of nuclear weapon testing in the Pacific, Australia, Algeria, Kazakhstan, the United States—it was and remains rather shocking that the ICJ could not just declare nuclear weapons categorically illegal. Every rule of international law developed to prevent harm and suffering is somehow negated by the idea that these weapons—weapons that are proven without doubt to destroy entire cities, melt human bodies, condemn survivors to a slow and painful death, and threaten entire generations—may somehow be "necessary" for security.

Indeed, the technostrategic discourse that ultimately governed opinions such as the ICJ's refused to take into account the multifaceted physical, political, social, economic, psychological, and moral consequences of nuclear weapons for which antiwar feminists would want us to account.[63] Instead, those espousing the dominant theories of deterrence and strategic stability rely on their self-contained production of "knowledge" and reality to determine how nuclear weapons should be treated in international law. They resist the humanitarian discourse because it focuses on what nuclear weapons actually do to human bodies, to societies, to the planet. Such evidence undermines the abstraction of nuclear weapons as "deterrents" and refocuses our attention on the fact that they are tools of genocide, slaughter, extinction.

DISRUPTING REALIST MYTHS WITH HUMANITARIAN REALITIES

"It may seem illogical," wrote Alva Myrdal in 1976, "but neither reason nor the political will of the majority of nations is enough to wrest these most powerful weapons from the minority of most powerful nations."[64] But logic has never been the strong suit of the nuclear-armed states or their nuclear-supportive allies. They claim a monopoly on realism, insisting on their credibility as deterrence doctrine defenders. But they could not contend with the emerging discourse on the humanitarian impacts of nuclear weapons. They could smell it coming, having been through it before on landmines and cluster bombs. They knew what this discourse shift meant and the threat it posed to their grip on the status quo of nuclear fiefdom. But they couldn't stop it, despite some serious attempts to do so.

Part of the success of this discourse shift was that many actors were far out in front, publicly and relentlessly pushing for a resurgence of humanitarian research and advocacy. Activist and advocacy groups affiliated with ICAN, and research groups such as UNIDIR, were ready to support and assist governments developing the humanitarian initiative. As soon as the language on IHL was adopted in the final outcome of the 2010 NPT Review Conference, WILPF was using it to make the case that it "reinforces the moral unacceptability and presumptive unlawfulness of any use of nuclear weapons, which is a powerful challenge to their possession by any state."[65]

Activists were not alone in this thinking. If no clear progress toward eliminating nuclear weapons comes soon, the Austrian delegation to the 2010 NPT Review Conference warned, "we will discuss with partners the feasibility of a global instrument to ban these weapons."[66] Similarly, the Swiss delegation argued that states must question at what point they will need to yield to the interests of humanity over their own narrowly defined concept of national security. "In the long term we must outlaw nuclear weapons, specifically by means of a new convention."[67] Although not yet ready to draw a direct line to any particular course of action, the Norwegian government was clear in its message that the humanitarian dimension is "as valid for nuclear weapons as for conventional weapons," with the deputy foreign minister arguing to the UN General Assembly in October 2010 that "weapons that cause unnecessary suffering and unacceptable harm have no place in today's international security environment, and it is in our mutual interest to establish norms and legally-binding rules for the elimination of such weapons."[68]

Countless other governments were embracing this view, denouncing the nuclear-armed states' assertions that nuclear weapons provide stability and protection in an uncertain world. "Nuclear weapons are a source of insecurity, not security," warned South Africa's ambassador at the same UN General Assembly meeting in 2010. "They are illegal, inhuman, and immoral instruments that have no place in today's security environment—a new reality marked by growing interconnectedness and common threats that transcend traditional boundaries."[69] South Africa decided to end its nuclear weapon program in 1989, giving it some measure of moral authority to challenge the arguments that nuclear weapons are valuable or necessary instruments of security.

This reality, that nuclear weapons are not useful for national security, had for South Africa and the majority of the world already translated into action. Most governments actively refused to acquire nuclear weapons. They actively rejected these instruments of death as a means of terrifying others into submission or holding entire populations ransom to their whim. Many of these governments, it must be said, invested ruthlessly in so-called conventional means of violence: either by selling weapons to shed blood around the world for profit—not on their territories, not their problem, out of sight, out of mind; or by purchasing shiny new toys or worn used goods, still good for killing, round after round. Though not adverse to violence or war or weapons per se, they still exhibited revulsion at the type of killing a nuclear bomb caused: the type of killing where everyone dies; where yet-unborn children will suffer their whole lives; where the water and land are contaminated for generations.

It was, for the first time, the narrative of these victims and survivors that took hold in the UN conference rooms. For once, the stories of those who had lost everything, or who could explain how we would all lose everything, took center stage. The perspective of nuclear weapon survivors and governments that sought security through international cooperation and regional collaboration got to be heard. But it took quite some effort to build this space. This was not a change that occurred overnight. Building on decades of feminist and humanitarian discourse in other areas and the lessons of banning other weapon systems, governments and activists worked together to change the discourse on nuclear weapons, bit by bit. And they sought to leverage this discourse shift in real political change.

FROM WITHIN THE UN WEEDS

As the humanitarian initiative began its ascent, Austria, Mexico, and Norway put together a proposal to start work on multilateral nuclear disarmament initiatives through the General Assembly in 2011. As noted earlier, the forum where such work was supposed to be conducted, the Conference on Disarmament (CD) had not negotiated any treaties since 1996. It had not even been able to implement a program of work—its agenda for discussion—since then. Thus, asking the General Assembly to take up the work to break this logjam seemed reasonable enough. These three countries had worked together banning landmines and cluster munitions. Advancing disarmament on humanitarian grounds was becoming part of their normative multilateral identity.

Their proposal in 2011 was similar to a work-around that WILPF and the Lawyers Committee on Nuclear Policy had proposed earlier in the year in a joint position paper that called on the UN General Assembly to establish working groups on nuclear disarmament and other issues on the CD's agenda.[70] It used lessons from the Arms Trade Treaty process to build a case for advancing work within the most democratic intergovernmental body at the world's disposal.

Yet after a month of dialogue, consultations, and frustration, the three governments fostering this approach were forced to withdraw their resolution. The most frustrating thing of all was that not just the nuclear-armed states objected to this proposal. Some of the countries condemning the resolution were states that claim to have as their highest priority the complete elimination of nuclear weapons. They blocked the proposal because they want this work to take place only within the CD, a body that operates only by absolute consensus. The nuclear-armed states have used the consensus rule as an instrument of veto since 1996. But here we were in 2011, with a bunch of supposedly nonnuclear-armed states holding disarmament hostage to the preservation of an institution established during an intense period of arms racing. These countries accused the Austria-Mexico-Norway resolution as distracting from the "core task" of CD member states, which is to forge consensus on a "balanced" program of work. However, this task had, at that point, been attempted for fifteen years to no avail—which has in fact distracted from the CD's real core task, which is to negotiate disarmament treaties!

Activists and many other nonnuclear-armed states had grown weary of calls for "political will" to overcome the deadlock in the CD. That mantra had been repeated for decades without bringing us closer to nuclear disarmament. Meanwhile, we were all watching the goal of nuclear disarmament become more elusive as modernization programs were put into place and billions of dollars were sunk into the weapons laboratories. The continued economic, political, and security investment in nuclear weapons was corrosive, undermining the development of collective approaches to security and peace.

The sponsors of the withdrawn resolution were flabbergasted by the response to their resolution. "Since joining the CD in 1996, Austria has never seen one day of substantive negotiations there," remarked the Austrian ambassador to the meeting. "We are being told that security interests are at stake, as if the negotiation of disarmament treaties were a threat." This is odd, he argued, as we know that "the negotiation of disarmament treaties increases the security of the international community at large, especially of the vast majority of states not possessing nuclear weapons."[71]

This episode was depressingly reminiscent of the attempt by Canada and others in 2005 to establish working groups to take up the work of the CD, as described previously. The former Canadian ambassador who had led the failed attempt in 2005 to get the UN to start real work on nuclear disarmament commented poetically on the 2011 failure. He lamented, "It would appear that the prospect of actually coming to grips with the diplomatic disaster that is the [CD] induced vertigo amongst the decision-makers in several capitals, and instructions were issued to revert to the default setting of deferring action while admonishing the conference for the nth time to overcome its differences." Describing this failure as "kicking the can down the road," the former ambassador concluded that meaningful action was put off again for at least another year. "The metallic sound of tin scraping against asphalt echoed along First Avenue only briefly."[72]

Shortly after this epic show of powerful countries flexing their muscles at the General Assembly to delay progress, however, a boost came from a crucial civil society actor. In November 2011, galvanized by powerful statements from the ICRC president, the Council of Delegates of the International Red Cross and Red Crescent Movement adopted a new resolution on nuclear weapons. The resolution, which appealed to states to prohibit the use of and completely eliminate nuclear weapons,[73] was intended to "help position the Movement in the changing context of the nuclear disarmament discussion."[74] It also offered support to those Red Cross and Red Crescent National Societies that were already raising nuclear weapon issues at the national and regional levels, and to inspire others to do so.

In April 2012, just before the opening of the next NPT Preparatory Committee, the Norwegian government announced that it would host a conference in early 2013 to discuss the humanitarian impact of nuclear weapons. Referring to the increasing momentum on this topic, including the resolution adopted by the International Red Cross and Red Crescent Movement, foreign minister Jonas Gahr Støre announced to the Norwegian parliament that it would host "a conference in Oslo to highlight different aspects of nuclear weapons as a humanitarian problem."[75]

The nonnuclear-armed states parties of the NPT eagerly anticipated hearing about progress on the twenty-two Action Plan items dealing with nuclear disarmament that the nuclear-armed states had agreed to in 2010. But the nuclear-armed states had only marginally addressed any of these by the 2012 NPT Preparatory Committee, held in Vienna.[76] Although representatives of the nuclear-armed governments met in Paris in June–July 2011, ostensibly to discuss the actions they had committed to the previous year, the meeting did not go beyond declarations of "unconditional support" for and "reaffirmation" of the Action Plan.[77] In the meantime, they were pushing ahead with nuclear weapon modernization programs, investing billions more each year in the "refurbishment" of their arsenals.[78] The performance of supposed political will for nuclear disarmament—put on since Obama's Prague speech in 2009—was over.

Even the nuclear-armed states' closest allies were a bit perturbed by this intransigence. The Australian delegation to the 2012 Preparatory Committee expressed concern about the lack of transparency around the Paris meeting. The Australian representative noted that the references to transparency, confidence building, verification, terminology, and the development of a standard reporting form were all "somewhat vague." He acknowledged that the idea of nonnuclear-armed states asking for more information makes the nuclear-armed states uncomfortable, but he emphasized that the fundamental bargain of the NPT requires the nuclear weapon states to go beyond their comfort zones and the benchmarks they have set for themselves and to be more transparent about issues other than what they've reported on already.[79]

Ignoring this and countless other "expressions of concern," the nuclear-armed states walked into the 2012 Preparatory Committee proudly, bringing their nonproliferation game in full force. Arguing that they had done enough on disarmament for now, they brushed off criticisms from other countries that they had not yet begun to undertake the commitments to which they'd agreed in 2010. Without irony, the Russian representative argued, "Global events analysis shows the utmost need to strengthen the nuclear nonproliferation regime comprehensively. . . . A lot of work still has to be done to ensure that the non-proliferation requirements enshrined in the Treaty are respected everywhere."[80]

What he didn't reflect on was the fact that in February 2011, the Russian government had announced more details for its decade-long military modernization plan, which included the deployment of various new nuclear weapon missiles.[81] Both the Russian and Chinese delegations were warning that the United States' development of antiballistic missile programs would effectively preclude multilateral nuclear disarmament. They called for the international community to focus on "creating the conditions" for nuclear disarmament by maintaining "strategic stability" and "undiminished security for all."

The lack of preparation and obnoxious positioning of the nuclear-armed states, however, was vastly overshadowed by a bold move from a small group of nuclear-free governments. Sixteen countries led by Switzerland launched a joint statement on the humanitarian dimension of nuclear disarmament. Switzerland had been a leader in getting the language on humanitarian consequences into the 2010 NPT outcome document and wanted to make sure it received prominence in the years ahead. The joint statement questioned the idea that nuclear weapons can help solve traditional or new security challenges and asserted that nuclear weapons raise both grave humanitarian concerns and important legal issues. "It is of utmost importance that these weapons never be used again, under any circumstances," proclaimed the sixteen countries, calling on all states to "intensify their efforts to outlaw nuclear weapons and achieve a world free of nuclear weapons."[82]

The United Kingdom and France tried to justify their policies in response. The UK delegation said that since "the threshold for the legitimate use of nuclear weapons" is extremely high, it would only consider using such weapons in extreme circumstances of self-defense, including defense of NATO allies.[83] The French delegation said that its nuclear weapon policy is in line with international law.[84] However, both also argued that the 1996 International Court of Justice advisory opinion did not unanimously conclude that the use of nuclear weapons is unlawful in all circumstances. The U.S. delegation concurred, arguing that it is impossible to discuss the "hypothetical" use of nuclear weapons and that the issue has to be considered in a specific context.[85]

This style of defensive engagement, with the nuclear-armed states clearly on their back foot trying to justify their positions and policies, was reminiscent of how many users and producers of landmines and cluster bombs reacted to the discourse shifts on those weapons. Claiming that those weapons were indispensable tools of war for their militaries, some governments tried to argue that their policies and practices for use of landmines and cluster munitions were entirely within the bounds of the rules of war, and that humanitarian concerns had to be kept in balance with "security concerns"—that is, the deaths of civilians need to be weighed against the value of achieving military objectives.

But these claims could not withstand the compelling logic of the humanitarian initiative. By the end of the NPT Preparatory Committee in May 2012, a definite shift was afoot. The nuclear-armed states had for decades been saying that nuclear disarmament is everyone else's responsibility. Their consistent line was that it is up to the rest of the world to "create the conditions" for the most powerful countries on the planet to forgo their nuclear hedge. So, we made use of this. Turning this rhetoric of responsibility on its head, a handful of states and some in the activist community argued that it was clearly time for the rest of the world to take matters into their own hands—the hands of the nuclear free.

"There is a pressing need to develop new ideas and approaches if we are to achieve our common goal of a world without nuclear weapons," said Norway's representative to the next conference, the annual UN General Assembly meeting on disarmament.[86] In this spirit, Norway, together with Austria and Mexico, once again decided to table a resolution seeking to break the logjam in the Conference on Disarmament. This time, they called for the creation of a UN working group, open to all countries, that would convene in Geneva for up to three weeks during 2013 in order to develop concrete proposals to take forward multilateral negotiations for the achievement and maintenance of a world without nuclear weapons.[87]

The Austrian delegation explained its motivation for this approach, arguing that over the past few years, everyone has had to work within "flawed multilateral processes that are dominated by tactics to maintain the status quo for as long as possible."[88] Many activists were similarly outraged with the status quo and the practices working to preserve it. Twenty-two activist groups issued a joint statement to the General Assembly meeting arguing that the abuse of the rule of consensus has ensured that no real nuclear disarmament negotiations are taking place. In addition, the manipulation of consensus has undermined the security of those that depend on the rule of law rather than rule of terror for their protection and has permitted unhindered increased investments in military-industrial complexes around the globe.[89] The simple beauty of the Austrian-Mexican-Norwegian proposal was that it declared an end to this game. It offered a straightforward, inclusive way for all countries to talk about how to advance real work on nuclear disarmament.

In response, the United States criticized the increasing demands for "wholesale approaches to achieve a world without nuclear weapons." The delegation complained, "Disarmament is hard work. There are no shortcuts and no practical alternatives to the step-by-step approach. Trying to accomplish everything at once will distract us from more realistic efforts."[90] The Norwegian delegation shot back, "There is no doubt that nuclear disarmament is not easy and requires hard work. That is why we cannot allow the current impasse in the machinery to prevail. And just as nuclear weapons concern us all, so the responsibility to work for a world without nuclear weapons rests with all UN Member States."[91]

This was another sign of the revolt underway. The status quo, in which the tyranny of the minority can threaten the security and survival of the vast majority, was no longer accepted. Efforts aimed at placating those frustrated with the situation, and dissuading anyone from undertaking activities to change it, were no longer landing their marks. The willingness of a few key states such as Norway, Switzerland, and Mexico to stand up and gather others for collective action was having an impact. The nuclear-armed were no longer able to suppress dissent to the same degree. They had started losing their grip, even if they didn't recognize it yet.

An overwhelming majority of states, 147, voted to adopt the resolution tabled by Austria, Mexico, and Norway. Unlike the previous year, even those that consistently support the maintenance of the CD as the so-called "sole multilateral disarmament negotiating body" supported the resolution. The nuclear-armed states, however, would not budge. France, Russia, the United Kingdom, and the United States voted no, and China, India, Israel, and Pakistan abstained. They proclaimed that a working group would have no value, that it would distract from their alleged implementation of the 2010 NPT action plan, and that, in the words of the Russian delegation, it would only create the appearance of moving forward and destabilize existing mechanisms for progress.[92]

Well, most the rest of the world's governments—including many of the nuclear-armed states' closest allies—were not buying this anymore. Although the "existing mechanisms" had been able to contribute in the past to the development of norms and treaties, said the Canadian delegation, "these achievements are rapidly fading from memory, to be replaced by ridicule and a lack of credibility."[93] There was no excuse for sitting in meetings going nowhere year in, year out. A working group on nuclear disarmament, while not revolutionary in itself, provided a new opportunity for real work.

This seemingly minor revolt in the basement of the United Nations in New York must not just be seen against the backdrop of frustration within established disarmament forums but should also be seen in the context of broader global change. By 2012, our new century was characterized by interconnectivity and international solidarity. People across the Middle East were at this time challenging authoritarian governments while also reaching out to each other in mutual respect to assure each other that they do not want war in the region. Citizens from the United States were marching in Pakistan to show that they opposed their government's use of armed drones. Activists from around the world were protesting with villagers on Jeju Island, South Korea, in an attempt to prevent the construction of a U.S. military base intended to service naval destroyers and their antimissile systems. The idea, in this context of international cooperation and solidarity, that a handful of governments could continue to possess weapons of terror and claim they were for purposes of "security" seemed outrageous to most people—and most of their governments.

The key message coming from the overwhelming support for a seemingly benign "open-ended working group" in the United Nations was that a handful of countries would no longer be allowed to hold back the rest of the international community in tackling the problem of nuclear disarmament. This message was bolstered by the rising support for a concerted consideration of the humanitarian impact of nuclear weapons. An additional nineteen countries subscribed to the joint statement that Switzerland initiated at the NPT Preparatory Committee in May 2012, bringing the number up to thirty-five. The statement once again expressed concern with the humanitarian impacts of nuclear weapons, as well as with the "perceived political value and prestige attached by some States to these weapons," which it identified as "factors that encourage proliferation and non-compliance with international obligations." In this context, the signatories reiterated the call on all states to "intensify their efforts to outlaw nuclear weapons and achieve a world free of nuclear weapons."[94]

It was this call that galvanized the next phase of the humanitarian initiative's work: using the growing emphasis on the humanitarian consequences of nuclear weapons to finally ban the bomb. In order to take this step, activists and diplomats needed to work together to build the case for the ban and to build the community to deliver it.

4

KARAOKE AND CAMPAIGNING

Building a Case and a Community

The recognition in the 2012 joint governmental statement on the humanitarian impacts of nuclear weapons that certain states attach to these weapons a "perceived political value and prestige" was rather profound. It aligned the thirty-five governments signing on to the statement[1] with analyses of nuclear weapons discussed in the opening chapter, in particular the perspectives of feminist, postcolonial, and anticapitalist academics and activists who locate the perpetuation of the nuclear age in patriarchy and political economy as well as racism and colonialism. Such perspectives would also help inform the process and politics of banning nuclear weapons. The shared understanding among diplomats and activists working together on this project was that we were going out on a limb, against the interests of a handful of incredibly economically, militarily, and politically powerful governments, to create meaningful change that would alter the legal, political, social, and economic contexts of the most destructive weapons in the world.

Arguably, the humanitarian initiative and the efforts to create a new treaty prohibiting nuclear weapons were feminist projects, even if most of the diplomats and even activists engaged in this work did not realize or acknowledge this. Banning the bomb was about standing up against power in the interests of the majority of people on the planet, people whose voices and perspectives were traditionally either excluded entirely or dismissed by the nuclear policy elite as irrelevant or irrational. To some extent, it was also about flipping the script on where "power" was located or how it was perceived: it turned the outside into the inside, in that those of us normally locked out (metaphorically and literally) of decision-making spaces were at the center of the work, while those who typically dominated every discussion found themselves standing outside the rooms in which the treaty was developed and adopted. As will be described later, this quite ironically resulted in the U.S. ambassador standing physically outside of the UN General Assembly protesting the critical mass of governments, activists, and humanitarian agencies inside the room negotiating the treaty.

To build a new center of influence and to bring people outside of the normative frameworks related to nuclear weapons, it was crucial for those engaged in this project to build up the arguments for the ban and to build a community to take these arguments forward and initiate a process to develop a new treaty. This chapter looks at how certain activists and diplomats made the case for banning nuclear weapons on the basis of humanitarian harm, drawing on the lessons from banning landmines and cluster munitions. Some of the earliest thinking about the nuclear ban was developed by WILPF and other ICAN partners, setting much of the stage for treaty negotiations and the development of the actual text once we reached that point. This chapter also explores how activists, academics, diplomats, and representatives of international organizations built a community of actors to carry forward the humanitarian initiative and start to lay the groundwork for banning nuclear weapons. It looks at the culture of resistance developed in meetings and writing from those at the heart of the project to ban nuclear weapons and how that resistance from working-level officials within government institutions helped foster change at the highest levels. It also shows how these efforts related to some of the theoretical work on paradigm shifts, social movements, and feminist perspectives explored previously in the book.

LEARNING FROM THE PAST

By 2010, we had learned from other processes that had successfully changed the discourse on particular weapon systems or practices. In particular, the treaties on landmines and cluster bombs were groundbreaking. They stigmatized entire weapon systems on the basis of the humanitarian harm they caused. The treaties prohibited the weapons and facilitated their elimination, establishing a widespread though not universal end to their production and use. These treaties also set the standard for a new concept of humanitarian disarmament, which has emerged as a leading approach and community of practice to disarmament. It is people-centered, focusing on preventing and remediating human suffering and environmental harm from the development and use of weapons.[2]

These two treaties also set new precedents in terms of economic divestment: facing pressure from well-organized campaigns, banks and pension funds withdrew financial investments from companies that produced these weapons. Importantly, the processes for both treaties began with the development of a narrative that highlighted the humanitarian impacts of these weapons over their alleged military utility. Activists and survivors worked to compile evidence and testimony about the effects that landmines and cluster bombs had on civilians, including in post-conflict environments. All of these elements helped guide those now seeking to ban nuclear weapons.

On the tenth anniversary of the Mine Ban Treaty in 2007, Felicity Ruby, one of the cofounders of ICAN and former WILPF director, argued that key to the success of the campaign to ban landmines was that a broad range of civil society groups, "including humanitarian, peace, disability, medical, de-mining, arms control, religious, environmental, development, and women's organizations from more than seventy-five countries reframed landmines as a humanitarian issue rather than an arms control or disarmament debate."[3] She saw this as applicable to the work that needed to happen on nuclear weapons, but she warned that the nuclear-armed states knew this kind of process was coming. They were "once bitten twice shy," she noted, and were actively cautioning civil society groups and other governments against pursuing a ban on nuclear weapons the way they had with landmines and, later, cluster bombs. "These governments were determined, forewarned, and alert to anything that smelled like evolution," Ruby noted.[4]

For a while, governments and activists abided by the pressure not to attempt "doing a landmines" on nuclear weapons. Most government and even activist critics had for years scoffed at the credibility of pursuing a legal prohibition on nuclear weapons when the countries that possessed them were investing billions in maintaining their arsenals. Time and energy were spent explaining how nuclear weapons are different from landmines. The standard rhetoric went: Nuclear weapons are much more complicated than landmines. Nuclear weapons are not used in conflict and thus cannot be cast in a humanitarian light. They are a security issue, not a weapons issue. They are so much more interwoven into the structures of international relations and the identity of certain states. Several activists participated in the perpetuation of this rhetoric, perhaps in an attempt to appear "credible" to the nuclear-armed states and their allies. Some NGOs tried to assure such states that antinuclear activists understood the difference between how we could address landmines and nuclear weapons.

But others refused to play this game. WILPF, for example, had consistently argued for a "shift of language away from that which focuses on so-called national security—which in reality is the economic security only of the elite, technologically proficient classes of the state—to that which focuses on human security."[5] We saw that, to a large extent, this shift was happening in the context of other disarmament and arms control measures, including through the ongoing Arms Trade Treaty process as well as the bans on landmines and cluster bombs. This shift to humanitarian disarmament was a direct affront to the arguments typically put forward by those justifying or defending the use and possession of certain weapons. Putting forward humanitarian concerns and human rights commitments as counterclaims to "military necessity" has since come to guide a number of disarmament campaigns. The activist and diplomatic community espousing humanitarian disarmament includes those challenging the international arms trade, the use of explosive weapons in populated areas, and seeking prohibitions on certain weapon systems. But before 2010, this concept was in its infancy, being shaped by the collective thinking of a number of activists, academics, and diplomats.

In November 2008, the United Nations Institute for Disarmament Research (UNIDIR) and the Geneva Forum convened an informal symposium in Glion, Switzerland, with representatives from governments, intergovernmental and civil society organizations, and academic institutions. The objectives of the symposium were to identify and elaborate key lessons that could be drawn from the landmine and cluster munition processes, to explore how any such lessons might be adapted and applied to multilateral action in other areas of disarmament and arms control, and to reflect on how human security thinking could benefit disarmament policy making generally and suggest possible next steps toward common disarmament and arms control objectives.[6]

One of the findings of the symposium was consistent with Felicity Ruby's assessment that those working to abolish cluster munitions and antipersonnel landmines reframed the discourse and acceptability of these weapons in broader terms than before. Activists focused on the human impacts of the weapons alongside their purported military advantages and consciously shifted the burden of proof for the continued acceptability of a weapon onto users and producers. They established a direct link between the weapons and their impact on human beings. "The importance of reframing an arms control issue in humanitarian terms cannot be underestimated," explained UNIDIR researcher John Borrie in his history of the ban on cluster bombs. Previous efforts to restrict landmines and cluster munitions had enabled many states to retain these weapons in their arsenals "while, if possible, restricting the ability of potential adversaries, rather than concerns about vulnerable human beings being maimed or killed."[7]

Guided by these lessons, in 2008 WILPF argued that because conventional weapon processes were benefiting from the consideration of humanitarian implications of weapons, nuclear disarmament initiatives could likely benefit from such an approach as well.[8] In 2009, we called on diplomats at the United Nations to debate the humanitarian merits of nuclear weapons. "Getting away from Cold War deterrence theories, we are interested in hearing a debate on the moral, legal, and humanitarian justifications for the retention or elimination of nuclear weapons."[9] For WILPF, this approach to nuclear weapons also took lessons from feminist movements, queer politics, and civil rights initiatives. As a nearly hundred-year-old feminist organization, we recognized that successfully challenging power and privilege is not something that is achieved overnight. It builds on other successful attempts to chip away at the status quo, often starting with a confrontation of dominant narratives and focusing on the harm the current way of doing things has on human beings. As feminist scholars such as Carol Cohn and Sara Ruddick have noted, antiwar feminism has always examined the social costs and the "long-term physical, psychological, socioeconomic, environmental, and gendered effects" of war.[10] As described in chapter 1, feminists critique the "technostrategic discourse" on nuclear weapons, which restricts thinking about these weapons to "the destructive effects when, *and only when*, they are detonated, and to the possible deterrent effects of possessing these weapons," ignoring the "potential suffering of targeted societies" and the "moral significance of willingly risking such massive, total destruction."[11]

In 2010, this kind of feminist analysis was brought squarely into the world of international nuclear diplomacy with the humanitarian initiative, as described in the previous chapter. Further, an arguably feminist, queer, and antiracist approach to confronting power and taking action without "permission" began to emerge in these circles. In a 2010 speech mentioned in the previous chapter, the then-foreign minister of Norway argued that not all countries have to be on board an initiative in order to make progress. "I believe it would be possible to develop norms against the use of nuclear weapons, and even to outlaw them, without a consensus decision, and that such norms will eventually be applied globally," suggested Jonas Gahr Støre. Further, "We cannot leave it to the nuclear weapon states alone to decide when it is time for them to do away with these weapons. Their destructive power would affect us all if put to use—and their threat continue to affect us all—therefore they are everyone's business."[12]

These would become foundational arguments for the process ahead to ban nuclear weapons. Of course, calls to "ban the bomb" were not new. What was new was the idea of doing it in the immediate future, even without the support or the participation of nuclear-armed states. If that sounds ridiculous to you, the reader, then you're certainly not in a minority. It sounded ridiculous to a lot of government officials and fellow activists when the idea was first introduced. In fact, those of us believing this could work were, for a very long time, in the minority. But a few of us believed that a treaty that prohibits nuclear weapons—not just their testing, their proliferation, or their development, but their use and their very possession—could be instrumental in stigmatizing, outlawing, and ultimately eliminating nuclear weapons.

BUILDING THE IDEA

The early conceptions of a nuclear ban treaty involved building on the humanitarian reframing offered by the language in the 2010 NPT outcome document, to bridge the gap between aspirations for nuclear disarmament and the seemingly intractable legal and political landscape surrounding nuclear weapons. The thinking of the leadership of ICAN at the time,[13] together with a handful of diplomats and academics, was that a new legal instrument could provide a framework for the prohibition and elimination of nuclear weapons. Although participation of all states would be welcomed, such a treaty could be developed even without the participation of the nuclear-armed states and would still have significant impact in normative as well as practical terms. Regardless of the participation or approval of the states that possessed nuclear weapons, such a ban could alter the international legal, political, social, and economic environment, which in turn could help facilitate nuclear disarmament. It would draw a clear line around nuclear weapons for what they are—instruments of violent death and irredeemable destruction.

Those of us pursuing this angle saw the treaty as a tool that would help make unconscionable the concept of these weapons providing security or preventing conflict or deterring attack. As an instrument that would create legal, political, and economic obligations on the basis of this stigma. As a force of nature that would change the way nuclear weapons are treated by people, corporations, banks, governments, and others. Something to undercut the power, privilege, and profit that the few seek to derive from wielding weapons of mass destruction.

Certain groups within ICAN "had a clear idea of the ban from the beginning," noted one observer. "It wasn't hidden, it was carefully articulated, and it pushed the logic of the treaty in a particular direction."[14] WILPF and another of ICAN's steering group organizations put together a paper outlining the conception of a nuclear ban treaty.[15] We suggested that such a treaty would offer states opposed to nuclear weapons an opportunity to formalize a categorical rejection of the use or possession of nuclear weapons by anyone under any circumstances. Establishing a clear rejection of nuclear weapons would enhance the stigma against these weapons that already exists. The process of banning nuclear weapons would require governments to decide whether they want to continue to support nuclear weapons or reject them entirely. We also believed that such a treaty would have wide-ranging implications for nuclear weapon policies and practices, including in relation to financial investments in their maintenance and modernization, as well as to military cooperation and alliances involving nuclear weapons.

We took as our starting point the idea that under the NPT, it is the responsibility of all governments—not just the nuclear-armed states—to make progress toward negotiations on nuclear disarmament. We expected that a treaty banning nuclear weapons could be developed and adopted even without the nuclear-armed states, and despite their opposition to it. This would require a group of states to recognize the unacceptable consequences of nuclear weapons and begin negotiations to prohibit them, without being held back by states opposed to a ban. We also consistently argued that such a treaty should not be seen as antagonistic toward nuclear-armed states. By contributing to international stigmatization and rejection of these weapons, it should be seen as supportive to all disarmament and arms control efforts.

The main selling point for this approach, from our perspective, was that banning nuclear weapons is a pragmatic way to confront the risk nuclear weapons posed and is a logical evolution of nuclear disarmament discourse and process. The nuclear weapon free zone treaties, as regional prohibition agreements, already pointed in the direction of a global treaty prohibiting nuclear weapons. Finally, we believed that an international process to develop a global nuclear ban could transform civil society engagement in this area, develop a stronger community of states and civil society working together for the elimination of nuclear weapons, and provide unprecedented opportunities for political, legal, social, and economic pressure against the institutions currently supporting nuclear weapons.

The idea was to change the political environment in which nuclear weapons exist—to make it illegal to research, develop, test, manufacture, deploy, or possess nuclear weapons; and to raise the political and economic costs of maintaining nuclear weapons. Our assessment was that a treaty banning nuclear weapons, even if entirely negotiated, adopted, and implemented by nuclear-weapon free states, would affect the calculations of the nuclear-armed states. It would make it harder for them to justify their continued possession and modernization of these weapons.

At the core of the failure to make real progress on nuclear disarmament is a belief that certain states have the right to possess nuclear weapons. At various times, most of the nuclear-armed states have insinuated or outright declared that the NPT confers legitimacy on their possession of nuclear weapons. This disingenuous interpretation of the so-called cornerstone of the nuclear weapon governance regime has meant that for nearly half a century, five countries have refused to comply with their legal obligation to disarm. It has meant that four other countries have tried to assert their own claim to power through violence by acquiring nuclear weapons and shunning the NPT. It has meant a proliferation of programs and mechanisms to prevent others from acquiring nuclear weapons while billions of dollars have gone to upgrade and extend the lives of the ones already existing. It has also meant that some countries that don't possess nuclear weapons themselves support the retention of nuclear weapons by their allies, asserting that their allies' ability to threaten the rest of the world with massive nuclear violence provides them with security.

The treaties banning landmines and cluster munitions brought the international community to rightly perceive these weapons as illegal and immoral, causing even those governments that have not ratified the treaties to (mostly) follow their provisions. Although these weapons have not been completely eliminated and are still being used to great humanitarian harm in certain conflicts, the majority of the world has renounced them and condemns their use today. Even the policies and practices of governments outside of the treaty regimes have been affected. The United States gives money to land mine clearance. It has not produced landmines since 1997 or cluster munitions since 2007.

These treaties have also had an economic impact. Companies get and stay involved in the nuclear weapons business because it brings them large flows of cash without financial risk or investment. A treaty that prohibits the assistance of or investment in the development, production, or testing of nuclear weapon systems would go a long way to undermining these companies' rationale for being involved with the nuclear weapons business. The divestment campaign accompanying the treaty banning cluster munitions has been incredibly successful in affecting the financial interests of corporations producing these weapon systems and related components. One recent success case, for example, is that in 2016 the last remaining U.S. manufacturer of cluster munitions stopped producing them,[16] following pressure from international civil society groups that documented their use by the Saudi-led coalition during airstrikes in Yemen.[17] The ICAN leadership postulated that divestment from nuclear weapons will over time undermine the benefits companies currently derive from producing these weapons. In this way, a nuclear ban could have a significant impact on nuclear weapon modernization programs and financial investments in nuclear weapons, delivery systems, and related infrastructure. Further, the more pension funds, banks, and public investments that remove their material support from nuclear weapons producers, the greater the political effects will be, especially in nuclear-armed countries where corporations have become so intertwined with the political system, as described in chapter 1.

Those of us in the ICAN steering group and staff team also believed that a nuclear ban could have real implications for practices and policies related to nuclear deterrence. Accession to such a treaty by some states would generate the need to coordinate policy among allies, which in turn would raise the political costs of acts that breach the treaty and facilitate behavior that is in compliance with the treaty's provisions.[18] States' parties that belong to alliances that envision the use of nuclear weapons would be obliged to effectively renounce their participation in any doctrine or policy involving the stockpiling, deployment, use, or threat of use of nuclear weapons. While joining the ban treaty would not necessarily have to require any state to exit its alliance, this principle could compel them to ensure that their participation is compatible with their commitments and policies under the ban treaty.[19] Similarly, any bilateral arrangement involving hosting of nuclear weapons would need to be revisited. The ban treaty could make it clear that nuclear weapons are illegal and states' parties cannot plan to benefit from or support their use or continued possession. In this regard, relationships of "extended nuclear deterrence," in which a nuclear-armed state pledges to use nuclear weapons to "protect" an ally, would likely need to be renounced by states' parties.

Finally, we thought that a treaty prohibiting nuclear weapons would have domestic political costs. States opposed to the ban would have to justify their position to their citizens. An international process to develop a treaty banning nuclear weapons could provide a very different backdrop for national discussions on nuclear weapons. Even if such a process were to be dismissed by the nuclear-armed states as irrelevant, it would nevertheless provide a strong entry point for critiquing the wisdom and legitimacy of investing large sums of money in weapons that large parts of the world consider immoral, unacceptable, and have deemed to be illegal.

BUILDING THE COMMUNITY

This building up of an idea through conversation, through serious work in various spaces, is essential to developing international law. This is the main—and perhaps most surprising—thing I learned from my work both on the Arms Trade Treaty and the nuclear ban treaty. I think it's this way for two key reasons: one, if the initiative to curtail power or violence isn't coming from a place of human relationship, empathy, and compassion, it's less likely to succeed. Two, the community that is built through the process of these conversations is essential to the initiative's survival and success. Power and violence do not surrender lightly, as explored previously. They will fight back. Establishing trust and camaraderie among those with whom you are going take on that power and violence is the only way to sustain yourselves in the effort. And, in most cases, building a culture of resistance to power is necessary to shape the initiative and motivate the individuals engaged in it.

Trust and confidence are necessary to get people to take risks. Undertaking any action that upsets powerful entities that benefit from the status quo can be politically and even personally dangerous for those involved. This is frequently true for activists, who can face arrest, surveillance, deportation, refusal of visas or entries when traveling, firing from their jobs, and so forth. In the case of the pursuit of the nuclear ban treaty, other than the nuns and laypeople breaking into missile silos described earlier, ICAN's activists dealt with minimal bodily or material risk and exposure in these ways in relation to their ban treaty advocacy. However, some of the diplomats working for the ban, and even just for the change in discourse to the humanitarian consequences of nuclear weapons, experienced ridicule within their systems as well as pressure from external colleagues working for oppositional governments. Once again, this reinforced the lesson outlined earlier in this book that making institutional change requires grassroots and other forms of pressure from "outside" the established channels of power. "We need activists, we need people confronting and challenging cynicism," commented one diplomat from Latin America. "But for diplomats, it's risking our jobs. If you open your mouth [in support of something like this], you lose credibility, your salary."[20] Calls were made, jobs were threatened, certain bilateral and multilateral meetings became insufferable. But the community of actors that built up over time became solid enough to provide sanctuary and solidarity for those under pressure.

We knew this would be the case from the experiences of banning landmines and cluster bombs. "People willing to take risks and foster a common sense of purpose, commitment, and opportunity changed their institutions' positions," which contributed to collective reframing of the issues in humanitarian terms in the processes to ban landmines and cluster munitions, explains John Borrie in his history of the cluster bomb process. "This extended to politicians who in some countries overruled entrenched bureaucratic positions, for instance in their defence departments." And these efforts extended from one initiative to the next: "Potent networks of trust had been created among people representing diverse institutions in the [landmine] process; these relationships provided a basis for campaigning and diplomatic networks built on in the [cluster munitions] process."[21]

Building this community for the humanitarian initiative and the nuclear ban treaty involved years of meetings, gatherings, and discussions in various formulations. A few governments, activists, and academics began discussing new initiatives on nuclear weapons around the time of the 2010 NPT Review Conference. A ban on the use of nuclear weapons was one of the key items considered in these discussions. But it was outlawing nuclear weapons altogether that took hold after several meetings. A set of ICAN steering group members and colleagues from the International Law and Policy Institute (ILPI) from Norway then began to bring together a cross-regional group of working-level diplomats for a series of two-day retreats a few times a year over three years. Initially, these meetings brought together diplomats from various countries interested in the idea of a nuclear ban, as well as representatives of international agencies and a few academics. This was where the foundational ideas and elements for the ban were articulated. It's where several of the working papers that were submitted by governments to UN meetings were first drafted and discussed—papers that would become the basis for negotiations of a treaty banning nuclear weapons. It's also where many of the individuals who would go on to be leaders in the movement to develop the ban treaty learned to trust each other, work together, and build off of each other's energy and commitment.

For the most part, these meetings included working-level representatives from governments. Although ambassadors attended later meetings in this series, it began primarily as an initiative of enthusiastic junior diplomats eager to collaborate with activists, academics, and working-level people from international organizations. It was the "young wolves only," as one diplomatic participant described it.[22] Buy-in and support from top-level diplomats within government systems would become vital at later stages, but in the early days of thinking it required the attention of those whose primary portfolio of responsibilities included nuclear disarmament. This gave space for challenging the established narrative and reflecting on alternative perspectives, such as those elaborated in chapter 1, to inform thinking and then change policies. These meetings helped "sensitize" participants and build up "articulate and knowledgeable" argumentation for the humanitarian initiative and for the ban treaty.[23] For some participants, their views on nuclear weapons were shaped by the retreats.[24]

In addition to the substantive ground made at this series of meetings, they also provided some of the most crucial space for community building—between diplomats and activists, but also among the diplomats themselves. Many forged close friendships even if previously they hadn't necessarily been working in the same spaces. In my interviews with diplomats for this book, a resounding emphasis on trust came through. As the age-old feminist slogan suggests, the personal is the political. "Friendship made all the difference" to this project, said one participant. "Maybe other people could have gotten it done, but I'm not sure."[25] This kind of trust is built over time, through consistently positive interactions between individuals. Spending time together out of meeting spaces—taking walks or chatting at the pub, coffee shop, or the karaoke booth—provided important space for more informal conversations, building a sense of community and confidence. The brainstorming was continuous before and after formal meeting hours. Some diplomats questioned whether others in their position would have been able to keep their governments on track, arguing that the close relationships with individuals in ICAN were uniquely instrumental in staying informed and strategizing about next moves. Other participants in these meetings emphasized the importance of this friendship to make advocacy meaningful. "Advocacy has to come with the right message at the right time from the right person," one diplomat said:

> Advocating a cause relentlessly doesn't work. You need to build up personal connections. This can lead to things beyond the individual if you unlock it in a person—they will do the work! But first, you have to distinguish the topic in a way that relates to other issues and to diplomats' personalities. ICAN [activists] did that, in a way that's not pushy. They worked heart-to-heart, at the working level—real "grassroots diplomacy."[26]

For one representative of a country that came to be very influential in the pursuit of the ban, ICAN activists got her fired up about nuclear weapons. She remembers being asked, "So, what are we going to do about it?" Feeling involved in scheming quietly about what to do about nuclear weapons helped focus her energy and attention, she said.[27] People were so fed up with where we were internationally on nuclear weapons. Everyone at these meetings wanted to get cracking on a solution. That meant starting with their own governments, some of which had great rhetoric and good intentions but not a whole lot of action backing it up. They wanted to do something, participate, elevate, muck things up, but they didn't have space to do so. Held down by decades-old positions, a tedium created both by national inertia, international or regional alliances, and oppressive opposition of the nuclear-armed states, the idea of banning nuclear weapons offered a new hope. At the very least, it was something new and interesting to try.

During the same years that ICAN and ILPI brought together officials for cross-regional retreats, these groups were also helping to organize regional roundtables and workshops around the world, bringing together government officials of various levels of experience and capacity to talk about nuclear weapons. For many of the diplomats and officials participating in these regional meetings, it was often the first time they had been involved in work on nuclear disarmament. Others had spent frustrating years grappling with the perpetual stagnation within the UN on nuclear issues. At first, the regional meetings focused on raising awareness and establishing discourses on the humanitarian impacts of nuclear weapons. But the ultimate objective was to build a sense of empowerment among these governments to take action for nuclear disarmament in ways that had not yet been tried and in ways they may previously have believed to be impossible. These gatherings provided space for people to discuss the logic and potential of banning nuclear weapons and to figure out how to shift positions of big bureaucratic systems to support this seemingly radical idea of banning the bomb without the participation of any states that had them.

The regional meetings provided space for solidarity to grow among officials and activists of the region, solidifying the idea that nuclear weapons affect us all and that we all have a role to play in challenging and changing the status quo. In a few key cases, the participants in the regional meetings, inspired by the discussion about the humanitarian initiative and the possibilities for change, went home from the gathering and worked hard to change their government's policies from one of apathy or opposition to one of support. Moving from the comfortable position of demanding disarmament to one of taking real action to upset the forces that enable the status quo to continue was not an easy shift to undertake. Pretty much every government that ended up supporting the humanitarian initiative and then the nuclear ban treaty had to go through an internal reckoning with their past positions. Even in those countries that historically had supported nuclear disarmament, those higher up in government systems needed to be convinced that the ban was a real possibility and that it could have a real impact on nuclear weapons. One diplomat from a consistently pro-disarmament country reported that a senior official told her that she was naive for thinking she could make a difference.[28] Another said that he had to use a lot of capital and put his reputation on the line for this project. "I was really exposed and was seen as someone that pushes a humanitarian disarmament agenda or as being antinuclear. Some people within my government treated me as a tree hugger or an activist. I was seen as toxic by some."[29]

This isn't surprising or unusual. It took a long time for most people to come around to the idea that banning cluster munitions was feasible, including people who had been actively engaged in banning antipersonnel landmines the decade before. But once underway, argues John Borrie, completion of the task was fairly rapid. The Convention on Cluster Munitions' "achievement entailed factors such as post-conflict evidence, greater focus on the human impact of the weapon, and the right combination of individuals, organizations, and governments working in partnership, all of which contributed to a gradual but steady reframing of expectations about what could be achieved."[30]

The same was true of the humanitarian initiative. "The first challenge was overcoming lethargy," noted one diplomat who has been involved in the nuclear weapons issue for years. We needed to understand that "something is happening to get over our disbelief that something is possible." For many inside his governmental system, he said, the attitude was "don't waste our time." He personally had reservations for a long time about the idea of banning nuclear weapons. Refocusing on the humanitarian impact of nuclear weapons made sense to him, he said, because it was necessary to "create a different environment for having conversations" about nuclear weapons. But for most of the build-up to the ban negotiations, his government was clear that "our participation in the humanitarian initiative did not mean we're 'on the ban-wagon.'"[31]

However, setting out to change the paradigm, as Kuhn described in the previous chapter, meant dismantling the old and creating something new. "The ICAN movement on the side allowed us to participate in the process," one participant explained. His government's involvement was inevitable because of its history, he said: "when the choice was put there," to participate or not participate, "there was no way we couldn't support it." The jury is still out for some of his colleagues, he noted, explaining that not everyone is enthusiastic that his country supported the ban. "But the determining factor for our support was that the choice was between doing something or doing nothing." His government, like many others, was frustrated with the status quo, and they wanted to do something positive without destroying anything else. "The notion that this isn't the end but a step that can be taken now" was important to convincing officials to join the process.[32]

BUILDING A CULTURE OF RESISTANCE

This reasoning worked for many government officials. As they listened to the arguments for the ban throughout this process, it became increasingly obvious to many that if they did not act, nothing was going to happen. "The dismal cycle of NPT review conferences was not ever going to change unless we took control of it and started steering."[33] The humanitarian initiative and the movement for the ban was "a revolt from the bottom, a revolution. This was about injustice, frustration. Instead of begging, we were doing something."[34]

For some who remained unsure about the ban treaty's potential until the time negotiations began, it was not until they thought of the ban as a tool rather than an end in itself that he saw its value. "I realized it was a pressure tool," said one person. "If enough people demanded it, it would scare the nuclear-armed states into getting more serious about nuclear disarmament." It also became clear, he said, that the treaty had value in empowering new countries to take action. "The intellectual basis for the ban was that it showed countries that weren't really active on nuclear disarmament that it matters, that you can have a say."[35]

These arguments were apparently important for many countries. Most were facing pressing priorities in other areas, and the diplomats trying to make the case for the ban had to elevate the issue and sell it as a winning move. "We have to be on the right side of history" was a compelling argument internally for many governments.[36] They had to listen to disbelievers within their systems, and be prepared for debates, but at the end of the day they needed to convince the higher-ups that this would be good for their country both morally and politically. This work was, fundamentally, a concerted effort to achieve a Kuhn-like paradigm shift, by challenging the dominant "realist" theories of nuclear weapons and even of international relations more broadly.

For many governmental representatives working on getting internal support for the ban, this was the key. For so long, "nuclear-free countries just had to plead with the nuclear-armed states to take action and report back on it. If you tried to say more, you were begging for trouble."[37] In the 1960s, when Latin America and the Caribbean decided to become a nuclear weapon free zone, these states "were saying we no longer play by your rules of the Cold War. It was a declaration of freedom," which the ban treaty mirrors today. "The NPT is the [nuclear-armed states'] domain. The ban treaty is *our* agenda."[38]

The obvious injustice and hypocrisy within the NPT review cycle were influential in bringing some skeptics around to supporting the ban. For several nonnuclear-armed governments, continuing to accept the nuclear-armed states' double standards year after year was already upsetting. They didn't need to be convinced that the status quo was unacceptable or untenable, but they weren't necessarily ready to accept that the answer was then to join another treaty that would not immediately impact the nuclear-armed states. Convincing them that new international law could solve some of the problems of existing international law proved to be an uphill battle. But the logic of the ban, in almost all cases, ultimately prevailed. And the building up of regional support for the treaty through the joint ICAN-ILPI-government meetings around the world proved instrumental. Officials from governments that did support the treaty were, in most cases, able to convince their counterparts from more skeptical countries that prohibiting nuclear weapons was the right move morally, as well as politically, legally, and economically.

In one case, this mostly took the determined efforts of a single government representative. She attended one of the regional meetings as someone new to the nuclear disarmament portfolio. Her government traditionally had been very quiet on the issue of nuclear weapons. At the meeting, we had wildly productive conversations with her. She asked all the right questions, had great analysis of the regional and national dynamics within which she was working, and had immense enthusiasm for driving things forward. She was keen to wake up her ministry and get things moving. It took a lot of effort on her part, but in short order she had helped influence changes in position and policy on nuclear weapons, and her government ended up becoming a leader in the ban treaty process. Her efforts provide compelling evidence of the value of one person's determination to make a difference wherever they happen to be situated. For her, it was as a diplomat who managed to help steer the bureaucracy of her foreign ministry toward championing new international law and disrupting the "perception of privilege and power" associated with nuclear weapons noted at the beginning of this chapter.

Shifting norms about the acceptability of nuclear weapons was a main motivation for negotiating the nuclear ban treaty. Most of the leaders in the process to outlaw nuclear weapons believed that this would impact norms around possession and the threat of use of these weapons.[39] This was a direct challenge to theories of nuclear deterrence and the idea that nuclear weapons provided security or stability, as explored in chapter 3. It threatened the very basis of the justifications for the possession of these weapons of mass destruction. But norms are not static, as explained earlier in reference to the work of scholars such as Seyla Benhabib and Nick Ritchie, among others.[40] Norms are constructed and evolve over time in response to debates about competing meanings of the norm and in interaction with an external environment, which consists of other norms that are themselves in process. Not all actors have a similar voice in defining norms, due to structures of social, economic, and political inequality. Power "is integral to the processes of social construction, determining what can and cannot be said—and, as a result, who can and cannot speak," as Mona Lena Krook and Jacquie True note.[41] But all of this can be challenged. The norms themselves can be reconstituted or reinterpreted based on new evidence, debates, and the amplification of alternative perspectives.

There were already strong norms of nonproliferation and of cumulative progress toward nuclear disarmament—norms that were enshrined in the NPT and all review conference outcomes. In this sense, said one person interviewed, "the humanitarian initiative and the ban haven't created something new—but they have reformed these existing norms. They took them forward, and in confrontation with the nuclear-armed states."[42] The effort of encouraging nonnuclear-armed states to confront the nuclear-armed states and to shift the dominant norm away from "limited" possession to absolute rejection of nuclear weapons was also about reframing norms of who has power and about how political change can occur. Along with reframing nuclear weapons as murderous, genocidal, and illegitimate for all, those engaged in the effort to ban nuclear weapons also sought to reframe ideas about processes of change.

Activists in particular were adamant that the delegitimization of nuclear weapons "by a majority of relatively disempowered actors would have an impact over time."[43] Similarly, one of the Costa Rican diplomats involved in the process argued publicly that it was imperative for nonnuclear-armed states "to rewrite the normative framework and find political leverage in processes where the nuclear powers have traditionally stymied progress."[44] While noting that some "think that it is too difficult a task to change the minds of the nuclear states who still clutch tightly to the theory of nuclear deterrence," she argued that moving forward, "we have two options: we can maintain our course and merely hope that we avoid nuclear catastrophe, or we can try to achieve real change."[45]

This idea of change—that the "weak" can influence or affect the "powerful"—is central to any resistance movement. This is how I thought of the joint efforts of diplomats and activists on this project—as a resistance. Nick Ritchie and Kjølv Egeland also argue that the humanitarian initiative and ban process constitute collective resistance to entrenched power structures.[46] More simply put, we worked together to take on the nuclear-armed states.

Resistance movements, argue Ritchie and Egeland, oppose or challenge existing power. They tend to rely on unorthodox, creative methods to level the playing field with the powers that be by changing the structure and rules of the game. The aim of such movements is usually to contest the legitimacy of existing practices and power structures, as outlined in previous chapters including in relation to the role of social movements and "outside" pressure. Resistance, in this context, "is often mobilized by a sense of common struggle and solidarity against injustice and oppression, giving voice to the marginalised and silenced, and faith in the possibility of change through an alternative vision of politics."[47]

The aim of our collective resistance was to challenge and change the dominant nuclear weapon discourse, norms, and actions so that states without nuclear weapons and activists, rather than those who perpetuated nuclear violence, could together set the terms for progress. To mount an effective resistance, activists and diplomats needed to be coordinated, consolidated, and committed to a clear path, a unifying idea of how to best disrupt the dominant narratives. This meant developing a network of state and civil society actors that could work together to develop a common narrative about the catastrophic humanitarian impact of nuclear weapons and about the strategy for change—which for us was the nuclear ban treaty.

In academia, a campaign such as ICAN is likely to be described as a "transnational advocacy network" (TAN)—a loose grouping of people advocating for specific change across borders.[48] The idea is that when acting within a TAN, domestic groups operating within states that are ignoring their demands are able to connect to transnational allies, who lobby their own states or international organizations to put pressure on the recalcitrant state from the outside. Through this so-called boomerang effect, "local activists can gain access, leverage and information that they would not have had on their own, thereby instigating dramatic changes in the scope and recognition of international norms."[49]

This isn't exactly what happened with the nuclear ban, although the concept of a TAN is useful. Using the framework of this theory, a more accurate description of the nuclear ban movement is that activists, academics, Red Cross advocates, and government officials, particularly diplomats, formed a TAN together. Working as a network, we were able to move states that were—in relation to the nuclear-armed states—relatively disempowered, in order to change the norms that were allowing the powerful to maintain their dangerously privileged position. This enabled our network of diplomats and activists to put pressure on the nuclear-armed and nuclear-supportive states to affect their normative (as well as legal, political, social, and economic) relationship with nuclear weapons.

One person interviewed for this book argued that the most fascinating aspect of this network was "the reinforcing circular quality of the dynamic between the diplomats and the activists." Many ICAN partners had a clear idea of the ban from the beginning, he explained. "It wasn't hidden, it was actually very carefully articulated. It pushed the logic about the ban in a particular direction and was strategically simplistic." Having a few nongovernmental organizations pushing ahead in a particular direction was helpful for diplomats, he suggested. "Because of the humanitarian reframing offered by the NGOs, enough states started to move towards the middle and momentum gathered. The NGOs created politically safe space for them. It became normal to talk about the ban treaty. They made it seem plausible first, then actionable." On the other hand, "The diplomats wouldn't push, they were conservative-minded, even the most progressive among them. But the NGOs created a 'slipstream' of political space. And there was a self-reinforcing aspect to all of this: the diplomats encouraged the NGOs to do this, because they wanted this space! So it's not that this effort was NGO-led. It was a collaboration."[50]

A diplomat involved in the process likewise emphasized the complementary role of states and civil society. "NGOs can put in the limelight information" in a different way than states can. If we share an objective, we can work together, in different roles, he said.[51] This again reinforces some of the theory about social movements and political change explored in chapter 2, in which both activists and politicians made the case for the importance of having pressure applied to decision makers by those outside of established institutions. But the lessons of banning nuclear weapons also speak to the potential of collaboration between those on the "inside" and those on the "outside"—which I think, based on experience, is really only possible when the trust, camaraderie, and shared goals exist, as described earlier. Without that, it's more likely that those on the inside will end up paying lip service to the contributions of activists while pursuing their own agendas and interests.

Building this kind of trust in a diverse network of actors is not simple. Nor did it work the same way for every government or bureaucracy. In many of the cases where governments supported the ban, it seemed that having eager and influential people operating within their system—individuals who were willing to push the envelope—was important. For one diplomat, having someone in charge who had no background on disarmament—and thus no biases—but plenty of other multilateral experience was really important. Her boss "enjoyed a good David versus Goliath fight," she quipped, noting that the dynamics of some of the least developed countries in the world taking on the most developed countries over their weapons of terror really appealed to him. He quickly became personally and professionally committed to the ban, bringing the entire government's position along with him.[52]

For some governments, it was a process of constant reaffirmation and justification about why we should take an active role.[53] People in high positions throughout the ministry move around, so there is no continuity; working-level officials have to keep talking new supervisors or bosses through the process and the objectives. Lack of institutional memory is also a challenge—with people cycling through portfolios, only general positions remain while nuances are lost. In this context, framing the initiative as resistance to power can be useful for building up institutional buy-in through individuals interested in taking up this task.

It was thus important for those working within government systems to keep clear documentation of their positions and policies and those of their allies and neighbors. The case for supporting the ban had to be built—the logic had to be clearly shown, and the progression of policy and leadership had to be drawn inch by inch. One diplomat explained that every memo she sent to the foreign minister's office about the ban or the humanitarian initiative "referenced the past ten meetings and traced the logical development of the issue and the government's position on it."[54] Ministers don't like to backtrack, so as long as you can keep reminding them of how their position developed, they're unlikely to question it. But those working on this issue full-time also have to keep educating and convincing the layers of people who advise top ministers—and these people change all the time.

A key obstacle some diplomats faced was that nuclear policy questions are in the hands of military or national security advisers with foreign or defense ministries. This meant that it was important to get those advisers on board with the ban to make it easier to get support from those making decisions within their ministries. Some diplomats maneuvered to bring such officials along to important meetings, such as the humanitarian impact conferences and UN meetings, so that they were informed and inspired from external partners and could feel the growing momentum for themselves.[55] Others focused on getting high-level officials to support the ban in internal meetings or even public speeches, in order to solidify their commitment to the process.[56]

For some, it became important to show how this process was mounting a credible challenge to the privilege that established centers of power exercised and exploited.[57] "In nuclear politics, those engaged in the diplomacy of resistance have connected *nuclear* structures of power, *nuclear* inequalities and *nuclear* violence with a wider set of global structural hierarchies, inequalities and violent practices," observed Ritchie and Egeland.[58] Countering these global inequalities reportedly was important to some of the diplomats involved in the ban process and certainly important to many of the activists.

More broadly, supporting this treaty, from the perspective of several diplomats, was important for their countries' stake in other issues. "Consistency with our positions on international humanitarian law and global governance meant we needed to be engaged and supportive of this process."[59] Most countries supporting the ban had long supported other nuclear disarmament initiatives, had opposed nuclear testing, and had even joined regional nuclear weapon free zones. Their past practices and positions conveyed evidence of their commitment to nuclear weapons, which helped convince high-level officials that they support a prohibition on nuclear weapons.

Several governments active in the nuclear ban process were previously involved in prohibiting landmines or cluster munitions, such as those of Austria, Ireland, Mexico, and South Africa. They were able to draw on those experiences and the logic of those processes. "We needed to impose reality on the powerful," a diplomat of one such country argued. "They don't come up with ideas for change. We have to make it happen."[60] This diplomat said she became convinced about the logic of the nuclear ban because of working previously on landmines and cluster munitions. Others found that arguments about the impacts nuclear weapons would have on development, climate change, and human rights were compelling—and many sold the ban internally within their systems by emphasizing the inconsistency between their position on those issues and not pushing further for nuclear disarmament.[61]

Some government representatives worked hard, in coordination with activists, to craft clear positions against arguments that a ban treaty could weaken existing treaties such as the Comprehensive Nuclear Test-Ban-Treaty or the NPT. This "was a central element of our regular engagement with our Ministers," for some representatives, "both in keeping them informed on, and ultimately seeking their endorsement for, the various stages leading up to the negotiation and its outcome."[62] She suggested that the arguments her team prepared for their own government might have also been useful to others. "I'm not sure I would say that our focus on this truly changed anyone else's position, but it certainly reduced the potency of arguments that the ban would undermine the NPT, and in fact did make a number of [opponents] at least back off from continuing to put the argument forward."

For others, opinions were changed on questions of process and institutions. This helped flip some skeptical governments into supporting the treaty. One such country, Brazil, went from publicly expressing doubt about the utility of a ban to joining the core group of states championing the new treaty. Many Brazilian government officials were initially not convinced that a prohibition treaty—especially one negotiated outside of traditional venues or without the nuclear-armed states—would be effective. They weren't alone; other skeptical governments such as Cuba and Egypt felt the same way. But the rising chorus of government and nongovernment voices for the ban and further elaboration of its potential benefits reportedly helped shift perceptions within these government systems toward the understanding that prohibition could helpfully come first, before elimination of nuclear weapons. For some governments, the Arms Trade Treaty (ATT) negotiating process apparently also helped change minds. A process in the style of the landmine or cluster bomb bans might have been a step too far for certain government, but the ATT format of negotiating within the UN General Assembly offered a reasonable compromise between the Conference on Disarmament and an "outside the UN" process. "We felt like we shouldn't go outside the UN on this one."[63] Even understanding the challenges and risks to operating within UN forums, and having experienced the benefits of stand-alone processes such as those on cluster munitions and landmines, some felt staying inside the UN would bring the most countries along.[64] Many countries within the Non-Aligned Movement (NAM),[65] for example, had a disingenuous belief in the virtue of the "multilateral system"—which to them didn't mean a multilateral process but only a process that took place within the established system.

Meanwhile, building up the arguments in support of negotiating a new treaty outlawing nuclear weapons through any forum was a slow process for most countries. One representative from a country championing the development of the treaty described the "slow burn" toward the ban through the humanitarian initiative as necessary to prevent scaring off certain governments. "We had to keep the rhetoric far from the ban—we didn't want to jump too fast, so that the rest could follow."[66] No one was sure how fast things would go, he noted, but some delegations knew that's what they wanted from the very beginning. The goal was to bring as many other countries along with them as possible. This involved, at times, having weaker language in working papers, statements, or pledges, and seeking higher numbers of signatories over the strongest possible language.

Some participants said they felt that a key obstacle to securing support for the ban within their government systems was existing alliance or regional positions, or even experienced pressure from otherwise supportive allies. With two nuclear-armed states and several governments skeptical of the ban treaty within the NAM, for example, it was impossible for other NAM countries to get unified agreement on supporting the humanitarian initiative or the ban treaty. "We knew we couldn't be bound by a NAM position" on the ban, said one diplomat from Southeast Asia, because it wouldn't be supportive of the ban.[67] When one NAM member tried to establish an unfavorable position for the alliance, others reacted strongly against it and managed to maintain a vaguely supportive position that allowed members to engage with the ban process to the extent that they wanted. Group dynamics were important, but at the end of the day the decision to support the ban was a national decision—and those choosing the ban managed to bring many of their allies along with them.

SKEPTICS AND NON-SUPPORTERS

Unfortunately, not everyone was able to bring their government's position fully on board with the idea of banning nuclear weapons, even if they personally believed in its possibilities. For some of these diplomats, not being able to support the development of the ban process or participate in negotiations was personally devastating. One diplomat who found himself in this position explained that he had been engaged in early thinking about the ban treaty, but when his government shifted course and became less supportive of the initiative, he had to stop coming to the meetings. He was excited about developments in the process but couldn't convince his government to support it. For some, it became a full-time job to keep their governments engaged at all, even if they couldn't be overtly supportive. "I constantly had to make sure that our position didn't undermine us. It was a constant uphill struggle" to at least stay part of the humanitarian impact joint statements and to stay positive on relevant UN resolutions. "Others in the government hierarchy would have had no problem just walking away from the whole thing." Those of us who believed our country should be part of this "had to be careful," and had to forge alliances with internal and external colleagues.[68]

In some cases, supportive diplomats were able to keep their skeptical governments involved by talking more about technicalities and historical positions rather than black-and-white questions about nuclear weapons. Some emphasized how the ban was consistent with international humanitarian law. Some focused on how the ban would strengthen the NPT. Others argued that their government had a general principle of participation and inclusion, and that to not engage in the process would mean walking away from an important characteristic of their country. For these governments in particular, the involvement of the International Committee of the Red Cross was apparently instrumental, as well as the participation of other regional partners and even other skeptical governments. But it was lonely, said a diplomat who felt that they could not join their traditional friends and colleagues in being fully supportive of the process.

For diplomats working within governments that did not support the ban, the questions were more about whether to engage at all, rather than how to engage. "There was no question about changing my government's position," said one such representative. "The only question for us was tactical—do we attend to help shape things, or not. We knew we wouldn't participate in good faith, but there was an appetite to know what was going on" inside the negotiating room.[69] In some of these countries, an internal debate even questioned whether they would participate in the humanitarian initiative. Most government officials from countries unsupportive of the ban treaty felt that the humanitarian impact conferences and joint statements were a "slippery slope"—yet, at the same time, they did not want to be seen to be boycotting the issue entirely. One diplomat from an unsupportive country found that the policy discussions within his government were "very top down." The main conversations were happening in the capital, without input from diplomats who had spent time in the UN meetings dealing with nuclear weapons. This made it more difficult to convey or have taken seriously the momentum around the idea of banning nuclear weapons and some of the key arguments in its favor.

Then, of course, consider the nuclear-armed states and the governments of countries who support their retention of nuclear weapons. For the most part, as will be seen in later chapters, they self-selected their exclusion from the process, opting out of participating in the humanitarian initiative, various UN working groups, and/or the treaty's negotiation. What is perhaps most interesting about their refusal to engage, or their attempts to undermine, slow, or stop the process to ban the bomb from moving forward, is that they seemed to fully believe they would win. The arrogance with which they dismissed the arguments for a ban and the momentum growing among the majority of states and other actors was absolute. Even those who could sense what we had set out to do, and were aware that it had been done before on landmines and cluster bombs, still thought they held all the cards when it came to nuclear weapons. This hubris is part of why the process got away from them and even motivated some states to join it, as will be discussed later. But this attitude is also likely related to the regrowth of activist engagement in this issue with the rise of ICAN. Governments of nuclear-armed states have succumbed to pressure from activism before at different points through the nuclear age, as shown in chapter 2, but have always managed to avoid the ultimate demand of civil society: the total abolition of nuclear weapons. Perhaps they felt they could once again sidestep the pressure from the activists and continue on their merry way.

The next chapter, then, looks at the growth of ICAN, including within the context of social movement theories and the history of antinuclear organizing examined in chapter 2. This growth was happening simultaneously with the development of the wider transnational network of diplomats and others working to ban the bomb, which also helped shape the direction and nature of the campaign.

5

REVITALIZING A MOVEMENT

On 28 July 2012, eighty-two-year-old Catholic nun Sister Megan Rice, Vietnam veteran Michael Walli, and housepainter Greg Boertje-Obed broke into the Y-12 Nuclear Security Complex in Oak Ridge, Tennessee. With flashlights and bolt cutters, the three activists made their way to the inner sanctum of the facility where the United States keeps its fuel for nuclear weapons. They cut through a chain-link fence, decorated the walls of the uranium-storage facility with blood and spray paint, knocked a piece of concrete off the building with a sledgehammer, and sang religious songs for about half an hour. Nuclear experts have described it as the biggest security breach of the country's nuclear complex.[1]

The three activists were following in the tradition of the Plowshares movement inspired by Catholic workers Dorothy Day and Daniel and Phillip Berrigan. Nuns, priests, and Catholic laypeople had for decades undertaken similar actions across the United States. All three involved in the Y-12 action were arrested and imprisoned for destroying government property and committing sabotage. In defense of their actions, they highlighted the criminality of the seventy-year industry of nuclear weapons. After serving about two years of their sentences, they were released from federal prison in May 2015 when a court of appeals panel threw out the government's sabotage convictions.[2]

Shortly after the break-in at Y-12, more than one hundred activists from thirty countries participated in an ICAN campaign meeting in Hiroshima in August 2012. They talked about reframing the nuclear disarmament debate in humanitarian terms and developed practical ideas for generating a groundswell of public support for a treaty banning nuclear weapons—already, in our minds, the next big stage of the campaign.[3] What was not overtly visible at the time was the connection between the Plowshares action in Tennessee and the ICAN campaigners meeting in Hiroshima. Although those who founded ICAN in Australia had done so with the express purpose of revitalizing the global anti-nuclear movement, and although the campaign was actively reaching out to new actors to get involved, the nature of the campaign and its movement-building potential were heavily contextualized in the wider political situation and constraints on activism. "When we began ICAN," explained cofounder Dimity Hawkins in a public speech in 2018, "it wasn't out of the blue, a one-off lightning bulb moment where we thought we'd 'have a go' . . . We knew well from close work, decades of experience, how hard it would be to begin a new approach to nuclear disarmament."[4] But wherever people first engaged with the ideas around banning nuclear weapons, what made it a sustainable idea was the building of community and friendship around it. The early formation of ideas for the initiation of ICAN or the pursuit of a new treaty "were forged in the shared sense of purpose, to re-engage with the issue from the grassroots up," said Hawkins.

Thus, at the same time that ICAN was working with diplomats, academics, and UN officials to build the case for the ban and the community to deliver it, we were also building our own campaign—a movement to generate the energy, ideas, and sustenance to carry this project forward. Antinuclear activism had largely been on the decline since the end of the Cold War, as described earlier. Nevertheless, it persisted.[5]

This chapter examines how activists revitalized and built a transnational network of campaigners and diplomats to ban the bomb through an international treaty as a key step toward the abolition of nuclear weapons. Working—in some cases consciously, in other cases without proper recognition—from the legacy and lessons of feminist, queer, Indigenous, antiracist, and postcolonial activism to challenge knowledge production, activists with ICAN sought to challenge the status quo, confront power, build alternative narratives around nuclear weapons, engage a new generation of activists and diplomats, and learn from those who had come before—including from those who participated in the processes to ban landmines and cluster munitions. This chapter discusses some of the struggles ICAN faced, but also highlights some of its key successes.

INTERGENERATIONAL AND INTERSECTIONAL

For those of us in ICAN partner organizations such as WILPF, who were thinking about broader issues of organizing and movement building and the relationship of this work with international advocacy in the diplomatic sphere, we did not necessarily find ourselves purposefully designing our style of activism for ICAN. Some engaged in the project understood that we were building a sort of transnational advocacy network, but we did not necessarily engage in the theoretical foundations of such organizing. We tried, sometimes successfully and sometimes not, to allow a broad enough scope in the work of the campaign so that different people could contribute with different activities at different points. In this way, we sought to "reclaim our time" not only from the arrogant narratives of nuclear deterrence and nuclear security, as described in chapter 3, but also from those who had prioritized elite institutional relationships over grassroots mobilization and demands for radical change. We sought—as feminists as well as queer, Indigenous, antiracist, and postcolonial activists have always done—to challenge the idea that only certain people could produce knowledge on certain subjects, or that some voices and ideas were more credible based only on where those people were situated or what bodies or institutions they inhabited.

In this work, some of us in ICAN were determined to mobilize a broader, more diverse constituency of activists on the issue of nuclear weapons. This work also included engaging a more diverse constituency of diplomats and government officials—those who were considered marginal rather than central to decision making and power when it came to nuclear weapons. This helped us develop a clear, concise goal for our work, with a strategy aimed at weakening particular nodes of power politics, rather than directly working to immediately change the positions or policies of those in power. That is, instead of continuing just to demand that nuclear-armed states eliminate their weapons, we wanted to build up a groundswell of activists and diplomats from around the world to pull the rug out from under them, changing norms and international law to make the status quo increasingly untenable.

To some extent, these lessons were learned once again from the campaigns to ban landmines and cluster bombs. Both processes involved a broad partnership among activists, governments, and intergovernmental

134   *Chapter 5*

organizations. "Although not free of inherent tensions, these partnerships served overall to advance a common goal using the various tools at the disposal of the different actors," found the participants in the 2008 United Nations Institute for Disarmament Research (UNIDIR) symposium looking at lessons from banning landmines and cluster munitions.[6] The processes also earned legitimacy from their involvement of survivors and those affected by the use of landmines and cluster munitions. Geographical balance and inclusiveness within the campaigns "promoted ownership in the process among all participants and ensured that the process was (and was perceived as being) representative, transparent, and credible."[7]

Governments were also keenly aware of the value of including and promoting involvement of survivors and other activist groups. In 2009, Norway's representative had argued at a UN General Assembly meeting that disarmament "can only be achieved if states listen to, learn from and include strong voices from civil society that advocate change."[8] He noted that this needs to include women's groups, humanitarian agencies, and people directly affected by the weapons. In this vein, the 2008 UNIDIR symposium had found that credibility for the humanitarian reframing of weapon systems needed to be established through research and practice. "Both the Ottawa and Oslo processes were described as data-driven. . . . The experience and expertise of humanitarian field workers, clearance personnel, and survivors were also heavily drawn on and helped to focus the debate on the humanitarian effects of weapons," symposium participants noted.[9]

The participation of survivors and others with lived experiences of the bomb was a crucial, life-changing experience for many people engaging with antinuclear activism—both in terms of activists and diplomats. Survivor testimony has been crucial to raising public awareness since the first bombs were dropped on Hiroshima and Nagasaki and continues to play an important role in engaging people today. ICAN worked to ensure that this was a central part of its organizing by including survivors from the atomic bombings of Hiroshima and Nagasaki, as well as of nuclear testing in Australia, the Pacific, and Kazakhstan, as part of its delegation to meetings in the humanitarian initiative and nuclear ban processes. "Focusing on survivors was morally correct and also strategically clever," said one North American ICAN activist.

"Hearing testimony from survivors generates visceral reactions and changes the nature and style of international discussions."[10] It is also important to ensure that survivor testimony reaches outside the halls of the United Nations. Hibakusha Stories, an ICAN partner in New York, has for years brought atomic bomb survivors into New York City high schools. Hearing the testimony of those who suffered and survived the U.S. bombings of Hiroshima and Nagasaki has had an impact on many students' lives. A student from Queens said that before hearing from a survivor, the atomic bombings were just something that happened in World War Two. "They didn't really mean anything to me. When you can put a face to the story, it really changes your perspective."[11] ICAN campaigners and diplomats alike reported having the same reaction to hearing survivors speak about their experiences.

At the same time, however, for some survivors the focus on the impacts of nuclear weapons through the humanitarian initiative was puzzling at first. "It wasn't new," said one ICAN campaigner from a country in the Pacific that has suffered from the legacy of nuclear-weapon testing in the region.[12] "The particular goal of prohibition and disarmament of nuclear weapons through a treaty was new, though, and seemed hypothetical." From this perspective, activists from countries impacted by nuclear testing or use sometimes needed to grapple with why the humanitarian initiative was such a breakthrough in the realm of nuclear disarmament. But as time passed, she said, "I found ICAN [to be] a practical, focused campaign that needed specific actions by countries at particular times, to get a process going for a ban treaty. I focused on that, and the best entry points for Pacific support." This, she determined, was reminding the Pacific governments "of the region's profoundly intense experience of nuclear weapons and that it could, as a region, come out strongly in favor of prohibiting these weapons, as the region had unwillingly been drawn into their development." She and other representatives of affected communities engaged with ICAN firmly believed that survivors must not only be used for their victim testimonies. "They must themselves represent the region and their peoples—this is basic good politics in the twenty-first century—and can be involved at the highest levels in disarmament discussions."

The humanitarian aspects of nuclear weapons have proven time and again to be the catalyst for most people to engage in antinuclear work.

The inhumanity of the bomb is reflected not just in the immediate suffering of its direct victims, but also in the broader injustices it generates for many generations. It wasn't until she moved from Ireland to the United Kingdom, a nuclear-armed state, that one ICAN campaigner got involved in antinuclear activism. "Before that, nuclear weapons were an abstract horror but very much in the periphery of my life and not something tangible or frightening in my reality," she explained.[13] It was the injustice of nuclear weapons that drove her to action. It was not just the idea that the UK government could end the lives of millions of people, but also that it was spending precious resources to ensure its ability to do so:

> When I moved to the UK, suddenly it was impossible for me not to have an opinion on nuclear weapons. They were in the news, reference to "our deterrent" was constant; at the same time, the UK was continuing a policy of austerity measures where the levels of inequality were growing rapidly. In the same news program, they would cover the exponential growth of people needing food banks and then the hundreds of millions of pounds that the government was, at that time, hoping to put into Trident.[14]

It is a natural reaction for many people to feel overwhelmed by the magnitude of the problem and the seemingly ubiquitous power of the structures of political economy sustaining the nuclear enterprise. But key to any campaign, including ICAN, is not balking at the gravity or magnitude of the problem, but instead embracing it as a challenge to be overcome through courage and creativity. One European-American campaigner was drawn to the challenge the nuclear ban treaty mounted to traditional structures of power. "I liked how ICAN was vocal about the fact that entities in power on this issue, like the nuclear-armed states, shouldn't dictate the pace of progress," he said. The idea of going for a ban treaty without those countries "would be something that flipped the script." He liked being a part of a campaign that led rather than followed. Even when it seemed like things were stuck, "we nevertheless managed to keep the flame burning until we found the next opportunity."[15]

Creativity was always a big part of the campaign, together with relentless hope and optimism. From its beginning, ICAN sought to stigmatize nuclear weapons using "humor, horror, and hope."[16] We held up legacies of relentless activism achieving change over time—the abolition of slavery, the civil rights, women's rights, queer rights movements, and more. There was never any misconception that the abolition of nuclear weapons would be immediate or even near term. Each social justice movement mentioned has not achieved absolute success—that is, the abolition of slavery has not eliminated racism or discrimination; women's rights and queer rights movements have by no means resulted in gender equality or even an end to gender- and sexuality-based violence. Further, any grounds made for social justice are usually subject to pushback and retrogression. We can see this for every equality and rights-based movement out there. But each of these efforts to change the world for the better has resulted in significant shifts culturally, socially, politically, and economically. By choosing an achievable goal—in ICAN's case, a treaty banning nuclear weapons, even without the nuclear-armed states on board—and by building confidence that it is attainable through collective action, human society is able to achieve meaningful change.

The possibility of change was critical to ICAN's success as a campaign. The possibility of the ban treaty, the possibility of standing up to the most powerful countries in the world, the possibility of working across borders, across lines dividing "civil society" and "governments" to create something new, was enough to draw in and sustain many young people in the campaign for the nuclear ban. Engaging a new generation of antinuclear activists was crucial to ICAN's success. Many young people around the world view their current political systems as broken. Although they may want to improve social conditions, they do not necessarily see traditional politics as an effective way to do that.[17] "Politics is an elite institution that excludes many people," writes Helen Berents, who has spent of much her academic career exploring representations of youth in politics. In many cases, the terms of debate are "set up to pre-emptively discount young people's experiences, voices and contributions. No place is being left at the table for them."[18] When there is no room at the table, and your views are consistently dismissed as naive, it's not easy to figure out how to get involved or make change. But many young people do anyway—particularly when alternatives are available to them, such as organizations or campaigns that will welcome and even encourage their contributions and give them a chance to challenge the structures and attitudes that prevent their involvement in more traditional spheres of political action.

One of ICAN's activists found that she was attracted to the campaign's approach "of the pursuit of a tangible goal, a win—not just a vague win but a hard-hitting win that would provide a tool to begin dismantling the structures that tell me I'm naive, that acting for justice or equality is, at the end of the day, an inevitable loss." It took a while, but she eventually realized that "if I was willing to contribute and could figure out how best to do that, then my contribution would actually make a difference."[19] Another noted the way that his "range of activities" shifted from an activist folding paper cranes and organizing public demonstrations to a lobbyist interacting with diplomats at the United Nations and organizing international meetings.[20]

ICAN tried to encourage everyone of any age to take part in whatever aspects of the campaign's work they wished. Want to lobby a government? We'll give you a crash course and send you on your way. Want to do some research on nuclear policy or monitor and analyze the government discussions? Bring your laptop and write something for our publications. Want to go to a nuclear facility and talk to the workers about the treaty?[21] Yes, please! "For us new ones with no experience, only with a lot of enthusiasm and engagement for this cause, ICAN was really a place where we were allowed to be a part, contribute with what we could and learn and develop a lot," explained one activist. She added, "It didn't matter if you had done this work for six months or sixty years, everyone was welcome."[22] Another campaigner said he hopes that some of the other established antinuclear organizations learn from ICAN's engagement of a younger generation. "Peace activism tends to attract an older crowd," he said, noting that as someone in his late thirties he was often the youngest person at antinuclear meetings until ICAN came along. "It was pleasantly refreshing to see more diversity in the participation and the leadership of this campaign, and it lays the groundwork for decades to come."[23]

This intergenerational effect was indeed essential to ICAN's success. "ICAN is not a youth organization," ICAN's very first volunteer in Australia says regularly. "We're an inter-generational campaign. Indeed, that's one of our greatest strengths. We have octogenarians working alongside school students. No one is too young or too old to contribute to a world free of nuclear weapons."[24] He started at ICAN at the age of twenty-one, helping to get the campaign off the ground in Melbourne. But ICAN was not the beginning of his activism against nuclear weapons. He was ten years old when he got started in this work. "I remember learning about the atomic bombings of Hiroshima and Nagasaki and being horrified. How could such acts be committed? Each year, my class would fold a thousand origami cranes in support of disarmament. I guess that was the beginning of my anti-nuclear activism." He feels that he was part of ICAN's founding even as a young volunteer, explaining that he and the others starting the campaign "were convinced that the only way to bring about lasting, meaningful change was through public mobilization." With the success of the nuclear ban treaty, he notes, "We have shown, I think, that people power is greater than military power."

This was part of the reason another Australian campaigner got involved. Previously, she had worked with Traditional Owners of the land, Indigenous groups that were active in resisting nuclear waste dumps and uranium mines. She came to know about ICAN through this work but wasn't involved in weapons issues because it "didn't feel as present" to her. "It was more of an intangible idea that others were dealing with, rather than lands being smashed and people affected" every day by other aspects of the nuclear chain.[25] She considered herself to be an activist whose learning and experience was "geared more towards tactics for direct action, like forest blockades and legal strategies." But when a paid gig opened up with ICAN, she jumped at the opportunity to learn something new. "Being paid to work on antinuclear issues is rare," she laughed. One of the most important aspects of the work from her perspective was able to bring her connections with Indigenous communities around the country into ICAN's national and international campaigning on the humanitarian impacts of nuclear weapons and for the ban treaty.

Building networks across borders is something that antinuclear activism has always offered. In the 1980s in particular, protesters in Western Europe and North America were connected in their opposition and even in many of their actions. ICAN sought to reinforce the transnational character of this work—and to include activists from countries that traditionally hadn't been very active in antinuclear work. An activist from Kenya said she was drawn to the "synergy and complementarity among campaigners" in ICAN.[26] "Sharing research and knowledge, undertaking collaborative campaign actions" across countries, she describes ICAN as "a coalition of dreams of hope of a people to achieve one objective—banning nuclear weapons." She was also encouraged by the "unity in diversity and accord amongst campaigners of different ages, nationalities, religious or political affiliations," to which she attributes keeping "the momentum of the campaign alive."

ICAN also tried to ensure diversity not just of age, but also of sex, gender identity, and sexual orientation. "As a feminist, the seamless participation and contributions by women as leaders in the campaign, as experts, analysts, strategists and writers, thinkers, is welcome, noticeable, and achieved without any apparent strain within ICAN," said one campaigner.[27] In addition to having parity between those identifying as men and women on the steering group, some of ICAN's staff, steering group members, and campaigners identified as LGBTQ+. This was not really something ICAN as a campaign highlighted and some within the staff and leadership body may not really have thought about this one or way or the other. But in 2017, some ICAN activists initiated a spin-off group, IQAN—International Queers Against Nukes. "Coming out" at Pride March in New York City that year, they unveiled a banner and Twitter account. Although not a formal structure, IQAN has since been present at several pride events in different countries and aligns itself with organizations and campaigns against other weapons and forms of violence, such as Gays Against Guns. Since 2017 it has continued to raise connections between queer liberation and the abolition of nuclear weapons, situating the possession of the bomb, as many feminists do, in the machinations of the patriarchy and its heteronormative, racist underpinnings.[28]

Overall, ICAN as a campaign sought to provide community—a chance to make friends, network intergenerationally, learn from each other, and work together on an equal footing toward a shared goal. Beyond its founding, the promise of collective action and the possibility of change is what continued to bring young people to ICAN. One activist said she was drawn to ICAN because of its international community, explaining that it was "an amazing feeling of being part of a group of people and organizations that are actually making a change in our society. Working by yourself in your own country can sometimes feel a little hopeless, but then every time we get together at an international arena with everyone, you understand that you are part of something much bigger."[29] Another said that the collective growth of ICAN was also a personal growth for him. He found that work became a lot more fun and social once he joined ICAN, which helped quench his thirst for doing something significant and international. "I became addicted to the work," he said. "I could see the power of change, and I liked being involved."[30] Meeting everyone internationally was also inspiring, he explained. Being connected across borders helped him realize the benefits of working nationally with a broader global community. "To be honest, I thought the idea of banning nuclear weapons was kind of crazy," said one North American campaigner, "but there was no way to deny the energy of the campaign and so I ended up just going with the flow."[31]

NOT ALL SINGING, ALL DANCING

Of course, the positive aspects of the campaign, the things that ICAN got right, or tried to get right, should not override the things the campaign got wrong. From my perspective, and the perspective of several ICAN activists I interviewed, these foremost include ensuring racial and regional diversity in policy-making roles and being sufficiently democratic in our consultations and decision making.

Although ICAN has done a consistently excellent job of ensuring gender and age diversity among its campaigners, it did less well when it came to racial or regional diversity. Even while dedicating resources and thought to how to be inclusive and supportive of activists from around the world, the campaign is still largely white and Western, especially among its leadership body—the international steering group, represented by ten of the campaign's partner organizations, and the paid staff team.

"ICAN is a bit Eurocentric," said one activist from the global south. "If we're talking about the campaign being international, then sometimes it was like the 19th-century style of internationalism, where the decisions are made by the Europeans."[32] Throughout the campaign leading up to treaty negotiations, the international steering group was comprised mostly of European-based organizations and representatives, with two international groups represented by North Americans and Australians, and only one group each from Africa, Asia, and Latin America. Small grants programs ensured that funds were sent to partner organizations for campaigning in the global south, and sponsorship programs ensured that activists from those countries could attend international and regional meetings. But some people within the campaign expressed concern that the decisions about policy, practice, and funding were made predominantly by the international steering group and staff team, which was not adequately representative of the broader campaign.

Some ICAN activists, including some of those in the steering group, argued for more diverse inclusion within the steering group and staff team and for better integration of the leadership's activities with the broader campaign. Some steering group members and some on the staff team attempted to set up campaign partner surveys or organize opportunities at campaigner meetings to listen to and work with feedback from those outside the steering group. But overall, the campaign continues to suffer from white, Western dominance of its leadership.

"I would like to see ICAN reflect its global collective," said one campaigner, "and have this appear as part of ICAN more, at the center, in publications and its publicizing international commitments and actions for nuclear disarmament." For many from the global south, she noted, nuclear disarmament is a minority concern, not the issue of choice in activist movements. "I think the time has come for nuclear disarmament to really be known and owned by many more countries across the world." Unfortunately, as it stands, she said, "The knowledge and analytical base is also heavily Northern-centric. If ICAN could consciously increase its representation of other sources of analysis and expertise on nuclear issues, international relations, disarmament processes, speakers etc., that is probably important for changes in ICAN's membership, to really convey to the world different power lines other than North-South."[33]

This regional and racial imbalance led to what some campaigners viewed as mistakes in terms of which organizations or individuals the campaign leadership chose to work with or engage in certain regions. "I offered to help map out [activists in my region]," said one campaigner, but ICAN staff "just did what they wanted. Mistakes were made. ICAN had an asset on the ground and didn't use it."[34] She expressed gratitude that ICAN helped secure a budget for her work, allowing her to engage full-time on nuclear issues. Yet at the same time, she lamented, "In ICAN I was sometimes feeling the burden of not being white." Attending her first ICAN campaigners meeting, she felt that the way the agenda and regional work were set up erased regional campaigners' identities. "Whoever decided the agenda didn't give us time to talk amongst ourselves," she said. "We all came with a lot of experience, but we were just talked at by people with less experience."

It wasn't just activists who noticed this phenomenon. A few diplomats from the global south noted that although some ICAN campaigners from their regions were participating in international meetings or regional workshops, a lot of visible national or local campaigning wasn't necessarily happening. One said he wasn't very happy with the minimal representation of ICAN in Africa, though he understood that part of the problem was resources.[35] Another more bluntly pointed out that overall, ICAN "looks very western."[36]

In addition to problems of regional and racial diversity, the campaign also at times struggled with socioeconomic and class issues. Although many partner organizations were funded for their work on the ban, others were not. And although the participation in the work of representatives of some of these groups was enabled through small grants or sponsorships, not everyone benefited. Resources are not unlimited, which meant that some activists had to self-fund to attend international meetings or to organize actions in their countries. Although not a bad thing on its own, it did at times lead to tensions between those who were funded and those who were not—especially when at international meetings some were sleeping on floors and others were being put up in hotels, or some had thousands of dollars granted by the campaign to organize a local meeting whereas others had to raise the funds themselves or put in out of pocket.

The variable resources also led to feelings of alienation among some activists at international meetings—especially for those used to a different style of activism. This was particularly true in regard to the series of meetings held in Norway, Mexico, and Austria on the humanitarian impacts of nuclear weapons, to be described in the next chapter. Some activists pointed out how strange it was to have a meeting about nuclear weapons at a resort in Mexico, for example, and how out of touch this felt with the idea that people are donating thirty dollars out of their limited budgets to support the campaign. Those raising these types of concerns understood that the locations for meetings were chosen by the government hosting them, not ICAN, but wondered if more could have been done by the campaign to find alternative accommodation for those who couldn't afford to stay at the official venue.

Some activists also found ICAN's style of mobilizing campaigners to be rather divergent from what they were accustomed to. As described earlier, most ICAN activists interviewed for this book reported feeling engaged, supported, and part of a growing collective. Most felt welcome regardless of their level of knowledge about nuclear weapons before joining the campaign. But not everyone shared this experience. One activist noted that she had previously been involved in participatory movements and found ICAN's style too top-down. Another reported that he sometimes felt treated as a "low-level employee," given orders from above that were supposed to be followed without question. But at the same time, most of those conveying these concerns said they felt able to push back on this when it happened. The level of friendship within the campaign allowed people to call each other out on inappropriate demands. Still, the idea that demands were being made at all was troublesome. One activist mused that it sometimes seemed some people wanted hierarchy within the campaign—some wanted to be told what to do, others wanted to tell them. "It's important to draw from and respect experience," she noted, "but it's also important to encourage more autonomy and growth. That's how to build a movement."[37]

Some of us in the international steering group also struggled with what at times felt like a top-down, hierarchical organization rather than a movement or a campaign. We had to recognize our own place in the campaign structure and struggle against that—sometimes to no avail; other times we were able to push through changes that were beneficial to the wider movement. At the end of the day, those of us experiencing this struggle had to try to act as the best version of ourselves, to behave as members of a campaign we wanted to be part of, rather than just rail against what we felt was wrong. We were operating within an international, institutional world order that still tends to privilege white, Western voices. It was important not to accept this and blindly benefit from it, but to recognize it and take every possible opportunity to challenge it by trying to create space for alternative perspectives and for diversity at all levels of the campaign. But there was a constant underlying—and sometimes overt—tension between efficiency and democracy in the campaign's operations.

This tension meant that many activists felt cut out of decision making. The steering group, or segments of it, would sometimes make decisions without wide consultations. At moments a small majority within the staff and steering group would try to prevent discussion or debate over points of substance or process by agreeing with each other on a course of action and ensuring that quick votes were taken, stifling debate by arguing that there was no time for discussion, and asserting that the only alternative to this was allowing every single partner organization to have an equal voice, which would make it impossible to advance.

This false dichotomy—between absolute equal participation of hundreds of people or a handful of people making decisions behind closed doors—is not unique to ICAN. It is the bane of all democratic-minded, participatory collectives and movements the world over. Much of the social movement theory explored in chapter 2 grapples with this problem. But many of us in ICAN still believe that transparency, inclusiveness, and consultation did not have to be sacrificed on the altar of efficiency as often as it tended to be.

Collectives, especially ones as large as ICAN, can rarely have a perfect system of consultation or democratic participation. But those of us in the leadership mechanisms should have learned from early mistakes of taking actions or operating in ways that resulted in people feeling like they had been left behind. When ICAN first started in 2007, it was very inclusive, welcoming all organizations that supported the goal of nuclear abolition to join. In the early years, ICAN's goal remained an instrument negotiated by all states, including the nuclear-armed states, through which they would commit to the total elimination of their nuclear weapon programs. But after discussion with like-minded governments and other partners, the leadership of ICAN decided to shift course around 2010, pursuing a nuclear ban treaty to prohibit the weapons even without the participation of the nuclear-armed states—for all the reasons explained in the previous chapter.

This decision was vehemently rejected by some nuclear abolitionists, especially those who had been active on the scene for decades.

Those in opposition felt that the pursuit of any nuclear disarmament measure without nuclear-weapon-possessing states was useless. Similar to the nuclear-armed and nuclear-supportive states, they accused the campaign's new objective of being ridiculous and naive. Most of these same people, however, eventually supported the ban—once states had agreed to negotiate the treaty, or in some cases, the day the treaty was adopted. But when we first started advancing the idea, some refused to believe that such a treaty could ever be developed. A few argued, and continue to argue, that it will never be effective as a disarmament instrument. Some have even asserted, as the nuclear-armed states do, that it was harmful to other initiatives, or that it set back progress in nuclear disarmament.

I believe that the motivation behind these arguments was based more on ICAN's shift away from consensus-based decision making in the wider antinuclear movement than it was about the substance of those arguments. The problem, it seemed to me, was less about the perceived potential of the ban treaty and more about the fact that certain activists in the nuclear abolition movement felt that they had not been part of the decision to pursue a ban treaty. This was in part the fault of ICAN's leaders in 2010, including me, for failing to widely consult, discuss, and debate the merits of such an approach with all of the activists who considered themselves to be important players in the international diplomatic conference circuit. But more broadly, and as clearly persisted over time, the problem was entitlement. Certain people felt that they had not "approved" this course of action.

This reflection is based on repeated conversations with some of these individuals. Even after some of my ICAN colleagues and I made genuine efforts to mend bridges, to bring folks along, to converse across divides, we were accused of disrespecting our elders and of being naive. Some of us tried to do damage control and see if we could hear out people's concerns in a way that would help them find ways to support our initiative even if they hadn't been part of the process in deciding on the path forward. But we were sometimes met with ageist and even racist critiques of the campaign—we were too young to know what we were doing and we were involving activists from regions without an antinuclear organizing history, who, we were told, were just getting involved because ICAN had money to bring them to the United Nations.

Part of this hostile reaction, I think, is probably due to the fact that many of the activists opposing the ban had for years been suffering from lack of funding. ICAN was able to raise money for its campaign, which caused tensions with groups that were scrambling to support one or two staff people. "ICAN was given financial and administrative help to set up and run an office in Geneva and was made the Norwegian government's official civil society partner at the Oslo Conference on the Humanitarian Impact of Nuclear Weapons in March 2013. This prepared the grounds for a reorganization (or re-networking) of the nuclear disarmament NGO community," wrote academics Ritchie and Egeland.[38] They and others pointed out that Norway's interest in the ban changed the anti-nuclear game. The political opportunity arising out of the Oslo humanitarian conference, and the resources that Norway was willing to put into this process, seemed to shift the balance of power within ICAN toward new ideas. "This is what got ICAN taken seriously. It had resources, it had a plan, and it had opportunities to promote its objective."[39]

But it also brought resentment from those who felt that money had been taken from them, who saw the funding situation as a zero-sum game where if ICAN "won," they "lost." Of course, where there is money, there is power. Issues arose over power distribution within and external to ICAN: issues of control, of exclusion, of discipline. Anyone skeptical or critical of a nuclear weapon ban treaty was excluded from ICAN, argued Ritchie and Egeland.[40] It was true that those against the ban were not warmly welcomed into policy discussions. But this was not just because they did not support the ban. It also had to do with the ways in which they opposed the ban and ICAN—where they *situated* their critique. The idea that ICAN would spend money building capacity in regions that traditionally had not engaged as much with antinuclear activism, that the campaign would bring activists to the United Nations from the global south to international meetings, that it would help them organize roundtables or meetings in their countries—in these countries that did not have nuclear weapons!—was apparently not OK. Those of us in ICAN's leadership were also told we were all too young—most of the steering group and all of the staff team, including me, was at this time under the age of thirty-five. What could we possibly know about proper activism? (As noted earlier, of course, ICAN is an intergenerational campaign, including in the steering group.)

For some of us in ICAN at this time, this attitude drove us further down our path of pursuing something that was becoming increasingly seen as radical—even though it wasn't really radical at all. It was the most logical thing in the world for us to pursue, we believed: it was a partial measure, a step to something bigger, a tool to break the perpetual logjam that had plagued international nuclear disarmament efforts for decades. It also motivated us to try to bring as many people along who had previously been excluded from antinuclear activism. Despite its challenges with diversity noted above, ICAN did recognize this problem and try to bring new voices and perspectives into the international debate about nuclear weapons. There was no intentional effort to displace those already operating in this space, but as we can see from other movements toward rights, equality, and diversity, sometimes those who have traditionally held a space feel threatened when others begin to assert themselves within it.

Despite the early tensions, many initial critics of the ban eventually came around—realizing, perhaps, that the only obstacle to their participation and contribution to banning nuclear weapons was themselves. But resentment lingered, and in some cases grew. It was here that assertions about inclusivity and participation came to be blurred with consensus and unanimity. Some NGO ban opponents questioned why we couldn't all just support each other's efforts as complementary; others insisted that we all had to get behind and work on things in total agreement. Both approaches were problematic for the same reason that the idea of "consensus" in intergovernmental meetings had become so fraught. Consensus had become synonymous with deadlock.

Consensus as a process is intended to be cooperative rather than competitive, to facilitate compromise rather than zero-sum approaches, and to ensure that the "tyranny of the majority" cannot silence the concerns of a minority. Consensus as an outcome offers an aura of unity. It suggests that the final product is satisfactory to all participants, which will make its implementation easier, because everyone involved agrees with it. But from the perspective of someone working in and around the United Nations for nearly fifteen years, it is painfully clear that consensus is not about getting along to get along, or about reaching compromise. It is about preventing progress. It privileges and empowers blocking.

At the Conference on Disarmament (CD), where no substantive work has occurred since 1998, the rules of procedure stipulate that the conference shall conduct its work and adopt its decisions by consensus. This has led to a stalemate that one delegation or another has perpetuated using the consensus rule as a veto to block the commencement of work. In effect, consensus as currently practiced in the CD avoids tyranny of the majority by empowering a tyranny of the minority.

This is an important question for activists as much as governments. Does consensus mean compromise? Does it mean tyranny? Does it afford the opportunity to promote cooperative approaches? Are there other, better ways to bring folks along, perhaps the use of "rough consensus," where people can voice concerns, register discomfort with decisions, but move forward and not prevent anyone else from acting?[41]

POSITIVE ENGAGEMENT, POSITIVE RESULTS

These questions remained valid and vexing throughout the campaign for the ban treaty and will likely remain so for all movements and initiatives. But one thing was clear for most of the activists engaged in ICAN's work: being part of a bigger whole, part of a movement, was fulfilling, challenging, life changing, inspiring, frustrating, and significant. "It's hard to be a campaigner. Other people are going to get credit for your work, and you're not even getting paid for it," said one ICAN activist. "But if you look at the bigger picture, it doesn't really matter. Even with all the disagreements, ICAN is still a very unified campaign. We have a clear message and understanding of what we want, both of which helped us achieve our goal."[42]

This idea of a "bigger picture" helped many of us in ICAN deal with our concerns with certain aspects of the campaign's style and leadership to "get the work done." While continuing to call out or try to help resolve the problematic organizational elements, we tried to focus on building the movement and advocating for the treaty. In this work, being part of ICAN had many benefits.

Despite the hierarchies and tensions some activists felt, most valued the relatively flat structure of the campaign. "You can talk to anyone, there's no difference between the staff, the steering group, and the

campaigners. You don't feel intimidated by anyone."[43] Others highlighted the benefits of working with a team with varied experience
and expertise. Several were enthusiastic about the helpful campaign
resources from the ICAN staff team as well as WILPF's reporting on
the intergovernmental processes, noting that these materials helped
them feel prepared and informed. Some spoke about the attention and
assistance they could count on from staff and the steering group in their
regional or local work. "Looking back, my sense is that the painstaking
perseverance of the campaigners and their remarkable spirit of solidarity
with each other are among the important virtues that helped the cause
immensely," said one campaigner.[44] Others noted the benefits of working collectively on an important issue. "Working with the campaign
meant feeding off each other," one campaigner remarked. "There's an
additive value to your actions—whatever you do is a grain of salt in a
movement."[45]

The global nature of ICAN's movement was imperative to its success. Although the antinuclear movement has always been global, the
national, local, and international efforts of activists were not always as
well connected as they became through the ICAN network. The following provides a brief taste of some of ICAN's activities around the
world.

As mentioned, ICAN was founded in Australia in 2007, and
national partners and staff there have been extremely active locally and
internationally ever since. They have organized public meetings and
events, including art exhibits and auctions. They wrote op-eds, journal
articles, and did countless media interviews. They lobbied parliamentarians and government officials in Canberra and around the country,
urging them to work to change the government's position to support
the ban treaty. The Australian activists were not shy about direct action,
climbing on top of the Foreign Ministry building with a banner calling
on the government to sign the treaty, standing outside of Parliament
urging members to sign ICAN's Parliamentary Pledge, or riding their
bikes hundreds of kilometers from Melbourne to Canberra to promote
the ban. In addition, they ensured activists from First Nations groups
were on their delegations to the United Nations and humanitarian
impact conferences, as well as ICAN campaigner meetings, to engage
directly with diplomats and other campaigners. Many of these activists

had been engaged in antinuclear activism for generations, and their voices and experiences were indispensable to the global movement to ban the bomb. Australian campaigners were also active in policy making and advocacy coordination at all moments.

Campaigners in Brazil were active throughout the Latin American and Caribbean region, helping to organize and participating in round-tables in Punta del Este, Uruguay; Montego Bay, Jamaica; and San José, Costa Rica. They advocated frequently with the Brazilian government, parliamentarians, and diplomats throughout the humanitarian initiative process to bring it on board the ban treaty strategy. They also hosted events and activities with students at the Federal University of Pampa who were part of the Grupo de Práticas em Direitos Humanos e Direito Internacional, which featured mobilization on the streets and an academic approach. They also hosted an action in the park that divides Santana do Livramento (Brazil) with the city of Rivera (Uruguay). They engaged local television and radio to discuss the humanitarian impacts of nuclear weapons. They also participated in academic events and published papers on nuclear disarmament.

In Canada, campaigners worked to keep opposition parliamentarians, as well as government officials, informed about the humanitarian initiative and the process to ban nuclear weapons. They helped organize an open letter from Order of Canada recipients to the prime minister calling for him to join the nuclear ban, and a letter from the Canadian Council of Churches to the foreign minister about Canada's absence from the negotiations. Canadian ICAN campaigners also worked with colleagues in Australia to ensure that First Nations perspectives and voices were heard during the nuclear ban negotiations. They also worked to promote the perspectives and participation of Hiroshima atomic bomb survivor Setsuko Thurlow, a Canadian citizen and advocate for the nuclear ban.

In Costa Rica, campaigners participated in a global ICAN paper crane project, folding and sending a thousand paper cranes to their foreign affairs ministers as the basis for raising awareness and recruiting new members. They organized visits of antinuclear activists from other countries, meetings with parliamentarians and government officials, and worked closely with diplomats at the United Nations. They also helped organize and participate in regional initiatives.

In Fiji, campaigners have historically engaged in pan-Pacific activism against nuclear weapons. "Pacific islanders have had to face the impacts of radioactivity across the region, as we understood early that there are no boundaries to it, in the air or sea," said one activist.[46] Because of this, campaigners in Fiji found that they spend time interpreting the campaign and initiative for Pacific states, providing information on the ideas and intentions of the ban treaty. Campaigners from the region lobbied governments in capitals but also at their missions in New York, which some found to be a good source of people who had expertise on the United Nations, international law, and relevant issues such as human rights and the environment. They also wrote policy papers and briefed campaigners on the impacts of nuclear testing in the Pacific, linking the Pacific experience to the testimonies of others and, in this context, advocating for the ban treaty. They also helped coordinate a Pacific regional statement at the Nayarit humanitarian impacts conference, did media work, and worked locally to rebuild a network of antinuclear civil society organizations.

In Germany, young campaigners who founded an ICAN chapter there hosted an Action Academy for youth in 2014 and annual workshops called Nukipedia ever since. In 2014, they organized the Berlin Sessions on Humanitarian Disarmament, which brought together more than 150 people from seventy organizations working on various disarmament and humanitarian issues to learn about nuclear weapons and the ban agenda. The ICAN Germany crew has also been active in the nuclear weapon divestment campaign, pressing dozens of European Central Banks on their transparency and accountability arrangements. One activist was also involved in advocacy with the European Parliament, working with members of European Parliament to get a resolution in support of the nuclear ban. In 2016, a big effort resulted in the adoption of a resolution that welcomed the initiation of negotiations on the ban treaty and invited European Union member states to participate constructively in the negotiations.

In India, campaigners organized public events and roundtables with politicians about the humanitarian impacts of nuclear weapons and the nuclear ban treaty. They also invited ICAN staff and campaigners from other countries to meet with local activists about the nuclear ban initiative in the lead-up to treaty negotiations.

In Israel, ICAN's partners had to be particularly creative to get the ban on the public or political agenda. The first obstacle to overcome was that many people, including leftists, did not think they were allowed to talk about nuclear weapons. The government's consistent policy to never confirm nor deny its possession of the bomb meant that most activists were anxious about discussing the issue in public. With most concerned about the occupation, they did not want to risk whatever access or standing they had by talking about a comparatively abstract problem. The growing international discourse about the humanitarian impacts of nuclear weapons, however, opened space for campaigners in Israel. They argued that because Israel had nuclear weapons, concerned citizens had an obligation to discuss the humanitarian consequences of their development and use. They used moments of tension with Iran to mount conversations about Israel's own nuclear possession and encouraged the Israeli government, "Don't Bomb, Talk."

This helped the Israeli Disarmament Movement, the main ICAN partner, to hold a weekly demonstration in front of ministry buildings, get into newspapers, and hold lectures on the dangers of nuclear weapons. They even took a case against the prime minister, minister of energy, and nuclear energy commission to the Supreme Court, calling for legislation and independent oversight of the Dimona nuclear reactor. Although the campaigners knew they would lose the case, the win for them was seeing their day in court, putting the government on notice, and making their concerns public. At the same time, Israeli campaigners have been working to get Israel to the table to discuss the proposed weapons of mass destruction free zone in the Middle East. They have promoted this along with the ban treaty, arguing that at least Israel has accepted such a zone in principle.

In Japan, partner organization Peace Boat ran a "Hibakusha Appeal," promoting a signature campaign in support of the ban treaty. They engaged with government officials and politicians, gave lectures at universities and public events, initiated dialogue with Japanese banks on divestment from nuclear weapons, and sought to create and maintain momentum with media by giving interviews and press conferences. Peace Boat also used its "Global Voyage for a Nuclear Free World" to engage policy makers and catalyze public support for the nuclear ban treaty. As part of the project, *hibakusha* delivered public testimony about their experiences of the atomic bombings and met with national, regional, and municipal government officials. Peace Boat also organized educational programs and led interactions with activist groups in most ports the ship visited.

In Kenya, activists with ICAN partner African Council of Religious Leaders—Religions for Peace organized a regional roundtable for youth leaders from Ethiopia, Kenya, Malawi, Nigeria, Tanzania, and Uganda. They also hosted an awareness event on the humanitarian impact of nuclear weapons, launched an interfaith booklet on banning nuclear weapons, and worked to build the capacity of religious, women, and youth leaders on nuclear disarmament through peace education workshops.

In Nigeria, activists with the national WILPF Section hosted a side event at an African Union meeting about the gender dimensions of nuclear weapons and the role of women in pushing for the ban treaty. They also participated in advocacy at international meetings in support of the ban, encouraged the Nigerian government to host a regional roundtable at the UN in New York on nuclear weapons, and contributed to articles and information materials to give an African perspective on the humanitarian impacts of nuclear weapons, including on the environment and food resources.

In the Philippines, campaigners with the Center for Peace Education and Pax Christi student club organized film screenings, poster-making and petition-signing sessions, and prayer circles to raise awareness about nuclear weapons and the call for a nuclear ban. The Center also hosted a public forum on the humanitarian impacts of nuclear weapons and organized workshops on campaigning against nuclear weapons for education and youth conferences. The Center also organized students and faculty to visit parliamentarians and advocate for the treaty, hosted exhibitions, participated in global advocacy at the UN, and wrote articles. Finally, it also hosted one of the ICAN-ILPI regional roundtables for government officials of all Southeast Asian nations.

In the United States, groups affiliated with ICAN across the country were engaged in many diverse activities. WILPF coordinated UN activities in New York for ICAN campaigners around negotiations and provided analysis of nuclear negotiations and discussions. It also organized the Women's March to Ban the Bomb in New York before the final round of negotiations—more than one hundred solidarity marches and actions took place around the world. Hibakusha Stories brought atomic bomb survivors into New York City high schools to raise awareness about the history of the bombings, the impacts of nuclear weapons, and the ban treaty. The Los Alamos Study Group incorporated promotion of the ban treaty in its information and educational materials about the nuclear weapon labs in New Mexico. Physicians for Social Responsibility released a report looking at the global health impacts of a nuclear weapon detonation or nuclear war. Nuns and laypeople with the Catholic Plowshares movement engaged in direct actions at missile silos and other nuclear sites—and once the treaty was adopted, they started taking copies with them to hand deliver to base commanders. Among other things their actions resulted in one of the best newspaper headlines about our campaign: "Anti-Nuke Nuns Return to Crime Scene with a Treaty and a Nobel Prize."[47]

ICAN activists were engaged in diverse types of work in many more countries than this. By the time of treaty negotiations, ICAN had 468 partner organizations in 101 countries. Those numbers are still growing today. Although not all of these groups were active all of the time, they had engaged at some point in a direct action, educational initiative, public demonstration, or advocacy engagement with government officials, parliamentarians, or diplomats. The work of ICAN was diverse, global, and relentless. And it was this work that provided the backdrop for diplomats, activists, and others pushing the humanitarian initiative forward at the intergovernmental level, as will be explored in the next chapter.

6

FROM DETERRENCE TO DISARMAMENT

How the Humanitarian Initiative Disrupted the Nuclear Weapon Orthodoxy

> You love the bomb
> You say its protection
> Feels more like a bulls-eye
> Attracting your enemies
> We don't want no part
> In weapons that mass destruct
> There is no excuse
> Time to disarm your nukes
>
> Let's ban nuclear bombs together
> Cold war just can't last forever
> You said that peace is your friend
> So bring this stand off to an end
> Now we're determined more than ever
> Let's ban nuclear bombs forever
> Don't want your nuclear umbrella
> Don't want your nuclear umbrella

This is the opening verse and chorus of ICAN Australia's rendition of Rihanna's *Umbrella*, written, sung, and performed by antinuclear activists and their long-suffering friends in Melbourne in 2014.[1] This piece of performance art is one of the best in a long list of excellent public stunts ICAN activists orchestrated over the years, in keeping with the original strategy document's emphasis on humor, along with horror and hope. But it is also a highly accurate account of the positions of the nuclear-armed states as well as those under what is known as the "nuclear umbrella"—countries that do not possess nuclear weapons themselves but that include the nuclear weapons of others in their security doctrines. These include countries that are members of the North Atlantic Treaty Organization, as well as Australia, Japan, and South Korea—all of which claim that U.S. nuclear weapons provide them with protection.

The song highlights the cognitive dissonance around nuclear weapons—that government officials from these countries claim they want peace but love the bomb; that they simultaneously seek protection from and through weapons of mass destruction. This dissonance, and the efforts to shift the paradigm around the dominant thinking of nuclear weapons as described earlier, is what enabled the majority of other governments to move forward, inch by inch, toward a ban on nuclear weapons.

This chapter explores the humanitarian initiative's international process from Oslo to Nayarit to Vienna and the UN-based discussions occurring over the same years. Keeping in mind the cross-regional and regional meetings going on over this same period, as described in chapter 4, this chapter also explores how governments began to move from the humanitarian initiative, which focused on changing the normative discourse around nuclear weapons, to the idea of banning nuclear weapons through an international treaty. Although still in the formative stages, the conception of a ban treaty was emerging as a possible pursuit by several governments in 2014 and 2015. Confronted with the nuclear-armed states' refusal to comply with their legal obligations and political commitments to disarm, as well as their continued boycott of international discussions about the humanitarian impact of their weapons of mass destruction, the majority of the world was gearing up for action.

Fair warning: this chapter may be a bit in the weeds of international processes. But it tries to provide an accurate historical record of the key twists and turns of our path to the ban without being too overtly wonky.

RAISING THE HUMANITARIAN LENS

Norway hosted the first conference on the humanitarian impact of nuclear weapons (HINW) in March 2013.[2] Ahead of the conference, WILPF released a collaborative study on the humanitarian impact of nuclear weapons. The collection, authored by experts in various areas, explored impacts of nuclear weapons on health, the environment and agriculture, economies and development, law and order, and more.[3] It sought to provide and support the data-driven approach to outlawing weapons that previously had been successful.

This analysis fed directly into the conference, at which 127 states, several UN agencies, the International Red Cross and Red Crescent movement, and ICAN representatives presented findings on the environmental, developmental, and health consequences of nuclear detonations. Participants concluded that no international response plan could effectively be put in place to respond to the use of nuclear weapons. The Norwegian foreign minister's closing summary highlighted that nuclear weapons have demonstrated devastating immediate and long-term effects and that such effects will not be constrained by national borders.[4]

As the facts and evidence sank in, many states expressed their recognition of a shared responsibility to act to prevent any accidental or intentional use of these weapons of mass suffering. This conference was the first time that governments had come together to seriously address the catastrophic humanitarian impact that the use of nuclear weapons caused. It also marked a significant change in perspective for many nonnuclear-armed states, which recognized that the mainstream discourse on nuclear weapons had been insufficient to address the grave threats they pose to human existence and that the challenge that nuclear weapons posed to human and planetary survival must be addressed through preventive measures.

Austrian Ambassador Alexander Kmentt, who would go on a year and a half later to organize a related conference in his own country, wrote in a journal article, "The facts and findings presented clearly left an impression even on delegates with long experience of working on nuclear weapons." The experience "underscored that it is one thing to talk about nuclear weapons in the context of abstract security policy concepts and quite another to look in concrete terms at the evidence of what would actually happen to people and human society in the event of a nuclear detonation."[5]

The conference differed from standard meetings on nuclear weapons, such as those within the NPT review cycle or the Conference on Disarmament. Discussions remained focused on the weapons themselves and avoided to a large extent the recycled rhetoric that polarizes typical nuclear weapon debates. This was in no small measure because the nuclear-armed states were, for the most part, not in the room.

Only two nuclear weapon-possessing states, India and Pakistan, attended the meeting. The other countries with nuclear weapons— China, France, Israel, North Korea, Russia, United Kingdom, and the United States—refused to attend. The five permanent members of the UN Security Council said that the conference would "divert discussion and focus" away from other forums. The same day as the humanitarian impact conference was held, these five countries were sitting in Geneva at the Conference on Disarmament watching the paint dry.

The boycott backfired. Rather than influencing other countries to stay away, the absence of the nuclear-armed states sent a dismissive signal. In particular, the decision by France, the United Kingdom, and United States to boycott a conference organized by a fellow NATO member "astonished a number of delegates."[6]

Rather than being distracting, the Oslo meeting gave all participants a chance to zero in on the reality of nuclear weapons. The idea that addressing the humanitarian impact of nuclear weapons could prevent work in other forums such as the Conference on Disarmament was particularly disingenuous, considering that at that point, countries had been unable to even agree on an agenda for work for more than fifteen years. In stark contrast to the stalemate there, the humanitarian impact conference in Oslo welcomed contributions from activists. Before the intergovernmental conference convened, ICAN hosted a Civil Society Forum for campaigners and the general public. Some 450 people from seventy countries participated in the forum. ICAN also hosted a campaigners' meeting with those who would be participating in the Oslo conference, in order to prepare advocacy strategies and statements.

The ICAN interventions to the Oslo conference focused on the urgency of developing a new treaty banning nuclear weapons. Several governments participating in the conference called for a ban as well, though interpretations varied as to what exactly that meant.[7] ICAN, in contrast, was very clear. Refusing "to be anaesthetized by all the technical and institutional barriers that impede the total elimination of nuclear arsenals,"[8] ICAN pointed out that the fact that nuclear weapons "have not already been clearly declared illegal—to sit, outdated, alongside the other weapons of mass destruction—is a failure of our collective social responsibility."[9]

ICAN was already starting to agitate for a treaty to prohibit nuclear weapons to be negotiated, even if the nuclear-armed states didn't want to participate. As ICAN staff member Tim Wright wrote coming out of the Oslo conference, the focus on humanitarian impacts "has the potential to lead us to a negotiating process for a ban on nuclear weapons." For both landmines and cluster bombs, "the major producers and users claimed they were essential for their national security. But disarmament campaigners, humanitarian relief agencies and like-minded governments demonstrated that, from a humanitarian standpoint, bans were necessary. In a few short years, treaties were negotiated and brought into force."[10]

Bolstering this confidence that a ban was coming, the Mexican government announced during the Oslo meeting that it would host a second humanitarian impact conference. This decision was welcomed by all states issuing closing statements in Oslo, as well as by activists in the room and around the world. We saw that the follow-up meeting would be a key opportunity for all governments, international organizations, and activists to continue this discussion and to "deal decisively with nuclear weapons," as the representative from the International Federation of Red Cross and Red Crescent Societies said. Wright used the analogy of a train journey to describe what began in Norway in March 2013:

> We have left the platform in Oslo. Before too long, we will arrive in Mexico; and there will be a series of further stops. Along the way, some governments will get off; others will come on board. But the momentum will continue throughout, sustained by the overwhelming will of the world's people to achieve a more peaceful future, free from the threat of radioactive incineration. That momentum will take us to our destination—a ban on nuclear weapons. Reaching that place is an urgent humanitarian necessity.[11]

Although a number of governments and ICAN partner organizations had been talking about outlawing nuclear weapons for a while, it wasn't really until 2013, after the Oslo conference, that some countries started to discuss the idea more publicly. It was clear by this point that the humanitarian approach had helped catalyze a new change in discourse and increasingly creative thinking about how to achieve nuclear disarmament. Researchers and analysts with the United Nations Institute for Disarmament Research (UNIDIR) noted around this time that "for the first time in many years, discussions about the need to eliminate nuclear weapons have taken on a note of urgency, and some states have moved from lamenting their disempowerment and the state of the nuclear weapons control regime to actively considering how they can best strengthen momentum towards elimination based on fresh assessments."[12]

By the NPT Preparatory Committee in April 2013, the momentum of the humanitarian approach was undeniable. Seventy-seven countries endorsed the joint statement on the humanitarian impact of nuclear weapons, up from thirty-five at the UN General Assembly in October 2012. Delivered this time by the delegation of South Africa, the statement reflected that this subject was now firmly on the international agenda.[13]

Never before in NPT history had such a large cross-regional group of states delivered a joint statement on one issue. Seventy-seven countries delivered one simple message: any use of nuclear weapons would cause unacceptable harm, and thus the weapons must never be used again, under any circumstances. The statement dropped the previous reference to outlaw nuclear weapons, as some of the governments joining were not yet convinced that this was a feasible way forward, but nevertheless continued to press upon states the imperative of taking immediate action for nuclear disarmament. The updated statement also welcomed the conference in Oslo and Mexico's announcement that it would host a follow-up meeting.

In response, the nuclear-armed states performed the diplomatic equivalent of pouting and stamping their feet. They spent most of the Preparatory Committee complaining that the so-called step-by-step approach, as laid out in the 2010 NPT action plan, was the only credible path to nuclear disarmament and that the humanitarian perspective would undermine their ability to achieve any progress. This assertion was not grounded in fact. In reality, this position was ridiculous, and most governments very well knew that.

First of all, examining the humanitarian horrors that nuclear weapons posed was meant to provide urgency to the disarmament agenda, not undermine it. Second, the laundry list of items included in an incremental approach has existed since the 1960s, yet its provisions have yet to be fulfilled because of the ongoing nuclear-armed gamesmanship. Third, the nuclear-armed states' activities to implement the action plan had at this point been extremely underwhelming, to say the least. They decided, after much hemming and hawing, that they would report on a new project of a "nuclear definition glossary." In two years' time, they announced this with a smugness that suggested the other conference participants should be delighted at their ambitious agenda. We weren't.

By April 2013, the nine nuclear-armed states were collectively spending about US$100 billion a year on their nuclear arsenals.[14] They were not implementing the steps for nuclear disarmament that they had agreed to in 2010, or 2000, or 1995 at NPT review conferences. They were spending more time whining about other governments examining the horrifically brutal impacts of their treasured weapons than they were spending on doing any of the work they had agreed to do. As the Irish delegation said in 2013, the "persistent underachievement" in nuclear disarmament was not acceptable.[15] The discourse focusing on the humanitarian impact of the use of nuclear weapons had sharpened the opposition to the continued possession of these weapons, especially while it remained apparent that the risk of their use was as high as ever. The Swiss and New Zealand delegations to the 2013 NPT meeting expressed confusion about how nuclear-armed states could accuse those talking about the humanitarian impact of nuclear weapons of undermining the NPT or its action plan. The decision by the nuclear-armed states to not participate in initiatives supported by the overwhelming majority of countries in the world, said the Swiss ambassador, does not help improve transparency or confidence, and does not advance disarmament.[16] "We cannot approach nuclear weapons through a strategy of denial," argued the Norwegians. "As long as the probability of a nuclear weapons detonation exists . . . it must be a humanitarian concern."[17]

THE DIPLOMATIC INCH FORWARD

Some states advanced this line of thinking at a UN open-ended working group in Geneva, which met for fifteen days in May, June, and August 2013. It was, at the end of the day, another talk shop—fairly unremarkable and certainly not reported upon by any press. But as the meeting was boycotted by all but two of the nuclear-armed states (India and Pakistan), it did provide space for other governments and activists to throw around a few new ideas and to ramp up the humanitarian narrative.

The Austrian delegation to this meeting urged nonnuclear-armed states to explore the contributions they could make to nuclear disarmament. Austria included the development of the humanitarian initiative in its list of suggested actions, noting that nonnuclear-armed states "can play a key role in transforming and reframing the discourse into a human security debate which addresses the security concerns and needs of peoples and societies." In this context, Austria encouraged its fellow nuclear-free governments to challenge "the patterns of attaching value and special status to nuclear weapons" by developing a broad political discourse that undermines existing dominant narratives.[18] Thus, the working group in 2013 began to open space for nuclear-free governments, as well as activists, to more formally present some new political and legal options for pursuing nuclear disarmament.

Ireland and Switzerland together called on the working group to consider how nonnuclear-armed states "can advance the process of stigmatizing nuclear weapons" and "which weapons-related activities or principles (use, possession, development, production, transfer, assistance, etc.) would require to be prohibited in order to facilitate nuclear disarmament."[19] They put forward a menu of options for moving forward, which included the option of a nuclear weapon ban treaty. It was the first time a ban treaty was suggested by governments in an official document. Neither country provided details about what they thought such a treaty might entail, but rather encouraged discussion of elements that might be necessary. In this vein, the cross-regional New Agenda Coalition[20] argued that elimination of nuclear weapons requires complete destruction of stockpiles, but also "a comprehensive set of prohibitions banning the development, production, acquisition, possession, stockpiling, retention, testing, use and/or transfer of such weapons under any circumstances and at any time."[21]

Some partners of ICAN supported this discussion at the working group. WILPF submitted a working paper outlining the rationale and possible effects of a treaty banning nuclear weapons, arguing that even without the participation of the nuclear-armed states, a global legal prohibition of nuclear weapons "would stigmatize the weapons, provide an impetus for financial institutions to divest from companies involved in nuclear weapons production, and build pressure for disarmament."[22] This was supported by other presentations to the working group, such as that by the Acronym Institute for Disarmament Diplomacy, which articulated ICAN's perspective on such a treaty "not as the codification of the end-phase of nuclear disarmament but as a transformative and necessary legal step to mandate, enable and accelerate the process of disarmament."[23]

The working group's final report noted that participants agreed that all states have a responsibility to act "in the light of the catastrophic humanitarian consequences of nuclear weapons," and that nonnuclear-armed states have a role in promoting global nuclear disarmament. This is one of the main successes of the working group. It managed to empower nonnuclear weapon states to consider what could be done immediately, even if nuclear-armed states were not engaging constructively.

This sense of empowerment was set to continue. On 26 September 2013, the UN General Assembly hosted a high-level meeting on nuclear disarmament, which provided an opportunity for heads of state and government, foreign ministers, and other high-level officials to outline their policies and priorities for nuclear disarmament. Although some of the statements were pulled out of the recycling bin for reuse, the high-level meeting turned out be yet another significant sign that the discourse around nuclear weapons was changing. Most participants highlighted the humanitarian impact of nuclear weapons, indicating a growing confidence and resolve that this was a credible path toward overcoming the challenges associated with making progress on nuclear disarmament.[24]

The overwhelming majority of countries spoke with alarm about the grave threats that nuclear weapons posed. Several significant group statements on this topic came from the African Group, the Community of Latin American and Caribbean States (CELAC), the Association of Southeast Asian Nations (ASEAN), as well as the cross-regional New Agenda Coalition and Non-Proliferation and Disarmament Initiative. In addition, national statements by states including Algeria, Austria, Belarus, Botswana, Brazil, Chile, Denmark, Egypt, Germany, India, Ireland, Japan, Kazakhstan, Malaysia, Mexico, Montenegro, New Zealand, Nicaragua, Norway, Paraguay, Philippines, Switzerland, Thailand, and Uganda focused on concerns about the humanitarian impact of nuclear weapons.

The Irish foreign minister noted that the reemergence of the humanitarian consequences narrative offers an opportunity to return to the original principles of the NPT, arguing that the humanitarian imperative for nuclear disarmament is "written into the DNA" of the treaty.[25] Indeed, the NPT recognizes the catastrophic consequences of nuclear weapons in its preamble, calling for "every effort to avert the danger" of nuclear war and to "safeguard the security of peoples." The foreign minister also used the opportunity to call out the differences in approach by governments to nuclear weapons and chemical weapons. The General Assembly meeting on disarmament came on the heels of the first horrific use of chemical weapons during the conflict in Syria. A number of governments, condemning this use, drew attention to the inconsistencies in state policies toward chemical and biological weapons on the one hand and nuclear weapons on the other. Both biological and chemical weapons had already been outlawed by international decree. Nuclear weapons, the most destructive of all weapons, remained safely ensconced in arsenals and security doctrines of a few states. The heads of several organizations affiliated with ICAN wrote an op-ed ahead of the high-level meeting, noting, "Weapons that cannot discriminate between military targets and civilians, between armed combatants and infants, are anathema to any sense of human dignity."[26] Yet whereas chemical weapons have been banned, they argued, nuclear weapons have not. This makes nuclear weapons an anomaly among weapons of mass destruction.

Although government reactions to the idea of prohibiting nuclear weapons varied at this point between those who understood it as simply another call for nuclear-armed states to disarm and those who understood it as a potential initiative that would go ahead without the weapons' possessors, an increasing number of countries were calling for a ban. "Our collective efforts to move away from the nuclear abyss have remained too modest in ambition and brought only limited success," warned the president of Austria. "Nuclear weapons should be stigmatized, banned and eliminated before they abolish us."[27] The foreign minister of Nigeria similarly argued, "Efforts to outlaw, eliminate and consign nuclear weapons to the dustbin of history must start now."[28] These comments were amplified by messages from the African Group, the Arab Group, ASEAN, CELAC, the New Agenda Coalition, the Non-Aligned Movement, and more. Many of these groups, as well as individual states including Brazil, Burkina Faso, Costa Rica, Malaysia, Mongolia, Mexico, Nicaragua, and the Philippines, called for a treaty to prohibit nuclear weapons.

In contrast, in a defensively worded joint statement France, the United Kingdom, and United States expressed "regret" that some states and civil society have put so much effort into highlighting the humanitarian consequences of nuclear weapons. "While we are encouraged by the increased energy and enthusiasm around the nuclear disarmament debate, we regret that this energy is being directed toward initiatives such as this High-Level Meeting, the humanitarian consequences campaign, the Open-Ended Working Group, and the push for a Nuclear Weapons Convention."[29] Reusing their arguments from the 2013 NPT Preparatory Committee, they argued that energy should instead be directed to existing processes and making progress on the step-by-step agenda.

But what didn't sell in April definitely wasn't selling in September. By this time, the step-by-step process had become widely synonymous with foot dragging. Despite rhetoric in favor of a nuclear weapon free world, the nuclear-armed states had done little to concretely implement their obligations, and this was clear to everyone else participating in the high-level meeting. It was also clear that any credible path toward a world free of nuclear weapons must begin with a clear agreement within the international community that all nuclear weapons are unacceptable and should not be legal to possess. Countless delegations quoted UN Secretary-General Ban Ki-moon's recent remark that "there are no right hands for the wrong weapons."[30] Consensus was nearly universal that nuclear weapons must no longer exist, for all of our sakes.

TURNING UP THE VOLUME

This is about when the humanitarian initiative, and the rhetoric against it, got seriously fierce. When 125 states collectively raise their voices to say that it is "in the interest of the very survival of humanity that nuclear weapons are never used again," and that the only way to guarantee this "is through their total elimination," it is time for serious action.[31] That's what happened with the joint statement at the UN General Assembly in October 2013. In only a few months, support for the humanitarian discourse went from 80 countries to 125.

Even Japan finally joined the humanitarian statement. Japan had been one of the strongest resisters to the humanitarian discourse shift, and in particular rejected the suggestion that nuclear weapons must never be used again "under any circumstances." If this sounds incredible coming from the only country to have been attacked with nuclear weapons, you're not wrong. The vast majority of the Japanese public support nuclear abolition, but its government has an agreement with the United States that the U.S. military would use nuclear weapons on Japan's behalf if Japan were attacked. The leaders of the humanitarian initiative refused to delete the language from the joint statement saying that nuclear weapons must never be used "under any circumstance," which is what Japan objected to, but Japan finally decided to join anyway. This shift in position was due, at least in part, to a public protest by ICAN and *hibakusha* (the Japanese term for survivors of a nuclear weapon explosion) outside the Japanese mission in Geneva, when the government refused to join the iteration of the joint statement at the 2013 NPT Preparatory Committee earlier in the year.[32]

Most nuclear-free states by this point saw the humanitarian discourse as an effective means to delegitimize, or stigmatize, nuclear weapons. And they weren't letting up. This was exactly why the nuclear-armed states were so upset about the progress being made in developing this narrative. Registering its fury with the humanitarian initiative, the Russian delegation complained that it "turns a difficult issue into public diplomacy" and is out of line with "true needs and priorities."[33] It claimed that because "children in school already understand" how horrific nuclear weapons are, we should "not waste time on such useless topics." Instead, as the nuclear-armed states kept insisting, we should refocus our attention on all of the glorious actions they had already taken to reduce their arsenals to still-world-destroying levels. Any further actions or demands would be naive, proclaimed the Russians. Anyone asking for more is a "radical dreamer" who has "shot off to some other planet or outer space."[34]

Yes, that was really the content of a speech given by a government official in a diplomatic meeting.

The UK delegation, in a much less dramatic fashion, also expressed its alarm with the idea that other governments might want to prohibit the possession of nuclear weapons, arguing that "any attempts to establish a new conference or body to discuss such approaches risk undermining the full implementation of all three pillars of the Non-Proliferation Treaty."[35] But at least 125 countries disagreed with this sentiment, as expressed through the joint humanitarian statement. Such claims by the nuclear-armed were easily refuted. In another joint statement, for example, Austria, Ireland, Liechtenstein, Malta, New Zealand, and San Marino argued that the efforts of the humanitarian initiative are "entirely consistent" with the 2010 NPT action plan. Noting that action 1 of the plan obliges states' parties to pursue policies that are fully compatible with the NPT and with the objective of achieving a world without nuclear weapons, these countries highlighted the relevance and appropriateness of all actions that promote nuclear disarmament. They also emphasized their interest in pursuing "any set of effective measures to achieve the objective of complete nuclear disarmament and the maintenance of a world without nuclear weapons, regardless of how such measures might be elaborated."[36]

"The willingness of the world as a whole to move forward in a constructive manner to eliminate nuclear weapons has never been more evident," explained an archbishop from the Vatican speaking at the General Assembly. "Yet a very small number of States stand in the way, trying to block progress and to find a comprehensive solution to the problem that goes on year after year in paralysis and obfuscation."[37] Nuclear-free countries were mounting an increasingly coordinated resistance to the disingenuous, misleading accusations and assertions of the nuclear-armed states. Although in the years since 2010 most nuclear-armed states and all of their allies had spoken about needing to reduce the role of nuclear weapons in security postures, and about their desire to one day eliminate nuclear weapons, it was clear that all of these governments continued to value nuclear weapons and to act in the interest of their perpetuation, not their elimination. Some of these governments exhibited extreme cognitive dissonance about nuclear weapons. They recognized the catastrophic humanitarian and environmental consequences that nuclear weapons cause when detonated. They worried about proliferation because they knew that more nuclear weapons would make the world even more insecure. Yet, at the same time, they continued to act as if the nuclear weapons that do exist—at least some of them, the ones in the "right hands"—keep them safe.

The incongruity of these positions and policies means that although these governments know that nuclear weapons are dangerous, destructive, and despicable, they want to keep them around because the world is insecure. The tools they see as being the best response to insecurity are those that cause the most insecurity. These governments, by defending the continued existence of nuclear weapons and their inclusion in security doctrines, were saying that they are ready to use nuclear weapons while knowing full well the inevitable results. They refused, and continue to refuse, to draw the ineluctable conclusion that the way to increase security, prevent proliferation, and preclude the unspeakable suffering that the use of nuclear weapons would cause is to prohibit and eliminate these weapons once and for all.

The arguments of the nuclear-armed states also were at odds with the history of disarmament and arms control. The Arms Trade Treaty was adopted at a time when the global arms trade was increasing. The prohibition and elimination of other weapon systems were at this moment taking place in regions of conflict and in countries with financial investments in those systems. Excuses that the "conditions" are not yet "ripe" are unjustifiable and unacceptable and do not conform with success in other areas.

The conditions that the nuclear-armed states want—such as solving all other international and national challenges—will likely never exist. Are we then to assume that nuclear disarmament is never to be achieved? According to the UK delegation in October 2013, we need an environment "in which no state feels the need to possess nuclear weapons."[38] But, as has been shown throughout the atomic age, the overwhelming majority of countries in the world do not feel the "need" to possess nuclear weapons. Those that do feel this "need" are outliers of the robust international norm against the possession of such abhorrent weapons. What is this "need" based on—a need for power, for violent coercion? The rest of the world uses the multilateral system and international law. Why do a few states insist that they "need" anything more than that?

This is the classic cognitive dissonance that Kuhn described in his theory about paradigm shifts, as explored in chapter 3. He argued that even when confronted with "severe and prolonged anomalies," scientists are unlikely to renounce the paradigm or theory that they have held for so long until they have a new theory ready to take its place.[39] Those in government policy making are in much the same position: despite the fact that their theoretical framework of nuclear deterrence or the effects of nuclear weapons can and have been systematically refuted by the majority of other governments, they cling to their beliefs. Thus, the challenge for advocates for nuclear disarmament is a paradigm shift, which is precisely what nuclear-free countries and ICAN activists were attempting with the humanitarian initiative.

Suggestions that the humanitarian initiative or the push to prohibit nuclear weapons are unproductive or unrealistic were meant to distract governments from the reality that the days of nuclear weapons are over. So were the days of the rest of the world putting up with rhetorical commitments to disarmament without any meaningful accompanying actions. The time had come for states to decide if they wanted nuclear weapons to be legal or illegal, for them to exist or not exist. As the ambassador of Kenya warned at the General Assembly meeting, "So long as we continue to practice Orwellian double-speak, we may end up blowing ourselves to extinction." He declared, definitively and without hesitation, "It is time States considered a legal ban on nuclear weapons, even if nuclear armed States refuse to participate."[40]

THE POINT OF NO RETURN

This comment set the stage nicely for the second conference on the humanitarian impact of nuclear weapons, hosted by Mexico in Nayarit in February 2014.[41] Some 146 countries attended the conference. As with Oslo before it, the meeting in Nayarit exposed nuclear weapons as dangerous and destructive. The evidence that UN agencies, academics, former military officials, and civil society organizations presented again reinforced that the continued possession and deployment of nuclear weapons is a reckless and unsanctionable gamble with the future of humanity and the planet.

The Nayarit conference built on the findings from Oslo the year before, and further dug into the long-term consequences of the use of nuclear weapons on human health, the climate, food security, economics, and society. The meeting also explored the risk of the use of nuclear weapons, whether by accident or design. Studies on the vulnerabilities of command-and-control structures and practices provided new context to the discussion on humanitarian consequences. "Many participants appreciated for the first time the extent to which mere luck rather than planning had saved the day on several occasions in the past," explained the Austrian ambassador attending the meeting.[42]

Yet even still, a handful of nuclear-dependent states such as Australia, Canada, Germany, Netherlands, and Turkey spoke with trepidation about any new initiatives to confront the challenges that nuclear weapons posed. Signaling once again their inclination to stand outside the growing norm in favor of taking concrete action even without the nuclear-armed states, they argued that "simply banning" nuclear weapons would not guarantee their elimination and was more likely to "antagonize" the nuclear-armed states than to bring them into a multilateral process.

Yet the path these countries continued to espouse—pressing for implementation of the NPT action plan, continuing to promote the "step-by-step" approach to nuclear disarmament, and insisting on the participation of nuclear-armed states—has failed to achieve the elimination of nuclear weapons. By 2014, incremental steps agreed upon over the previous twenty years had not been implemented, and the actions of some nuclear-armed states had actually resulted in steps backward. Thus, the motivation for the conference and the development of new narratives and approaches.

"It seems clear to us that inevitable and unavoidable policy implications arise from what we now know about the extent of the risks involved," argued the Irish delegation at the Nayarit meeting. Similarly, most governments taking the floor during the conference argued that it is now time to examine ways forward that, as New Zealand's representative said, do not simply rely on implementation of the NPT or a hope of compliance with international humanitarian law.

At least twenty governments participating in Nayarit articulated the way forward to a ban on nuclear weapons. At the end of the conference, the chair of the meeting, Mexican Vice-Minister for Multilateral Affairs Juan Manuel Gómez-Robledo, announced, "Nayarit is a point of no return."[43] In some ways, this comment can be read as a declaration of defiance by the Mexican government. According to one diplomat familiar with the situation, the U.S. government warned Mexico to tread carefully even before making the formal announcement at the Oslo conference that it would host the second conference. The Mexicans knew that they could not afford to be clumsy with this process. U.S. officials were reportedly calling relevant government ministries daily while simultaneously visiting Mexico's diplomatic missions in New York, Geneva, and Vienna. The pressure, however, came not just from the nuclear-armed states, but also apparently from some nuclear allies such as Australia and Japan, which have investments in Mexico.[44]

But first and foremost, the declaration of a "point of no return" was meant for nuclear weapons themselves. In his summary of the meeting, the chair called for the development of new international standards on nuclear weapons, including a legally binding instrument:

> In the past, weapons have been eliminated after they have been outlawed. We believe this is the path to achieve a world without nuclear weapons. In our view, this is consistent with our obligations under international law, including those derived from the NPT as well as from Common Article 1 to the Geneva Conventions. The broad-based and comprehensive discussions on the humanitarian impact of nuclear weapons should lead to the commitment of States and civil society to reach new international standards and norms, through a legally binding instrument. It is the view of the Chair that the Nayarit Conference has shown that time has come to initiate a diplomatic process conducive to this goal.[45]

ICAN celebrated. This was exactly what we had been advocating for the past few years. But the Austrian government started sweating. It had announced at the beginning of the Nayarit meeting that it would host a third conference on the humanitarian impact of nuclear weapons later in the year. This wasn't the conclusion that Austria had anticipated. It had agreed to host a meeting that would, as the Mexicans suggested, "deepen the momentum" and anchor the conference's conclusions and take them forward. By the end of the Nayarit meeting, some governments considered the Mexicans to be "way out in front." "They weren't alone but they were in the minority"—none of the other states that would come to form the core group pushing for the ban treaty were there yet.[46]

The Nayarit conference had already added more of a political and policy dimension than the Oslo conference, in part because about eighty states delivered statements outlining their position on the questions at hand. A lot of these countries expressed disappointment with the lack of progress on nuclear disarmament and suggested ways forward. The continued boycott of most of the nuclear-armed states further aggravated participants, which only gave more impetus to finding creative solutions to break the logjam and push for progress.

ICAN's presence also grew at the Nayarit conference, with a larger number of activists permitted to attend and participate in the meeting, including in official panels and interventions. ICAN was also adamant in its consistent calls for the discussions on the humanitarian impact of nuclear weapons to lead to a diplomatic process to ban these weapons.

This is what those clinging to nuclear weapons wanted to prevent from happening. The nuclear-supportive states "expressed support for the humanitarian focus but were, at the same time, at pains to reconcile this support with their role as 'umbrella' States," explained the Austrian ambassador.[47] Those governments that are protective of the nuclear-armed states emphasized the "security dimensions" of nuclear weapons and the need to proceed with "realistic steps" in an "inclusive manner"—meaning with the NPT nuclear-armed states, on their terms. In this vein, the Australian foreign minister, Julie Bishop, published an op-ed during the Nayarit conference titled "We Must Engage, Not Enrage Nuclear Countries." In it, she argued, "The global community needs to engage those countries that have chosen to acquire nuclear weapons and address the security drivers behind their choices. They are the only ones that can take the necessary action to disarm."[48]

This narrative was at odds with the majority perspective in two ways. First of all, it was not the nonnuclear-armed states that chose to disengage from the nuclear-armed states. It was the other way around. Second, the idea that only the nuclear-armed states could take "necessary action" was counter to the sense of agency that had been growing over the past two years with the focus on the humanitarian impact of nuclear weapons. Bishop's recommended approach was aimed at putting the power back in the hands of those with nuclear weapons. She even used the tired but true patriarchal technique of calling those engaged in the humanitarian initiative emotional: "Some will seek to use this week's conference to push for a ban on nuclear weapons. Their argument 'to ban the bomb' may be emotionally appealing, but the reality is that disarmament cannot be imposed this way."[49]

This provided an excellent example of how those who are worried about losing their grip on power seek to downplay or undermine their perceived opponents' position—and how women can be co-opted into using gendered techniques to do so. It also provided a useful standpoint from which nuclear ban proponents could flip the script. As one diplomat from the global south said in an interview for this book, the humanitarian initiative in fact "takes out the emotions and the politics" from nuclear weapon discussions. "It starts at the technical level, building slowly with evidence and testimony."[50] Other diplomats interviewed pointed out how the humanitarian discourse was about both facts and emotions, in a positive way. "Some of our team members were motivated by the risk factor. Others really felt the 'duty of care' arguments," one explained. "Either way, our response—to support the nuclear ban— was both an emotional and an evidence-based response."[51]

As diplomats came to understand how their perspectives were being undermined by gendered language and assertions, some from Western countries also had similar realizations about the pressures typically experienced by their colleagues from the global south. Those representing non-Western countries have long been subjected to an attitude from their Western counterparts that their interests and positions are subordinate to those with more money, more weapons, and more power in the geopolitical world order. Before the Swedish government changed and adopted a position more sympathetic to banning nuclear weapons, the foreign minister in 2013 charged that countries supporting the humanitarian initiative are "not serious states."[52] This type of attack was perhaps new to some of the European countries involved in the humanitarian initiative, but not so much to those from the global south. As an ambassador from Kenya astutely noted, "The crux of the matter is that there are those who always want to have a dominant position for the purpose of national security to the exclusion of the interests and concerns of others," and in this context, "It seems there are those who wish to continue maintaining their own set of rules outside of international norms."[53]

Australian foreign minister Julie Bishop was not finished. She followed her op-ed about not "enraging" the nuclear-armed states a few weeks later with a speech to the Conference on Disarmament. Acknowledging that the "horrific human impact of nuclear weapons use" has led to "support in some quarters for a near-term nuclear weapons ban treaty," she argued that such a treaty "would not provide a short-cut to some form of security nirvana."[54] This absurd remark was panned by activists, including comedian-activist Wildfire, an initially anonymous online commentator who was later revealed to be a former Australian diplomat.[55] He spent a great deal of time ridiculing governments that maintained pro-nuclear policies and highlighting their hypocrisies in order to point out that they have been standing in the way of disarmament while hiding behind the nuclear-armed states.[56] In addition, the phrase "security nirvana" also made its way into the music video that ICAN Australia produced, as described in the beginning of this chapter.[57]

The point is that no one supporting a nuclear ban had ever suggested that such a treaty would solve the world's problems, let alone bring nirvana. The activists and the governments supporting the idea of such a treaty had only ever suggested that it was an achievable tool that could help facilitate further progress for nuclear disarmament, rather than simply waiting for the nuclear-armed states to change their mind and get on board. Despite the warnings and absurd caricatures that Bishop and her like-minded counterparts from other nuclear-supportive countries lobbed, the majority was moving ahead. The tides had shifted way too far to put the power back in the hands of countries whose interests clearly did not lie with humanity. The nuclear-free nations of the world were standing up and fighting back in new and creative ways. The resistance was building and was now turning from rhetoric to law.

BUILDING MOMENTUM AGAINST
INTENTIONAL INERTIA

This new attitude of resistance shone brightly in the Marshall Islands' Nuclear Zero case at the International Court of Justice (ICJ). In April 2014, the Marshall Islands filed lawsuits against all nine nuclear-armed states for their failure to comply with their obligations under international law to pursue negotiations for the elimination of nuclear weapons. The suits were filed against all nine governments at the ICJ, with an additional complaint against the United States filed in U.S. Federal District Court. Activists with groups such as the Lawyers Committee on Nuclear Policy and Nuclear Age Peace Foundation supported, as did prominent feminist international lawyer Christine Chinkin and other legal scholars.[58]

"International law—and legal obligations—are not hollow and empty words on a page, but instead the most serious form of duty and commitment between nations, and to our collective international purpose," argued Marshall Islands Foreign Minister Tony de Brum in a speech to the NPT Preparatory Committee in April 2014.[59] The government brought the lawsuits on behalf of humanity but in court stood alone against the nine nuclear-armed nations. Given the Marshall Islands' status as a state that has entered a Compact of Free Association with the United States, it was a particular act of bravery to confront the United States and other nuclear-armed countries in this way.

The Marshall Islands has had firsthand experience with the humanitarian impacts of nuclear weapons. The United States used it as a testing ground for its nuclear weapons from 1946 to 1958, detonating sixty-seven nuclear bombs over the islands. Castle Bravo, the largest bomb ever tested by the United States, was about one thousand times larger than the bomb used on Hiroshima. The Marshallese people suffered horrific health effects and environmental contamination because of the testing. Many were forcibly relocated, never to return to their homes. "Several islands of my country were vaporised and others are estimated to remain uninhabitable for thousands of years," said de Brum, who was nine years old when he witnessed the nuclear tests.[60]

Ultimately, the lawsuits didn't go through. The ICJ, by a narrow margin, ruled in October 2016 that there was no evidence that the Marshall Islands' government had a prior dispute with any of the nuclear-armed states that were subject to the court's jurisdiction or had sought negotiations on the matter.[61] Thus the merits of the claims were never tested. In February 2015, the U.S. Federal District Court also dismissed the lawsuit on jurisdictional grounds. The Ninth Circuit Court of Appeals affirmed this decision in July 2017, ruling that Article VI of the NPT is "non self-executing and therefore not judicially enforceable."[62] Nevertheless, the spirit in which the Marshall Islands attempted to hold the nuclear-armed states to account could be read as a clear warning signal of the coming revolt of nuclear-free countries everywhere.

Within this context, the next NPT Preparatory Committee in April–May 2014 was another point of reckoning. Although this UN conference was again not on the public's radar, it was a moment for governments and activists seeking change to make yet another important advance institutionally. Diplomats were supposed to report on their countries' progress implementing the 2010 NPT Action Plan. But with billion-dollar nuclear weapon modernization plans in the works, indications that the nuclear-armed five had only been working on a glossary of terminologies rather than what they actually signed up to do, and the continued failure to hold a conference on establishing a weapon of mass destruction free zone in the Middle East, the review of implementation was not promising.

Some states were starting to whisper that the Action Plan should be seen as a long-term roadmap, rather than something that was supposed be implemented by the 2015 NPT Review Conference the following year. The nuclear-armed were clearly receding from their rhetoric for disarmament in 2010. Just a few weeks before the PrepCom began, the Russian government also structurally diminished its commitment to disarmament, abolishing its Department for Security and Disarmament and replacing it with the Department for Nonproliferation and Arms Control. This change, made on 3 April 2014, was due to the government's perception that "disarmament in the 'classical' sense is in many ways becoming a thing of the past."[63]

The cross-regional New Agenda Coalition introduced a working paper to the meeting that further developed the one submitted by Ireland and Switzerland to the 2013 open-ended working group on nuclear disarmament. Ireland was part of this group, whereas Switzerland was not. But having a broader group of countries advancing concrete ideas was an indication that more governments were getting serious about moving forward. The New Agenda Coalition's paper suggested that, among other things, NPT states' parties establish "a series of legal prohibitions against the development, testing, production, stockpiling, transfer, use and threat of use of nuclear weapons" and "an unequivocal and legally binding obligation to enter into a transparent, irreversible and verifiable process of complete nuclear disarmament."[64] The paper argued, "early consideration should be given to the practical, technical, legal, financial, administrative and other arrangements required for the creation of a treaty body" to oversee such measures.[65] It then set out four iterations of such a body: a nuclear weapons convention to effectively eliminate all nuclear weapons, a nuclear weapons ban treaty to establish the key prohibitions necessary to achieve and maintain a nuclear weapon free world and facilitating nuclear disarmament, a framework arrangement of mutually supporting instruments, and a hybrid arrangement.

Although the 2013 version of this paper had put forward the nuclear weapon ban treaty for the first time in an official document from governments, working paper 18 was the first articulation by state officials about what such a treaty might entail. It suggested that the treaty could be a short, legally binding instrument codifying in simple terms the prohibitions implicitly assumed by nonnuclear-armed states under the NPT. The authors also suggested that the treaty could, but wouldn't have to, prescribe the legal and technical arrangements that would be necessary to eliminate nuclear weapons. Either way, the treaty would need to make provisions for the eventual elaboration of the disarmament obligations and arrangements needed for the accession of nuclear-armed states, such as verification and reporting requirements.

Those who worked on this paper, which had its origins in discussions at some of the retreats with activists and others, felt that they had not "broken cover" by championing a ban treaty, but instead were focused on getting the ban into the room and onto the table. Once it's in the room, the logic went, it can't come out. The paper constituted "about fourteen pages of protection and about four of substance."[66] It was frustrating for ICAN that governments were still treading so carefully within the confines of the NPT review cycle. But for the governments of the New Agenda Coalition and other sympathetic countries, it was all about laying the groundwork at this stage.

It was, indeed, a slow burn to the ban, but the momentum in its favor was undeniable. By the 2014 NPT meeting, many more states were openly calling for a ban treaty. The clearest-sounding cry came from Costa Rica, which demanded that nuclear weapons must be prohibited and subsequently eliminated like the other weapons of mass destruction. Noting that the Oslo and Nayarit conferences had demonstrated the increasing will of states to make substantial progress, Costa Rican representative Maritza Chan said that the NPT states' parties must decide to "commence negotiations to adopt a legally-binding framework for the achievement and maintenance of a world free of nuclear weapons."[67]

During the next UN General Assembly meeting on disarmament matters in October 2014, Costa Rica went even further. Chan announced that her government was ready to join a diplomatic process, as proposed by the chair of the Nayarit conference, to negotiate a treaty prohibiting nuclear weapons, even if the nuclear-armed states are unwilling to participate. She argued that such a treaty would establish a strong legal norm against the use, possession, and deployment of nuclear weapons and represent a significant step toward their complete elimination.[68]

Other countries started signaling their support for this approach. Palau's delegation agreed with the utility of a ban, noting that such a treaty could compel states to reject any role for nuclear weapons in their military doctrines, prevent nuclear sharing, and prohibit investments in nuclear weapons production.[69] "Naturally, the talk of banning nuclear weapons is the next logical step," said Kenya's delegation. "It should not cause anxiety."[70] The Thai delegation likewise expressed a firm conviction that it was time to "initiate negotiations on a legal instrument to comprehensively ban nuclear weapons."[71]

Not only were individual governments calling for a nuclear ban treaty by this point, but also three of the largest regional groups in the world had declared their support for this approach. The African Group,[72] the Caribbean Community,[73] and the Community of Latin American and Caribbean States[74] called for a treaty banning nuclear weapons as an effective measure for nuclear disarmament. At the same time, 155 states signed up to support the latest joint humanitarian impact statement.[75] By this point only a handful of states, generally among the wealthiest in the world, were consistently resisting progress toward nuclear disarmament. Perhaps finally realizing the extent to which they had lost control over the narrative, those opposing the humanitarian initiative started getting organized. Or, at least they tried to.

Australia initiated an "alternative" humanitarian statement. It was presented as not being in competition with the statement with 155 signatories but "as giving voice" to those U.S. allies that "wanted to express themselves on the humanitarian dimension" for which the original humanitarian statement "was too strong."[76] Twenty countries signed onto the alternative statement, which called on states to address the "important security and humanitarian dimensions of nuclear weapons." This statement suggested that working "methodically and with realism" is the way to "attain the necessary confidence and transparency to bring about nuclear disarmament."[77]

By this, the twenty countries were referring to the "step-by-step" or "building blocks" approach. Later on, these countries would refer to it, without irony, as the "progressive approach." Whatever you call it, all it meant was more of the same. The blocks or steps included, among other things, entry into force of the nuclear test ban treaty, negotiation of a fissile materials cutoff treaty, reducing the role of nuclear weapons in security doctrines, increasing transparency of and de-alerting nuclear forces, and arsenal reductions. These steps have been on the UN's agenda since the 1960s. This insistence on continuing along the same path that had led nowhere for decades was a clear attempt to return the power to nuclear-armed states by trying to revert the discourse to one that puts countries with nuclear weapons at the center of the discussion and that privileges their interpretation of the "security dimensions" of nuclear weapons.

What was particularly annoying about this joint statement wasn't just that its supporters tried to position themselves as offering a "reasonable alternative" to the original, majority-supported humanitarian statement. More frustrating, the countries signing on to support the building blocks statement had refused to put most of these blocks in place themselves. Some of them host U.S. nuclear weapons on their soil without acknowledging their presence. Most of these states include nuclear weapons in their security policies via the North Atlantic Treaty

Organization's strategic doctrine or other extended nuclear deterrence relationships.

It wouldn't be the last time this particular group of states would clamor to be seen as sympathetic to those worried about being blown to bits while still wanting to be seen as credible to the nuclear-armed states. In fact, it would become a recurring trend with increasingly hilarious and counterproductive results in the course of the process to ban nuclear weapons. But at that moment in 2014, it was just obnoxious. And highly patriarchal. As discussed in chapter 1, the desire to appear credible for many actors means fitting into the dominant paradigm—the paradigm that insists violence and weapons are the best ways to ensure security and power.

The alternative joint statement also gave some clear insights into the fears of the nuclear-armed and their nuclear-supportive allies. The statement lashed out at the idea of a new international treaty prohibiting nuclear weapons, arguing, "Banning nuclear weapons by itself will not guarantee their elimination without engaging substantively and constructively with those states with nuclear weapons." As Austrian Ambassador Kmentt pointed out in a journal article, "the notion of a 'ban' without 'engaging nuclear weapon States' was never part of the original humanitarian statement." He suggested that this language in the alternative statement "demonstrates the concern of many States under the US nuclear umbrella, as well as the nuclear weapon States, that the humanitarian initiative could develop into a diplomatic process towards a prohibition of nuclear weapons possibly without the participation of nuclear weapon States."[78]

Those countries supporting nuclear weapons were right to be afraid. But the Austrian ambassador was also correct in pointing out that those leading the humanitarian initiative had not mentioned the possibility of banning nuclear weapons without the nuclear-armed states in any of their statements. It hadn't even been what the chair of the Nayarit conference had called for in his summary. At least, it wasn't exactly what he had called for. Of course, it *was* exactly what ICAN had been encouraging for a few years. But in 2014, it was still about building the knowledge about the humanitarian impact of nuclear weapons and getting those ducks in a row to finally do something about it.

SOWING THE HUMANITARIAN SEEDS

Soon after the General Assembly meeting was over, most of the world headed to Austria for the third conference on the humanitarian impact of nuclear weapons.[79] Just ahead of the meeting, the International Physicians for the Prevention of Nuclear War (IPPNW) released a new study on the global impact of a limited nuclear war.[80] This report built on recent research into the effects of the use of nuclear weapons on the climate. It demonstrated that previous studies had significantly underestimated global declines in food production and the number of people at risk of mass starvation. Ambassador Kmentt, who led in the organization of the Vienna conference, said this study "underpinned the generic concerns about the humanitarian consequences of nuclear weapons in diplomatic documents and statements with up-to-date scientific research about these consequences."[81]

Also, right before the conference, Canadian folk band The Burning Hell released a song called *We Don't Do That Anymore*. I had asked lead singer Mathias Kom, a former history teacher, if he would write a song for ICAN. A year later, without any input from the campaign, he delivered a country song highlighting some of the most horrific practices in human history that have long been outlawed. The song points out, "We don't do that anymore / But we're apparently still basically okay with the threat of nuclear war / It's a little odd considering all the other crazy stuff that we used to do before / It's high time we didn't do this anymore," and advocating, "I know it's upsetting / But let's not be forgetting Armageddon / Yet I'm still a hopeful man / And I'm a big fan of the plan to ban nuclear weapons."[82] Personally, I think that both the IPPNW study (horror) and The Burning Hell's musical gift to the campaign (humor and hope) were instrumental in the success of what came next.

ICAN once again hosted a Civil Society Forum before the main conference, drawing hundreds of people and preparing activists for the advocacy ahead. Some 158 states participated in the Vienna conference—more than at the previous two humanitarian impact conferences. The outcomes delivered at this meeting would turn out to be a major turning point in the process to ban nuclear weapons. But at the time, it was considerably challenging for some of the Austrian officials involved.

According to diplomats familiar with the situation, Austria's difficulties started after the chair of the Nayarit conference presented his summary report. With Austria already in line to host the next conference, the nuclear-armed states had a clear target. Most of the pressure reportedly came from the Europeans, in particular France. But other countries within the European Union (EU) were extremely unpleasant, toward both Austria and Ireland, the other EU country clearly interested in pursuing a new path forward. Although neither country had publicly called for a treaty banning nuclear weapons, both were emerging leaders in the intellectual development of the project. Ireland held the pen on drafting working paper 18 at the NPT that year, and Austria's president in 2013 had already called on states to "stigmatize, ban, and eliminate" nuclear weapons.

Beginning in 2013, EU meetings were tough, reported some of the diplomats involved from various countries. In his public article after the conference, Ambassador Kmentt said that nuclear-supportive states "undertook frequent diplomatic démarches to Vienna to seek clarity on what exactly the Vienna Conference was going to be and whether a diplomatic/political outcome was the goal for the conference, underlining that they would not support such an approach." He noted that these states "asked for reassurance that 'their views' would be adequately reflected in any outcome or summary document."[83]

But despite these "concerns" and occasional lash outs in meetings, the Vienna conference was the first humanitarian impact conference to be attended by any of the five NPT nuclear-armed states. The United Kingdom and United States decided to attend, whereas the others continued to keep their distance. This was due in no small part to the painstaking outreach by Austrian officials, who sought to assure the nuclear-armed states that they would deliver a "fair" outcome from the meeting. After the Mexican government's strong statement about the "point of no return" earlier in the year, Austria felt it had to convince the nuclear-armed states that the conference would strictly focus on the humanitarian impact of nuclear weapons and not advance any political agenda. The Austrian government gave assurances that the conference "was not intended to initiate a diplomatic process and that the chair would attempt to reflect all views appropriately."[84]

Even with those assurances, the participation of the UK and U.S. governments was an indication of the changing power dynamics. Their decision to show up and engage, even in a defensive way, illustrated how much the power had shifted to the nuclear-free court. Ambassador Kmentt believed this signaled that solidarity among the five NPT nuclear-armed states had weakened since Nayarit and that the deterioration of relations between Russia and the United States helped the U.S. government to somewhat soften its rhetoric against the humanitarian initiative.[85]

This, in turn, meant that it was slightly more acceptable for U.S. think tanks and NGOs to encourage their government to attend. Previously, the mainstream U.S. groups had ignored the humanitarian impact initiative, because the "inside the beltway" thinking completely discounted anything led by any country other than the United States, especially countries of the "global south" or even Western countries they considered to be unimportant. Now that the United States was expressing some willingness to engage, some of the beltway groups were eager to participate, too.[86] This is in keeping with the dynamics explored in chapter 2, in terms of long-held divisions between more grassroots or activist groups and better funded, more institutionalized organizations that prioritized their "access to influence" over pushing for what might be considered "radical" change. Although their newfound engagement in the humanitarian initiative was welcomed by many, unfortunately it also meant that, in some cases, the panels at the Vienna conference took a decidedly more conservative tone than in Nayarit or Oslo. The panel on nuclear weapon risks, in particular, focused primarily on keeping U.S. nuclear weapons "safe and secure," for example, rather than on drawing conclusions about the urgent need for their elimination.

However, in addition to panels examining the effects of nuclear weapon explosions and testing, the risks for deliberate or accidental use, and the challenges of responding to a nuclear detonation, participants also engaged in a discussion about moral and ethical considerations. In his presentation during the final panel of the conference, philosopher Nobuo Hayashi noted what many states and ICAN had highlighted before: that the law does not address the legality of nuclear weapons in the way it does biological and chemical weapons. "It is as though we can strangulate this beast from all directions," remarked Hayashi, "but not quite strike directly at its heart."[87]

Some states, such as Ireland, have repeatedly questioned this distinction among the weapons of mass destruction (WMD). Why should nuclear weapons be viewed as somehow more "necessary," "legitimate," or "justifiable" than other WMD, asked the Irish delegation at the Vienna conference. "Is that because of a belief in their value as a deterrent? Then why has this deterrent failed to prevent conflicts breaking out in various regions in which the parties directly or indirectly involved have nuclear weapons in their arsenals?"[88]

The assault on nuclear deterrence that had begun years before continued in force at the Vienna conference, with most states reiterating long-held views that nuclear weapons bring insecurity and instability, not safety and protection. Only a handful of states argued that nuclear weapons provide some "security benefit" that must be taken into account when considering legal or policy options. Yet, as several delegations pointed out, despite the consistent and overwhelming objections to the concept and practice of nuclear deterrence, human society has still failed to establish law prohibiting and setting out a framework for the elimination of nuclear weapons the same way it has for biological and chemical weapons.

It is not because nuclear weapons have some sort of inherent, magical value that other WMD do not have. It has much more do with the way nuclear weapons are positioned within the political-military-academic-industrial nexus than anything else, as described in chapter 1. Any "magic" these weapons are perceived to possess has been falsely granted to them by those who benefit from them materially or politically. But like all magic, the illusion can be unmasked and its power taken away.

Essential to this process is learning from survivors who have direct lived experience of nuclear weapons. As highlighted in chapter 5, survivor testimony can provide meaningful connections for people to truly understand the gravity of the nuclear weapon issue. To this end, the Vienna conference featured survivors of nuclear weapons use and testing, which, as the chair's summary said, "exemplified the unspeakable suffering caused to ordinary citizens by nuclear weapons."[89] One diplomat described it as a "defining moment" to see history, personal testimony, and scientific studies come together at the Vienna conference. "It seemed inescapable that the international community was going to have to do so something a bit bolder" coming out of this conference, she remarked.[90] At the conference, Lithuania's delegation remarked that the testimony of survivors was a powerful "moral deterrent" against any use of nuclear weapons.[91] The voices of survivors from Australia, Japan, Kazakhstan, the Marshall Islands, and the United States at the Vienna conference indeed could not be denied. Even the U.S. delegation, after a rather callous delay, thanked those who brought personal testimonies to the conference.

But the question remained: *will* these voices deter, as Lithuania suggested? Will they deter the use of nuclear weapons? Can they deter the threat of use? Possession? Speaking at the ICAN Civil Society Forum the weekend before the Vienna conference, investigative journalist Eric Schlosser described nuclear deterrence as a "psychological threat to annihilate the population of another country." If we cannot conceive of accepting the use of nuclear weapons and the suffering it will bring, how can we accept the ongoing practice of nuclear deterrence? How can we accept that the use of these weapons is written into "security" doctrines of states? That they are deployed, on alert, ready to use? That they still exist, in any hands? These were the underlying questions of the humanitarian initiative, and governments and NGOs were agitating for an answer.

"Indiscriminate weapons get banned," declared ICAN in its statement to the Vienna conference. "We have done it before with other weapon systems, including biological and chemical weapons."[92] Categorically prohibiting nuclear weapons—for everyone, under all circumstances—is the logical outcome of the examination of the risks and consequences of the use of nuclear weapons, argued ICAN. It is the logical progression of the law regulating nuclear weapons, including the NPT and the Comprehensive Test Ban Treaty, as well as other WMD, including the Chemical Weapons Convention and Biological and Toxin Weapons Convention. It is the logical conclusion of a moral assessment of the human and environmental suffering that would be caused by any use of nuclear weapons. It is a meaningful, feasible, achievable option that can be negotiated now and that would have wide-ranging normative and practical impacts.

ICAN was not alone in calling for the ban treaty at the Vienna conference. Twenty-nine states called for negotiations of a legally binding instrument to prohibit or ban nuclear weapons, including Chad, Colombia, Comoros, Congo, Costa Rica, Cuba, Egypt, El Salvador, Guinea-Bissau, Jamaica, Kenya, Libya, Malawi, Malaysia, Mali, Mexico, Mongolia, Nicaragua, Qatar, Saint Vincent and the Grenadines, Samoa, Senegal, Timor-Leste, Togo, Uganda, Uruguay, Yemen, Zambia, and Zimbabwe. Thailand thought states might draw experiences from the Mine Ban Treaty in developing a new instrument. Brazil, Burundi, Ireland, New Zealand, Niger, South Africa, and Thailand also noted the need for new legal instruments on nuclear weapons, though did not specify their preferred option for moving forward. Austria, Bangladesh, Philippines, Switzerland, and the International Committee of the Red Cross (ICRC) noted that there is a legal deficit when it comes to nuclear weapons and highlighted the need for prohibition.[93]

The chair's summary of the conference reflected these views, noting that many delegations "expressed support for the negotiation of a new legal instrument prohibiting nuclear weapons constituting an effective measure towards nuclear disarmament as required also by the NPT." The summary also noted that the responsibility of such negotiation rests with all states' parties of the NPT and that the inability to make progress on some measures is not an excuse to not pursue other options.

Beyond impacts and risks, the Vienna conference also went on to explore the corresponding normative and legal framework governing these weapons. The "inescapable conclusions" that the Austrian government noted at the end of the conference included the conviction that nuclear weapons raise profound moral and ethical questions that go beyond debates about their legality and that efforts are needed now to stigmatize, prohibit, and eliminate these weapons of terror.

Some key new findings in the chair's summary drawn from the substantive sessions included the recognition that nuclear testing has left a legacy of serious health and environmental consequences; the risk of a nuclear weapon explosion either by accident or intention is unacceptable and increasing over time; nuclear deterrence entails preparing for nuclear war, and limiting the role of nuclear weapons to that function does not remove the possibility of their use or address risk of accidental use; and international environmental law and international health regulations can pertain to nuclear weapons.

But what really made the conference was the introduction of the "Austrian Pledge" to "identify and pursue effective measures to fill the legal gap for the prohibition and elimination of nuclear weapons."[94] Prepared separately from the chair's summary, but still in a solely national capacity, the Austrian government's pledge to pursue the prohibition and elimination of nuclear weapons was to become a profound moment in the history of the ban process. But when it was first introduced, it was done so cautiously.

By presenting the pledge as Austrian, rather than as something coming from the conference as a whole or from a particular group of states, the Austrians hoped to assuage some of the inevitable anger about what would be seen by the United Kingdom, United States, and other nuclear-supportive governments as a political move. The chair's summary, they argued, reflected both the majority and minority positions and did not posit a political way forward for the humanitarian initiative. But the pledge went beyond the summary, indicating the Austrian government's perspective on what it saw as "the *inescapable conclusions* that needed to be drawn from the humanitarian evidence."[95]

This was not well received by the nuclear-armed or nuclear-supportive states that had participated in the Vienna conference. Reportedly, some of these governments accused Austria of "betrayal" and expressed outrage at the "unacceptable line" put forward at the conference.

For a while after the pledge was introduced, it was not clear what was to become of it. The Austrians had tried to shelter themselves by introducing it as a national instrument. In advance, ICAN leaders had urged Austrian officials to offer something that others could sign onto or that would more firmly put in motion a diplomatic process to ban nuclear weapons. The national pledge could be seen more or less as a compromise between a desire to meet the the ambition of the activists and the fear of nuclear-armed pressure.

Once the pledge was introduced, ICAN cooperated with the Austrian government to encourage other countries to endorse it. This took some time, but by the time the 2015 NPT Review Conference commenced, more than seventy countries had formally associated themselves with the Austrian Pledge. By the end of the Review Conference, 107 had joined. Twenty more joined after the conference. The Austrians retitled the document the Humanitarian Pledge during the Review Conference to reflect its international nature. As one person interviewed for this book said, the pledge was a transition, "helping the humanitarian initiative become an impetus for action."[96]

Developments such as this don't just happen. The Austrians drafted the Humanitarian Pledge after years of strategy discussions with activists and other diplomats. Although some activists initially were disappointed that the document was issued only in a national capacity, ICAN campaigners worked hard to make sure it would be internationally meaningful. The global endorsements that followed were the product of a collective effort between ICAN and the Austrian government. One ICAN campaigner in particular spent countless hours on the phone to countries asking them to contact the Austrians to endorse the pledge. His efforts even facilitated the establishment of diplomatic relations between Austria and Niue, which previously had had no formal contact with each other.

Overall, ICAN activists were hopeful that the pledge would be a platform from which we could launch a diplomatic process to ban nuclear weapons. Although the pledge itself didn't explicitly call for a ban, it was clearly grounded in that approach, built up over the previous few years of discourse shift in the international diplomatic scene. But we were still some ways from getting from a pledge to act, on the one hand, to real action on the other. Although ICAN's demand for a prohibition of nuclear weapons, even without the nuclear-armed states, was as clear and strong as ever, it wasn't clear that the majority of governments were ready yet to make the necessary moves to negotiate a treaty like that. It also wasn't clear, at this point, where such a treaty could or would be negotiated.

Throughout the history of the United Nations there has been significant diversity of negotiating practice in multilateral disarmament and arms control agreements. Some treaties have been developed in consensus-based forums; others have not. Some have been negotiated within standing UN bodies; others have been developed and adopted outside of these forums. Nuclear-armed states and some others claim that the only acceptable place to negotiate disarmament treaties is in the

Conference on Disarmament (CD), but that is simply a false assertion meant to curtail progress.

The Comprehensive Nuclear-Test-Ban Treaty was negotiated within the CD, but when participants were not able to adopt the final text by consensus—as is required by the CD's rules of procedure—they took the treaty to the UN General Assembly to adopt it by a vote. The Chemical Weapons Convention was negotiated in the CD, whereas the Arms Trade Treaty was negotiated in a conference established by the UN General Assembly. Governments negotiated the treaties prohibiting anti-personnel landmines and cluster bombs through conferences established outside the UN structure after the Convention on Conventional Weapons (CCW), the established treaty body typically used to negotiate "conventional weapon" agreements, proved incapable of appropriately addressing these weapons because of its strict demand of consensus as unanimity.

When it came to banning cluster munitions in a process outside the United Nations, explains a historian of the process who was involved in the negotiations, many governments accepted this as necessity. "They had become convinced that the standing CCW machinery was incapable of delivering a meaningful response," and they recognized "that this did not reduce their moral or political culpability for failing to tackle the hazards cluster munitions pose to civilians."[97]

Among those supportive of negotiating a nuclear ban treaty, there was at this time a lot of discussion about how and where negotiations should take place. Some thought negotiations on a nuclear weapon issue would have to either include all countries in the world, including all of the nuclear-armed states, or at least be conducted in forums in which they participated. This overlooked the fact that numerous nuclear non-proliferation and nuclear security agreements had already been negotiated outside of such forums. The Global Initiative to Combat Nuclear Terrorism, the G8 Global Partnership Against the Spread of Weapons and Materials of Mass Destruction, the Proliferation Security Initiative, and the Nuclear Security Summits represent ad hoc processes established by like-minded states trying to address specific concerns related to nuclear weapons. Such initiatives were not branded as undermining existing forums for work on nuclear weapons.[98]

In ICAN, we consistently said that regardless of forum, negotiations of a nuclear ban treaty must be "open to all, blockable by none."

That is, the process should be open to all states and inclusive of activist groups and international organizations, and that the pursuit of consensus must not lead to the acceptance of a lowest common denominator agreement, or no treaty at all. We also argued that initiatives launched by like-minded groups of states should not be seen as lacking legitimacy. In international negotiations it has been natural for like-minded states—often supported by civil society and international organizations—to take the lead.[99] For example, the development of the Framework Convention on Climate Change, the International Criminal Court, and the Framework Convention on Tobacco Control were proposed and negotiated by groups of states in cooperation with civil society and others.[100]

Before the Vienna conference, the South African government had indicated that it might be interested in hosting a fourth humanitarian impact conference. But it was also clear, by the end of the Vienna meeting, that any follow-on meeting would have to advance the political groundwork laid by the Austrian, then Humanitarian, Pledge. South Africa's reluctance, however, did not stem just from hesitancy around this. Part of the challenge was reportedly the desire of some within the South African government to wait and see what happened at the 2015 NPT Review Conference.

"UPRISING" AT THE UN

And indeed, we had to wade back into the breach once more. The eagerly awaited 2015 NPT Review Conference. The moment of final reckoning for the 2010 Action Plan.

For more than a year, it had been increasingly clear that the outlook was not good. The five nuclear-armed states' parties had not been implementing the agreements from five years prior; their spending on nuclear arsenals and related infrastructure was on the rise, as were tensions among them; and they were already suggesting that the 2010 Action Plan was a long-term objective rather than an intermediate agreement meant to be fulfilled by the next Review Conference. Unsurprisingly, then, the five countries arrived at the Conference with a glossary of nuclear terms—and nothing else.

The nonnuclear-armed countries were unimpressed.[101] The glossary of nuclear terms was a joke. In a context when the nuclear-armed were serious about disarmament, it may have been accepted as a credible step toward beginning an effort of elimination. But when the only thing they could come up with after five years was agreement on what a nuclear weapon is, it was really just salt in the wounds caused by decades of stalling and backtracking. The nuclear-armed supportive governments were disappointed with this lack of progress, though they were careful in their criticisms. After expressions of frustration, the diplomats got down to work trying to update and renew the Action Plan for another five years. But it was rough going. The nuclear-armed states did not want to accept any new obligations and, in fact, tried to walk back considerably from commitments they made in 2010. The majority of countries, which over the past five years had revived a humanitarian discourse about nuclear weapons along with several proposals for creating new international law, were unwilling to accept any outcome that ignored all of this progress. It seemed at times that no agreement could be reached, but after late-night consultations that the president of the conference hosted, a compromise was reached.

This process in itself was problematic. It meant that the final outcome text was developed in a room outside the United Nations among a handful of states, with the nuclear-armed bullies reportedly deploying some heavy-handed pressure tactics to intimidate the pro-disarmament delegations in the room and back in their capitals. Activists were not able to attend the meeting, so it's hard to gauge how much the final text reflects discussions in that room. But it did demonstrate quite clearly, once again, that the NPT is a treaty of the nuclear-armed states.

The language on disarmament was weak. In keeping with the power politics described in earlier chapters, it arguably sold out potential progress on nuclear disarmament and instead served those who seek to preserve and embolden the nuclear-armed states' position. The critique of the state of play on nuclear disarmament expressed in the text was weak. It made no reference to the slow pace of nuclear disarmament. It suggested that only nonnuclear-armed states and activists had learned anything about the humanitarian impact of nuclear weapons over the previous three years and argued that it is only the perception of some states that there could be no adequate response to a nuclear weapon detonation.

The text regressed from even the most minimalist understandings and commitments made in 2010. It removed the reaffirmation that states must at all times comply with applicable international law, including international humanitarian law. It no longer called for a review of military doctrines in order to reduce or eliminate the role and significance of nuclear weapons. The reporting provisions provided an escape clause through the not-so-ambiguous reference to "without prejudice to national security"—which translates to: "You don't have to report on anything, really. We understand."

Some activists, including me, urged nonnuclear-armed states not to accept it. "Refusing to accept this text would not be an act of obstruction," I argued at the time. "It would be an act of courageous leadership by governments that believe that nuclear weapons are unjust, indefensible, horrific, catastrophic, unacceptable weapons of terror. It would signal to those militarily powerful, often violent countries that want to impose their vision of the world on the rest of us, that enough is enough."[102]

At the end of the day, the nonnuclear-armed governments decided to go along to get along. Rather than reject the outcome, they wanted to honor multilateralism and stay in relationship with the other countries participating in the process. This is arguably a feminist approach to getting things done: putting the process above individual (or, in this case, even majority) interest in order to not rip apart the fabric of previous agreements.

Despite this decision, the drama was not over. Those with nuclear weapons decidedly chose *not* to stay in the relationship, and in fact, to undermine it as fatally as possible. Late in the afternoon on the final day of the Review Conference, the United States, United Kingdom, and Canada[103] blocked the adoption of the outcome document—because Israel didn't like it. The Israeli government reportedly asked its allies to block the outcome because of references to a process to establish a zone free of weapons of mass destruction in the Middle East. This was an issue that had caused havoc on the nuclear agenda for decades and cannot be adequately explained here. But the important thing to understand in this context is that Israel *is not even a party to the NPT.*

This, as the South African ambassador said in the wake of this upset, "leaves us in a perverse situation, in which a state that is outside of the Treaty has expectations of us and expects us to play by rules it will not play by and be subjected to scrutiny it will not subject itself to."[104] This describes not simply Israel's influence over the Review Conference outcome, but also the NPT nuclear-armed states' attitude toward the rest of the treaty's membership. The engagement by the nuclear-armed delegations over the course of the Review Conference was at times hostile, at times ridiculing toward nonnuclear-armed states that were calling for concrete measures to ensure implementation of disarmament obligations and commitments.

This is the short version of a month-long conference. A month of statements. A month of finger-pointing and sometimes name-calling. A month of too much caffeine and too little sunshine. But it was also a month where 159 states—80 percent of the NPT's membership—joined the joint humanitarian statement reiterating that nuclear weapons must never be used again, under any circumstances.[105] A month where many more states joined Austria's pledge to "fill the legal gap for the elimination and prohibition of nuclear weapons." As Palau said in its closing remarks, the Humanitarian Pledge "provides a strong foundation from which to launch negotiations on a treaty banning nuclear weapons."[106] Thus May 2015 was a month of failure only in terms of the nuclear-armed states—and their nuclear-supportive allies—to follow through on their commitments made five years earlier and to advance global security and community. It was an extremely successful month in terms of building irrefutable and irreversible momentum to ban nuclear weapons. It was a month of what the *Washington Post* called an "uprising" of activists and governments "seeking to reframe the disarmament debate as an urgent matter of safety, morality, and humanitarian law."[107]

This was the first time that mainstream media reported what ICAN and many diplomats had been witnessing for some time. Speaking together in a joint statement on the final day of the conference, forty-nine countries noted a clear shift in the parameters, focus, tone, and balance of discussion on nuclear weapons. "Non-nuclear weapon states are today more empowered to demand their security concerns be taken in consideration on an equal basis," they noted. Yet they also recognized the continuing dominance of the nuclear-armed states and critiqued,

"The exchanges of views that we have witnessed during this review cycle demonstrate that there is a wide divide that presents itself in many fundamental aspects of what nuclear disarmament should mean. There is a reality gap, a credibility gap, a confidence gap and a moral gap."[108]

Rather than "compelling urgent action for disarmament" as the investigation of the humanitarian impact of nuclear weapons sought to do, the NPT had once again been misused as a shield against transparency and concerted action to fulfill the treaty's objectives. It is this that South Africa's Ambassador Mxakato-Diseko referred to when she said, "There is a sense that the NPT has degenerated into minority rule, similar to what we had in South Africa under apartheid," in which "the will of the few will prevail, regardless of whether it makes moral sense."[109]

By the end of the 2015 Review Conference, it was clear to the majority of countries in the world that they needed to find what Ambassador Diseko called "moral courage" in order to begin a process to prohibit nuclear weapons. Ironically, the adoption of a weak outcome document might have set back this realization by years. The nuclear-armed states' decision to crash the NPT conference opened an opportunity for action—and now it was time for courage. "Despite what has happened at this Review Conference, there is no force that can stop the steady march of those who believe in human security, democracy and international law," said Costa Rica's representative Maritza Chan in her closing remarks in 2015. "History honors only the brave, those who have the courage to think differently and dream of a better future for all."[110] This courage came to define the actions of the states pushing the ban forward, as will be discussed in the next chapter.

7

COURAGE, MY LOVE

How Nuclear-Free States Fought for the Ban

In *The Myth of Sisyphus*, philosopher Albert Camus posits that while although is absurd and a constant struggle, it is still worth living. Not only that, but that human beings have an obligation to choose to live despite the absurdity and the struggle. That, in fact, recognizing this absurdity and finding meaning in the struggle is the source of life. Living is about revolting against absurdity in a way that "challenges the world anew every second," he argued. "That revolt is the certainty of a crushing fate, without the resignation that ought to accompany it. . . . That revolt gives life its value."[1] He asks us to imagine Sisyphus, forever pushing that rock up the hill, happy.

Although Camus was writing here against suicide, the philosophical position is applicable to political struggle, as he explored later.[2] In our context, the obstacles to peace and disarmament seemingly are stacked against us. The global system of political economy and power undeniably is built in favor of those with military might and financial privilege. Yet those of us who seek to prioritize people over profit and pursue security through means other than the threat and use of violence, have an obligation, collectively and individually, to try to change this system. To make every effort to create obstacles and alternatives to this system—in our case, to the development and retention of weapons of mass destruction and radioactive genocide. This requires the "moral courage" that South Africa's Ambassador Mxakato-Diseko referred to in 2015, as noted in the previous chapter. It was finding this courage, locating it in the uphill, Sisyphean struggle against nuclear weapons and the nuclear deterrence orthodoxy, that led us to ban the bomb.

This chapter explains how the countries championing the ban treaty pushed the agenda forward through a series of UN meetings while facing increasing pressure from the nuclear-armed states and their nuclear-supportive allies. It demonstrates how the sexist and racist bullying deployed by those trying to prevent the prohibition treaty from becoming a reality actually served to propel many governments further toward negotiations. Hubris backfired. The work of building community and trust undertaken over several years provided enough solidarity and support to diplomats and other government officials so that they could ultimately withstand the pressure they faced. And by the end of 2016, we had agreement to negotiate new international law on nuclear weapons.

BRINGING THE BAN INTO THE UN

The behavior of the nuclear-armed states at the 2015 Review Conference of the Non-Proliferation Treaty (NPT) was the last straw for many governments. As described in the previous chapter, the nuclear-armed states came with their glossary of terms about nuclear weapons; refused to adopt new commitments for disarmament or to justify their lack of implementation of the commitments they had made five, ten, fifteen years ago; accused the humanitarian initiative of undermining the NPT; and, in the end, crashed the conference because a non-state party with nuclear weapons, Israel, asked them to.

"The Review Conference helped a LOT in shifting from the humanitarian impacts to the ban," said one diplomat from a nonnuclear-armed state.[3] The failure of the conference to adopt an outcome document, and the lack of transparency or cooperation from the nuclear-armed states, was a good summary to send back to the capital that made it clear another path was needed. It was this experience that really convinced many people in many countries about the ban. "The Review Conference's failure was the nail in the coffin. That's when we joined the Humanitarian Pledge."[4] For others, the writing was on the wall well before the 2015 Review Conference. "Our team was absolutely sure we wouldn't get successful implementation of the 2010 NPT action plan," a government official from a nuclear-free state recalled. "We didn't want to be seen as walking away from the action plan, but our worries about that decreased as it became clear that the nuclear-armed states weren't doing anything on their end."[5]

Those who were involved in some of the late-night discussions that the chair of the Review Conference hosted, described in the previous chapter, also cited those closed-door meetings as solidifying support for the ban. This is when "I became totally disillusioned with the NPT," said one participant.[6] Coming out of the humanitarian impact conferences, he wasn't really sure about what the next best step was for the process. Then he realized that the best chance for those wanting progress was to "call the bluff of the nuclear-armed states—to hold firm on the humanitarian initiative discourse and on the demands for disarmament." When the conference crashed over the Middle East issue, he said he was relieved that he and other humanitarian disarmament proponents had stayed strong.

Not only did the nuclear-armed states not deliver on their commitments, but they acted with extreme arrogance once they got to the meeting. The "belligerence at the Review Conference from the [nuclear-armed states] pissed folks off. There were always a few of us who were activist diplomats sold on the concept [of the ban], but we had to be careful. But the absolute refusal by the other side to engage built up support [for the ban]."[7]

Brazil is a good example of a government that was previously skeptical about banning nuclear weapons but came around to it after the 2015 NPT Review Conference. Back in 2012, the Brazilians had indicated some early support for a prohibition approach. Speaking to the NPT meeting that year, the Brazilian delegation argued, "The international community has already been wise enough to ban the other two categories of weapons of mass destruction: biological and chemical. Yet is has been lackadaisical at best about the deadliest [weapon] of all." The ambassador asked, "Has there ever been a more propitious time to put an end to the presently groundless addiction to nuclear weapons?"[8]

Yet once ICAN and some governments started seriously talking about prohibiting nuclear weapons, the Brazilians seemed less keen on this as the solution. They preferred an approach that would ensure the nuclear-armed states' participation, despite all the evidence that such an approach was, under present circumstances, impossible. Brazil participated in regional roundtables on the ban treaty and in all of the humanitarian impact conferences, but they kept a healthy distance from the idea of negotiating a ban without the nuclear-armed states. But after the 2015

Review Conference, this stance seemed to change. Their statements to the General Assembly in October that year indicated more interest in conducting business through that democratic forum rather than the consensus-based Conference on Disarmament.[9] Then in 2016, Brazil tabled a working paper with nine other countries calling for negotiations of a ban treaty.[10] (More on that later.) Although the government still had some skepticism, it seemed that the paradigm shift had taken hold for most Brazilian officials.

A few months after the debacle at the 2015 NPT Review Conference, governments convened once again for the UN General Assembly's committee on disarmament. It was here that the real momentum for the ban treaty began—even though at the time, many states and even some activists didn't recognize it. After things had gone so wrong at the Review Conference, said one diplomat, we really wanted to do something positive at that year's General Assembly.[11] Her delegation supported a package of different resolutions that were all about the implementation of the NPT's disarmament obligations.[12] "We weren't being prescriptive, we were mapping and thinking about possibilities," she argued. Another diplomat described this package of resolutions as a "full-frontal assault." We got the Humanitarian Pledge endorsed by the United Nations, he said, and we got agreement to establish a conference to discuss next steps.[13]

This conference, a second open-ended working group (OEWG), was the product of a resolution that Austria and Mexico tabled at the General Assembly's disarmament committee in 2015, after the Review Conference.[14] The first OEWG, described in chapter 3, had not led to any concrete conclusions or outcomes when it met in 2013. Yet at the 2015 General Assembly, establishing a second round became an obvious solution, said one diplomat.[15] After the NPT Review Conference failure, and without any other governments stepping forward to host another conference on either the humanitarian impacts or the ways forward, this offered a UN-based process to move everything to the next phase. "There was a specific role for contingency and serendipity at play here," argued one person interviewed. The second OEWG "wasn't on anyone's agenda as a strategy"—it "seemed to be more about people responding to circumstances and opportunity."[16]

A few diplomats and activists expressed concern that another OEWG would just drag things out for another year, preventing the initiating of negotiations of a ban treaty. But most seized upon the new OEWG as an opportunity to make real progress—to advance across the field of play. The resolution establishing the group determined that it would meet in Geneva for up to fifteen working days under the General Assembly's rules of procedure. This last specification was crucial: the General Assembly allows for voting, meaning that the OEWG would not be held hostage to consensus as unanimity.

"How do you eat an elephant?" one diplomat asked, using a decidedly non-vegan metaphor. "One bite at a time."[17] She remembers hoping the OEWG would bring states closer to the goal of the ban. Others were even more confident in the possibilities that a new OEWG offered. "Once we had agreement on a new OEWG, it was smooth sailing. It was clear to me that we would have the ban when we prevailed on the OEWG resolution."[18] However, it wasn't exactly smooth sailing to set up the second OEWG—the nuclear-armed states made sure of that.

The idea of hosting another OEWG had been raised at the 2015 NPT Review Conference. In the outcome document that was never adopted, diplomats involved in the backroom negotiations of the final text had provisionally agreed to a recommendation that the General Assembly establish an OEWG to "identify and elaborate effective measures" for the full implementation of the NPT's disarmament obligations, operating on the basis of consensus. This provided some context for calling for such a body in a General Assembly resolution.

But the nuclear-armed states quickly voiced concerns about the language in the resolution that Austria and Mexico tabled, in particular because its stated use of General Assembly rules of procedure. The diplomats from nuclear-armed states argued that a "take it or leave it" approach is not inclusive; that seeking piecemeal solutions outside of existing "machinery"—that is, the international forums set up to deal with disarmament—is not the right way forward; that the *aim* of the resolution was to "subvert established disarmament machinery"; that an open-ended working group without consensus will not succeed; and that any initiative without their participation has no future—and that they would definitely not be participating.[19] To top it off, in classic patriarchal fashion, the Russian delegation even accused the resolution's sponsors and supporters of being . . . wait for it . . . emotional. "Most if not all initiatives are based on disappointment or disillusion," cajoled Mr. Yermakov of the Russian Federation, "but emotions are the worst adviser in this kind of very serious work."[20]

In the midst of this shrill reaction to the resolution that Austria and Mexico proposed, Iran tabled a separate resolution calling for the establishment of an OEWG. Their version of the group was to operate in New York instead of Geneva and would operate on the basis of consensus.[21] "We were taken aback by Iran's resolution," said one of the supporters of the Austrian-Mexican text. Those calling for an OEWG had not anticipated that Iran—which was skeptical about the ban approach and also a staunch defender of operating exclusively within established disarmament machinery—would suggest establishing a new body to discuss ways forward. It was also not anticipated that nuclear-armed states, in particular the United States, would support an Iranian initiative. But this was just a few months after the U.S., Iranian, and other involved governments had finally reached agreement on what was known as the Joint Comprehensive Plan of Action on Iran's nuclear program.[22] Some diplomats and others watching this unfold considered that the nuclear deal may have encouraged Iran to help the nuclear-armed states attempt to stop the Austria-Mexico working group from going forward. "We were lectured by certain states to follow the constructive approach of Iran," said one diplomat whose government supported the Austria-Mexico OEWG. "We were accused of threatening world peace, just because our mandate for an OEWG didn't insist on consensus."[23]

At first, it actually appeared that Iran's proposed resolution had legs. The nuclear-armed states were faced with the reality of three major international conferences on the humanitarian impact of nuclear weapons, a growing group of states—by this point, more than 120—endorsing the Humanitarian Pledge to fill the legal gap on the prohibition and elimination of nuclear weapons, a groundswell of support at the General Assembly for a ban,[24] and clear support for the establishment of some kind of OEWG. Against this backdrop, the nuclear-armed states appeared rather keen to endorse the Iranian proposal. Perhaps they saw such a body as a way to slow down the diplomatic process to negotiate a ban treaty. If so, it was a testament to the concern nuclear-armed states held that a nuclear ban would have meaning and would erode the legitimacy they seek to ascribe to their continued wielding of weapons of mass destruction.

However, when states finally voted on the two resolutions, the Iranian approach fell apart. First, Iran had not wanted a vote on its resolution at all. It had anticipated that it could be adopted by consensus, in the spirit of the body that the resolution intended to establish. But the delegation of Israel called for a vote and voiced its opposition to the text. After this, China, France, Russia, United Kingdom, and United States delivered a joint statement asserting that the NPT and existing UN disarmament machinery have proven to be "a solid framework to advance nuclear disarmament and provide all opportunities for launching a constructive and mutually respectful dialogue." Saying that although they "remain open" to other channels of discussion, "not excluding an appropriately-mandated OEWG," they asserted that a consensus-based approach is the only way to achieve "productive results."[25]

Following this joint statement, Iran withdrew its resolution, declaring, "It is evident that nuclear weapon States are not willing at all to commit themselves to a consensus-based and inclusive approach. In the absence of such willingness, which is essential for having a meaningful and comprehensive discussion on nuclear disarmament in the framework of the United Nations, there will be no justification for keeping this proposal on the table."[26] In response, the French delegate reiterated the section of the joint statement stressing that their objections would only have applied to the OEWG contained in the Austrian-Mexican resolution. But this was clearly insufficient to assuage the Iranians, who were perhaps looking for a way out of this mess anyway. The resolution remained withdrawn.

Following this drama, the Austria-Mexico version of the OEWG was the only option left on the table. The resolution was adopted with 135 in favor and only 12 nuclear-armed and nuclear "umbrella" states opposed.[27] "It was nail-biting until they withdrew," said one diplomat supportive of the Austria-Mexico resolution.[28] And, of course, immediately after its adoption, those opposed—including Australia and Japan—slagged it off as being useless.[29] But it was too late. Things were moving forward.

BACKFIRING BELLIGERENCE

The OEWG began its work in February 2016 and met again in May and August that same year.[30] It was an "evolutionary experience," said one participant.[31] We learned a lot during the humanitarian initiative, she said, explaining how the OEWG continued this process. "The way the meeting was structured, the side events, the exchange of significant information, and the impact of the interventions" all propelled us forward. The arguments for the ban "became unanswerable" by its opponents, she noted. "It was an organic process flowing in the direction of the ban. We didn't drive it there, but we could read the room. There was a sense of empowerment at that meeting, and a sense of responsibility."

Some participants highlighted the discussions within the OEWG as essential to building the case for the ban. For one diplomat from a ban-supporting country who was personally still skeptical at this point in time, it was the intellectual turning point. In particular, he said, it was a diplomat from another country who convinced him that the call to prohibit nuclear weapons without the nuclear-armed states was not too ambitious and, in fact, was morally and legally necessary. He was compelled to work collectively with other representatives from around the world to advance this case.[32]

At the same time as they built the case for the ban, the treaty's supporters "tried hard to encourage everyone to be there," said one diplomat.[33] But most of the nuclear-armed states boycotted the meeting. Nonnuclear-armed NATO states participated in full, and the sense for some participants certainly was that these countries were speaking at times for the nuclear-armed states. "It became a binary conversation—which side are you on?" said one participant. "Well, there was only one place we could be."[34]

The choice of which side to be on was aided not just by the obnoxious nuclear-armed boycott, but also by the belligerence and bullying of their proxies. Like the nuclear-armed states, representatives of several so-called nuclear umbrella or nuclear-supportive states issued patriarchal objections to the ban and dismissed the concerns of those governments who wanted to see concrete progress on nuclear disarmament. They argued that a nuclear weapon ban would undermine the NPT. Skirting the fact of the imbalance in the NPT's provisions, through which very few of the disarmament commitments made over the past fifty years have been implemented, these governments insisted repeatedly that the treaty would somehow negatively impact this long-standing regime. "The political uncertainty [the ban] may create around already existing institutions, its indirect impact may even put at risk already achieved results," suggested the Hungarian government.[35] Poland went further, claiming that the ban treaty, "with unknown efficiency," would not enjoy the participation of the nuclear-armed states but would instead "destroy the NPT system."[36]

Underpinning this line of argument was the assertion that a nuclear weapon ban treaty will not have any positive effect whatsoever on nuclear disarmament, but that it will anger the nuclear-armed states so greatly that they might become even more intransigent about retaining nuclear weapons and make even fewer commitments to disarmament, or that they might even use nuclear weapons or start a nuclear war. Others argued that the ban treaty is not a "quick fix" for nuclear disarmament and does not "guarantee" the elimination of nuclear weapons—which is a strange argument coming from countries that support incremental measures on nuclear disarmament, or that have previously championed prohibitions on other weapon systems such as landmines, cluster munitions, chemical weapons, and biological weapons.

The reality is that the problem with the ban treaty for these countries was and currently remains that the ban is incompatible with the possession of nuclear weapons. Even though they do not possess nuclear arsenals themselves, they support the United States at the very least retaining these weapons and continuing to offer them "protection" through the extended nuclear deterrence arrangements discussed earlier. The potential of the ban's impacts on their nuclear practices and politics frightens these states and drove some of the extreme rhetoric against the ban treaty and its proponents. Also, in some cases, it drove these governments deeper and deeper into a vocal defense of nuclear weapons. We can revisit Kuhn's argument, presented in chapter 3, about people's resistance to letting go of their theories even in the face of mounting evidence against them.[37] The clearer it became that the nuclear ban was going to happen, the harder these governments dug in against it, relying on their belief that nuclear weapons provide security to defend their refusal to accept a prohibition, despite evidence to the contrary that the humanitarian initiative provided.

At the OEWG in 2016, countries that previously had a strong rhetorical commitment to nuclear disarmament began to speak more and more about the importance of nuclear weapons. Take Japan, for instance. In 2009, a Japanese ambassador to the United Nations emphasized that "possessing nuclear weapons *per se* should not grant states any political advantages in international politics."[38] As the only country atomic weapons have been used against during a time of war, the vast majority of Japan's population is staunchly antinuclear. Japan has supported U.S. possession of nuclear weapons since the end of the war, but it has had to try to balance this with the desire of its citizens for total nuclear abolition by running educational programs and giving a lot of lip service to nuclear disarmament. But as the process to ban nuclear weapons gained momentum, the Japanese government opposed its negotiation and was even extremely reluctant to sign on to the joint intergovernmental humanitarian statements expressing that nuclear weapons should never be used again, under any circumstances.

Even more acutely, the Norwegian government's position radically shifted after the beginning of the humanitarian initiative. In 2010, Norway's foreign minister delivered a statement in which he strongly criticized the nuclear-armed states' approach to nuclear disarmament. "During the Cold War, the disarmament community was often portrayed as idealistic and even naïve by the security policy establishment," he noted. "Disarmament was seen—by some—as irreconcilable with state security. And, as a consequence, as an attitude and act of irresponsibility."[39] Rejecting this analysis, he called on the North Atlantic Treaty Organization (NATO), of which Norway is a part, to reconsider its deterrence doctrine. "We cannot credibly expect others to renounce the nuclear option, while we maintain that nuclear deterrence is still vital to our own security, twenty years after the end of the Cold War," he pointed out.

Later that same year, Norway's ambassador for disarmament outlined a policy of "impatient realism." Speaking to the UN General Assembly, she said, "When non-nuclear weapon states call for more ambitious commitments on part of the nuclear weapon states towards this goal, we are told to be realistic and patient. But is patience really what is called for in today's situation? We *have* been patient." She pointed out that nuclear-armed states committed themselves to the elimination of their nuclear arsenals forty years ago when they joined the NPT and that the Cold War ended twenty years ago. "No wonder patience is wearing thin. And why should it be unrealistic to expect more from the nuclear weapon states? What we are asking for is fully achievable. Most states have never possessed nuclear weapons, some have renounced them. It is a matter of political choice and direction."[40]

Norway went on to host the first humanitarian impact conference in March 2013 and to help fund ICAN's work for several years. But a change of government led to a systematic defunding of the antinuclear movement, including ICAN, and to the new government distancing itself from the very process the previous government had started. In 2015, the new government reiterated its commitment to the "factual conclusions" of the humanitarian conferences, but said, "Unfortunately, the emerging common understanding of a fact-based humanitarian initiative has now been undermined, and the initiative is by many associated with efforts to achieve a legal instrument banning nuclear weapons."[41]

This revisionist history ignores the fact that, as shown in chapter 3, the Norwegian government actually initiated many of the early conversations about pursuing a treaty banning nuclear weapons. But it also shows how the Norwegian position went from one of confronting the pro-nuclear narrative that demands for nuclear disarmament are naive and utopian to fully embracing that hegemonic perspective and apportioning blame on those states seeking security through the abolition of nuclear weapons. Thus, Norway went from calling on its fellow NATO members to revise the alliance's strategic doctrine away from nuclear weapons, to grouping itself with NATO in opposition to the ban treaty, arguing that the treaty and related processes led to "a further polarization of the international community."[42]

Norway's shift over the ban may be the most acute, but it is illustrative of a broader trend of NATO and other U.S. nuclear-supportive allies reifying nuclear weapons as important for security and characterizing disarmament as unrealistic and emotionally motivated. Some representatives of these countries delivered rather overwrought speeches justifying their support for the continued existence of nuclear weapons. Poland, for instance, described the threats it faces from a "neighboring country"

(Russia): "I've heard very often that our situation is unjustly privileged because we rely on nuclear deterrence capability of our allies," said the Polish delegation at the 2016 working group. "Having in mind what I already said about our constant threat and strategic reality, do you really think we are privileged? Really? . . . We currently rely on nuclear capabilities of our allies not because we want to, but because we have to."[43]

NATO allies stuck to their argument that nuclear weapons are necessary for European security, reiterating again and again how this is an essential element of the NATO strategic doctrine that any (at that point) future ban treaty would undermine. But this position is broadly ahistorical. Have NATO states forgotten their own resistance to nuclear weapons? They did not ask for them to be introduced to Europe and were, in fact, not consulted when they were brought there by the United States. They were reluctant to approve the U.S. strategic doctrine and exerted what former Swedish diplomat Alva Myrdal described as "considerable pressure" to assert control over the nuclear weapons the United States stationed on their territories. The most they could get was agreement to establish a Nuclear Planning Group for joint consultations over issues such as nuclear weapon targeting. Yet as Myrdal reported back in the 1970s, there has been scant public discussion since the 1960s over these weapons, and European official postures have become frozen in a kind of silent approval of the status quo.[44]

No longer silent, NATO states now seem to wholeheartedly embrace U.S. strategic doctrine involving nuclear weapons and nuclear war. They have defended the "deterrence" value of these weapons for European security and have derided those pursuing the ban treaty as undermining this security. Also writing in the 1970s, Herbert York, director of defense research and engineering under Presidents Eisenhower and Kennedy, lamented, "Today's Western Europeans have chosen to buy current political stability by placing the awful risks described above over their lives and their future."[45] Unfortunately, today's European leaders that are part of NATO continue to make the same choice.

Then, of course, there were the nuclear-armed states. They had already boycotted most of the humanitarian impact conferences, and now they refused to show up to the open-ended working group. The idea that the rest of the international community would spend five years researching and discussing the reality of nuclear weapons, and that the nuclear-armed states would just reject that evidence, was frustrating to more than one delegation. It showed "they were afraid of people power," said one diplomat. "We were always confused and perplexed that the nuclear-armed states stayed away" from the humanitarian initiative and the OEWG. "We kept reaching out to them, but they always rejected our efforts. Maybe they thought we wouldn't persist. But we did. And they left us with nowhere to build a bridge to."[46] The nuclear-armed states' boycott "really pissed off countries," said one observer.[47] It actually gave momentum to the humanitarian impact conferences—made it more legitimate for "constructive dissent" from the NPT, the Conference on Disarmament, and other forums. Countries wanted to change the game, and the boycott opened space for them to do so.

But the nuclear-armed didn't learn from this. They didn't even learn from a similar experience in the process to ban cluster munitions. "Contingency plays a major role" in these circumstances, said one person who had participated actively in the process to prohibit cluster munitions. In that process, "opponents made mistakes," he said. "The way the United States played the cluster munition process was so arrogant. Wikileaks cables show how unaware U.S. diplomats were of the changing dynamics."[48]

And so the nuclear-armed states continued to boycott and ridicule discussion about the humanitarian impacts. On top of this, there was their failure to implement the 2010 NPT action plan steps related to disarmament, and of course their behavior at the 2015 Review Conference—their pride in delivering a dictionary instead of disarmament, and then walking away from an agreed outcome at the last minute. And now, here in yet another OEWG that the nuclear-armed states were boycotting, the Australians, Japanese, and NATO states were doing all they could to prevent any further movement toward the negotiation of a nuclear ban treaty.

But the opponents to the ban finally went too far in Geneva, resulting in some of the most memorable moments from the entire ban process. Their opposition backfired spectacularly. Rather than halting or delaying progress, the belligerence propelled momentum for the ban to a point of no return.

One of the greatest examples of this phenomenon is the moment the Australian delegation tried to challenge the chair of the

OEWG—Ambassador Thani Thongphakdi of Thailand—over his assertion that a majority of participating states supported the establishment of a conference to negotiate a legally binding treaty prohibiting nuclear weapons.[49] This language was drawn from a working paper submitted by states[50] and a working paper submitted by two ICAN partners (including WILPF).[51] All of these papers offered suggested elements of a prohibition treaty. One of the governmental working papers called for the UN General Assembly to establish a negotiating conference in 2017.[52]

The Australians weren't having it. When the chair of the OEWG released his draft report of the group's work, which reflected the majority support for a ban treaty, the Australian delegation said it did not agree that a majority was in favor of this option. The Mexican ambassador then pulled out a notepad with dramatic flourish and asked the chair to conduct a poll.

The Association of Southeast Asian States was the first to speak, clearly outlining its members' support for negotiations. Ten countries. The Latin American and Caribbean states spoke next. Thirty-three countries. Then the African Group chimed in, saving until the last sentence of their statement their declaration of support for a negotiating conference. Fifty-four states. This made up the majority. Fist pumps in the air were visible around the room—including from diplomats. A few European states—Austria, Ireland, Liechtenstein, San Marino—added their names to the tally, as did Fiji, Palau, and Samoa from the Pacific, but the results were already in. For the first time, we had on record all of these countries saying they supported the negotiation of a treaty banning nuclear weapons.

"We couldn't have pushed the envelope further from the supportive side," commented one diplomat. But the "bully mentality" exhibited by Australia and some of the NATO states to "dare" smaller states into making their positions known worked wonders, she said.[53] Sometimes this bullying works to shut things down, but not on the question of nuclear weapons—this is an issue of principle and of security. "Security for our people means no nuclear weapons," she said. "We wanted to be on the right side of history."

This was a common narrative at the OEWG, and a strong one at that. For many, perhaps for most of the diplomats involved, it was the first time they had considered seriously what a ban treaty could be, what such a treaty could offer the world. For some, it was also the first time they heard a *hibakusha*, an atomic bomb survivor, speak. If they had not been at the humanitarian impact conferences, they would not necessarily have heard firsthand testimony of the experience of living through a nuclear weapon detonation. This had an impact on proceedings, as did the strong, coordinated activist presence.

"ICAN had prepared the ground well," said one participant. They provided "good materials and reports explaining what the ban could be, which provided crucial resources to those who still had no idea what it was about. From February to May 2016, those materials better informed delegations more than [opponents] thought they would."[54] ICAN partners tabled working papers, delivered coordinated statements, held side events, and worked directly with governments to help bring them up to speed on the logic of the ban. A presentation by Nick Ritchie, an academic from York University in the United Kingdom who delivered a blistering analysis of the threat of massive nuclear violence inherent in the nuclear-armed states' opposition to the ban, was widely welcomed by many government delegations.[55] The ambassador of Mexico even jokingly said he wanted the chair to reflect in the official record Ritchie's presentation as being the position of the Mexican delegation.

Overall, the discussions at the 2016 OEWG shed a stark light on the reality of the situation. Several diplomats spoke about their realizations at this meeting that there was really only one option for moving forward. There was clear "disparity between the weight of the intellectual arguments, facts, and emotions," said one diplomat. It came down to "needing to do more versus maintaining the status quo." Those delegations opposed to the ban "had nothing else on offer, just empty, stale rhetoric."[56] From listening to the nuclear-supportive states, the OEWG was an Orwellian doublethink[57] world, in which nuclear weapons are safe; states clinging to a decades-old agenda entangled in a decades-old stalemate are "progressive";[58] and the most important thing is to engage states that haven't even shown up to the talks.

With the nuclear-armed states out of the room, it appeared to be the task of their nuclearized allies to oppose the ban and to object to anything that challenged the dominance of those possessing or supporting nuclear weapons. These states, including Canada, Belgium, Germany, Italy, Japan, the Netherlands, Norway, Poland, and Spain, argued against the prohibition of nuclear weapons. In their interventions and working papers they described banning nuclear weapons as premature, irresponsible, and ineffectual. In a classic demonstration of doublethink, they simultaneously asserted that they support a nuclear weapon free world while trying to prevent feasible actions to attain it. They also complained that the chair's synthesis paper was not "balanced" and did not reflect their "progressive approach" adequately. Representing 14 percent of states in the world, they delivered 29 percent of the statements at the February session of the OEWG. This would seem to suggest overrepresentation of a minority-held view, making the call for "balance" in a chair's summary seem rather undemocratic. At the same time, these states blamed others—for example, the overwhelming majority of states in the world—for being "divisive." This patriarchal discourse was so starkly obvious that the Mexican delegation at one point asked if the nuclear-armed allies participating in the OEWG had any say over security measures, or if those are left to the United States alone. Mexico also asked whether their so-called progressive approach is really about retrenchment of the status quo.

Tensions ran pretty high at this meeting. Everyone could see that the stakes were high, that the international community was at a turning point in the history of nuclear weapons. But the rich discussions during the February and May sessions of the 2016 OEWG, and the antics of Australia's denial of reality over support for the ban in May, led Ambassador Thongphakdi as chair of the meeting to retain the negotiating conference for the ban in his next draft of the recommendations released mid-August.[59] That document was discussed late into the night at the end of the August session of the OEWG. Ambassador Thongphakdi had delegations for and against the ban over to his residence to discuss the outcome. At the end of the day, the revised draft "recognized that there was a recommendation which received widespread support for the General Assembly to convene a conference in 2017" to negotiate the ban treaty.[60] This was diluted from the previous language, which stated, "A majority of States supported the convening by the General Assembly of a conference in 2017." Both versions acknowledged that "a group of states" believed such negotiations would be premature. It was a compromise all sides had to be willing to live with in order to respect the wishes of the majority while not completely overriding the concerns of the minority.

But then . . . Australia intervened. Again. The final day of the OEWG, everyone—including all of Australia's allies that opposed the ban—had assumed that the recommendations would be adopted by consensus, as agreed the night before. But at the last moment, the Australian delegation called for a vote. It said it could not accept the document as written and asked for a vote to be held.

After a brief moment of stunned murmuring throughout the conference room, the Guatemalan delegation asked for the floor. It suggested that since a vote had been requested, states should be able to vote on the language they actually wanted, rather than compromise language that had been watered down to accommodate Australia and its allies. The chair called for a recess, and when the session resumed, a vote was held on Guatemala's proposed amendment and on the draft report as a whole. The night ended with 107 states—the vast majority of participants at the working group—voting in favor of the ban. The twenty-two NATO states and the other nuclear-supportive countries participating in the meeting were divided. Some abstained, some voted against. They were all upset with Australia. They had not wanted to have to go on the record so early in their opposition to the ban. They understood that for their domestic audiences, it would look very, very bad for them to object to negotiations to outlaw heinous weapons of mass destruction. Australia had apparently not consulted or informed any of its allies that it was going to pull this move, leaving them flailing to figure out how to respond when it was too late.

"The nuclear-supportive states were freaking out at the OEWG," said one observer. "They couldn't boycott and be credible to domestic audiences. Then they were outmaneuvered by Australia's mistakes."[61] The nuclear umbrella and the nuclear-armed states "miscalculated everything," a diplomat agreed.[62] They only succeeded in creating more divisions among each other, not in stopping the ban.

Once again, Australia had failed spectacularly in its attempts to thwart the ban treaty. It was such a bad performance—even threatening its diplomatic credibility with its closest allies—that some diplomats and activists speculated whether the Australian delegation was secretly trying to help the ban treaty! Most likely, however, the "own goals" of the delegation were just the efforts of a failed bully.

Those who start bullying do so because they are pushed into a corner, said a diplomat. "When you're in a position of power and you feel like you're in a corner, you resort to tactics you know."[63] The bullying also indicates fear, said several diplomats and others. One person theorized that this level of intimidation—which was applied to governments as well as UN entities—was in part due to changing global dynamics and the uncertainty this instilled in those used to having their way. "In the 1960s and '70s, the world was a bipolar system—everyone knew the rules of the game," he said. "You could be as critical as you liked, because the paradigm was a superpower arms race. That's why there's so much hostility to the ban. In the post-post-Cold War era, US hegemony is in doubt; a new world order is emerging. The US doesn't want its alliances undermined by a ban."[64] He suggested that the bullying is similar to how the United States approached New Zealand's decision to become nuclear free decades previously. They wanted to "stop the rot," he said. But as with New Zealand, the bullying didn't work. It just galvanized increasing solidarity among those governments at the receiving end.

Some of us really felt that we were "sticking it to the nuclear-armed states," said one diplomat.[65] The recommendation to start negotiations on the ban at that meeting "told the nuclear-armed states and their allies—who were being disrespectful—that we were going ahead with this." For him, and possibly others, at this moment in time this frustration was more of a motivation to support ban negotiations than "a real expectation that such a treaty would advance nuclear disarmament." Ban supporters had a subliminal message for the world: "We can do something that we know you big guys don't like."[66] The fact that so many countries in the global south stuck to supporting the ban in the face of some extreme pressure shows how important the idea was that the ban was not only the right thing to do but that it signified a standing up to power.

The bully tactics were so demeaning and totally unnecessary, said another participant. "You have your position, so engage in negotiation, don't bully—the UN is a democracy, you can't just discount sovereignty. Bullying means you're not treating each other as equals."[67]

Countries of the global south were routinely told that they did not have "interests," recalls one diplomat. "Well, our interest is in international law, and in global governance that works," she said. Those countries defending nuclear weapons "don't see this as a national interest. But for us, this is not a principled position, this is in our interest—it is our choice to be nuclear free, not a political destiny."[68]

In this regard, some states were just as frustrated with the nuclear-supportive states as they were with the nuclear-armed ones, because of their protection of powerful countries wielding extreme violence. Many developing countries, small island states, and others, which work closely with certain NATO countries on the implementation of the Sustainable Development Goals (SDGs), couldn't accept the hypocrisy of their erstwhile allies. "We were involved in the SDG process at the same time" as the OEWG and humanitarian initiative, said one diplomat. In the SDG context, these countries were "promoting a holistic approach. This means putting people first. And now you support nuclear weapons?! Get real!"[69]

By the end of the OEWG in August 2016, it was clear that patriarchal, racist techniques of gaslighting and bullying were no longer sufficient to suppress the resistance's move for a ban treaty. So, the nuclear-armed states decided it was time to turn up the pressure outside the conference rooms.

THE PRESSURE TURNS UP

The date 27 October 2016 should go down in history as the moment when the majority of United Nations member states made a dramatic stand against the violent posturing and pressure of the most militarily powerful countries in the world. On that day, 123 governments voted for a resolution in the UN General Assembly that established negotiations on a treaty banning nuclear weapons.[70] They did so despite threats, warnings, and demands issued by several of the nuclear-armed states. This moment wasn't just a step toward a nuclear weapon prohibition. It also represented a revolt of the vast majority of states against the violence, intimidation, and injustice perpetuated by those supporting these weapons of mass destruction.

Not surprisingly, the efforts to crush this revolt were intense. In the weeks leading up to the vote on the resolution, several of the nuclear-armed states actively lobbied their allies to vote against the resolution. This pressure varied greatly in degree, with—unsurprisingly—former colonies experiencing the most pressure from their former colonizers. The other group of states to experience the most pressure was the European countries championing the ban, in particular Austria and Ireland. This was a clear attempt by the French and British governments to police other European Union members.

One diplomat from Southeast Asia said that pressure on her country didn't really start until after the 2015 NPT Review Conference. Most of the pressure on this diplomat's country, and others in the region, apparently came from Australia. Officials from Australia tried to spread misinformation at an Association of South East Asian Nations (ASEAN) Regional Forum meeting after the Review Conference, saying that the conference had produced an outcome. When the Southeast Asian members of ASEAN reacted to that, the United States started paying visits to their government ministries and raising the issue of the ban treaty during bilateral meetings. In one case, the U.S. State Department reportedly sent a top-level official who tried to dissuade a ban-supportive country in the region from continuing to pursue the treaty. "He talked about the humanitarian initiative as if it was a virus people caught," a diplomat from the country reflected.[71] But officials from that country pushed back hard and made it clear that it was going to continue to support the initiative. The U.S. official "was surprised to be contradicted," the diplomat noted. The Americans "stepped up the pressure after that with démarches at the capital level, but it wasn't very hostile."[72]

Diplomats from some other pro-ban countries reported similar experiences. "The Americans knew where we stood, and they didn't bother us too much," said one.[73] Another suggested that his country's overwhelming support for nuclear disarmament and for the humanitarian initiative was clear through their statements, workshops, and events. His country had "created a clear impression that we were unmovable," he said. "Pressure didn't materialize in a significant way."[74] Some experienced "low-level démarches" but didn't find that it was a serious issue. One even said that he "always managed to maintain good contact with the Americans . . . we just agree to disagree."[75]

Others had a different experience. One diplomat said that her delegation and others faced "put downs" and were told it would never happen or that it would be useless.[76] Another said her government's military adviser in Geneva faced some "snarky comments" from his French counterpart, and her government received a few démarches from the nuclear-armed states. The worst pressure came from Russia, she noted. "They kept complaining long after it made sense."[77] Another said more pressure came from France than any of the other nuclear-armed states. "The United States and France were the most interventionist in their opposition to the ban," she recalled, "but the US delegation eventually stopped applying pressure on us—they clearly decided we were a lost cause, especially after the open-ended working group."[78] But the French, she said, became even more engaged in pressuring us after the treaty was adopted, trying to persuade us not to sign or ratify. "The French are particularly exercised in a way that the others aren't," she commented, musing, "It's interesting that their reaction is so strong. They clearly feel there is a threat to their nuclear weapons from this treaty, that their status as a great power being based on nuclear weapons is at risk."

One diplomat reported experiencing pressure from Japan's delegation, which asked her why she had to "speak so strongly" during one of the meetings related to the ban.[79] China also reportedly raised a fuss with a few delegations, and India poked around a bit trying to find out where the ban was headed.[80] Some diplomats and activists were worried about the dynamics of BRICS—an economic grouping of Brazil, Russia, India, China, and South Africa. With Brazil and South Africa in the core group of states campaigning for the ban treaty, and Russia, India, and China all possessing nuclear weapons, some people were concerned that the two champion states would come under serious enough pressure to perhaps change their positions. Although Russia in particular did apparently use BRICS meetings to apply pressure against the ban—including at the highest levels—Brazil and South Africa stood firm. "We created the impression [within BRICS] that we are so solid that if you try to raise this with us, we'll be irritated," said one diplomat.[81]

Although some of those interviewed reported moderate exposure to pressure, others experienced a much more aggressive approach. One diplomat said that at least a dozen countries had calls from U.S. President Obama himself, for example, asking that they ease off their support for the treaty.[82] He also suspected that the communications of his government ministry were being surveilled. Diplomats within the European Union (EU) also experience pressure there. "EU partners were trying to put us in a corner," branding supporters of the ban as "unrealistic, ridiculous, endangering security" and using words such as "betrayal" and "unacceptable" in reference to pro-ban countries.[83] Many in this situation noted that the French officials were the most absolutist and aggressive.[84] "It can't be overestimated how much pressure Austria and Ireland were put under between the Nayarit conference and the 2015 NPT Review Conference," said one observer. They faced "daily hostility and disapproval." Importantly, "if they hadn't been able to withstand that pressure, the humanitarian initiative would have crumbled."[85]

African countries reportedly faced the most pressure. At the UN General Assembly, at the UN open-ended working group, and at the negotiations of the treaty itself, many African countries were confronted by pressure from certain nuclear-armed states. During the 2016 UN General Assembly, ahead of the vote on the resolution establishing ban negotiations, the U.S. delegation called a meeting of the African Group delegations in New York and asked them not to support the resolution. The French government also reportedly put pressure on Francophone African states, and some diplomats indicated that the Russian government was also involved. "The démarches were highly critical," one diplomat familiar with the situation explained. The nuclear-armed states "said the ban was dangerous and that supporters are undermining everything. The pressure went to a high level within many African countries."[86]

But, for the most part, the region stood strong. One diplomat familiar with the situation noted that between support and solidarity from other governments of the region, and active lobbying by ICAN in New York and back in capitals, most of Africa was able to stand strong. At critical times, ICAN and the International Committee of the Red Cross provided an important buffer to nuclear-armed pressure, by saying "you're doing the right thing," said one diplomat. "If someone was faltering under the pressure, they could ask ICAN to follow up and support them back in capital," he explained. "Without South Africa, ICAN, the ICRC, and the Pope, we wouldn't have been able to keep African countries on board." The countries of concern are politically independent, he explained, but the influence and economic pressure from external allies have major impacts.[87]

When it came to voting on the UN General Assembly resolution to initiate ban treaty negotiations, and to the negotiations themselves, the French were successful in peeling off a few Francophone African countries. For the most part, however, the region was able to stand united against this pressure. At the end of the day, the most successful lobbying against the ban came from the Obama administration toward its NATO allies.

In mid-October, the U.S. government warned other NATO members that efforts to negotiate a treaty prohibiting nuclear weapons or to delegitimize nuclear deterrence "are fundamentally at odds with NATO's basic policies on deterrence." In an unclassified memo, the U.S. government strongly urged allies and partners to vote no on the resolution, and "not to merely abstain." The memo also said that "if negotiations do commence, we ask allies and partners to refrain from joining them."[88] The document shows that the United States believed a treaty prohibiting nuclear weapons, even without the participation of nuclear-armed states, would indeed have a significant impact.[89]

The NATO states did all vote against the establishment of nuclear ban negotiations.[90] However, the Netherlands ended up participating in negotiations. A strong national ICAN effort inspired a parliamentary debate, and the Dutch parliament ended up supporting a motion that the government must actively work on the start of negotiations on a treaty banning nuclear weapons.[91] Although the Netherlands' participation in negotiations did not result in meaningful contributions to the treaty, it was a clear demonstration of the power of the people that the government participated because of public pressure.

MOVING AHEAD

The nuclear-armed and their allies kept up the pressure throughout the process to ban nuclear weapons. Even on the day of the vote of the UN General Assembly resolution establishing negotiations, Russia's representative warned of the "fatal, destructive repercussions" of adopting the resolution, describing the initiative to prohibit nuclear weapons as "hasty" and at risk of "plunging the world into chaos and dangerous unpredictability."[92]

But ICAN kept up the pressure, too. Throughout the October 2016 session of the General Assembly, we met with governments, wrote reports and analysis of the ongoing deliberations, and even distributed a collectible series of amusing posters calling on delegations to "Vote for L.41," the resolution to establish negotiations, featuring memes based on films including *War Games, Star Wars, Lord of the Rings, Napoleon Dynamite*, and even *Sharknado*. We were once again keeping the humor alive amid the horror of nuclear weapons and the hope for the ban.

With support from ICAN and several ban-champion states, and after the discussions and the theater at the open-ended working group, the majority of countries were ready to go. They knew that the nuclear-armed states would not have cared if they really thought this treaty was irrelevant. The pressure from those opposed to the ban only showed exactly how meaningful it would be.

"There comes a time when choices have to be made and this is one of those times," said Helena Nolan of Ireland before the vote on L.41. "Given the clear risks associated with the continued existence of nuclear weapons, this is now a choice between responsibility and irresponsibility. Governance requires accountability and governance requires leadership."[93] Several delegations had shown such leadership and even sought to assuage colleagues from states opposed to the ban. "We appreciate that a major factor contributing to resistance to change is often the fear of the unknown and apprehension to depart from a known course of action, even in the face of failure," noted Shorna-Kay Richards of Jamaica in her closing remarks at the OEWG. "But we daresay that a global prohibition on nuclear weapons is not an unknown—as mentioned during the course of our deliberations, 'history has shown that a key element for the elimination of scourges created by humanity has been their prohibition.'"[94] Further, she argued, those calling for prohibition and elimination of nuclear weapons also have fears, for their security and their survival:

Indeed, we fear that the "grand bargain" which enabled the coming into the being of the NPT, which is not being implemented in both letter and spirit as well as the backtracking on commitments freely undertaken, keeps us on the brink of massive nuclear violence and threatens the very survival of humanity.[95]

This fear, however, brought courage. The demand for prohibition in the face of pressure from nuclear-armed states and their nuclear-supportive allies was a bold, historic move. The moment of victory was not lost on those who had long campaigned for nuclear disarmament. In the United Nations, activists and diplomats celebrated loudly, causing the chair of the meeting to call the room to order with his gavel—with a big grin on his face. Around the world, others who had worked for this moment were glued to their laptops, watching the vote on the UN webcast. "I watched the vote with my daughter," one diplomat who wasn't there said. "I was so nervous, but it was special to share this moment with family. When the numbers climbed from 100 to 123, we were both cheering. I couldn't stop smiling for days."[96]

This was courage that Camus could celebrate. It had taken seventy-one years to get to this moment: seventy-one years since the first nuclear weapons were used by the United States against Japan. Seventy-one years of living with the existential threat of nuclear weapons. Seventy-one years of antinuclear activism and diplomatic maneuvers and incredible pressure from the most militarized states in the world—governments that felt they had a divine right to rule the world according to their image and interests. It took courage to initiate negotiations on a treaty outlawing nuclear weapons, and it would take courage to see it through to the end, as explored in the next chapters.

8

GETTING OUR BAN ON, PART ONE

The What

Negotiations of the nuclear ban treaty began on 27 March and ended 7 July 2017, with about four weeks of meetings, several draft texts, and lots of late nights. Outside the conference room, there wasn't much awareness of what was happening. It wasn't exactly invisible, but it also wasn't like the mainstream news was giving it much coverage—other than the United States' strange protest of the negotiations. On the opening day of the talks, the newly appointed U.S. ambassador to the United Nations, Nikki Haley, stood outside of the UN General Assembly Hall to belittle the participants negotiating this treaty. Talking to reporters with what others have described as a "ragtag band of about 20 diplomats" standing behind her,[1] she framed her opposition to the ban in the most patriarchal, patronizing way possible:

> First and foremost I'm a mom, I'm a wife, I'm a daughter. And so I always think of my family first, as everyone one of the people behind me do as well. Then we go and we look at our positions. What are we supposed to do in our jobs? Our jobs is [sic] is to protect the people in our countries. Keep them safe. Keep the peace. And to do it in a way that brings no harm. . . . Now, suddenly the General Assembly wants to have a hearing. To ban nuclear weapons. As a mom, as a daughter, there's nothing I want more for my family than a world with no nuclear weapons. *But we have to be realistic* . . . Today when you see those walking into the General Assembly to create a nuclear weapons ban, you have to ask yourself, are they looking out for their people? Do they really understand the threats that we have?"[2]

Ambassador Haley's statements are classic patriarchy, fully in line with the gendered discourse about nuclear weapons explored in chapter 1. She situates her desire for nuclear weapons disarmament within what she considers her primary feminine or female identities—mother, wife, daughter—but rejects this position as unrealistic. A more rational perspective, she argues, is retaining nuclear weapons for the indefinite future. She frames this as being the only logical way to "look out" for "one's people." Thus, she portrays the experience of being someone's mother, wife, or daughter as a weak position, as offering a perspective that is somehow not realistic or rational when it comes to considering issues of security and weapons. She positions her perception of her feminine identities as irrelevant or even harmful to the true security needs of her nation and people.

Haley's remarks are also a classic example of the dismissal of lived reality of those who have suffered from nuclear weapons—described in chapter 1 as a form of gaslighting. Criticizing Haley's framing that being a mother is an unrealistic position from which to make security decisions, and that the job of protecting the nation requires nuclear weapons, Fijian antinuclear activist Vanessa Griffen pointed out that this was a slap in the face to every woman who has given birth to "jellyfish" babies as a result of U.S., UK, or French nuclear weapons testing in the Pacific Islands or Australia. "Pacific women—mothers and non-mothers alike—have spoken out against nuclear weapons repeatedly and want them banned," she wrote. "Anyone who knows the impact of nuclear weapons knows their effects on women, and on children."[3] The idea that nuclear weapons are about protecting people, keeping the peace, and *doing no harm*—an oath that doctors take—is an incredible affront to anyone who has suffered from nuclear weapon use and testing. Overall, Haley's performance was offensive—but also embarrassing.

The U.S. government had tried to get all of its NATO allies to accompany Haley at this press conference, but only France, the United Kingdom, Australia, South Korea, Turkey, and a handful of Eastern European diplomats showed up. Other NATO members, even those that had abided by the U.S. directive to boycott negotiations, did not want to participate in this absurd spectacle. Ambassador

Haley opened her remarks saying, "We wanted to stand here just to have our voices heard." It was an intriguing reversal of usual roles, in which the most powerful country in the world staged a protest outside a multilateral institution while the majority of governments were inside working together with activists and others to address one of humanity's greatest threats. Typically, we activists are outside the rooms where decisions are being made, wanting to have our voices heard. In this case, the U.S. government was admitting that it had lost control of the nuclear weapon narrative. Its voice was no longer dominant on this issue.

The states inside the General Assembly Hall were moving forward regardless of the condemnations of the nuclear-armed states. They were standing up for security—a security rooted in what Ambassador Amr Aboulatta of Egypt described as "*collective* security as opposed to *selective* security."[4] In another episode of How Those Opposed to You Help You Through Their Hubris (for which the Australians wrote the playbook during the open-ended working group in 2016, as described in the previous chapter), the theatrical protest by the U.S. delegation only helped advance the cause of the ban. It brought a lot of press coverage not just to the protest outside the room, but to what was happening inside, helping to spread the word around the globe that countries were banning nuclear weapons.

This chapter takes a dive inside the UN conference rooms, highlighting the critical debates as the treaty text developed through negotiation. After so long living in the space created by the nuclear-armed states, by their assertion of power and authority, it was refreshing, as activists and nonnuclear states, to have our own space to discuss with each other what we need to achieve a nuclear weapon free world. Although the atmosphere of these negotiations was much more positive than many other multilateral disarmament negotiations, some serious points of contention still had to be talked through. This chapter tries to provide a concise historical record of these debates, while also providing my own thoughts on them and without trying to get too lost in the details. Hopefully it provides a taste not only of the substantive arguments but also of the ways in which diplomats and activists managed or struggled to resolve them.

SETTING UP THE PROCESS

The work began with what the UN calls an organizational meeting.[5] About one hundred countries convened on 16 February to discuss and, when possible, make decisions on key procedural issues for the negotiating conference. Ambassador Elayne Whyte Gómez of Costa Rica was confirmed as the president of the conference. Though she was the permanent representative of Costa Rica to the United Nations in Geneva, she was new to the disarmament beat. Some governments were a bit wary of her taking up the mantle. She hadn't been part of the process to get negotiations underway, and she was unfamiliar with both the political dynamics and the technical issues surrounding nuclear disarmament. Others saw her newness as a potential advantage. She would not have biases toward particular content for the treaty, or toward particular states. She would approach the negotiations from a fresh perspective.

The first test for the president was adopting the rules of procedure and other arrangements for the negotiations. Most of the organizational meeting was taken up with discussion around nongovernmental organization (NGO) participation and with the participation of Palestine and the Holy See as UN observers rather than member states.

On the issue of NGOs, most states were supportive of activists being involved in the conference. Liechtenstein and Ireland pointed out that without civil society, states wouldn't even be negotiating this treaty. But a few others, such as Iran and Syria, wanted to debate whether activists should be able to "participate" or just to "attend." The majority view was that of course NGOs should be able to participate—to give interventions, table working papers, and monitor discussions. But governments did agree to a compromise in which states could veto the participation of particular NGOs.[6] In the end, this didn't happen to any groups, but it was an unsettling precedent drawn from a high-level meeting on migration and refugees the year before.

On state participation, the problem was that the UN General Assembly resolution establishing negotiations encouraged all UN member states to participate in the conference.[7] But UN observer states, including Palestine and the Holy See, wanted to be able to participate as well. Palestine requested the rules of procedure for the conference refer to "states" instead of "member states" so as to be open to the widest possible participation.

The president received advice from the Office of Legal Affairs, but also had to contend with various governments' interpretations of the resolution. She also had to navigate the murky waters of states perhaps using this procedural question to stall the beginning of negotiations. During Arms Trade Treaty negotiations in 2012, the question of the participation of the Holy See and Palestine set back negotiations a week, and in the end the negotiating conference had to be reestablished for an extra two weeks. Avoiding this situation was critical.

Discussion on this matter took place behind closed doors, but when the final version of the rules of procedure were adopted, it was with a footnote explaining that the term "state" in reference to states participating in the conference "is understood as the Member States of the United Nations and the Holy See and the State of Palestine as the observer States of the United Nations," and that both countries "will participate on an equal basis with Member States, including with the right to vote."[8] Reaching this agreement was reportedly not easy, but in the end Ambassador Whyte was able to gavel it through, meaning the formal work of the conference could begin as scheduled on 27 March.

DECIDING ON THE ELEMENTS

As most UN conferences do, the negotiations began with high-level government representatives delivering rhetorical remarks about their countries' commitment to the issue and determination for success. Typically rather boring and sometimes redundant, this particular high-level segment was actually rather significant. So much effort had been put into getting to this point that it was nice to take a moment (or in the UN world, a day and a half) to reflect on that. As the ambassador of Trinidad and Tobago said, "We stand on the precipice of history as we seek to shatter the chronic stalemate that has existed in the field of nuclear disarmament and non-proliferation for far too long."[9] Many governments saw this negotiating conference as "a pivotal point in our international relations," as the ambassador of Ireland put it. She described the conference as a time to take stock and honor the testimony of the past, to decide what sort of present we wish to live in and what sort of legacy we wish to leave for future generations. We are not just writing a new and complementary treaty here, we are taking the opportunity to write a new history and in so doing to create a new, more stable, more secure and more equal future for all.[10]

During the opening March session, many governments outlined in detail (in many cases for the first time) what they saw as the preferred scope of the treaty, shedding more light than ever on the possibilities for this instrument. The vast majority of countries described a strong, comprehensive treaty that would prohibit a wide range of nuclear weapon-related activities and that would carve out space for future negotiations on nuclear disarmament and related verification measures. Creating that space was a sign to nuclear-armed states that negotiators had faith in this treaty. That they believed it would be effective in its normative, legal, political, economic, and social transformation of the nuclear world order and that it would help compel nuclear-armed states to eliminate their genocidal weapons.

After the high-level statements and expressions of support for the negotiations, participants spent the rest of the week exploring various elements of the future treaty. They worked their way through the preamble, the prohibitions, the question of what to do about nuclear-armed or nuclear-supportive states that want to join the treaty, questions about victim assistance and environmental remediation, arrangements for how the treaty enters into force and whether countries have the right to withdraw, and structures for future conferences of states' parties to the treaty.[11] In a move that was innovative for the nuclear field, Ambassador Whyte and the UN Secretariat arranged interactive panels with civil society experts, including two ICAN representatives, who delivered presentations and fielded questions from diplomats. I was honored to be one of these representatives, who alongside the International Committee of the Red Cross and the Lawyers Committee on Nuclear Policy was able to have a three-hour formal conversation with governments in the room about the treaty's preamble and prohibitions.[12]

From this first week of negotiations, it became clear that the elements of the ban treaty were really about pathways: closing off the pathways to develop, retain, or support nuclear weapons; and opening pathways for nuclear disarmament. The overarching objective of the treaty is to facilitate the elimination of nuclear weapons. This meant it needed to set out prohibitions and obligations that stigmatize nuclear weapons so that doctrines of "nuclear deterrence" are no longer legally, politically, and socially sustainable. Drawing on the paradigm shift that activists, academics, and diplomats had been shaping throughout the humanitarian initiative, we sought to craft international law that would firmly reflect the perspectives of those who rejected nuclear weapons as tools of security and saw them instead of weapons of mass destruction that must be outlawed alongside weapons in this category. For this to take shape, the treaty also needed to affect the economic incentives for nuclear weapon production and maintenance and provide legal prohibitions of any activity that supports the existence of nuclear weapons. Although we need to construct an instrument that would help alter social and cultural understandings of nuclear weapons, a political economy-based critique of nuclear weapons, such as that offered in chapter 1, meant that we also needed to take on the nuclear weapon enterprise where it would feel it the most: in terms of money.

Negotiators of this treaty also understood that it needed to be part of the larger architecture of disarmament, peace, security, and human rights. Essentially, all supporters of the ban treaty agreed that this instrument was not to be an end in itself, but a tool to advance peace, justice, and the prevention of humanitarian and environmental harm. In this sense, it needed to be a disarmament treaty—not just a normative prohibition, but something that could be used to help achieve and maintain a nuclear weapon free world.

During the first week of negotiations, some states were clearly operating under old rules. They still felt the weight of the nuclear-armed states bearing down upon them. But the activists in the room were there to remind them of how far they had already come. Negotiating this treaty was already a breakthrough. Diplomats had to risk a lot to get here. Now they had the space to design something off the charts, with imagination and creativity. There was no point in writing a new treaty that was either implicitly or explicitly permissive of the behavior of a comparatively small number of states that have either chosen or been instructed not to participate in the negotiations. It was the time to set out new law that would fundamentally change the way the world does business when it comes to nuclear weapons.

To encourage governments in this direction, in addition to the publications, inputs, and testimony offered inside the negotiating room, activists also offered up some street support outside. Between the March and June rounds of negotiations, WILPF worked with other partners to organize a Women's March to Ban the Bomb in New York City. About a thousand people turned up in a torrential downpour to march from Bryant Park to the United Nations on 17 June 2017, while around the world people in more than one hundred other locations held sister solidarity events with marches, vigils, teach-ins, or poster-making activities. Diplomats joined in the New York City march, and *hibakusha*, activists, and the president of the negotiations spoke at the rally in the rain. It was the biggest moment of public mobilization for the treaty. Throughout the negotiations, direct actions continued with activists of faith leading morning prayer vigils outside the United Nations, and a group of protestors sat outside the U.S. mission for an afternoon shaming it for boycotting the negotiations. Activists also visited the missions of the other boycotting states and performed vibrant street theater in bomb costumes and with masks of the heads of state of the nuclear-armed countries.

NEGOTIATING THE CRITICAL ISSUES

This activism outside the United Nations helped set the stage for the next round of negotiations, reminding everyone why we were there and bolstering energy in the room. The conference president released a draft treaty text on 22 May, which became the basis of discussions during negotiations in June and July.[13] After the March session, there was clearly a lot of convergence on the treaty's elements, but also some key points of divergence. These included whether or not the treaty would prohibit threat of use of nuclear weapons, financing, transit, or testing; and how the treaty would deal with nuclear-armed states joining, as well as issues such as safeguards for nuclear materials and verification of the implementation of the treaty's provisions.[14] The following sections outline some of the discussions on each of these.

Threat of Use

Many states, and several NGOs including WILPF and legal groups such as the Lawyers Committee on Nuclear Policy, argued that the treaty should prohibit the threat of use of nuclear weapons along with the use of nuclear weapons. South Africa's delegation argued that the threat of use needed to be included because it "would be key to the effort to delegitimse the concept of nuclear deterrence."[15] Academic Nick Ritchie agreed, noting that "nuclear weapons are not just individual physical things, but part of a system of organisations, ideas, and practices in which the possibility of perpetrating massive nuclear violence makes sense to their possessors." Thus, the physical existence of nuclear weapons is intimately connected with doctrines of nuclear deterrence and operational planning for the use of the weapons. "It is this system that needs destabilizing, delegitimizing, and disestablishing."[16]

A few states, including Austria and Mexico, argued that prohibiting threat of use of nuclear weapons would not be necessary because, as the Austrian ambassador said, there "is already a general prohibition on the threat of use of (armed) force in the UN Charter" and that including a prohibition of threat of use of nuclear weapons in this treaty "could be seen as calling into question the validity of that more general norm."[17] Some ICAN steering group members agreed with this perspective, while others did not, and thus ICAN did not have an official position on whether to include the threat of use in the treaty.

Opinions differ on whether nuclear deterrence doctrines constitute a permanent threat of use. In their submissions to the International Court of Justice hearings in 1996, described earlier, some states that believe the use of nuclear weapons is legal in some circumstances "invoked the doctrine and practice of deterrence in support of their argument."[18] Thus, some lawyers suggested that in the nuclear ban treaty, states should commit never to threaten to use nuclear weapons, including by having nuclear weapons in their security doctrines.[19] Others argued that the threat of use could be considered to be included in a prohibition on assistance, encouragement, or inducement of other prohibited acts in the treaty.

Threat of use was not included in most draft texts of the treaty produced by the president, but it was included in the final text after intense negotiations among states. Ecuador, Cuba, and several other governments felt it was imperative to the treaty and held firm to this view throughout the negotiations.

I think the inclusion of the threat of use in the treaty is positive and has already proven useful. Since the adoption of the treaty, even some people who expressed opposition to including it in the treaty have pointed to this provision as important in the face of renewed threats of use of nuclear weapons made by the U.S. and North Korean leaders in late 2017 and early 2018. It also, as several people argued during negotiations, gets to the heart of nuclear deterrence. If this treaty is meant to be useful as a tool to help embed alternative thinking about nuclear weapons, then it needs to challenge head-on the core justifications of nuclear weapons. As outlined in chapter 1, the main argument nuclear weapon advocates use is that these weapons are not meant to be used but are meant to deter attacks by imposing an enormous threat to the survival of the attacking state and its citizens. Outlawing threat of use helps us start to unravel the idea that threatening to use nuclear weapons, through deterrence doctrines or through direct threats, is some kind of benign behavior. Far from being benign, it is an aggressive action that can lead to absolute catastrophe.

Planning and Preparations to Use Nuclear Weapons

Some states argued that planning and preparations to use nuclear weapons would be covered by a prohibition on assistance, but others thought it would be useful to specify this. Existing nuclear weapon alliances, such as NATO, and bilateral relations vary in terms of the level of cooperation and coordination in planning and preparation activities.[20] Any related activities—such as planning operations, developing policy and strategy, and constructing related infrastructure or installations are not compatible with a prohibition on nuclear weapons. In the memo it distributed to NATO members in October 2016, the U.S. government noted that many potential elements of a future nuclear weapon ban treaty, in particular those related to nuclear war planning; targeting; use or threat of use; training personnel for use; and assisting, encouraging, or inducing prohibited actions would "make it impossible" for the United States or other nuclear-armed states to "defend" their allies with nuclear weapons. The memo notes that such prohibitions would "destroy the basis for US nuclear extended deterrence."[21]

The debates over planning and preparation to use nuclear weapons got to the heart of one of the key challenges of negotiating the ban treaty: how states in military alliances such as NATO could possibly engage with the treaty. ICAN and legal experts argued that although joining the ban treaty would not require any state to exit any particular military alliance, a prohibition on the planning and preparation for use would require them to ensure that their participation in any alliance is compatible with their commitments and policies under the ban treaty.[22] This may not be as difficult politically as it seems. No mutual defense policy requires its parties to retain a nuclear posture, nor does it require the use of nuclear weapons in any circumstance.

In the end, planning and preparation were not explicitly prohibited by the treaty. ICAN and the International Committee of the Red Cross (ICRC) both advocated for its inclusion, and Indonesia led an initiative to get delegations to sign on to a statement supporting it. But opposition from Austria eventually led ICAN and the ICRC to back off so as to not hold up negotiations. Austria's position was that inclusion of these elements could give NATO members an easy excuse not to join the treaty. But those of us pushing for its inclusion believed that it would have been important to ensure that NATO members could not join the treaty without changing their policies in relation to nuclear deterrence. As with threat of use, we wanted to make sure that the treaty would actually lead to meaningful change in nuclear weapon policy and practice. That said, even though the treaty does not include a specific prohibition on this issue, activists and states' parties argued that the prohibition on assistance definitely includes planning and preparations for nuclear weapon use.

Transit

The debate on transit was particularly sticky. Nuclear weapon deployment and preparations to use nuclear weapons may entail the transit of such weapons through other countries' airspace and waters. Ending the possibility of nuclear forces to be temporarily present in or to transit through national territory and airspace could curtail some avenues in which nuclear-armed states are able to engage in nuclear brinkmanship. Prohibiting transit could also end a means by which nonnuclear-armed states can assist nuclear weapon programs, by facilitating training activities of nuclear-capable military units.

The U.S. government's memo to NATO allies specified that prohibitions related to transit, port visits, overflights, deployment, and stationing "could make it impossible to undertake . . . nuclear-related transit through territorial airspace or seas." The memo also admitted that because the United States "neither confirms nor denies the presence or absence of nuclear weapons on U.S. naval ships," such prohibitions "could make it impossible for these ships to conduct port calls in signatory countries."[23]

Public safety arguments also prohibit the transit of nuclear weapons. If transit or visitation occurs during a period of hostilities between nuclear-armed states, the country or region where the nuclear weapons are transiting through or porting could be targeted. Further, any accident involving transiting nuclear weapons could have sudden and devastating consequences for local populations, especially given the lack of transparency with respect to these movements and the policy of nuclear-armed states not to disclose the presence of nuclear weapons on their ships and aircraft.

The Caribbean Community, which has long expressed concern about transit-related accidents involving radioactive waste, supported the inclusion in the treaty of a prohibition on transit and transshipment. So did Argentina, Cuba, Ecuador, Guatemala, Iran, Kazakhstan, Peru, Nigeria, and others. But Austria argued that it was too complicated to demarcate maritime and airspace, saying that states could not be expected to know the contents of every single shipping container brought into their territories. However, as the delegation of Ecuador pointed out, the 1979 Convention on the Physical Protection of Nuclear Materials obligates states parties to "not allow the transit of its territory by land or internal waterways or through its airports or seaports of nuclear material."[24] Ecuador asked, if states can be expected to not permit the transit of nuclear material, why could they not be expected to do the same for nuclear weapons?

Similarly, as some activists pointed out, UN Security Council resolution 1540 already obligates states to "develop and maintain appropriate border controls and law enforcement efforts" and to "establish, develop, review and maintain appropriate effective national export and trans-shipment controls" in order to "detect, deter, prevent, and combat" the proliferation of "nuclear, chemical, or biological weapons and their means of delivery."[25] In this sense, including an obligation for states to not permit transit or port visits of nuclear weapons would seem to be consistent with and reinforce existing nonproliferation obligations.

The New Zealand Nuclear Free Zone, Disarmament and Arms Control Act of 1987 prohibits nuclear explosive devices within a zone that includes the land, territory, territorial waters, inland waters, and the airspace above all. A New Zealand activist with ICAN partner Disarmament and Security Centre pointed out that the law "bans the government from permitting (as opposed to requiring that it actively prevent) visits by nuclear explosive devices to internal waters." This formulation "sidesteps some of the verification and enforcement challenges raised by delegates with regard to a transit ban." Further, the government's protocols for complying with its legal obligations "also create an official paper trail, publicly accessible pursuant to freedom of information law, asserting that any visiting military ships or aircraft are not carrying nuclear weapons," which mounts "a direct challenge to the US 'neither confirm nor deny' policy regarding the presence of nuclear weapons on its ships." Arguably, the New Zealand law "thus constitutes a direct challenge to nuclear deterrence as it is practiced by the Western alliance—a point highlighted in much of the Western opposition to the New Zealand law."[26]

Interestingly, the New Zealand delegation at the negotiations was not in favor of including transit in the nuclear ban treaty. Neither were most of the countries of Southeast Asia, which are party to the Southeast Asian Nuclear Weapon Free Zone. (Thailand, however, did suggest adding a prohibition on transporting nuclear weapons.) These countries agreed with Austria that it was too difficult to include in the ban treaty. The issue was debated in open plenary meetings, addressed in civil society statements and a formal expert presentation, and became a dominant point of debate in one of the closed-door, small-room meetings established by the president of the negotiating conference, Ambassador Whyte, to reach agreement on the core prohibitions of the text. Reportedly, discussions on transit were particularly tense in these meetings, with the delegation of Ecuador even walking out at one point.[27]

In the end, transit was not in the final treaty text. Cuba and Ecuador said they will interpret transit to be covered by assistance and asked for this to be reflected in the conference records. ICAN had a position supporting transit for a time, but as with planning and preparations to use nuclear weapons, backed off officially advocating for it after the Austrian delegation complained that the issue of transit was holding up negotiations. Not all ICAN partners agreed that this was the correct response, and some continued to advocate for transit to be prohibited by the treaty. Apparently, this confused some government delegations. One diplomat interviewed for this book said that he even got questions from other delegates asking what ICAN's position on transit was, because some groups affiliated with the coalition were asking for it to be included after the campaign as a whole had stopped including it in its position papers.[28]

This dissension within ICAN is a good example of the tensions between efficiency and democracy within social movements, transnational advocacy networks, or campaigns, as discussed in chapter 5. Internal disagreements can be healthy, leading to more impactful outcomes, or can limit the coherence and effectiveness of a collective effort. This will be explored further in the next chapter.

Financing

In the midst of the nuclear ban negotiations, the Center for Public Integrity released a new installment of its report about workplace hazards at the U.S. nuclear weapon laboratories, revealing a "litany of mishaps" across the eight sites. These mishaps included workers inhaling radioactive particles, receiving electrical shocks, being burned by acid or in fires, splashed with toxic chemicals, or cut by debris from exploding metal drums.[29] Los Alamos National Laboratory, where the plutonium cores for nuclear warheads are produced, "violated nuclear industry rules for guarding against a criticality accident three times more often" in 2016 than any of the country's other twenty-three nuclear installations combined.[30]

Contractors run Los Alamos and the other nuclear weapon labs. These corporations make between $15 and 60 million a year in profit. The work of making nuclear weapons is viewed as "extremely low risk," financially speaking—"contractors commit 'virtually no financial investment,' contribute only a limited number of top executives, enjoy legal indemnification protections, and have 'relatively few' costs that are not completely reimbursed," explains the report.[31] Violating safety standards and exposing workers or local communities to risk does not seem to hamper these profits at all. Los Alamos's critical safety shortcomings have been so persistent that two years ago the National Nuclear Security Administration (NNSA) threatened to fine the lab's managing contractors more than a half million dollars. However, "In the end, the NNSA administrator decided to not to impose the fine, exemplifying what critics allege is a climate of impunity for mistakes."[32]

Before Los Alamos took over the production of the plutonium component for U.S. nuclear bombs, Rocky Flats near Denver, Colorado, was the country's sole facility for plutonium core manufacturing. This facility, which various contractors managed, had a series of serious "mishaps," including multiple fires; two major accidents involving plutonium in 1957 and 1969; on-site storage and burial of transuranic materials in leaking drums and unlined trenches contaminating the land and groundwater; radioactive contamination of nearby creeks and reservoirs; plutonium trapped in building ductwork, missing plutonium, and so-called infinity rooms deemed too highly radioactive and dangerous to enter; and the incineration of plutonium contaminated waste. Eventually, these highly dangerous incidents brought the attention of the Federal Bureau of Investigation, leading to a raid.[33] In 1989, Rocky Flats shuttered its operation, the buildings were taken down, and much radioactivity was borne away from the site—but much also remains. The first six feet of level earth were partially "cleaned" of contamination, but below that, any amount of plutonium and other radioactive and toxic materials have been left on-site.[34]

These cases clearly demonstrate that while a handful of corporations make profits from building the bomb, their workers and the surrounding public suffer immediate, direct health-related costs. Meanwhile, the rest of the world lives under the risk of environmental and humanitarian catastrophe. All of this is in keeping with the political economy-based critique of nuclear weapons explored in chapter 1. And this is the basis upon which some states and ICAN activists advocated for an explicit prohibition on financing. We argued that this would help provide clarity and guidance toward treaty implementation, which could include national prohibitions on financial or material support to public and private enterprises involved in any of the activities prohibited by the treaty.[35] As explained in chapter 4, when we were setting out the logic for the ban treaty, we believed that this could reduce the incentives for private companies to accept any work related to nuclear weapons. In this regard, the nuclear ban treaty could raise the political and economic costs of maintaining nuclear weapons. It could also help remove the influence of private interests from any decision-making processes related to nuclear weapon production and disarmament. It could also increase the societal stigmatization of nuclear weapons, including through public divestment programs.

Other states raised questions about how this would work in practice, concerned that it would be too much of a legislative burden. The treaties banning cluster munitions and landmines do not explicitly prohibit financing, but legal interpretations of those instruments suggest that financing is included under assistance.[36] Several states at the nuclear ban negotiations said they would view a prohibition on assistance in the ban treaty as having "implications for the regulation of the investment of our public monies," as Ireland put it.[37]

ICAN pushed hard for financing to be included, and many states promoted it. But as with transit and planning and preparations to use nuclear weapons, ICAN dropped it before the end of the negotiations at the urging of certain delegations that were worried that it would prevent negotiations from being concluded on time. By the end of the negotiations, there was not an explicit prohibition on financing, but a number of delegations expressed their view that it would be covered by assistance.

When it ratified the treaty, Cuba said that it interpreted the prohibition on assistance in this way, and other states are reportedly considering adopting legislation to accompany their ratifications that would explicitly prevent government funds from contributing to nuclear weapon production. "I didn't understand the logic about not including financing," said a diplomat from a country that advocated for its inclusion. "But we can always include it in our own legislation when we ratify. We have an article in our criminal code that criminalizes financing of weapons of mass destruction."[38]

Since the treaty's adoption, a number of government pension funds as well as banks and other financial institutions announced that they would divest from nuclear weapons. These include institutions within countries that did not participate in the treaty's negotiation. Many of these banks and pension funds have cited the treaty as the reason for their divestment decisions.[39] This indicates that our logic of the potential impacts of the ban on the political economy of nuclear weapons was right on the money, so to speak!

Testing

Although many governments and activists showed broad support for including a specific prohibition on nuclear weapon testing in the treaty, some delegations expressed concern that this would undermine the 1996 Comprehensive Nuclear-Test-Ban Treaty (CTBT). However, given that the CTBT has not entered into force, others argued that prohibiting testing in the ban treaty—as it has been prohibited in all of the regional nuclear weapon free zone treaties—would serve to reinforce and strengthen the norm against nuclear weapon testing.

Some states believed that a prohibition on development of nuclear weapons would include testing, though, as Ireland said, this does not preclude the need for an explicit testing prohibition. Overall, for many delegations the point of the ban treaty was to build upon and deepen global norms against the existence and maintenance of nuclear weapons. They saw a prohibition on testing as an important element of demonstrating the renunciation of nuclear weapons and were concerned that omitting testing from the prohibited activities in the ban treaty could leave a crucial gap in the treaty's core prohibitions that would be instrumental in preventing future development or reconstitution of nuclear arsenals.

In response to the initial draft treaty, which prohibited "any nuclear weapon test explosion or any other nuclear explosion," the Netherlands and Switzerland called for a direct reference to the CTBT. The Netherlands urged that the treaty also call for the ratification of the CTBT. Sweden and Mexico, on the other hand, wanted to delete the reference to testing altogether.

Cuba, meanwhile, pointed out that the CTBT doesn't prohibit testing by nonexplosive means, which has allowed subcritical and other nonexplosive forms of nuclear weapon testing to continue. Cuba argued that the nuclear ban treaty offered a chance to close this loophole by prohibiting all forms of nuclear weapon testing. Ecuador, Egypt, Iran, Singapore, Venezuela, and Viet Nam supported this.

The discussion on testing got so intense it had to be taken out of the small-room discussions on prohibitions into an even smaller room. Some delegations complained about this, saying that they weren't even aware this had happened and thus weren't part of the final days of discussion about testing. In the end, the treaty does prohibit the testing of nuclear weapons. It keeps things simple, just sticking to a prohibition on "testing" without mentioning the CTBT, or subcritical nuclear testing, or any other matters.

Most of us in ICAN were satisfied with this outcome, as were most governments. We felt that it was important to strengthen the global norm against nuclear weapon testing by including it here and do not view it as undermining or being redundant to the CTBT. In a time of rising tensions among nuclear-armed states, we need all the law against testing and every other nuclear weapon activity that we can get.

Dealing with Disarmament

All states agreed that the possession of nuclear weapons must not be allowed under this treaty, but the question persisted of whether the treaty should deal with setting out provisions for the elimination of stockpiles or whether it should leave that for later negotiations with nuclear-armed states. There was also discussion of whether nuclear-armed states had to eliminate their nuclear weapon programs before they could join the treaty—known as "destroy-and-join"—or whether they should be able to join the treaty with nuclear arsenals and reach an agreement for verified elimination with the other states' parties—known as "join-and-destroy." The parameters for each became topics of the most difficult debates during the negotiations.

In March 2017, a very small minority of states seemed to think that the ban treaty should try to address detailed disarmament processes. The first draft reflected this, simply stating that countries that have nuclear weapons need to eliminate them and cooperate with the International Atomic Energy Agency (IAEA) to verify "the completeness of its inventory of nuclear material and nuclear installations." Arrangements for this verification would be negotiated between the state in question and the IAEA within 180 days of the state joining the treaty and making a declaration of its inventory. For states that still have nuclear weapons, the treaty simply says future protocols could be negotiated "for the verified and irreversible elimination of any remaining nuclear weapon programs under strict and effective international control."

The problem with this arrangement was that it only provided for verification of the declared nuclear inventory, not for the stockpile destruction itself. That is, it would mean a state could promise to eliminate its nuclear weapons without explaining how this would happen or providing that it had. It also left out entirely the join-and-destroy option, leaving it obliquely referred to in the paragraph about dealing with such issues in a future protocol. Austria, Ireland, Mexico, New Zealand, and others argued that the treaty should be open to all states to join, including through a join-and-destroy option.

South Africa suggested that any state may join the treaty after submitting a declaration about the status of its nuclear weapon possession and other relevant activities. If a state joining the treaty possessed nuclear weapons, stationed nuclear weapons on its territory, or engaged in any planning, training, or military preparations for the use of nuclear weapons, it must cease these activities within an agreed time frame specified by the treaty. But Ireland argued, "It is not the mandate of this conference, nor is it feasible in the time available, nor is it in fact necessary, to negotiate detailed arrangements for the elimination of nuclear weapons now." It suggested that a state that is not in a position to submit a declaration that it has not manufactured, possessed, or otherwise acquired nuclear weapons could still express its intention to join the treaty. A meeting of states' parties could then establish the parameters for the process of negotiating the terms and conditions of their accession to the treaty. This might take the form of an additional instrument "to address the transparent, verifiable and irreversible elimination of their nuclear weapons programs and arsenals."[40]

The second draft of the treaty, released on 27 June, did include a join-and-destroy option.[41] But the formulation was problematic. As

New Zealand noted, the language in this section allowing nuclear-armed states to join the treaty seemed to contradict the prohibition against possession of nuclear weapons. Even so, the join-and-destroy option was stronger than the destroy-and-join option. States joining the treaty and then submitting a plan for elimination were required by this draft to do so in a time-bound, verifiable, and irreversible manner. In contrast, those joining the treaty after destroying their nuclear weapons would only have to cooperate with the IAEA on verifying the correctness and completeness of their inventory of nuclear material, not facilities or activities related to nuclear weapons.

The next text, released 30 June, further developed and somewhat improved both the destroy-and-join and join-and-destroy options.[42] This draft provided an option for states to eliminate their nuclear weapon programs and then join the treaty. This required an agreement to verify that nuclear materials and equipment were not diverted anywhere and to provide assurance on the absence of undeclared material or activities. In addition, it specified that states' parties would designate a competent international authority to verify the elimination of nuclear weapon programs, including facilities, for states choosing either the destroy-and-join or join-and-destroy option. These two processes are potentially quite different given ambiguities about the verification body. There was some discussion over whether to use the IAEA or set up a new mechanism.

The 30 June draft also set out the details of join-and-destroy. The first step was removing nuclear weapons or devices from operational status and destroying them, as well as elaborating a time-bound, irreversible, verified plan for the elimination of its entire nuclear weapon program, including related facilities. The parameters of this plan, and the manner in which it would be agreed, were flexible. As with the destroy-and-join option, any state choosing join-and-destroy must also conclude an IAEA safeguards instrument to verify their nuclear material and undergo verification of the elimination of their programs and facilities. Most participants seemed to agree that nuclear weapon programs include nuclear materials and delivery systems, though this was not made explicit in the treaty text.

The most vexing issue here was the concern that nuclear-armed states might join the treaty and try to carve out some justification for their continued possession of nuclear weapons while engaging in some long, drawn-out, ultimately inconclusive disarmament program—much as they have done already with the NPT. But to most participants in these negotiations, it seemed useful to have states sign on to the prohibition against the use, testing, and other nuclear weapon-related activities while engaging in a disarmament process. This is the approach taken by the Chemical Weapons Convention (CWC), which allows states that possess stockpiles of chemical weapons to join the treaty and eliminate those weapons and related facilities while being bound by the treaty's prohibitions and to provide, negotiate, implement, and conclude a process for verified and irreversible elimination of its program.

The next draft cleared this up. The text released 3 July—which remained the same in the final version—mandated the verification of the elimination of nuclear weapons for any nuclear-armed states using the destroy-and-join option.[43] As for join-and-destroy, a key change was that states using this option were required to "immediately" remove nuclear weapons or nuclear explosive devices from operational status and destroy them, "as soon as possible but not later than a deadline to be determined by the first Meeting of States Parties." The rest of the paragraph remained unchanged, mandating that the legally binding, time-bound plan for the verified and irreversible elimination of nuclear weapon programs be submitted within sixty days of the treaty entering into force for that particular state. The plan was not to just be accepted, though—it would be negotiated with the verification authority and then approved by other states parties.

This was a *lot* of detail and received some raised eyebrows from states and other participants that anticipated that a prohibition treaty would provide for a much simpler structure for dealing with nuclear-armed states. However, once the majority of conference participants expressed their determination to allow for a join-and-destroy approach, this level of detail became more or less inevitable. Another option, in which a space is simply carved out in this treaty to negotiate parameters like this later, punts those decisions down the road to a time when nuclear-armed states would be engaged in designing the parameters. The way the article was set up in the end, it left all of the details of the actual elimination plan to be negotiated with the particular nuclear-armed state that is joining the treaty, but it establishes a firm expectation and a framework for ensuring that these states cannot simply join the treaty and retain their nuclear weapons indefinitely or eliminate their programs without oversight and involvement of states' parties and international authorities.

This is arguably the best formulation nonnuclear-armed states could come up with in this context. It leaves the space for nuclear-armed states to come on board the treaty and negotiate with other states' parties the details of eliminating their nuclear weapons but does not leave space for them to drag it out forever. It also leaves open the possibility that nuclear-armed states could abolish nuclear weapons through other agreements or processes and then join the treaty. Either way, the nuclear ban is set up to allow everyone to come on board and to facilitate the achievement and maintenance of a nuclear weapon free world.

Dealing with Nuclear Weapon Alliances

The first draft of the treaty didn't have anything explicit to say about countries in nuclear weapon alliances. Several delegations argued that the declarations required from states joining the treaty should reflect the treaty's prohibitions—that is, they should have to declare the absence or cessation of any nuclear sharing, participation in nuclear war planning, or reliance on nuclear security doctrines. Later drafts thus specified that states joining the treaty that have nuclear weapons belonging to other countries stationed on their territories (i.e., Belgium, Germany, Italy, the Netherlands, and Turkey, all of which station U.S. nuclear weapons on their soil) have to get rid of them. Under a draft tabled on 30 June, these states would have to propose the "prompt removal" of such weapons "within a timeframe . . . to be . . . approved by the next Meeting of States Parties or Review Conference." There was no means of verification, and it said nothing about dismantling or converting nuclear weapon support facilities or providing a mechanism whereby states' parties can negotiate this.

The 3 July version of the draft treaty fixed these issues. The updated text allowed for states that have nuclear weapons in their territory to "ensure the prompt removal of these weapons," to be completed "as soon as possible but not later than a deadline to be determined by the first Meeting of States Parties." One remaining issue was that no verification mechanism was specified for how a state can show it has complied with its obligation to remove the weapons it had been hosting. The state only needs to declare that it has done so. Because such states have nuclear weapon-related facilities (for instance, the dedicated nuclear weapon storage vaults at airbases), activists recommended that a simple fix would be to require the designated authority to verify that these storage facilities have been eliminated or converted. Unfortunately, this wasn't taken up in the final draft, but meetings of states' parties could elaborate this once the treaty has entered into force.

Safeguards

Another point of contention was how the treaty would deal with safeguards to prevent diversion of nuclear material to weapons. Under the NPT, states are allowed to have fissile materials and uranium enrichment technology for the purposes of nuclear energy. The IAEA has a mandate to verify that such equipment and material are not being used to develop nuclear weapons. The IAEA has signed a safeguards agreement with every nonnuclear-armed state party to the NPT, but the five NPT nuclear-armed states are exempt. The IAEA also has something called an "additional protocol" with most NPT states' parties, providing for a stricter set of inspections. For those that subscribe to it, the additional protocol is considered to be the "safeguards standard," but it is a voluntary agreement; and several countries, including ones such as Brazil that were champions of the ban treaty, have refused to sign it as a matter of principle. As long as nuclear-armed states refuse to disarm, they do not see why they should have to sign up to even stricter nonproliferation mechanisms.

All of this history is important to understanding the debate over safeguards in the ban treaty. Some countries wanted to use the ban treaty to make the additional protocol the standard, not just in practice but in law. This perspective was driven primarily by the European states that were known as "skeptically constructive" about the ban—Switzerland and Sweden—as well as the Netherlands, which was participating in negotiations against its government's desire but at the will of its citizens and parliament. Other delegations just wanted to replicate the NPT language about safeguards agreements verbatim.

Although most states participating in these negotiations agreed that new verification mechanisms are not necessary for this treaty, most also agreed that the current IAEA safeguards system should be reinforced. There was also broad agreement on referring to the "safeguards system" rather than specific arrangements, some of which are now several decades old (e.g., the forty-five-year-old IAEA model comprehensive safeguards agreement or the twenty-year-old additional protocol). Many delegations emphasized that ban treaty negotiations were not the place to renegotiate the safeguards system, however imperfect. The Malaysian delegation argued that the ban treaty must be dynamic, retaining the ability to incorporate protocols or other instruments at a later date as necessary. It was important to allow for various options, without pre-negotiating them. As Ireland noted, "We cannot see into the future, we can only allow for it."

In the end, the treaty says that each state party shall, at a minimum, maintain its IAEA safeguards obligations that are in force at the time of entry into force of the ban treaty, "without prejudice to any additional relevant instruments that it may adopt in the future." If a state doesn't have an IAEA safeguards agreement when it joins the ban, then it needs to get one.

The safeguards provision of the treaty has come under the most criticism by states that didn't participate in the negotiations. Some of the nuclear-armed states and nuclear-supportive countries—and some think-tank folks within those countries—argued that the treaty sets up a two-tiered safeguards system.[44] In reality, as a legal adviser with the ICRC points out, the treaty takes the same approach as the NPT and even goes beyond it by requiring nuclear-armed states to have any safeguards at all. Further, she argues, "what is currently stalling progress on nuclear disarmament is not the reluctance of a small number of states to adopt [additional protocols] (for which they have no obligation), but the failure of nuclear-weapon states to implement their commitments under the NPT." In this context, differentiated safeguards standards are warranted, "considering how much easier it would be for a state having possessed nuclear weapons to conceal or re-acquire nuclear weapon-grade material and relevant technology, or to divert material to non-peaceful uses and/or to convert nuclear facilities, compared to a state that was not previously in possession of such weapons."[45]

Victim Assistance

Activists and several governments also pushed to ensure that the nuclear ban would continue the legacy of other humanitarian disarmament treaties such as the prohibitions on landmines and cluster munitions, as well as the rights of persons with disabilities, by including provisions for assistance to survivors and victims of nuclear weapon testing and use. Victim assistance in these contexts is intended to "respond to the physical and non-physical harms that victims experience" and requires states to "dismantle barriers and put in place measures to ensure victims' full and effective participation in society."[46]

The first draft treaty text recognized the responsibility of states where victims live to work toward the fulfillment of their human rights. It also called on "states in a position to do so" to provide such assistance. Some delegations such as Egypt, Iran, Cuba, Malaysia, and Viet Nam, among others, argued that the primary responsibility for victim assistance should lie with the states that created the victims in the first place. Malaysia argued that international customary law supports this, including the Articles on the Responsibility of States for Internationally Wrongful Acts. However, as other states and ICAN partners pointed out, the primary responsibility for ensuring that victims' rights are respected and needs are met lies with the country in which they live or work. This is consistent with states' sovereignty, general human rights obligations, and responsibilities toward any of their citizens.[47] Delegations of the Caribbean Community, as well as Brazil, Ghana, Holy See, Ireland, Mozambique, and the Philippines, among others, argued that the language of "being in a position" to provide assistance must be removed from the treaty.

This approach does not mean that affected states must face these issues alone or be solely responsible for addressing them. Establishing strong international cooperation and assistance provisions is crucial to helping affected states meet their obligations to victims and in order to establish responsibility for these matters among all states' party to the treaty. The provisions on victim assistance in the antipersonnel landmine and cluster munition treaties, which heavily affected states have joined, take this approach.

Human rights law requires all states to provide assistance to victims in areas under their jurisdiction or control, and ICAN as a coalition argued that this must be reflected in the treaty. This does not prevent affected states from pursuing redress for such harms through other peaceful means. ICAN also argued that the treaty should strongly encourage the states that have caused this humanitarian and environmental devastation to help affected states meet their victim assistance obligations.

Debate was minimal about what acts should be covered in the provision on victim assistance, though Mexico suggested replacing "use or testing of nuclear weapons" with "any detonation of a nuclear weapon or nuclear explosive device." Some activists argued that the provision should be expanded to also include production of nuclear weapons, given the humanitarian and environmental impacts of uranium mining, nuclear weapon production processes, and radioactive waste storage. ICAN also argued it should include other types of nuclear weapon development, including so-called minor trials that the UK government conducted in Australia. These did not involve detonations but did spread radioactive contamination. This was a minority view, however, and these activities were not included in the final treaty.

Still, in the end, affected states' parties are obligated to provide assistance to individuals affected by the use or testing of nuclear weapons. The caveat "in a position to do so" was deleted, and the treaty also requires user states as well as all other states' parties to provide international assistance to affected states' parties. The treaty also specified that a state party that has used or tested nuclear weapons "shall have a responsibility to provide adequate assistance to affected States Parties, for the purpose of victim assistance and environmental remediation."

This is extremely important for ensuring that the nuclear ban is consistent with other humanitarian disarmament initiatives of the past and future. It helps provide continuity of law banning weapons that cause indiscriminate harm and human suffering. The work done by several ICAN partners in allegiance with governments was an excellent example of our transnational network of activists and diplomats working together to make a significant difference in the treaty text.

Environmental Remediation

Work was done on environmental remediation. Many antinuclear groups and some states wanted to ensure that the treaty would address the environmental devastation that nuclear weapon use and testing caused. Although understanding that the environment cannot be completely rehabilitated from the radiation that nuclear weapons released, they argued that efforts could and should be made to decontaminate areas by separating radioactive material from the soil or preventing the spread of radiation by capping or solidifying radioactive soil. They also suggested that certain risk-reduction measures could be used to reduce human exposure to radiation, including by marking exposed areas, educating civilians about the risks, providing safe food products to affected populations, and monitoring radiation levels.[48]

Some states, including Cuba, Ecuador, Egypt, Iran, and Nigeria, argued that those responsible for causing the harm must provide for victim assistance as well as environmental remediation. Harvard Law School's Human Rights Program, which worked with ICAN during the negotiations, issued materials suggesting that, as with victim assistance, states should have the right to request and receive assistance for environmental remediation efforts. The group explained that although affected states' parties "should bear primary responsibility for victim assistance and environmental remediation in their territory, they should not have to bear this burden alone." Thus, it advocated for all states, including user states, to be obliged to provide technical, material, financial, or other forms of assistance to affected states' parties, which it argued "would not preclude affected states from seeking accountability and redress through peaceful measures separately from the nuclear weapon ban treaty."[49]

The ICRC suggested that the provision on environmental remediation should specify that each state party "shall take necessary and appropriate measures towards environmental areas so contaminated," which the Philippines, among others, supported. Switzerland suggested that it should say, "States should take steps towards environmental remediation," which Sweden supported.

This is more or less the language adopted in the final treaty, which set out that "Each State Party, with respect to areas under its jurisdiction or control contaminated as a result of activities related to the testing or use of nuclear weapons or other nuclear explosive devices, shall take necessary and appropriate measures towards the environmental remediation of areas so contaminated." As with victim assistance, other states' parties are obligated to provide assistance to this end, and states' parties that have used or tested nuclear weapons have a responsibility to provide such assistance.

Whistle-Blowers

Some activists also wanted to see protection of whistle-blowers included in the treaty. Information provided by nonstate actors, as a form of "societal verification," might assist in the detecting of undeclared nuclear weapon-related activities. In this context, WILPF argued the importance of ensuring that individuals within states' parties have the safety to report on their governments or relevant agencies they work for if they see violations of the treaty. We wanted the treaty to reflect the need for witness protection and other relevant measures, and found precedent in the field of human rights, with obligations of the International Criminal Court to protect witnesses.[50] In the end, this wasn't included in the treaty text, but meetings of states' parties could consider it in the future.

Establishing a "Treaty Body"

Some other disarmament treaties have "treaty bodies"—units that assist states with implementation, organize meetings of states' parties, encourage ratification, and educate the public about the treaties. ICAN and some states thought this would be useful for the nuclear ban treaty, but others pointed out the costs associated with such bodies and the difficulties that other treaty bodies were encountering in meeting their budgets each year. The final treaty text did not include a treaty body, but a meeting of states' parties could establish it in the future if it decides to do so.

Entry into Force

A treaty usually requires a certain number of states to ratify it before it can enter into force or become international law binding on its states' parties. The first draft suggested 40 ratifications would be necessary. Sweden wanted 100, then suggested 80. The eventual compromise reached was 50, so that the treaty would enter into force 90 days after the fiftieth ratification is deposited at the United Nations.

Withdrawal

A big fight over withdrawal only broke out on the penultimate day of the negotiations. The first draft stated that states' parties would have the right to withdraw "if it decides that extraordinary events, related to the subject matter of this Convention, have jeopardized the supreme interests of its country." The draft provision specified that the withdrawing state would have to give three months' notice, but that if the country is engaged in armed conflict after the three-month period, the provisions of the treaty would still bind the state.

ICAN and others argued that the treaty should not contain a withdrawal clause. Several delegations, including Ecuador, Palestine, and South Africa, agreed, and many others such as Brazil, Guatemala, Mexico, Mozambique, and New Zealand expressed concern with the withdrawal clause. As academic Nick Ritchie argued, the concept of withdrawing in order to develop nuclear weapons is "incongruous" with the treaty itself. "The very logic of the nuclear ban treaty delegitimizes the sovereign prerogative to understand security in terms of nuclear weapons," and a withdrawal clause dilutes that message.[51] The UN Charter does not have a withdrawal clause, because its negotiators understood the necessity of the organization's permanence. Similarly, the delegitimization of nuclear weapons is not meant to be temporary— "it must be, and be seen to be, a permanent and expanding process."

No multilateral disarmament treaty concluded in the past twenty-four years has included a reference to withdrawal in the case of "extraordinary events [that] have jeopardized the supreme interests" of the state party. The withdrawal clauses for the humanitarian-focused Mine Ban Treaty and Convention on Cluster Munitions do not include references to extraordinary events and supreme interests. This formulation also does not appear in older humanitarian-focused treaties, such as the Geneva Conventions, or in human rights treaties that contain withdrawal provisions. Thus, ICAN and several states argued that its inclusion in the ban treaty would run counter to the principles and goals of the treaty as set forth in the draft preamble. It would send the message that "supreme interests" override the treaty.

Many problems are associated with including a withdrawal provision based on a principle of "supreme interests" in the ban treaty. First, this principle is embedded in a regressive notion of state security. How would acquiring or using weapons to commit genocide contribute to a state's security? Second, the notion of supreme interests is completely subjective. A state may essentially decide for itself what constitutes extraordinary events or its supreme interests. Third, the principle runs counter to the humanitarian purpose of this treaty, which is to prohibit nuclear weapons for all on the basis of their catastrophic consequences.

Removing the withdrawal provision would not have explicitly indicated that withdrawal was prohibited, but instead would have meant that the Vienna Convention on the Law of Treaties would have applied. This, in turn, would have meant that states wanting to withdraw would need to prove that the intention of states' parties was to allow withdrawal from the treaty. This is an extremely strong position against withdrawal, as that may have been difficult to prove. Another "fix" would have been to just have a simple withdrawal provision that did not say anything about supreme interests or extraordinary events and just reflected the right to withdraw, period. ICAN also suggested that the treaty could state that any withdrawal from the ban treaty shall be treated as constituting a threat to international peace and security and shall lead to an emergency meeting of the treaty's states' parties and, if required, the UN General Assembly.

But Austria and Sweden argued that retaining the withdrawal clause as written in the first draft would make the treaty more "credible." Algeria, Egypt, and Iran also wanted to keep the withdrawal provision as it was.

Even though the initiative to remove or improve the withdrawal provision did not achieve this result, debate over withdrawal demonstrated without a doubt that the intent of negotiating states was that this treaty was to serve as a categorical rejection of nuclear weapons, and that no "supreme interests" or "extraordinary events" could ever override that. The brilliant appeals from Palestine and South Africa are in the public domain, as is the clear majority support they garnered from states in the room. Also on record is the enthusiastic applause that broke out when the conference president acknowledged this majority view and moved to remove the offending paragraphs from the text. She had support to do so; the minority of Algeria, Bangladesh, Egypt, Iran, the Philippines, Sweden, and a few others caused her to try to get agreement on the text as it stood. In the end, the states calling for the removal of the withdrawal provision let it pass, making their priority the adoption of the treaty as a whole.

Relationship with Other Treaties

Since the process to ban nuclear weapons began, its supporters have had to defend against accusations of undermining or even destroying the NPT. Such accusations are not based on any real risk or challenge to the NPT regime. But the language in the first draft of the treaty was problematic. It asserted that the ban treaty "does not affect the rights and obligations" of NPT states' parties. Article 30(2) of the Vienna Convention on the Law of Treaties notes that, "When a treaty specifies that it is subject to, or that it is not to be considered as incompatible with, an earlier or later treaty, the provisions of the other treaty prevail." Our concern was that, although the nuclear ban would be complementary to the NPT, the NPT's provisions must not prevail over the ban treaty's. One issue that several states raised during negotiations was that the nuclear-armed states would try to argue that their (erroneous) assertion that they have a "right" to possess nuclear weapons under the NPT would override the ban treaty's prohibition of these weapons.

One option was to delete the article referencing the NPT, as some states such as Egypt suggested. Another was to follow Malaysia's suggestion to use the formulation from article 26 (1) of the Arms Trade Treaty, which reads, "The implementation of this Treaty shall not prejudice obligations undertaken by States Parties with regard to existing or future international agreements, to which they are parties, where those obligations are consistent with this Treaty." This formulation was designed to assuage any concerns that the ban undermines the NPT while not subjecting the ban to the NPT's problematic elements or interpretations.

The Netherlands, on the other hand, called for stronger language to subordinate the ban treaty to the NPT. It felt that the draft did not make it clear as to how the new treaty would engage with nuclear-armed states.

In the end, the negotiators went with Malaysia's suggestion, taking language directly from the Arms Trade Treaty as outlined above.

Recognition of Gender Dimensions

WILPF and the delegation of Ireland worked hard to ensure that the treaty included language on the gendered impacts of nuclear weapons and the importance of gender diversity in nuclear disarmament. The first draft did reflect that ionizing radiation harms women and girls disproportionately but did not sufficiently reflect the myriad of ways in which the production, testing, and use of nuclear weapons impact women. Health effects from ionizing radiation are acute, but more broadly, women are also more susceptible physically to absorb radiation and socially to be exposed to it. Also, the social stigma around exposure to radiation has uniquely affected women and girls in some ways.[52]

In addition, we argued that it was important for the ban to highlight not just the physical impacts of nuclear weapons on women's health but also the need for women's effective and equal participation in disarmament forums. Building on UN Security Council resolution 1325 on women, peace and security,[53] UN General Assembly resolution 71/56 on women, disarmament, non-proliferation and arms control,[54] and the 2017 Non-Proliferation Treaty chair's factual summary (which encouraged states to actively support the participation of women in their delegations and through support for sponsorship programs),[55] we insisted that the nuclear ban treaty must say something—and do something—about the serious underrepresentation of women in nuclear disarmament.

The final text recognizes that the catastrophic consequences of nuclear weapons "have a disproportionate impact on women and girls, including as a result of ionizing radiation"—which allows space for the consideration of other impacts. It also recognizes "that the equal, full and effective participation of both women and men is an essential factor for the promotion and attainment of sustainable peace and security," and expresses commitment "to supporting and strengthening the effective participation of women in nuclear disarmament." This is the first time such language has been included in a weapons-related treaty and, as such, breaks barriers for pursuing better gender diversity in the future.

Of course, as explored in chapter 1, increasing women's participation in nuclear weapon negotiations or policy making is not sufficient to significantly challenge or change the political and economic systems that sustain these weapons. Much more is needed in terms of diversity: of sex, gender identify, and sexual orientation, as well as of race, ethnicity, class, ability, and other aspects that bring diverse views into the nuclear weapon debate. This is essential if we are to seriously take on the dominant narratives about what nuclear weapons are for and who credibly gets to speak about them. With more diversity in disarmament, U.S. Ambassador Haley's comments about how her "womanly concerns" are not realistic for her job as a representative of her state would have been revealed for the patriarchal nonsense that they are.

Recognition of Indigenous Peoples' Suffering

As also explored in chapter 1, due to racist and colonial policies and attitudes, Indigenous communities have borne the brunt of nuclear experimentation. There have been well over two thousand explosive nuclear weapon tests, as well "minor trials," at more than sixty locations around the world since 1945. Today, these sites continue to face persistent radioactive contamination. The tests have also irradiated downwind and downstream communities, increasing the risk that their people will one day develop cancers and other chronic diseases as a result. In many cases, those residing near test sites have been permanently displaced from their homes. Uranium mining, nuclear weapon production facilities, and nuclear waste storage sites have also historically impacted Indigenous communities disproportionately, due to targeting of politically disenfranchised communities.

As Sue Coleman-Haseldine, a test survivor from South Australia, testified to the nuclear ban treaty negotiations, "Aboriginal people were still living close to the test sites and were told nothing about radiation. Some communities were so contaminated that most people developed acute radiation sickness. High rates of cancer were eventually docu-mented in the 16,000 test workers, but no studies were done of Aborigi-nal people and others living in areas of fallout, many of whom were even more highly exposed."[56]

Coleman-Haseldine, other survivors, and several ICAN activists thus pushed for the treaty to recognize the disproportionate impact of nuclear weapons on Indigenous communities around the world. As with gendered impacts, we argued, recognition of the impacts on Indigenous communities is vital for ensuring that victims and survivors are afforded appropriate assistance. It is also essential for understanding their place in the nuclear legacy and for further motivating the prohibition and elimi-nation of nuclear weapons. Nick Ritchie also argued that the stigmatiza-tion of nuclear weapons, one of the core objectives of the nuclear ban treaty, "requires explicit recognition of the rights transgressed through nuclear weapon practices and the gendered and racial effects of these transgressions."[57]

In support of this, thirty-five Indigenous groups issued a joint statement reminding delegates that "Governments and colonial forces exploded nuclear bombs on our sacred lands," and that "Our land, our sea, our communities, and our physical bodies carry this legacy with us now, and for unknown generations to come."[58] The statement urged delegates to acknowledge this harm and to do everything in their power to ensure that no one else suffers as they have. The statement was coordinated by ICAN Australia and presented to the negotiating con-ference by Karina Lester, a Yankunytjatjara-Anangu second-generation nuclear test survivor from South Australia, whose father, Yami, had been blinded by British testing.[59] ICAN partners including WILPF and Mines Action Canada also pushed for the recognition of the disproportionate impact on Indigenous communities.[60]

In the final reading, the preamble recognizes "the disproportionate impact of nuclear-weapon activities on Indigenous peoples." Without the dedicated, active participation of First Nations people throughout the process, from the humanitarian impact conferences, to the open-ended working group, to the ban negotiations, this might not have been possible.

THE FINAL TEXT

As noted earlier, these were not the only points of contention of the treaty negotiation. There was a wide debate over many elements of the preamble, the institutional arrangements, and more. This is just a snapshot of a few of the key debates to give a taste of what was negotiated. How it was negotiated is another piece of this story. The next chapter will look at the process itself, leaning on interviews with diplomats, activists, and other participants in an effort to relay the thoughts and feeling of those most intimately involved in the negotiations about the process and the treaty itself. But what is most important here is the final text adopted.

The Treaty on the Prohibition of Nuclear Weapons (TPNW) is a carefully crafted, strong piece of international law oriented toward changing the landscape of nuclear weapons forever.[61] It may not be perfect, and it certainly has come under critique in particular by those who did not participate in the process. But it does what we need a treaty such as this to do and it creates space that did not exist before for achieving nuclear disarmament.

Very importantly, the development of this treaty represented a breaking point with the status quo, with subservience to the powerful, with the patriarchal world order of massive nuclear violence. This treaty prohibits the policies and practices that sustain nuclear weapons, including those related to nuclear "deterrence." Whatever is not explicitly prohibited in its provisions is implicitly prohibited through its spirit. It outlaws all aspects of nuclear weapon activities, from development to use and everything in between. It will help prevent future risks to humanity and will address the damage that past use and testing of these weapons has caused. It will affect even those states that did not participate in these negotiations. Nuclear-armed and nuclear-alliance states may not have been in the room, but they will be challenged by the new reality this treaty created. Their legacy of radioactive violence will be confronted with a future of vibrant political, legal, economic, and social opposition.

Above all else, the final product negotiated in 2017 asks of all governments the fundamental question: are they for nuclear weapons or against them? This question has, over the years, been drained of its stark vibrancy, black and white muddled to gray. This was deliberate. Concepts such as nuclear deterrence replaced the horrors of burning flesh, flattened buildings, and generations of cancers. Governments wanting to support their nuclear-armed allies did not want to assert in a resolute way where they stood—it made them uncomfortable, knowing how their publics might react and how their positions on nuclear weapons were incompatible with their stated commitments to peace, democracy, and the rule of law. The TPNW brought all of this into focus. Its underlying questions are: what kind of world do we want to live in? What kind of world do we want to actively build, against the interests of the structures of power that rely on violence, intimidation, fear, and hate to sustain themselves?

As the next chapter seeks to demonstrate, an alternative way to conduct international relations exists—not through violence and threats, but through cooperation, negotiation, and compromise. The negotiation process for the TPNW was by no means perfect. The activist campaign was not always as strong as it could have been. But this process sets a high standard for how governments, activists, academics, survivors, and international organizations can work together to create meaningful change in the world and provides insights for how the next process could be even stronger.

9

GETTING OUR BAN ON, PART TWO

The How

Activism against nuclear weapons has been fierce and determined for more than seventy years. But it wasn't until a few courageous diplomats in partnership with a group of activists decided to take a leap into the unknown that we managed to finally develop international law prohibiting these weapons of mass destruction. Working together, we foregrounded our actions in resistance and hope. Resistance to the pressure from nuclear-armed and nuclear-supportive states. Resistance to attitudes of cynicism and of defeatism. Resistance to staying the course, being placated, being told to be patient, that the "important" countries will handle this matter. Hope that change is possible. Hope that by working together we can achieve something that can disrupt some of the most powerful, heavily militarized structures and doctrines in the entire world. Hope that a shared sense of humanity could prevail against all odds. In his closing remarks to the negotiating conference, Irish Foreign Minister Simon Coveney quoted Seamus Heaney, noting that "hope is not optimism, which expects things to turn out well, but something rooted in the conviction that there is a good worth working for."[1]

This more or less unique context and way of working together meant that from the beginning to the end of the negotiations, the atmosphere was mostly constructive and always dynamic. Delegations supported and built off each other's suggestions, engaging in debate about the merits of particular proposals. It was more open and relaxed than most other UN conferences; activists were welcomed in most of the meetings, and most delegations were clearly genuinely committed and excited to be doing this work. Still, there were at times tensions between governments, between governments and the activists, academics, and international organizations providing input to the negotiations, and within the activist campaign. At the end of the day, we are human beings, imperfect creatures with individual personalities and varying perceptions. But what held us together was knowing that we all wanted the same thing: a ban on nuclear weapons.

This chapter goes through some of the process of the negotiations, looking at how deliberations were structured, who was engaged, the key challenges, the dynamics of gender and regional diversity, and how all of the various actors managed their relationships. It is not a story of unadulterated glory but, rather, of real life, including the inevitable ups and downs. It is told through the perspective of those involved, based on interviews with diplomats, activists, and other participants. People threw themselves into this process, which comes across clearly. Those engaged in this work truly cared about what they were doing. This can be gleaned from reading the treaty, but it also shines through in these interviews. These people did not just make a treaty—making this treaty transformed them.

HOW IT ALL WENT DOWN

Governments took different approaches to the negotiations, especially in the beginning. Some seemed to approach this treaty as they did UN General Assembly resolutions—as a text to set out their frustrations and their general commitments to disarmament. Others wanted it to break new ground and focus on specifics. Some clearly wanted to have a concrete impact on the activities and policies that facilitate the maintenance of nuclear weapons, whereas others seemed to hedge away from that objective, not wanting to add too many elements that would necessitate change in their own or other states' behavior.

These competing agendas meant that the draft text was pulled in various directions. This is bound to happen in negotiations, especially in a setting with well over one hundred participating governments. This was an incredibly open and inclusive negotiating process, but that meant that states that truly wanted this treaty to have an impact on current practices and help lead to the elimination of nuclear weapons needed to figure out, together, how to advance the text in this direction.

Most of the negotiations took place in an open setting, with full participation of states and activist groups. These meetings took place in a large conference room, with seats for about three diplomats per delegation and a large balcony for civil society, which had full access to the floor so that activists could visit diplomats at their desks if needed. NGOs, the Red Cross, academics, and others were able to intervene, table working papers, and monitor discussions alongside government delegations.

Toward the end of the negotiations, however, the president of the negotiations appointed facilitators for working groups on different aspects of the draft text. She chaired consultations on article 1 (the prohibitions), while representatives of Ireland, Chile, and Thailand facilitated work on articles 2–5 (dealing with nuclear weapons and safeguards), 6–8 (positive obligations and international cooperation and assistance), and 9–21 (institutional arrangements for the treaty), respectively. Other small groups to discuss prohibitions on transit and testing were also briefly established.

Most governments were happy with this approach. Trying to discuss everything in open plenary meetings was proving tricky, and to some it felt like we were going in circles debating similar points. The smaller discussions provided the opportunity for states to interact more freely with each other to talk through particular issues and come up with compromise language. The only problem was, these meetings were held in smaller rooms, and activists were not allowed. It wasn't just ICAN campaigners and other activists locked out—representatives of the ICRC, the UN Institute for Disarmament Research, and academics from Princeton, Harvard, York, and Pace Universities that were participating actively also weren't allowed in. It also meant that small government delegations with only one or two people had to choose which discussions to be a part of, whereas bigger delegations were able to send people to all of the meetings.

To follow what was going on, those of us outside the rooms had to rely on friendly delegations to keep us informed and share draft texts with us. Given the strong relationships of trust ICAN campaigners had built over the years with diplomats from many countries, this wasn't very difficult. A number of delegations sought the views of some of us outside the room, discussing the thrust of the debates with us and considering our input on the text. Still, it was frustrating to not be part of the discussions and able to intervene with our expertise in the moment of discussion. At various points, we resorted to WhatsApp diplomacy—diplomats in the room were texting some of us who were waiting in the hallways and coffee lounge, and we tried our best to feed into the discussions in real time that way.

Despite these complications, the small-room discussions did result in resolutions to tricky issues, and ultimately, a much stronger treaty. Most diplomats interviewed for this book said that the facilitators that the president appointed to take on pieces of the text were really good at bringing people together, listening to their views, and helping them find necessary compromises. Some irritation surfaced that the small-group discussion on testing happened without notice, and most states weren't invited to participate. Otherwise, participants found these meetings effective and crucial to getting a treaty as strong as we did.

"The exclusion of NGOs from the small room negotiations, especially since civil society was so instrumental in getting negotiations going, was of course difficult," said one diplomat. "But it's the price of agreement with sticky delegations, and the small room negotiations worked well. The big, open meetings could get quite difficult and tense. People found it hard to be heard. For example, some of the open negotiations around withdrawal and procedural issues were quite tough. But some of the small groups had very good facilitators and participants that strove to reach strong outcomes."[2] Another noted that although activists were upset about being excluded from some of the discussions, "some states are critical of their involvement at all, because NGOs have no treaty obligations or accountability." But, he said, the level of activist participation at these negotiations "was more dynamic," it "broke new ground." This should send "a message to others that there could be more flexibility for civil society participation."[3]

Despite these positive feelings about much of the process, some participants expressed concerns. "The negotiations were not a highlight" of the process to get the ban, said one diplomat ruefully. "I wish they were. But there were internal fights, and the dynamics in the room, including with the presidency, were not always positive."[4] Others also expressed dissatisfaction with the leadership of the president and her team. They "leaned heavily on the Secretariat, which is dangerous because they're not always sensitive to process," argued one person.[5] Some participants were unsettled by the process the president had for inviting certain delegations to her mission on the weekends, then talking to them individually instead of collectively as a group. A few felt that the president's team would seek advice widely but then sometimes it seemed that they would just go with the advice of whomever they had spoken to last. Others felt that members of the president's team did not listen to advice when drafting new pieces of treaty text and would even ignore agreements reached among delegations in the conference rooms, resulting in confusion when new drafts were published. "Negotiations were very confusing in the beginning," said one delegate. "The president wanted to make sure it was technically sound but involved too many experts with negative views of the treaty. Our position was that we were here to negotiate not with the UN Secretariat or with experts, but each other," he said.[6]

Others, however, thought the president did a great job. "It was a great choice of chair, we were very supportive," said one diplomat. "And the choice was vindicated—she showed great talent in choosing her facilitators for the small room negotiations. It was a strength of hers to know who could do this work."[7] A few participants questioned whether some of the criticism against the president might have been rooted in sexism, though others felt that this was not part of the dynamic.

It is important to note that women have not led many intergovernmental disarmament processes. A woman chaired the NPT Review Conference for the first time in 2015. In seventy-four years of the UN General Assembly, only one woman has ever presided over the disarmament committee's work. Thus, it is not something people are necessarily accustomed to, whether or not they recognize that consciously. Ambassador Whyte clearly felt the responsibility of the task at hand in chairing the nuclear ban negotiations and acknowledged her recent initiation to the subject matter. She tried to consult widely, though as indicated above, not everyone was impressed with her methods. Managing any process of this magnitude is a difficult undertaking. And there were real challenges in the process, including in terms of how the president and her team handled closing the small-room meetings to activists, in addition to the other issues noted above. Despite this, however, most participants seemed satisfied overall with the process.

Some said it was the most transparent negotiations in which they had ever been involved. "It shone a light in the corners—no one could hide."[8] One participant described a "precarious consensus" during negotiations. Everyone "advocated for their favorite approach," but generally the attitude was good.[9] Several felt the pressure was already off when it came to the negotiations, because the discussions at the open-ended working group in 2016 had set them up so well.[10] Others agreed that having a common project was helpful. "We didn't really have anyone to fight with during the negotiations."[11]

The only delegation participating that was definitely not part of the common project was the Netherlands. "The Dutch were interesting to deal with during the negotiations," said one participant. "They had some really outrageous positions on some things, but then in the smaller working groups would occasionally make a sensible point."[12] Among other things, the Netherlands argued that the ban treaty must be compatible with the obligations of NATO *as a nuclear alliance*. It was clear to everyone else participating in these negotiations that that would be clearly unacceptable for a nuclear weapon ban treaty. There could not be space for a state to join the treaty and continue justifying the potential use of nuclear weapons for its security. As Algeria's delegation clearly stated during negotiations, the ban treaty should explicitly reject the role of nuclear weapons on behalf of anyone's security, whether in national, regional, or international doctrines.

Most of the Netherlands' interventions focused on its ability to retain a nuclear deterrence doctrine, its insistence that the ban treaty be subservient to the NPT, and the importance of having a full verification and safeguards system. But although it was the most widely removed from the otherwise "precarious consensus," the Dutch weren't alone in feeling slightly outside of things.

A few other delegations also felt, at times, removed from the common project. Sweden and Switzerland seemed frustrated during the negotiations, particularly on points related to safeguards and nuclear testing. They were also concerned with the treaty's relationship with the NPT, though their positions on any of these matters weren't as extreme as the Netherlands'. Argentina and Colombia also raised sticky questions and put forward the same proposals repeatedly, noted some participants. And Singapore also raised some hard-line positions, particularly regarding transit. These later cases are interesting given otherwise strong regional support for an effective prohibition treaty. Views differed about what motivations these countries might have for objecting to certain prohibitions or pushing for things that seemed more compatible to a nuclear-supportive government's position. Some considered their relationship with the United States to be a possible factor.

But for the most part, the majority of delegations were clearly eager to develop a strong treaty. One of their main concerns in this regard was a lack of technical expertise available during the negotiations. In particular, this was a criticism of the International Atomic Energy Agency's refusal to participate due to pressure from the nuclear-armed states. The result was that the only guiding authority on issues such as safeguards and verification was provided by government delegations. "We could have benefited from having the IAEA involved in the negotiations," said one delegate. "But if we're honest with ourselves, the current verification system isn't adequate. So at least we didn't do worse or undermine or preclude anything."[13]

Interviewees also had mixed reactions about the core group. This included states that had been key drivers to getting the ban to the point of negotiations—Austria, Brazil, Ireland, Mexico, Nigeria, and South Africa were the ones identified at the time of the negotiations as making up the core group, though other countries such as Thailand and New Zealand came to be loosely considered to be part of a broader, "core group plus." Some participants felt that the core group had too much to say in terms of the treaty's content; others felt they were insufficiently coordinated to be effective; and some core group members felt they didn't have enough control over the process. "There was a core group for the cluster munition process," which had "a rigorous process of decision making," said someone who participated in both processes. "There really wasn't the same for the nuclear ban treaty. The core group was frustrated during negotiations. There wasn't really a core group or a champion state" taking the lead and guiding the process.[14]

For others, though, the core group was *too* involved. "The main problem with the process was the way, to a certain point, that the core group was seen as owners of the process," said one delegate. "The core group is important, but process should have been left more to interplay of all states involved in the negotiations." He felt that certain members of the core group even tried to shut down discussion on certain issues. "I was surprised by the coordinated opposition to taking language from the Chemical Weapons Convention [in relation to planning and preparations to use nuclear weapons], for example. It seemed like a coordinated effort to silence certain delegations," he said.[15]

This wasn't a feeling that those in the core group shared, however. Some representatives of governments involved in that grouping felt cut out of things. One participant argued that the problem was that the president didn't work enough with the core group. "We had concerns with early drafts," said one diplomat. "We talked it over and the president realized she needed to work with the core group more, after which it got better."[16]

Although some delegates were skeptical about how and why certain language was put forward in the early drafts, most seemed comfortable with the process of having debates followed by new drafts. A few, however, would have preferred a different method. "I would have preferred a rolling text and open process—put the treaty on the screen and let us work with it," said one delegate. "The final text should never be a Chair's text. A closed text is more efficient, but not democratic. It's always a trade-off."[17] But this is frequently the quickest (or slowest) way to kill a process, others argued, noting that it not only makes negotiations crawl to a grinding halt but does not necessarily mean you will have any more agreement on the outcome. Still, this point about efficiency versus democracy is an important one, and was something with which activists also had to contend.

One of the most difficult dynamics of the negotiations from our side was the division within ICAN over our positions on key issues. As described earlier, steering group members and other partners were torn on the prohibitions on threat of use, transit, planning and preparations to use nuclear weapons, and financing. ICAN never officially supported the inclusion of threat of use, even though some steering group members and many partner organizations did. On the other three issues, ICAN officially supported their inclusion but backed off in advocating for them after some core group diplomats told some individuals in ICAN that these issues were holding up negotiations.

ICAN's steering group and staff team faced several challenges in how to make decisions about policy on the fly. One was how to include views from coalition partners that weren't part of the limited-membership steering group. Each morning we held campaigner meetings open to all partners, but not all of the steering group or staff showed up to these meetings, which meant not everyone was there to hear their views, and certain steering group members had to relay these perspectives in the steering group meetings. Further, as some ICAN activists noted, these morning campaign briefs were mostly focused on the day's assignments: who to lobby about what, updates from the day before, ideas about what was working and where we needed more capacity or more information.

This element of our work was extremely efficient. ICAN set up regional leads with teams of campaigners willing to go around the room and talk to respective delegations advocating for certain priority issues each day. We also had a media and communications team recording and documenting and searching for opportunities to talk to the press about what was happening, as well as sharing the proceedings with the world over social media. These morning meetings set the tone of a collaborative campaign working efficiently and effectively within the limited resources we had. It brought people from around the world together as part of a team, and it fostered a community with a lot of laughter, joy, and integrity.

At the same time, at certain moments ICAN still suffered from a top-heavy approach to making decisions about key policy points. The steering group and staff team didn't effectively use the campaign meetings to make decisions about policy. To some extent, this was necessary to prevent hours-long debates and running around in circles. But we could have done more to ask and receive input on key points in a way that would feed into decision making without necessarily slowing it down, as discussed in chapter 5.

We also could have done a better job setting up things in advance. Although we didn't know exactly what the stickiest issues would be, we weren't prepared for how to deal with opposition to some of our core asks, such as financing and transit. ICAN as a coalition caved very early on this, while some partners continued pushing for it. Transit was not surprising, as a minority in the steering group opposed including it in the first place. But the entire steering group and staff team categorically endorsed financing, and some of us were really surprised when certain steering group members informed us that we'd been asked to back off by one of our key government allies. We had a vote on some of these decisions, which was unusual for how the steering group and staff team operated. We had for a long time operated on the basis of rough consensus, described in chapter 5. We had voted perhaps only once or twice since the steering group was established in its current form around 2012. During negotiations, we voted on almost everything.

The phenomenon of activists bending to a government's will is not altogether unusual, of course. In her September 2007 assessment of the activist landscape, ICAN cofounder Felicity Ruby argued that "proximity to power in a closer relationship with governments can seriously dilute NGOs' political resolve."[18] The analysis of social movements and institutional pressure explored in chapter 2 is highly relevant here. What we faced during negotiations is a common challenge that all activists must face: stand one's ground and experience pressure from your allies, or make compromises to maintain the relationships. The "authority trap" that we examined earlier was certainly a factor here: as ICAN grew in size and credibility, some people in the leadership team seemed to begin prioritizing perceived access and influence with governments over pushing for exactly what we as activists wanted out of the treaty. An additional problem for ICAN was that not everyone was privy to the information necessary to make the decisions. There was a lack of transparency from the steering group and staff team to the wider campaign, and even *within* the steering group and staff team. This made it difficult for everyone to understand what was happening, where the pressure was coming from, or what the real motivations were for shutting down advocacy on certain aspects of the treaty.

Another interesting thing was that ICAN had an internal fight about victim assistance and environmental remediation. Two organizations in the steering group were concerned that we were giving survivors the wrong impression. They worried we were suggesting that this would be a mechanism through which they could claim compensation for the use or testing of nuclear weapons. These organizations were also wary that calling for environmental remediation meant we were suggesting it was possible for an area to be cleaned after a nuclear attack, which is not completely possible. It took months to resolve these concerns. ICAN partners outside the steering group, most of whom desperately wanted

ICAN to call for victim assistance and environmental remediation, were really confused by this, and it created some friction and overall concern with the leadership body. Fortunately, after much discussion we were able to have unanimous support to advocate for both, though certain folks were still a bit uneasy at how it would be interpreted later.

So, although some government delegates were feeling that the negotiations were particularly acrimonious, so too were some of us in ICAN. It wasn't how most of us had anticipated things playing out. We made too many assumptions, perhaps, about being on the same page about critical issues. We had not anticipated pressure from friendly governments about our positions, and those of us who did not want to bend to that pressure did not anticipate that our colleagues would put government interest ahead of doing what the rest of us saw as our job—holding the line and advocating for the strongest treaty possible.

All of this demonstrated a clear division in understanding the role of activists. For some, it seemed to become primarily about appearing as credible negotiating partners, willing to compromise to achieve a result that our strongest allies desired. Those pushing for that approach felt that if we deliberated for too long on particular issues or refused to drop things we wanted in the treaty, we would hold up negotiations and perhaps risk the entire treaty. For others, we saw our role as providing cover for those governments pushing for the strongest language possible, so that they didn't come across as outrageous. We saw our job as activists as being to advocate for the treaty we wanted, rather than the one we thought we could get—leaving those compromises to the governments.

This is an important lesson and is not meant to suggest that we failed as a coalition. Coalitions take a lot of work and care. ICAN is composed of hundreds of partner organizations around the world as well as a steering group and staff team. The differences in perspectives of organizations and individuals involved made for a strong debate at times, which ultimately does not have to become divisive. ICAN is not a homogenous voice; we are strong *because* of our diversity of views and perspectives and experiences. Occasional difference of opinion or deviation of approach is not weakness—such things often lead to stronger outcomes, testing consensus and ensuring proper scrutiny of different perspectives.

At the end of the day, ICAN activists all rallied behind the treaty as a remarkable achievement, as something strong that we could all be proud of, and that did the job of comprehensively prohibiting nuclear weapons and setting the stage for their elimination in the future. Whatever reservations we had about the process of achieving it, we were thrilled to have been part of it.

We also made the most of our collaboration with diplomats that we had built up through the cross-regional retreats and regional meetings held over the past few years, as described in chapter 4. Several diplomats said that the cooperation with activists was essential to the treaty's success. For diplomats with big portfolios, it's hard to be an expert. ICAN partners provided analysis and substance that many delegations relied on to inform their positions. Almost all of my interviews with diplomats for this book emphasized the importance of NGO studies, papers, and presentations accompanying the political process as critical to helping build the narrative of the ban. "The concepts of massive nuclear violence being a social issue, of resolute normative leadership being all of our responsibilities, and the importance of changing the discourse towards humanitarian impacts" made it clear that we weren't after utopia but were working within real life. "It made us question our own approaches," said one diplomat, who also said that some of WILPF's editorials through the ban process "really called us to action. You gave us a sense of being equipped with all of the information, arguments, and moral authority we needed to make this happen."[19] She spoke about feeling compelled to work in overdrive during key moments of the process, staying up late and getting up early to make sure that she was prepared each day at conferences.

Some diplomats indicated they learned from ICAN activists how to pay attention to personalities—how they fit together, how to interpret advice, when to move or not move on information.[20] Sometimes, one diplomat said, she would text activists in the middle of the night for advice on certain language.[21] Another diplomat similarly said that the "magic" about this campaign "was its responsiveness."[22] Activists didn't just try to do their own thing: they cooperated with governments to sign up countries to the Humanitarian Pledge, to joint statements, and to resolutions, and they built a network around the world with connections to many governments.

A representative of one government said this was the closest he's ever been to NGOs in any initiative, where diplomats and activists were trying to find solutions together. We had a "fantastic team" in ICAN, he said, describing how his delegation was able to pool human resources with the campaigners. "It was more like a team extension than a foreign entity," he said.[23] Another described the effects of ICAN as being a "force multiplier" when working in concert with government representatives.[24] At critical moments, diplomats and ICAN activists would work the room separately, reinforcing each other's advocacy from government and civil society perspectives. This meant that delegations were hearing from local campaigners from their region or country as well as a cross-regional set of governments leading the process. Each gave credibility to the other and boosted one another's spirits. One participant said she holds ICAN up as a model for collaboration. "You always pushed us to go further," she said, but it never felt like you were pushing anything down our throats; we were working as partners.[25] "Working with ICAN was like having two hands on the potter's wheel," agreed another participant. "But that doesn't mean you [activists] didn't poke us once in a while."[26]

There was not always complete synergy, of course, between diplomats and activists, even if both wanted the same goal. Some felt that ICAN activists disparaged the NPT too much, or that they made showing up the nuclear-armed states too much of an objective. These strategies didn't work for every country. But, some diplomats from unsupportive countries still acknowledged the importance of activists in advancing the agenda. "When we can ally with civil society groups, it's a powerful force," said one such diplomat.[27] Several diplomats working in unsupportive or skeptical government systems maintained close contact and even friendships with ICAN campaigners. "The information sharing was extremely important," said one such diplomat. "We needed to anticipate moves to make sure we could be a part of this even if we weren't at the center."[28] At least one unsupportive government even officially acknowledged the "deft coordination" of ICAN with governments, describing in a cable back to the capital our joint work as a "well-oiled campaign."[29]

DIVERSITY IN PARTICIPATION

The nuclear ban negotiations, and the process leading up them, were also important and groundbreaking from the perspective of diversity. From setting up new forums such as the humanitarian impact conferences, to moving out of consensus-based venues such as the Conference on Disarmament to the more democratic General Assembly, activists and governments opened new space for conversations on nuclear weapons. In this effort, we also consciously opened new space for who could participate in those conversations. Women, as well as queer activists, activists and diplomats from the global south, and Indigenous atomic bomb survivors became central to the efforts to ban the bomb.

Women were leaders in ICAN, as they always have been in the broader antinuclear movement. Women also played a leading role among the diplomats in the process to ban nuclear weapons, with some delegations to the negotiations even being comprised solely or mostly of women, such as those of Ireland, New Zealand, and Sweden. Although not wanting to overstate the effect that "simply" adding women can have, as discussed in chapter 1, the ban negotiations illuminated how including a preponderance of women, in particular of different experience and perspective, can have a positive impact. Overall, the percentage of women participating in the ban treaty negotiations on behalf of governments was actually lower than that of women participating in the 2015 NPT Review Conference: 26.5 percent at the NPT, versus 17.9 percent at the ban negotiations.[30] However, what the statistics based on the list of participants don't show is the leadership of women within and between delegations, the more vocal participation of women of color, and the increased number of activists of color and of queer identities. These are variables that had an impact.

"The fact there were so many women involved in the negotiations—chairing, facilitating, participating—made such a difference," said one diplomat interviewed for this book. "It was such a change from other negotiations."[31] The women diplomats involved in this process had a tight network, one official noted. It was a trusted circle and seemed more collaborative than other experiences. "We shared more drafts with each other," she explained, and "felt freer, less caught up in ego," and "more results oriented."[32] Another noted the ways in which the higher-than-usual proportion of women was reflected in the nature of discussions. "When we had better gender balance, we had better, more diverse debates. It changed the tone of the discussion, made it freer and more open."[33]

Male diplomats recognized this difference, too, with one noting that the women who were facilitating discussions were not pushing their own egos, but instead were oriented toward talking things through and making sure everyone felt heard. "Some delegations had a hard time with women in leadership positions," he acknowledged, but "we may have muted them a bit. It did seem like a different process. The 'raw-raw' male ego stuff is mostly associated with the nuclear-armed and nuclear-supportive states, so it just wasn't there."[34]

Some government officials also appreciated the diversity within ICAN, describing it as important to changing the discussion on nuclear weapons. One explained how vital it was to hear in particular from those who had survived nuclear weapon use and testing, and from women who were willing to challenge patriarchal discourse about nuclear weapons:

> The women who participated in this process ensured a more diverse worldview than usual. Instead of a reiteration of well-known views on security, on nuclear disarmament as a technical issue, as bean counting, instead of the traditional discourse, we suddenly got all these perspectives approaching it from the effects of the weapons, the consequences, lived experiences. This really helped delegates focus, knuckle down to get the treaty adopted on 7 July. We knew we had to finish, this was our moment—and those voices, of survivors, of women, were very motivating.[35]

Several women who participated in the negotiations spoke about how empowering it felt to be part of this process. "We felt bold, had agency, could be part of the discourse in a meaningful way," said one.[36] She attributed this directly to the humanitarian approach and to the work that activists did to ensure women's participation in the process. Having so many women participating in the nuclear ban process opened up space for new perspectives. It also created a dynamic in which some diplomats began to recognize the traditionally gendered nature of the discourse. One woman noted, "We're usually accused of being emotional. But the fact is, women are able to have opinions and to have factual evidence to back them up. It's a question of being passionate about facts versus being emotional."[37] A male diplomat indicated that this process was eye opening for him in terms of gender dynamics, including the ways in which he and others were accused of being "emotional" for wanting to talk about the humanitarian impacts of nuclear weapons, as described earlier.[38]

Some participants also highlighted the importance of having a woman of color from the global south—Ambassador Elayne Whyte Gómez of Costa Rica—presiding over the negotiations. "Having a woman chair the negotiations was significant. It was different to see a woman sitting up there—it felt empowering."[39] Another agreed, saying, "If you look at photos of the NPT or First Committee, you see white men everywhere, talking about 'security,' measuring their arsenals against each other. To have a woman of the global south [chairing negotiations] was genuinely important."[40]

Some diplomats also highlighted the importance of having women of color as active participants, not just in the negotiations but in the process leading up to it. The Irish delegation pushed for a sponsorship program to the relevant meetings in order to ensure that women of the global south would be presented during discussions. The women diplomats from Palau and Jamaica, who were part of these sponsorship efforts, provided "powerful momentum" to the ban, one diplomat attending the conferences recalled. "When they spoke, you could hear a pin drop."[41]

Overall, people of color played a leading role in the nuclear ban. The process was galvanized and led by the nonwhite world, especially on the government side. One diplomat from the global south highlighted the importance for her country and broader region of becoming leaders in the process. "In the Arms Trade Treaty process, we saw a big voice from the global south," she said. "We were energized as victims, and on the basis of promoting development. But we haven't found our same voice on nuclear weapons. Because of the refocus on the humanitarian impacts, nuclear weapons became an easier sell for the global south. It was empowering."[42] She described the internal process for her government to go from rarely speaking out on nuclear weapons to becoming a leader in the ban process. "I started questioning things when I started to look at wider security concerns of small island states," she said. "When I heard about the humanitarian initiative through Latin American campaigners, I sought to engage with the issue. This was easy, but it was hard to get urgency from the capital. I used the angle of transshipment of nuclear waste through our region, which was already a big issue for us," to get traction on making the ban a priority. Countries of the global south haven't engaged as actively with the NPT, she noted, "but with the nuclear ban, we were involved in developing the strategy."

Some Western diplomats also acknowledged the importance of this being an initiative led by many countries of the global south. One described how his delegation actively sought to "cultivate relationships with the global south during this process. They were our allies, not western states. But we had to build up trust together."[43] He noted that having Brazil, Mexico, South Africa, and Nigeria in the core group, and other diplomatic leaders in the Caribbean and Southeast Asia, helped a lot to generate interest among countries of those regions. "Diplomats worked with who they knew—personal relationships really helped."

Building up new connections and trust between the pro-ban Western countries and those in the global south may go on to have ramifications beyond nuclear weapon issues. Certainly, the friendships and trust that developed between individual diplomats from these countries have been an essential element in the success of the ban (as discussed in the previous chapter). And it is really past humanitarian disarmament initiatives that have brought many of these countries together. Austria, Norway, and Ireland, together with Mexico and South Africa, were leaders in the bans on landmines and cluster munitions. The experience and trust gained from working together previously helped prepare them (with the exception of Norway, under a new government) to lead on this initiative as well.

These cross-regional relationships have historical precedent also in nuclear disarmament. For example, in 1954, in response to the U.S. nuclear test Castle Bravo, which killed Japanese fisherman with radioactive fallout, a number of non-Western states demanded a ban on nuclear testing. They were joined by Austria and Sweden, but the rest of the Western governments "led a vigorous resistance" to the idea of a nuclear test ban.[44] The world was split, notes Alva Myrdal, with "moral opinion" starkly imbalanced between the nuclear-armed states and the majority, "which constituted lesser powers."[45]

Today, that split is perhaps more acute than ever. And as noted in chapter 7, some governments that previously supported nuclear disarmament, if even just rhetorically, have become increasingly reticent in their defense of nuclear weapons and of the states that wield them. This shift has occurred dramatically even just within the past few years, within the context of the humanitarian initiative and the nuclear ban. The difference between 1954 and 2017, however, is that those "lesser powers" decided to stand up and fight back. The multilateral system has changed remarkably in this time. There are regional powers, not just two global superpowers. Economic, political, and military interests and alliances have shifted. Domestic politics and the identity of the nation have become important. In disarmament, the "lesser powers" have stepped up before and were willing to do so again.

FEELINGS ON THE FINAL PRODUCT

Creating this new type of process, where the typical voices dominating nuclear weapon discussions chose not to show up and where activists and diplomats collaborated across regions and identities, was instrumental to creating a good product. Those who participated in the negotiations generally felt that the final treaty is strong. Several wished they could have had more time to iron out a few sticky issues, mostly around the safeguards and join-and-destroy disarmament options, but all agreed this was the best possible result within the time frame. "We had little time," said one diplomat, "but it was the right move to finish when we did."[46]

Most delegates also pointed out that the treaty wasn't just the best within a time frame, but also the best version of a prohibition treaty that didn't include the nuclear-armed states as negotiating partners. "We couldn't write the future," in terms of how the nuclear-armed may or may not engage, "we could only provide for it."[47] In this context, the treaty "is already having a normative impact on our discussions, and on investments" in nuclear weapons. Another agreed, saying, "I see value in the normative effect of the treaty. The withdrawal of pension funds from nuclear weapons shows it's really working." They also argued, "The gender provisions of the treaty are really groundbreaking. I was pleased that it was relatively easy to get their inclusion. It's so useful to have this in an international instrument."[48]

A particular challenge of the negotiations was the orientation of many governments toward the world we live in today. Nonnuclear-armed states and activists have been promised "good faith" for so long and have become accustomed to bad faith. The nuclear-armed and nuclear-supportive states have abused the goodwill of the rest of the international community for decades. This generates unease about establishing parameters in this treaty for such states to join while still retaining their weapons and programs. But the way the nuclear ban is written, it can lock nuclear-armed or nuclear-supportive states that join it into the treaty's prohibitions and into time-bound, irreversible, verifiable elimination or removal of the weapons and weapon programs. This is a valid pathway to achieving the elimination of nuclear weapons and programs and the establishment and maintenance of a nuclear weapon free world. In the pursuit of such a world, we will have to build trust with and confidence in states that have previously let us down for so long and in so many ways. This will not be an easy thing to do, but staking out carefully guarded space for it in this treaty is a good start to that work.

As one participant noted, "The ways in which the treaty is valuable are impacted by the way it was negotiated."[49] Suggesting that it could only have been stronger on its technical provisions if others with particular expertise in these areas had been more involved, he argued that it can still be a blueprint for disarmament in the future. In the meantime, "its main value is political value," which will increase as more states sign and ratify it. "Even some of the opposition creating noise about the treaty can be beneficial," he argued. "It brings deterrence to the fore, helps situate many people and governments. If we see a crack in any opposing state, even one, that would be highly significant and will likely lead to more change. It's just a matter of time." From now on, said another participant, "We have to defend the treaty as the core of our nuclear disarmament efforts." The NPT is important, he acknowledged, but argued, "Now we have a comprehensive agreement. It's an effective symbol and will effect change. It has to be something that creates a reality."[50]

Speaking on the penultimate day of the negotiations, as the text was being sent to translation, an Australian senator from the Green Party took one last crack at the Australian government. Years before, the Australians, thinking themselves clever, had coined the phrase "simply banning nuclear weapons"—as in, simply banning nuclear weapons will not solve the world's problems. In his remarks to the negotiations, Senator Scott Ludlam noted that simply banning nuclear weapons is not simple at all. And speaking on behalf of activists from nuclear-armed and nuclear-supportive states, he said:

> Our work is only just beginning. We commit to all of you this morning to make our way home and to campaign for our governments to recognize that this treaty is the best chance we have to build a truly secure world free of nuclear weapons. One by one, we will bring them into the room. So please know you have allies and supporters in parliaments and civil society organizations in all of the nuclear-armed and umbrella states who are committed to bringing your work to fruition.[51]

TAKING RISKS

The story of the ban is the story of individuals working hard to change a well-established norm of political power and international security. This is part of the reason why it is difficult to tell this story without identifying those individuals. But it's important to recognize, in this context, how individuals needed the collective movement and the network of activists and diplomats to make real change: on their own, individual diplomats cannot make government policy. But working together, connecting with others within their system, or external allies such as officials from other countries and even activists, they were able to compel their governments to change positions and support the nuclear ban initiative.

All of the diplomats interviewed for this book felt it was worth the risk and the personal exposure to support the ban. Even a diplomat who said he now feels "toxic" within some of his government's agencies says that he felt he had to stand up for the ban in order to protect his country's reputation. "I was motivated to get the best possible position for my country."[52] Another said he felt threatened enough that he had long conversations with his partner, telling her, "I might go down for this—there's no one else to blame if it all goes wrong." A lot of colleagues were supportive within his own system, within ICAN, and within the broader community of actors. "I wouldn't have been able to do it without them," he said. At the end of the day, "I took the risk because I knew it was my one chance to contribute to something this important."[53]

For some, on the other hand, being involved in the ban process has actually helped their careers. One diplomat said that she's since been assigned a priority portfolio, explaining that her work on the ban made her more visible within the ministry. "I can only see good things about being in this process," she said. "Within eight and a half years [in the foreign service], this is the most important professional experience I've had. It will be difficult to surpass."[54] People within her system were supportive, as were friends and family—and she used her work on the ban as an opportunity to spread information to them about the need to abolish nuclear weapons.

Most diplomats engaged in the ban process found that it impacted them personally. They became passionate about the issue and now feel invested in seeing this through to elimination. This was "easily the most significant thing professionally that I've been part of, as a diplomat, but also a human being," said one person.[55] Another found being involved in this process provided her with "a source of happiness, joy, and confidence." It was "transformative."[56] Another described how she felt that being involved in the process helped her grow personally and professionally. "It showed that we could take action—not just complain, but actually do something to help move the disarmament process forward," she argued. On a personal level, she said, it also helped her build knowledge, as well as public-speaking and negotiation skills. "I was proud to be part of a process that seemed impossible but with energy and passion achieved success."[57] Others were not sure if they would encounter more meaningful work in their careers. "Other work may be more tangible, but this is global, and real."[58]

A number of diplomats described what they most liked about the work. Most of these comments centered around feeling like they were part of a bigger whole, working with friends, and most important, having fun. "I loved being part of the lobbying effort to get the numbers up on the resolution to establish negotiations, to see the country names up on the screen," said one.[59] "It was an unforgettable experience to do this work, to be part of this process," said another participant. It was "hugely rewarding—and exhausting," she said, laughing that by the end she was working in her sleep. "I would wake up at 4:00 a.m. writing speeches in my mind, so then I'd have to get up and write them down." This was "a chance to say something important," and she didn't want to miss that chance.[60]

Diplomats weren't the only ones who felt transformed from being engaged with this campaign. A number of activists I spoke to described the experience as one of learning, exploration, and adventure. It was certainly this for me. It offered a unique opportunity to bring feminist and queer theory to bear on my activism in a dynamic, revolutionary political process taking place inside an international institution, the United Nations, for which I cared deeply but had over the course of my career seen frustrated time and again by governments' competing interests. It was also the source of many lasting friendships, with other activists but also with diplomats and others. I learned a lot about interpersonal dynamics, diplomatic procedure, regional differences and similarities, and the importance of principles. Having a feminist orientation to process as well as substance at times meant I found myself at odds with the dominant current within the campaign, which at times had an "ends justifies the means" attitude toward how decisions were made or what those decisions were. But being part of this process, analyzing it while advocating for it simultaneously, has given me optimism for what is possible. In this, I am certainly not alone.

The hope this treaty brought to diplomats and activists alike cannot be overstated. It changed the sense of what is possible for a lot of people. "I've been involved in this issue for many years," said one diplomat. "On conventional weapons, we've had some measured success: the Arms Trade Treaty, the prohibitions on cluster munitions and landmines. But on WMD, especially nuclear weapons, things have been horrible."[61] He recalled the final day of the conference, reflecting that the treaty's adoption "gave me a sense that despite all the skepticism, it's like a victory. It was a victory over major forces, major interests—it gave a sense that it's possible to change all of this! I was skeptical right up to the end, but I wanted to make a difference, and we managed to pull it off. It was a real collective effort."

He wasn't the only one celebrating from afar. Other diplomats spoke about their reactions with friends and family watching the adoption in various time zones around the world. And those in the room, participating in the final dramatic moments, will have it etched in their memories forever.

THE MOMENTS OF ADOPTION

For the activists of ICAN, 7 July 2017 started early. We were in the conference room by 7 a.m., as soon as we could get through the security gates with our passes. Limited space in the gallery meant everyone wanted to be there early enough to secure a seat to watch history. We had spent the day and evening before running a phone bank to make sure that delegates would show up for the final day to vote for the treaty's adoption. The previous evening, we had been alerted that the Dutch delegation informed the president it was requesting a vote on the treaty, which meant our efforts to get people in the room were even more important. We needed as many supportive countries there as possible. Some of our Dutch ICAN campaigners had spent the afternoon before trying to prevent this—they'd been on the phone to the Dutch Red Cross and other civil society groups and parliamentarians in the Netherlands to try to pressure the government not to call for a vote, but given its opposition and its ties to NATO and U.S. nuclear weapon policy, most of us were not surprised when they did demand their opposition be put on the record.

Despite knowing this request came in, on the morning of 7 July the president moved to adopt the treaty by consensus. She delivered an eloquent speech, describing the work of the conference as having been bolstered by common determination. "We are just a few moments away from saying to the survivors, to our children that yes, it is possible to inherit a world free of nuclear weapons for future generations." She gaveled in the adoption of the treaty, and the room burst into applause. A few of the activists had been alerted by a delegation by text moments before that this would happen, so some knew this was just a play, but unfortunately others in the gallery believed we'd just adopted the treaty. Tears and hugs were flowing.

It was all gamesmanship, however. The Netherlands' delegates were wildly waving their arms trying to get the attention of the president and the Secretariat; one delegate had to dash up to the podium to "remind" the president that they wanted a recorded vote. The applause subsided as the president called the room to order and announced that there would be a vote. As the numbers came on the screen, the room erupted early. One opposed—the Netherlands. One abstention—Singapore. One hundred and twenty-two in favor.

The vote received a standing ovation, and the president was able to gavel in the treaty's adoption—for real, this time. Although her move had provided spectacular theater, it was an odd choice for the chair of a diplomatic conference to go so far outside the bounds of proper procedure. There were grumblings later from some delegations, not just the Netherlands, about these antics, but in the moment almost everyone was too exuberant to care. We'd just adopted a treaty banning nuclear weapons.

After the applause had finally died down, around forty delegations took the floor to deliver explanations of vote. Nearly every delegation spoke of the new treaty as groundbreaking, historic, and a significant step forward. Many referred to it as laying the foundation for the elimination of nuclear weapons and as a triumph of multilateralism. Trinidad and Tobago said that it has "shattered the chronic stalemate" in nuclear disarmament and nonproliferation. Several delegations highlighted the contributions of ICAN to making this treaty a reality. Egypt's delegation, not always one to support the participation of NGOs in intergovernmental meetings, said that although civil society is traditionally seated at the back of UN conference rooms, "their devotion places them at the forefront of our respect."

Abacca Anjain-Maddison from the Marshall Islands delivered the final remarks for ICAN, noting that this treaty is not just the product of those in the room who have created the language of the treaty text but also of those who have marched in the streets around the world.[62] And Setsuko Thurlow, an atomic bomb survivor from Hiroshima, delivered a powerful closing statement expressing joy at the adoption of this treaty, for which she has waited for seven decades. "We've always known that nuclear weapons are immoral," she said. "Now they are also illegal." She declared the treaty's adoption "the beginning of the end of nuclear weapons."[63] She received the third standing ovation of the day.

The Treaty on the Prohibition of Nuclear Weapons opened for signature on 20 September 2017. Forty-two[64] states signed the treaty that day, and many more have signed and ratified it since then. The numbers of those governments committed to outlawing nuclear weapons continue to grow.[65] That same year, ICAN won the Nobel Peace Prize in recognition of our work "to draw attention to the catastrophic humanitarian consequences of any use of nuclear weapons" and our "ground-breaking efforts to achieve a treaty-based prohibition of such weapons."[66] It was a remarkable year, but the work to abolish nuclear weapons is far from over. The conclusion looks at where we are now and what could help the work ahead.

CONCLUSION

After about seven years of concerted effort, and nearly seven decades of antinuclear activism and international diplomatic initiatives for nuclear disarmament before that, the world finally banned the bomb.

Along with a collaborative endeavor to challenge the dominant nuclear weapon discourse, through which we sought a paradigm shift from abstract but deadly theories such as nuclear deterrence toward an evidence-based, human-centered approach to nuclear weapons, leaders of the humanitarian initiative used the compelling narrative of catastrophic humanitarian consequences to stigmatize and prohibit nuclear weapons. This was, as one diplomat noted, "a victory for multilateralism, for working together . . . We could not do it alone. There is safety in numbers, especially when pitted against the so-called major powers."[1] The way in which like-minded governments, activists, and a few academics and humanitarian agencies such as the International Committee of the Red Cross came together on this project is indeed a testament to what can be accomplished when people cooperate in creative, innovative ways to solve a seemingly intractable problem.

But just as the work to achieve a nuclear ban is not the beginning of the story of antinuclear activism, the adoption of the Treaty on the Prohibition of Nuclear Weapons at the United Nations on 7 July 2017 is certainly not the end. Much remains to be done to secure the treaty's full and effective implementation, to bring as many countries on board as possible, to continue to stigmatize nuclear weapons as an effort toward social justice and human security, and, of course, to achieve the total abolition of these weapons once and for all. But as we engage in this work, it is helpful to remember, as E. P. Thompson wrote, that social movements "do not often attain their goals at their first moment of assertion. What they do, more often, is transform the climate of expectations and redefine the limits of what is possible."[2] Redefining the limits of the possible was a key goal and product of the ban treaty process. For so long, the nuclear-armed states dictated what was possible in the realm of nuclear disarmament—and after operating on their terms for decades, it was clear that on those terms, nuclear weapons would continue to be embedded in the national imaginations, as well as economies, politics, and conceptions of security, for the indefinite future. Changing this assertion, that progress on nuclear disarmament is not possible, was instrumental to achieving the ban treaty and remains imperative to achieving the elimination of nuclear weapons.

Our continued work to abolish nuclear weapons may also require shifts in the way we organize and who we organize with. As antinuclear activists, but also as diplomats, academics, and others, we need to reflect on the fact that we achieved this treaty by prioritizing the voices of those usually not treated as credible or relevant in this field. We actively sought to break down barriers, build up capacity, and bring people along, particularly those normally not engaged in thinking or acting against nuclear weapons. I think this needs to be at the core of our work moving forward. This means, among other things, centering our efforts to eliminate nuclear weapons in broader contexts and working with people addressing other issues. This does not necessarily mean that we need to try to re-create the mass movements for nuclear disarmament that we experienced in earlier decades. It also does not mean that we need to ask people to turn away from their campaigns on other issues and join ours. Quite the opposite. It means situating our analysis of the bomb in spaces and in language that can support and learn from other struggles for social justice—including, for example, Indigenous, queer, feminist, antiracist, anticapitalist, and environmental struggles. Struggles for human security, liberation, and justice.

Some of the ongoing work described in this chapter—such as seeking ratifications for the treaty's entry into force, urging economic divestment from nuclear weapons, adopting city council resolutions, and pursuing parliamentary engagement and public awareness—are being worked on in isolation of other struggles. But I believe that we can find connections between this work and the broader work of systemic change. When faced with the violence of settler colonialism, imperial intervention, war and armed conflict, mass incarceration, poverty, displacement, sexism, homophobia and transphobia, racism, environmental devastation, and violence in our homes and communities, nuclear weapons may seem like an abstraction. But these weapons are part of the spectrum of institutionalized violence. As objects they can manifest the most violence in a single moment—the most death, destruction, and despair. Even without being launched, they are used to project power and invincibility of their possessor. They are the pinnacle of a state's monopoly on violence, the ultimate signifier of domination. Thus, it is important for those resisting injustice and oppression to pay attention to the role nuclear weapons play in our world order, including at the intersection of patriarchal, racist, colonial, and capitalist oppressions. Even more so, it is crucial for those opposing nuclear weapons to pay attention to the ways in which the critiques and strategies of resistance of these oppressions can help inform, guide, and shape the work to abolish nuclear weapons.

THE PERSISTENT PROBLEM OF
POWER THROUGH VIOLENCE

As we continue or begin to engage in this work, it is important to take stock of where we are, even with the Treaty on the Prohibition of Nuclear Weapons (TPNW) now on the books. At the time of writing, the nuclear-armed states are continuing to invest billions in their nuclear arsenals. Tensions between them are growing, particularly between Russia and the United States. In early 2019, the U.S. government suspended its compliance with the Intermediate Nuclear Forces agreement, a treaty reached between Reagan and Gorbachev in 1987 that has for decades staved off the deployment of nuclear weapons in Europe. The U.S. government has also withdrawn from the Joint Comprehensive Plan of Action, an agreement reached in 2015 between Iran and the United States, China, France, Russia, United Kingdom, Germany, and the European Union over the Iranian nuclear program. These two incidents, coupled with the U.S. government oscillating between threats and apparent rapprochement with North Korea, as well as a general disdain from the current U.S. administration toward international law generally and nuclear disarmament specifically, have created a volatile and unpredictable atmosphere.

Amid of all this, it seems that the nuclear-armed states can only agree on one thing: that the TPNW is a Very Bad Thing. The only thing they hate more than each other's nuclear weapons, it seems, is the rest of the world outlawing nuclear weapons. Nuclear-armed and most nuclear-supportive governments have, since the TPNW was adopted, asserted that their retention of nuclear weapons is as imperative as ever, given the "strategic instability" and the negative "international security environment" as discussed in chapter 1. These governments argue, as they have for decades, that nuclear weapons are the only real security assurance they can count on. Several of these governments have said they will never join the TPNW—which in itself is an interesting speculation from supposedly democratic countries.

These governments' conception of security is one based on the patriarchal notion that violence is strength. Weapons, especially nuclear weapons, mean power. As discussed in chapter 1, this framing of security protects weapon industries and governments rather than human beings. The money poured into the development and maintenance of nuclear weapons, the damage that their use caused, and the risks they pose for our survival all undermine the security of human beings. But nuclear weapons are great for those making profits off their production or for maintaining privileged positions of power. In this context, nuclear disarmament is posited as something that will weaken security—in that it will undermine corporate profits or the nuclear-armed governments' perception of their place in the world order. Thus, the TPNW is painted as a security-destroying machination.

Of course, the purposeful shift to a humanitarian discourse about nuclear weapons and the resulting TPNW was not an initiative to undermine security but to increase it. The humanitarian initiative and the subsequent efforts to ban nuclear weapons "emerged from deep misgivings about nuclear order—the prevailing set of ideas, institutions, and practices that comprises the global politics of nuclear weapons," notes academic Nick Ritchie in an article more than a year after the treaty's adoption. In turn, this process "has generated fierce criticism for undermining that order."[3] Indeed, the unity of nuclear-armed states against the TPNW reeks of hypocrisy and gaslighting. This unity is based around a common narrative in which governments with the capacity to destroy us all are the ones who also have the best grip on stability and security for the entire world. That those who threaten to unleash a nuclear holocaust are the ones best suited to determine how to keep us safe. The nuclear-armed and nuclear-supportive governments have engaged in a kind of victim blaming, in which the "international security environment" forces them to retain nuclear weapons.

So, they use the same kind of rhetoric that certain men do to hold onto their power and privilege: they belittle, demean, and dismiss those who have the audacity to challenge their behavior or status. Their spokespeople, whether diplomats at the United Nations or mainstream media op-ed columnists, ridicule those who support the nuclear ban as being emotional and irrational.[4] They also assert that the negotiation of the TPNW was a futile endeavor—that it has only further polarized the international community without actually leading to the elimination of nuclear weapons. But the more they decry or desist from the treaty, the more obvious it becomes how threatened they feel, and the more they lose their clutch on the established narratives. It is only a matter of time before this translates into changing policies, practices, and politics.

THE CHALLENGE TO MONEY AND POWER

Cracks are already appearing. Although it is true that the nuclear-armed states have not yet been compelled by the TPNW to eliminate their arsenals, this is not the only possible measure of progress of the treaty's success. Banks, pension funds, and other financial institutions have already started divesting from nuclear weapon production. Even government pension funds within countries that have so far refused to join the TPNW have pulled money away from nuclear weapons.[5] For example, the Norwegian government announced that it will exclude investments in BAE Systems, AECOM, Fluror Corporation, Huntington Ingalls Industries, and Honeywell because of these companies' involvement in the production of key components for nuclear weapons.[6] The largest Dutch pension fund, the civil servants fund ABP, has decided to end its investments in producers of nuclear weapons. The pension fund recognizes that the TPNW was decisive in its decision.[7] Sweden's major pension funds have sold their stocks in nuclear weapon producers and announced that they will no longer invest in such companies, "in line with the aim for all countries to disarm nuclear weapons."[8]

National and local political resistance to nuclear weapons is also building. Parliamentarians and political parties within some nuclear-supportive countries are working actively to change their governments' position on the ban treaty.[9] Major cities in nuclear-armed and nuclear-supportive states, such as Baltimore, Los Angeles, Washington, D.C., Berlin, Paris, Manchester, Melbourne, Sydney, Toronto, and Vancouver,[10] have endorsed the TPNW and demanded that their federal governments join the ban. The number of cities joining the ICAN Cities Appeal grows every day and has been a great way for activists to raise local awareness about nuclear weapons and the TPNW.

With the treaty now firmly on the table, public debates about nuclear weapons are increasing. Action by city councilors and parliamentarians means new opportunities for public discussion about the nature of nuclear weapons, about the policies and practices that sustain them and put the world at risk, and about alternatives for global security. The awarding of the Nobel Peace Prize to ICAN in 2017 for its work on the humanitarian initiative and the TPNW also helped to generate media attention to the treaty and the issue of nuclear disarmament.

These conversations and debates have an impact. The process to ban nuclear weapons has exposed the cognitive dissonance of nuclear deterrence theory, illuminating its corrupt self-serving rationale and its influence over international affairs. Those engaged in the ban process took away the veil of legitimacy and authority of the nuclear-armed states—dismantling their arguments, disrupting their narratives, and ultimately standing up to their projection of power. The tension between many governments' stated commitment to achieving a nuclear weapon free world and their actual policies that support the maintenance of these weapons is becoming clearer and more public. Several governments, such as Norway, Italy, Sweden, and Switzerland, are undertaking investigations into the legal and political implications of joining the TPNW. Some government officials already seem to be struggling with the dissonance between their current policies and their own rhetoric.[11] Through the process to ban nuclear weapons, those who suffered from nuclear weapon use or testing, and those campaigning for disarmament, have been empowered, while "the nuclear possessors and their enablers were 'othered' as 'anti-humanitarian,'" write academics Nick Ritchie and Kjølv Egeland. "While the dependence of the nuclear-armed states and their allies on nuclear weapons was framed as illegitimate and oppressive, the humanitarian initiative was portrayed as legitimate and emancipatory."[12]

This kind of intellectual wrestling with being complicit with practices and policies that put the world at risk of annihilation is a product of the stigmatization of nuclear weapons facilitated by the humanitarian initiative and the TPNW's development. Together with divestment initiatives, ongoing political work in nuclear-supportive and nuclear-armed countries, public debates and street protests,[13] and signatures and ratifications of the TPNW, it's clear that progress is being made.

CHANGE THROUGH COURAGE, ACTION, AND HOPE

"After the energetically anti-nuke eighties and the end of the Cold War, nuclear holocaust—always unthinkable—became almost unmentionable," wrote Dr. Bill Williams, one of ICAN's cofounders. "A mass self-censorship, a mental no-fly zone, a cone of silence descended. Little wonder: no sane person wants to contaminate their dreams with this ultimate horror. But to finish this journey of survival—to abolition—we need to penetrate the fog of fear and denial, informing ourselves and our neighbours without inducing psychological paralysis." Dr. Williams passed away less than a year before the TPNW was adopted and before his campaign won the Nobel Peace Prize. But his words continue to resonate.

Some may find comfort in describing ICAN and the governments that share our vision and commitment as irresponsible or irrational. But we are not. We pursued an idea through to international law, despite being opposed by other activists, by many governments, and by being stripped of funding partway through the initiative. It took courage for the majority of governments to stand up to the power of the bomb wielded by a handful of heavily militarized countries with big economic and political influence. This was not an irresponsible or irrational choice made by officials in countries around the world: it was a bold decision, made possible through the collective effort, the building of trust described in chapter 4, and the determination of individual people to make a difference in the world.

Most of us—whether diplomats, activists, or academics—have had to live in the space created for us by the nuclear-armed states. They decided that they alone have the power and authority to determine when and where they will eliminate nuclear weapons. So far, their obligations and commitments have amounted to naught. Yet these states have controlled the narrative and even much of the scholarship for so long that most of the world believes they have the legitimate right to do so. But they don't. The adoption of the TPNW makes this very clear.

Global civil society and the majority of the world's states, following in the steps of feminist peace scholars and activists, rejected the dominant narrative to write something new. On the opening day of TPNW negotiations in March 2017, Ambassador Patricia O'Brien of Ireland said, "We are not just writing a new and complementary treaty here, we are taking the opportunity to write a new history, and in so doing to create a new, more stable, more secure and more equal future for all."[14] This is the crux of the TPNW. It was negotiated on the basis of courage and hope rather than on fear and inequality. It was a case of states and civil society coming together to stand up to power and violence, to say to the nuclear powers, "Enough."

The dominance of militarist, capitalist, predominantly white, Western masculinities persist in mainstream discourse upholding nuclear and other arms as necessary to the security of certain "rational" actors. But there are other rooms now, rooms full of diplomats and activists of diverse genders and ethnicities, talking about the prohibition and elimination of nuclear weapons. As described in chapter 8, these people have collectively flipped the script on who holds power, where that power is located, and what it looks like.

Taking a human-focused approach to disarmament, and thereby challenging the dominant state-centered approach to international peace and security, was instrumental in establishing negotiations for the TPNW.[15] The humanitarian initiative recognized that nuclear weapons represent a constant threat of terror and that they perpetuate inequity between countries, with broader implications for humanity.[16] Moving forward, further challenging the patriarchal, racist, colonial, and capitalist scaffolding upholding nuclear weapons will likewise help us to under-mine justifications and rationales for these weapons, exposing their roots in a world order that privileges a few over the many.[17]

Within this more complex critique, a feminist analysis is crucial to illuminating and challenging the structures of power that impose injustice and deprivation and sustain nuclear weapons. Just as the humanitarian discourse undermines the perceived legitimacy of nuclear weapons, a feminist analysis of nuclear discourse helps to deconstruct nuclear weapons as symbols of power and tools of empire. Feminist theories and activism, such as those explored in chapter 1, can show that the enshrinement of nuclear weapons as an emblem of power is not inevitable and unchangeable but a gendered social construction designed to maintain the patriarchal order. As Cohn, Ruby, and Ruddick wrote, a gender analysis that highlights the patriarchy and social constructions inherent in this valuation of nuclear weapons helps to "multiply, amplify, and deepen" arguments for nuclear disarmament and question the role of a certain kind of masculinity of the dominant paradigm.[18] Nuclear disarmament, sometimes cast by its detractors as a weak or passive approach to security, can instead be shown for what it is—rational, just, moral, and necessary for our survival. New conversations about security—what it is, who it's for, who gets to shape it—are ongoing and essential.

We have a responsibility to carry this forward and open the space even more. Campaigning for nuclear disarmament without also under-standing the racist, patriarchal, and capitalist injustice these weapons represent in international relations and local experiences does a disservice to fighting for both disarmament and justice. Our critique of nuclear weapons needs to also be a critique of the settler colonial state, which believes that it can conduct nuclear tests or store nuclear waste on stolen lands. It needs to be a critique of racism, with attention to the bodies and lands upon which nuclear weapons are tested and used. It needs to critique patriarchy, with a mind to how nuclear weapons are gendered, how they are used to reinforce social hierarchies, control, and domination.

An intersectional approach to nuclear disarmament also means ensuring that the voices and perspectives of those who experience the violence of nuclear weapons are leading our critiques and our work. This includes looking to the lessons of others that have struggled to make change from nonnormative and marginalized positions, learning from them and being led by them. It means not simply relying on established institutions to "allow" us to participate, or to settle for minor accommodations within those institutions. A critique of nuclear weapons in the locations and with the language of nuclear weapon proponents will not work. At best it may help achieve slight reductions in numbers of warheads or missiles, or the establishment of arms control regulations and nonproliferation initiatives. It does not get us to abolition. Only by situating our critique in the struggles of Indigenous, queer, feminist, antiracist, and anticapitalist activists can we start an honest accounting of what nuclear weapons are, what they do, and who they are really "for." Only by rethinking our relationship to existing institutions, which tend to co-opt participants into the status quo rather than providing opportunities for participants to change things "from the inside," can we start to think about alternative spaces and relationships to engage in meaningful processes.

Consciously or not, those engaged in the project of banning nuclear weapons have learned from other struggles. Much more work remains to be done, and the more we can learn from each other's theories and practices of action and participation, the better impact we will have across a range of social justice struggles. Nuclear abolition as a single-issue campaign worked for getting the nuclear ban treaty, but in order to advance it further and achieve elimination of these weapons of terror, it must be part of a broader, collaborative struggle for justice. This might seem too aspirational to many people but having worked in and around the UN system and as an activist across a spectrum of issues, I believe it is the best chance we have for meaningful change in our current world.

Perhaps most important of all is hope. It is often not clear where the impetus for change lies, and yet hope is essential. The radical notion of hope, as Czech political dissident-turned-president Václav Havel said in 1990, "is not a feeling of certainty that everything ends well. Hope is just a feeling that life and work have a meaning." In negotiating and adopting the TPNW, governments and activists worked together to bring this hope to action. "We acted on behalf of a grand coalition of committed activists, survivors, civil society, scholars and politicians," said the ambassador of Jamaica to the UN after the treaty's adoption. "They were the ones who steadfastly set aside the entreaties of the naysayers—that band of skeptics who at every turn told us we were embarked on a fool's errand."[19]

In doing this work as a grand coalition, I learned a lot about movement building processes and their interactions with institutions and individuals. These lessons, as I've tried to describe them throughout this book, have taught me about the importance of building the capacity of individuals to change institutions and policies. Governments are not monoliths, and neither are activist campaigns. Each is full of people with individual perspectives, skills, and motivations. Bringing together the ones who give a damn and building up their personal sense of capacity to create change seems to me imperative to any political process. As is not letting our human fallibility crush the overall growth of a movement or coalition or initiative. Ego, personality, personal agendas, fear, intimidation—these will arise. But relationships of trust and where possible, friendship, mean that activists, diplomats, and others involved can keep each other grounded and keep each other moving when the going gets tough.

The movement we built to change the discourse around nuclear weapons and develop an international treaty to ban the bomb is not perfect. It suffered from all of the stresses and tensions that any collective effort of human beings can suffer. But we did manage to bring people together, enhancing the diversity of perspectives and experiences and identities of people involved in the project of banning nuclear weapons. And several of us tried to be guided by intersectional feminist politics and processes—and tried to be accountable when we failed.

These lessons are important for developing campaigns and coalitions on any issue. And as we continue the work to eliminate nuclear weapons, we must continue to learn lessons from others. The story of the nuclear ban—why it could be achieved now and how we can carry it forward—must be seen in the much larger context of the broader global resistance to injustice and oppression. We are currently seeing First Nations' resistance to environmental disasters and political oppressions; protests and strikes to protect the rights of immigrants; professional athletes taking a knee to protest police violence against people of color. Around the world there have been initiatives to protect LGBTQ+ people, refugees, workers, human rights, the environment. Tech workers are standing up against their corporate bosses to try to ensure that the products they develop serve humanity rather than oppress it. The Women's March and the #MeToo campaign have smashed through layers of silence, exposing specific men but also disrupting the culture of misogyny, sexism, harassment, assault, and abuse.

Nuclear weapons are part of these bigger systems of oppression—systems that have been challenged throughout history and that are being challenged now in new ways, from new collectives of people around the world. As with all other social justice issues, laws will not fix everything, and certainly they will not fix them straight away. Further, whatever gains are made are assaulted by pushback from those who fear loss of their privilege and power. But things do change. The nuclear ban must be seen in this context: in the context of resistance to injustice, inequality, and oppression; and in the context of making meaningful change through acts of courage.

Key to this process is belief that change is possible. Throughout history, systems of oppression and inequality have cracked, crumbled, and been decimated. The changes necessary to achieve this were mostly not instant, but iterative. They happened because of the persistence of people who believed that change could and must occur, who fought even when the odds were stacked against them. People who took the smallest gains as immense victories because they could recognize that every chink in the armor of power weakens its foundations, making it more and more vulnerable to pressure.

The willingness and tenacity to keep trying to create change despite the obstacles is where hope lies and where change is achieved. Giving into the powerful is not an option, for it is only in giving up that we fail. The act of prohibiting nuclear weapons is an act of nonviolent, positive, courageous revolt. It is transformative. It is long-fought and hard-won, and it is certainly not over. It is a piece of the path of a long road of activism, sacrifice, and courage from people the world over for decades. It is an important piece, a critical node, and it will require more courage—from governments and activists—to carry forward successfully. As Ireland's Foreign Minister Micheál Martin said in 2010, quoting Irish poet Edmund Burke, "Never despair; but if you do, work on in despair."[20] You never know when change might happen, but the only way it will ever happen is if you keep working for it.

NOTES

ACKNOWLEDGMENTS

1. Nick Estes, *Our History Is the Future* (New York: Verso, 2019), 259.
2. Like this one: https://www.bbc.co.uk/programmes/p05wgqmr.

PREFACE

1. For the current status of signatures and ratifications of the TPNW, see https://www.icanw.org/signature_and_ratification_status.
2. See https://pledge.icanw.org.
3. See https://cities.icanw.org.
4. See https://www.icanw.org/polls_public_opinion_in_eu_host_states _firmly_opposes_nuclear_weapons.
5. Edith M. Lederer, "US Urges Countries to Withdraw from UN Nuke Ban Treaty," Associated Press, 21 October 2020.

INTRODUCTION

1. Peter Baker and Choe Sang-Hun, "Trump Threatens 'Fire and Fury' against North Korea if It Endangers U.S.," *New York Times*, 8 August 2017.
2. For details on each nuclear-armed state's nuclear weapon doctrine and forces, see the Nuclear Notebook published by *Bulletin of the Atomic Scientists* at https://thebulletin.org/nuclear-risk/nuclear-weapons/nuclear-notebook and the Stockholm International Peace Research Institute's Yearbook chapter on "World Nuclear Forces" at https://www.sipri.org/yearbook.

3. For details on nuclear weapon modernization programs, see *Assuring Destruction Forever: 2019 Edition* (New York: Women's International League for Peace and Freedom, 2019) and earlier versions of the report available at www .reachingcriticalwill.org.

4. See chapter 2 of this book for some examples.

5. ICAN was established in Australia in 2007 by the International Physicians for the Prevention of Nuclear War. The campaign has since grown to include more than five hundred nongovernmental organizations in more than one hundred countries. More information is available at www.icanw.org.

6. Hans M. Kristensen and Matt Korda, "Status of World Nuclear Forces," Federation of American Scientists, updated May 2019, https://fas.org/issues/nuclear-weapons/status-world-nuclear-forces.

7. For comparative investments and information about modernization programs across the nuclear-armed states, see *Assuring Destruction Forever: 2019 Edition* (New York: Women's International League for Peace and Freedom, 2019) and other editions of the report available at www.reachingcriticalwill.org.

8. Albert Camus, *The Myth of Sisyphus and Other Essays* (New York: Vintage Books, 1955).

CHAPTER 1

1. Thomas C. Schelling, *Arms and Influence* (New Haven, CT: Yale University Press, 1966).

2. See, for example, Robert Zarate, "Albert and Roberta Wohlstetter on Nuclear-Age Strategy," in *Nuclear Heuristics: Selected Writings of Albert and Roberta Wohlstetter*, edited by Robert Zarate and Henry Sokolski (Carlisle, PA: Strategic Studies Institute, U.S. Army War College, January 2009), 1–90.

3. George Orwell, *Nineteen Eighty-Four: A Novel* (London: Secker & Warburg, 1969).

4. Kenneth N. Waltz, "The Spread of Nuclear Weapons: More May Be Better," *Adelphi Papers* 21, no. 171 (1981).

5. Carol Cohn, "Sex and Death in the Rational World of Defense Intellectuals," *Signs* 12, no. 4 (Summer 1987): 688.

6. Cohn, "Sex and Death in the Rational World of Defense Intellectuals," 690.

7. Matthew Rowland, ambassador and permanent representative to the Conference on Disarmament of the United Kingdom, statement to the 2014 NPT Preparatory Committee, New York, 2 May 2014, http://www.reaching criticalwill.org/images/documents/Disarmament-fora/npt/prepcom14/statements/2May_UK.pdf.

8. Jean-Hugues Simon-Michel, ambassador and permanent representative to the Conference on Disarmament of France, statement to the 2014 NPT Preparatory Committee, New York, 2 May 2014, http://www.reaching criticalwill.org/images/documents/Disarmament-fora/npt/prepcom14/statements/2May_France.pdf.

9. Matthew Rowland, ambassador and permanent representative to the Conference on Disarmament of the United Kingdom, statement to the UN General Assembly First Committee on Disarmament and International Security, New York, 20 October 2014, http://reachingcriticalwill.org/images/documents/Disarmament-fora/1com/1com14/statements/20Oct_Uk.pdf.

10. Robert Wood, ambassador and permanent representative to the Conference on Disarmament of the United States, explanation of vote on A/C.1/73/L.54, united action with renewed determination toward the elimination of nuclear weapons, to the UN General Assembly First Committee on Disarmament and International Security, New York, 1 November 2018.

11. Andrew W. Cordier and Wilder Foote, eds., *Public Papers of the Secretaries-General of the United Nations: Dag Hammarskjöld, Volume III* (New York: Columbia University Press, 1972), 176–77. See also Randy Rydell, *Explaining Hammarskjöld's "Hardy Perennial"—The Role of the UN in Nuclear Disarmament* (London: United Nations Association—UK, February 2013).

12. Vladimir Yermakov, deputy director of the Department for Security and Disarmament Affairs, Ministry of Foreign Affairs of Russia, statement to the UN General Assembly First Committee on Disarmament and International Security, New York, 22 October 2013.

13. Matthew Harries, "The Real Problem with a Nuclear Ban Treaty," Carnegie Endowment for Peace, 15 March 2017, http://carnegieendowment.org/2017/03/15/real-problem-with-nuclear-ban-treaty-pub-68286.

14. Breifne O'Reilly, director for disarmament and nonproliferation of Ireland, statement to the Non-Proliferation Treaty Preparatory Committee, New York, 2 May 2014, http://www.reachingcriticalwill.org/images/documents/Disarmament-fora/npt/prepcom14/statements/2May_Ireland.pdf.

15. Ulf Lindell, minister-counselor at the Permanent Mission of Sweden in Geneva, statement to the UN General Assembly First Committee on Disarmament and International Security, New York, 20 October 2014, http://reachingcriticalwill.org/images/documents/Disarmament-fora/1com/1com14/statements/20Oct_Sweden.pdf.

16. See, for example, Ward Wilson, "The Myth of Nuclear Deterrence," *Nonproliferation Review* 15, no. 3 (2008): 421–39.

17. See, for example, Eric Schlosser, *Command and Control: Nuclear Weapons, the Damascus Accident, and the Illusion of Safety* (New York: Penguin, 2013);

and Joseph Gerson, *Empire and the Bomb: How the U.S. Uses Nuclear Weapons to Dominate the World* (London: Pluto Press, 2007).

18. See, for example, David P. Barash, "Nuclear Deterrence Is a Myth. And a Lethal One at That," *The Guardian*, 14 January 2018, https://www.theguardian .com/world/2018/jan/14/nuclear-deterrence-myth-lethal-david-barash; Nick Ritchie, "Deterrence Dogma: Challenging the Relevance of British Nuclear Weapons," *International Affairs* 85, no. 1 (2009): 81–98; and Ward Wilson, *Five Myths about Nuclear Weapons* (Boston: Houghton Mifflin Harcourt, 2013).

19. Daniel Ellsberg, *The Doomsday Machine: Confessions of a Nuclear War Planner* (New York: Bloomsbury, 2017), 332.

20. Ellsberg, *The Doomsday Machine*, 339.

21. Ellsberg, *The Doomsday Machine*, 20.

22. Ellsberg, *The Doomsday Machine*, 332.

23. Alva Myrdal, *The Game of Disarmament: How the United States and Russia Run the Arms Race* (New York: Pantheon Books, 1976), 22.

24. Myrdal, *The Game of Disarmament*, xvii.

25. Myrdal, *The Game of Disarmament*, 10.

26. Myrdal, *The Game of Disarmament*, 319.

27. Ellsberg, *The Doomsday Machine*, 348.

28. Cohn, "Sex and Death in the Rational World of Defense Intellectuals"; and Carol Cohn, "Slick 'Ems, Glick 'Ems, Christmas Trees, and Cookie Cutters: Nuclear Language and How We Learned to Pat the Bomb," *Bulletin of the Atomic Scientists* (June 1987): 17–24.

29. Cohn, "Sex and Death in the Rational World of Defense Intellectuals," 712.

30. Hugh Gusterson, *Nuclear Rites: A Weapons Laboratory at the End of the Cold War* (Berkeley: University of California Press, 1996).

31. Shampa Biswas, *Nuclear Desire: Power and the Postcolonial Nuclear Order* (Minneapolis: University of Minnesota Press, 2014), 122.

32. Biswas, *Nuclear Desire*, 122.

33. C. Wright Mills, *The Power Elite* (New York: Oxford University Press, 2000), 185–86.

34. Mills, *The Power Elite*, 276.

35. Karl Marx, *Capital: A Critique of Political Economy, Volume I* (London: Penguin, 1991).

36. Karl Marx, *Capital: A Critique of Political Economy, Volume III* (London: Penguin, 1991), 363.

37. James M. Cypher, "Critical Analyses of Military Spending and Capitalism," *Eastern Economic Journal* 11, no. 3 (July–September 1985): 274.

38. Paul Baran and Paul Sweezy, *Monopoly Capital: An Essay on the American Economic and Social Order* (New York: NYU Press, 1968), 213.

39. Scot Arnold, "Does DoD Profit Policy Sufficiently Compensate Defense Contractors?" *IDA Research Notes* (Fall 2008): 13.

40. Dina Rasor, "Heads Up, Supercommittee: Here's How to Cut Billions from Overpriced Weapons," *Truthout*, 2 November 2011.

41. Seymour Melman, *Pentagon Capitalism: The Political Economy of War* (New York: McGraw-Hill, 1970), 65.

42. Cypher, "Critical Analyses of Military Spending and Capitalism," 280.

43. See, for example, Allison Pytlak, ed., *Assuring Destruction Forever: 2019 Edition* (New York: Reaching Critical Will of the Women's International League for Peace and Freedom, 2019).

44. See https://www.sipri.org/databases/milex. These ten countries are the United States, China, Russia, Saudi Arabia, India, France, United Kingdom, Japan, Germany, and South Korea. Planned U.S. nuclear weapons expenditure exceeds the combined military expenses of the eighty-nine countries with the smallest overall military budgets.

45. See Jon Wolfsthal, Jeffrey Lewis, and Marc Quint, "The One Trillion-Dollar Triad—US Strategic Nuclear Modernization over the Next Thirty Years," James Martin Center for Nonproliferation Studies, January 2014, http://www.nonproliferation.org/wp-content/uploads/2016/04/140107_trillion _dollar_nuclear_triad.pdf; and Robert Alvarez, "Yesterday Is Tomorrow: Estimating the Full Cost of a Nuclear Buildup," *Bulletin of the Atomic Scientists*, 3 November 2017, https://thebulletin.org/yesterday-tomorrow-estimating -full-cost-nuclear-buildup11264.

46. Susi Snyder, *Shorting Our Security—Financing the Companies That Make Nuclear Weapons* (Utrecht: PAX and International Campaign to Abolish Nuclear Weapons, 2019).

47. Jacqueline Cabasso, "Putting Nuclear Weapons in Context: The Hidden Architecture of U.S. Militarism," in *The Challenge of Abolishing Nuclear Weapons*, edited by David Krieger (New Brunswick, NJ: Transaction Publishers, 2009), 119–40.

48. See, for example, Gusterson, *Nuclear Rites*; and Maggie Mort, *Building the Trident Network: A Study of the Enrollment of People, Knowledge, and Machines* (Cambridge, MA: MIT Press, 2002).

49. Robert W. DeGrasse, *Military Expansion, Economic Decline* (New York: Council on Economic Priorities, 1983), 32.

50. Greg Mello, "Does Los Alamos National Lab Help or Hurt the New Mexico Economy?" Los Alamos Study Group, 2006, 1, http://www.lasg.org/ LANLecon_impact.pdf.

51. "Quick Take: Women in Science, Technology, Engineering, and Mathematics (STEM)," Catalyst, 14 June 2019, https://www.catalyst.org/research/women-in-science-technology-engineering-and-mathematics-stem.

52. "Facts, Figures," Los Alamos National Laboratory, last updated July 2019, https://www.lanl.gov/about/facts-figures/index.php.

53. Cynthia Enloe, *Maneuvers: The International Politics of Militarizing Women's Lives* (Berkeley: University of California Press, 2000); and Cynthia Enloe, *Bananas, Beaches, and Bases: Making Feminist Sense of International Politics* (Berkeley: University of California Press, 1990).

54. Kumkum Sangari, Neeraj Malik, Sheba Chhachhi, and Tanika Sarkar, "Why Women Must Reject the Bomb," *Out of Nuclear Darkness: The Indian Case for Disarmament* (New Dehli: Movement in India for Nuclear Disarmament, 1998).

55. Philip Alston, the UN's rapporteur on extreme poverty and human rights, said, "If you got a group of misogynists in a room and said how can we make this system work for men and not for women they would not have come up with too many ideas that are not already in place." See Robert Booth and Patrick Butler, "UK Austerity Has Inflicted 'Great Misery' on Citizens, UN Says," *The Guardian*, 16 November 2018, https://www.theguardian.com/society/2018/nov/16/uk-austerity-has-inflicted-great-misery-on-citizens-un-says. See also Diane Elson, "The Impact of Austerity on Women," Women's Budget Group, 3 December 2018, https://wbg.org.uk/resources/the-impact-of-austerity-on-women; and Dawn Foster, "Britain's Austerity Has Gone from Cradle to Grave," *Jacobin*, 9 April 2019, https://www.jacobinmag.com/2019/04/britain-life-expectancy-austerity-conservative-party-tories.

56. Elizabeth Piper, "UK Nuclear Deterrent to Cost $256 Billion, Far More Than Expected," *Reuters*, 25 October 2015, https://www.reuters.com/article/us-britain-defence-trident-exclusive/exclusive-uk-nuclear-deterrent-to-cost-256-billion-far-more-than-expected-idUSKCN0SJ0EP20151025.

57. Spike V. Peterson, "How (the Meaning of) Gender Matters in Political Economy," *New Political Economy* 10, no. 4 (2005): 510.

58. Rosa Luxemburg, *The Accumulation of Capital* (New York: Modern Reader Paperbacks, 1968).

59. Marx, *Capital: A Critique of Political Economy, Volume I*.

60. For further discussion and examples, see Neta C. Crawford, *Pentagon Fuel Use, Climate Change, and the Costs of War* (Providence, RI: Brown University Press, 2019); and Murtaza Hussain, "War on the World: Industrialized Militaries Are a Bigger Part of Climate Change Than You Know," *The Intercept*, 15 September 2019, https://theintercept.com/2019/09/15/climate-change-us-military-war.

61. Mary Kaldor, "Warfare and Capitalism," in *Exterminism and Cold War*, edited by New Left Review (London: Verso, 1982), 262.

62. Karl Marx, *Grundrisse: Foundations of the Critique of Political Economy* (London: Penguin, 1993).

63. Robert J. Lifton and Richard Falk, *Indefensible Weapons: The Political and Psychological Case against Nuclearism* (New York: Basic Books, 1982).

64. Marx, *Capital: A Critique of Political Economy, Volume I*.

65. Anne Harrington de Santana, "Nuclear Weapons as the Currency of Power: Deconstructing the Fetishism of Force," *Nonproliferation Review* 16, no. 3 (2009): 327.

66. Nick Ritchie, "Relinquishing Nuclear Weapons: Identities, Networks and the British Bomb," *International Affairs* 86, no. 2 (2010): 466.

67. Biswas, *Nuclear Desire*, 124.

68. Biswas, *Nuclear Desire*, 125.

69. See, for example, Peter Lavoy, "Nuclear Myths and the Causes of Nuclear Proliferation," *Security Studies* 2, no. 3 (1993): 192–212; Scott Sagan, "Why Do States Build Nuclear Weapons? Three Models in Search of a Bomb," *International Security* 21, no. 3 (Winter 1996/1997): 54–86; Stephen Meyer, *The Dynamics of Nuclear Proliferation* (Chicago: University of Chicago Press, 1984); Jacques Hymans, *The Psychology of Nuclear Proliferation* (Cambridge: Cambridge University Press, 2006); Ritchie, "Relinquishing Nuclear Weapons;" and Nick Ritchie, "Valuing and Devaluing Nuclear Weapons," *Contemporary Security Policy* 34, no. 1 (2013): 155–59.

70. Joseph Masco, *The Nuclear Borderlands: The Manhattan Project in Post-Cold War New Mexico* (Princeton, NJ: Princeton University Press, 2006), 17.

71. Ritchie, "Relinquishing Nuclear Weapons."

72. Bryan C. Taylor and Judith Hendry, "Insisting on Persisting: The Nuclear Rhetoric of Stockpile Stewardship," *Rhetoric and Public Affairs* 11, no. 2 (2008): 314; Biswas, *Nuclear Desire*, 131; Carol Cohn and Sara Ruddick, "A Feminist Ethical Perspective on Weapons of Mass Destruction," in *Ethics and Weapons of Mass Destruction: Religious and Secular Perspectives*, edited by Sohail H. Hashmi and Steven P. Lee (Cambridge: Cambridge University Press, 2004), 19.

73. Darwin BondGraham, Jacqueline Cabasso, Nicholas Robinson, Will Parrish, and Ray Acheson, "Rhetoric vs. Reality: The Political Economy of Nuclear Weapons and Their Elimination," in *Beyond Arms Control: Challenges and Choices for Nuclear Disarmament*, edited by Ray Acheson (New York: Women's International League for Peace and Freedom, 2010), 9–10.

74. Ritchie, "Valuing and Devaluing Nuclear Weapons," 157.

75. Ellsberg, *The Doomsday Machine*, 219.

76. Myrdal, *The Game of Disarmament*, 124.

77. See, for example, Carol Cohn, Felicity Hill, and Sara Ruddick, "The Relevance of Gender for Eliminating Weapons of Mass Destruction," *Weapons of Mass Destruction Commission*, no. 38 (2006); and Cynthia Enloe, *Globalization and Militarism: Feminists Make the Link* (New York: Rowman & Littlefield, 2007).

78. See, for example, Carol Cohn and Sara Ruddick, "A Feminist Ethical Perspective on Weapons of Mass Destruction," 405–35; Maya Eichler, "Militarized Masculinities in International Relations," *Brown Journal of World Affairs* 21, no. 1 (2014): 81–93; Cynthia Enloe, "Beyond 'Rambo': Women and the Varieties of Militarized Masculinity," in *Women and the Military System*, edited by Eva Isaakson (New York: St. Martin's, 1988), 71–93; Enloe, *Bananas, Beaches, and Bases*; Kimberly Hutchings, "Making Sense of Masculinities and War," *Men and Masculinities* 10, no. 4 (June 2008): 389–404; and David H. J. Morgan, "Theater of War: Combat, the Military, and Masculinities," in *Theorizing Masculinities*, edited by Harry Brod and Michael Kaufman (Thousand Oaks, CA: Sage, 1994), 165–82.

79. See, for example, R. Charli Carpenter, "Recognizing Gender-Based Violence against Civilian Men and Boys in Conflict Situations," *Security Dialogue* 37, no. 1 (March 2006): 83–103; R. Charli Carpenter, "Women, Children and Other Vulnerable Groups: Gender, Strategic Frames and the Protection of Civilians as a Transnational Issue," *International Studies Quarterly* 49, no. 2 (June 2005): 295–344; Enloe, *Bananas, Beaches and Bases*; and Enloe, *Globalization and Militarism: Feminists Make the Link*.

80. Cohn, "Sex and Death in the Rational World of Defense Intellectuals," 693.

81. Cohn and Ruddick, "A Feminist Ethical Perspective on Weapons of Mass Destruction," 19.

82. Cohn, "Sex and Death in the Rational World of Defense Intellectuals," 696.

83. Cohn, Hill, and Ruddick, *The Relevance of Gender for Eliminating Weapons of Mass Destruction*, 6.

84. Zack Ford, "Media Fawns over President Trump's Strike on Syria," *ThinkProgress*, 7 April 2017, https://thinkprogress.org/trump-media-syria -attack-cd8bee9d61d6.

85. Associated Press, "North Korean Military Parades: 70 Years of Propaganda, Intimidation and Unity," *Los Angeles Times*, 8 September 2018, https://www.la times.com/world/la-fg-north-korea-military-parades-20180908-story.html.

86. Rowena Mason, Anushka Asthana, and Rajeev Syal, "Theresa May Would Authorize Nuclear Strike Causing Mass Loss of Life," *The Guardian*, 18

July 2016, http://www.theguardian.com/uk-news/2016/jul/18/theresa-may
-takes-aim-at-jeremy-corbyn-over-trident-renewal.

87. Heather Hurlburt, Elizabet Weingarten, Alexandra Stark, and Elena
Souris, *The "Consensual Straitjacket": Four Decades of Women in Nuclear Security* (Washington, DC: New America, 2019), https://www.newamerica.org/
political-reform/reports/the-consensual-straitjacket-four-decades-of-women
-in-nuclear-security.

88. David Brown, "How Women Took Over the Military-Industrial Complex," *Politico*, 2 January 2019, https://www.politico.com/story/2019/01/02/
how-women-took-over-the-military-industrial-complex-1049860.

89. Nancy Fraser, Tithi Bhattacharya, and Cinzia Arruzza, "Notes for a
Feminist Manifesto," *New Left Review* 114 (November–December 2018): 117.

90. Julian Hayda, "Women Now at Top of Military-Industrial Complex. A
Feminist Reaction," *WBEZ 91.5 Chicago*, 8 January 2019, https://www.wbez
.org/shows/worldview/women-now-at-top-of-militaryindustrial-complex-a
-feminist-reaction/900b5028-9f25-4fe0-b778-24b04f4a6115.

91. Ray Acheson, "Feminist Solution: Abolish Nuclear Weapons," in
Feminist Solutions for Ending War, edited by Megan Mackenzie (London: Pluto
Press, 2021).

92. Cohn and Ruddick, "A Feminist Ethical Perspective on Weapons of
Mass Destruction."

93. Cohn, Hill, and Ruddick, *The Relevance of Gender for Eliminating Weapons of Mass Destruction*.

94. Carol Cohn, "Wars, Wimps and Women: Talking Gender and Thinking War," in *Gender and War Talk*, edited by Miriam G. Cooke and Angela
Woollacott (Princeton, NJ: Princeton University Press, 1993), 226–46.

95. Sangari et al., "Why Women Must Reject the Bomb," 52.

96. Cohn, Hill, and Ruddick, *The Relevance of Gender for Eliminating Weapons of Mass Destruction*.

97. Catherine Eschle, "Gender and Valuing Nuclear Weapons," working paper for *Devaluing Nuclear Weapons: Concepts and Challenges*, University of
York, Department of Politics, 20–21 March 2012.

98. Clare Duncanson and Catherine Eschle, "Gender and the Nuclear
Weapons State: A Feminist Critique of the UK Government's White Paper on
Trident," *New Political Scientist* 30, no. 4 (2008): 545–63.

99. Runa Das, "Colonial Legacies, Post-Colonial (In)securities, and
Gender(ed) Representations in South Asia's Nuclear Policies," *Social Identities*
16, no. 6 (2010): 717–40.

100. Cohn, Hill, and Ruddick, *The Relevance of Gender for Eliminating Weapons of Mass Destruction*.

101. Zia Mian, "Beyond the Security Debate: The Moral and Legal Dimensions of Abolition," in *Abolishing Nuclear Weapons: A Debate*, edited by George Perkovich and James Acton (Washington, DC: Carnegie Endowment for Peace, 2009), 295–305.

102. Ray Acheson, "The Nuclear Ban and the Patriarchy: A Feminist Analysis of Opposition to Prohibiting Nuclear Weapons," *Critical Studies on Security* (30 April 2018): 1–5.

103. Ray Acheson, "Patriarchy and the Bomb: Banning Nuclear Weapons against the Opposition of Militarist Masculinities," in *The Gender Imperative: Human Security vs State Security*, edited by Betty A. Reardon and Asha Hans (New York: Routledge, 2019), 392–409.

104. *United States Nuclear Tests: July 1945 through September 1992* (Las Vegas, NV: U.S. Department of Energy, National Nuclear Security Administration Nevada Field Office, September 2015), https://www.nnss.gov/docs/docs _LibraryPublications/DOE_NV-209_Rev16.pdf.

105. Taylor N. Johnson, "'The Most Bombed Nation on Earth': Western Shoshone Resistance to the Nevada National Security Site," *Atlantic Journal of Communication* 26, no. 4 (2018): 224–39.

106. Kyle Mizokami, "America Has Dropped 1,032 Nuclear Weapons (on Itself)," *National Interest*, 30 August 2018, https://nationalinterest.org/blog/ buzz/america-has-dropped-1032-nuclear-weapons-itself-30042.

107. Dimity Hawkins, "Nuclear Weapons Testing in the Pacific: Lessons for the Treaty on the Prohibition of Nuclear Weapons," unpublished paper in author's possession, draft as of 21 May 2018, 11.

108. Hawkins, "Nuclear Weapons Testing in the Pacific," 11.

109. Indigenous statement to the UN Nuclear Weapons Ban Treaty Negotiations, June 2017, http://www.icanw.org/wp-content/uploads/2017/05/ Indigenous-Statement-June-2017.pdf.

110. Minor trials were nuclear tests intended to investigate the effects of fire or nonnuclear explosions on atomic weapons.

111. Nic Maclellan, *Banning Nuclear Weapons: A Pacific Islands Perspective* (Melbourne: International Campaign to Abolish Nuclear Weapons, 2014).

112. Jim McClelland, *The Report of the Royal Commission into British Nuclear Tests in Australia* (Canberra: Australian Government Publishing Service, 1985), 122.

113. McClelland, *The Report of the Royal Commission into British Nuclear Tests in Australia*, 118.

114. Hawkins, "Nuclear Weapons Testing in the Pacific," 10.

115. See, for example, Sebastian Pflugbei, Henrik Paulitz, Angelika Claussen, and Inge Schmitz-Feuerhake, *Health Effects of Chernobyl: 25 years after the*

Reactor Catastrophe (Berlin: German Affiliate of the International Physicians for the Prevention of Nuclear War, April 2011), https://ratical.org/radiation/Chernobyl/HEofC25yrsAC.html; Reiko Watanuki, Yuko Yoshida, and Kiyoko Futagami, *Radioactive Contamination and the Health of Women and Post-Chernobyl Children* (Chernobyl Health Survey and Healthcare for the Victims—Japan Women's Network, 2006); and Whitney Graham and Elena I. Nicklasson, "Maternal Meltdown: From Chernobyl to Fukushima," *Inter Press Service*, 26 April 2011, http://www.ipsnews.net/2011/04/op-ed-maternal-meltdown-from-chernobyl-to-fukushima.

116. Calin Georgescu, *Report of the Special Rapporteur on the Implications for Human Rights of the Environmentally Sound Management and Disposal of Hazardous Substances and Wastes*, Human Rights Council, Twenty-First Session, Agenda Item 3, Promotion and Protection of all Human Rights, Civil, Political, Economic, Social and Cultural Rights, Including the Right to Development, 2013, http://www.un.org/en/ga/search/view_doc.asp?symbol=%20A/HRC/21/48/Add.1.

117. Georgescu, *Report of the Special Rapporteur*, 73.

118. International Commission on Radiological Protection, *Report of the Task Group on Reference Man*, no. 23 (Oxford: Pergamon Press, 1975), 4.

119. Mary Olson, "Human Consequences of Radiation: A Gender Factor in Atomic Harm," in *Civil Society Engagement in Disarmament Processes: The Case for a Nuclear Weapon Ban* (New York: United Nations Office for Disarmament Affairs, 2016), 32.

120. Eric Frohmberg, Robert Goble, Virginia Sanchez, and Dianne Quigley, "The Assessment of Radiation Exposures in Native American Communities from Nuclear Weapons Testing in Nevada," *Risk Analysis* 20, no. 1 (March 2000): 101–11.

121. Laicie Heeley, "To Make and Maintain America's Nukes, Some Communities Pay the Price," *PRI*, 30 January 2018, https://www.pri.org/stories/2018-01-30/make-and-maintain-americas-nukes-some-communities-pay-price.

122. See "Nuclear War: Uranium Mining and Nuclear Tests on Indigenous Land," *Cultural Survival Quarterly Magazine*, September 1993, https://www.culturalsurvival.org/publications/cultural-survival-quarterly/nuclear-war-uranium-mining-and-nuclear-tests-indigenous.

123. Sangari et al., "Why Women Must Reject the Bomb," 48.

124. Biswas, *Nuclear Desire*, 167.

125. Hawkins, "Nuclear Weapons Testing in the Pacific."

126. "U.S. Relations with Marshall Islands," U.S. Department of State, Bureau of East Asian and Pacific Affairs, Fact Sheet, 27 December 2016, https://www.state.gov/r/pa/ei/bgn/26551.htm.

127. Gough Whitlam, *The Whitlam Government 1972–1975* (Melbourne: Penguin, 1985), 611–13.

128. "Algerians Take Steps to Prosecute France for Nuclear Tests," *Middle East Monitor*, 15 February 2017, https://www.middleeastmonitor.com/20170215-algerians-take-steps-to-prosecute-france-for-nuclear-tests.

129. Vincent Intondi, *African Americans against the Bomb* (Stanford, CA: Stanford University Press, 2015).

130. Intondi, *African Americans against the Bomb*, 22.

131. Jacqueline Castledine, *Cold War Progressives: Women's International Organizing for Peace and Freedom* (Urbana: University of Illinois Press, 2012), 17.

132. Ian Zabarte, "Indigenous Peoples Condemn Nuclear Colonialism on 'Columbus' Day," *PopularResistance.org*, 10 October 2016, https://popularresistance.org/indigenous-peoples-condemn-nuclear-colonialism-on-columbus-day.

133. See, for example, Johnson, "'The Most Bombed Nation on Earth," and "Protest, Dissent, and Witness at the Nevada Test Site," *Online Nevada Encyclopedia*, http://www.onlinenevada.org/articles/protest-dissent-and-witness-nevada-test-site.

134. Matthew Neisius, "Western Shoshone Nation Opposes Yucca Mountain Nuclear Repository," *Commodities, Conflict, and Cooperation* (Fall 2016 and Winter 2017), https://sites.evergreen.edu/ccc/warnuclear/shoshone-tribe-opposes-yucca-mountain-nuclear-repository.

135. Zabarte, "Indigenous Peoples Condemn Nuclear Colonialism on 'Columbus' Day."

136. Arundhati Roy, *The Cost of Living* (New York: Modern Library, 1999), 101.

137. Biswas, *Nuclear Desire*, 177.

138. Biswas, *Nuclear Desire*, 179.

139. Cohn and Ruddick, "A Feminist Ethical Perspective on Weapons of Mass Destruction," 19.

140. Pedro Motta Pinto-Coelho, permanent representative of Brazil to the Conference on Disarmament, statement to the 2014 NPT Preparatory Committee, New York, 2 May 2014, http://www.reachingcriticalwill.org/images/documents/Disarmament-fora/npt/prepcom14/statements/2May_Brazil.pdf.

141. Gerard Keown, director for disarmament and nonproliferation, Department of Foreign Affairs and Trade of Ireland, statement to the 2013 NPT Preparatory Committee, Geneva, 25 April 2013, http://www.reaching

criticalwill.org/images/documents/Disarmament-fora/npt/prepcom13/ statements/25April_Ireland.pdf.

142. This was the experience, for example, at the 2019 nuclear Non-Proliferation Treaty Preparatory Committee at the United Nations in New York, when the chair of the meeting had to keep asking the conference room for quiet when smaller delegations took the floor. See Ray Acheson, "Creating the Environment for 'New Thinking,'" *NPT News in Review* 16, no. 3 (6 May 2019): 1, http://reachingcriticalwill.org/images/documents/Disarmament-fora/npt/NIR2019/NIR16.3.pdf.

143. George Orwell, *Animal Farm* (New York: Harcourt Brace, 1945), 50.

144. Myrdal, *The Game of Disarmament*, 331.

145. Myrdal, *The Game of Disarmament*, 326.

146. Myrdal, *The Game of Disarmament*, 331.

CHAPTER 2

1. For deeper and broader history, see Lawrence S. Wittner, *Confronting the Bomb: A Short History of the World Nuclear Disarmament Movement* (Stanford, CA: Stanford University Press, 2009); David Meyer, "Peace Protest and Policy: Explaining the Rise and Decline of Antinuclear Movements in Postwar America," *Policy Studies Journal* 21, no. 1 (1993): 35–51; and David Meyer, "Protest Cycles and Political Process: American Peace Movements in the Nuclear Age," *Political Research Quarterly* 46, no. 3 (1993): 451–79.

2. John Hersey, "Hiroshima," *New Yorker*, 23 August 2016.

3. Rosalind Early, "How to Stop a Nuclear Bomb: The St. Louis Baby Tooth Survey, 50 Years Later," *St. Louis Magazine*, 20 September 2013, https://www.stlmag.com/How-to-Stop-a-Nuclear-Bomb-The-St-Louis-Baby-Tooth-Survey-50-Years-Later.

4. Amy Swerdlow, *Women Strike for Peace: Traditional Motherhood and Radical Politics in the 1960s* (Chicago: University of Chicago Press, 1993).

5. *Economic and Social Consequences of Disarmament*, E/3593/Rev.1 (New York: Department of Economic and Social Affairs, United Nations, 1962), http://undocs.org/E/3593/Rev.1, 1.

6. Bulgaria, Canada, Czechoslovakia, France, Italy, Poland, Romania, United Kingdom, United States, and Soviet Union.

7. Jaja Anucha Wachuku, representative of Nigeria, statement to the Eighteen-Nation Committee on Disarmament, ENDC/PV.3, Geneva, Switzerland, 16 March 1962, 26.

8. Jorge Castañeda, representative of Mexico, statement to the Eighteen-Nation Committee on Disarmament, ENDC/PV.430, Geneva, Switzerland, 21 August 1969, 5.

9. For more on these examples and others, see Nic Maclellan, *Grappling with the Bomb: Britain's Pacific H-bomb Tests* (Canberra: Australian National University, 2017); and Lawrence S. Wittner, "Nuclear Disarmament Activism in Asia and the Pacific, 1971–1996," *Asia-Pacific Journal* 5:25, no. 5 (15 June 2009), https://apjjf.org/-Lawrence-S.-Wittner/3179/article.html.

10. Randall Forsberg, "Call to Halt the Nuclear Arms Race: Proposal for a Mutual US-Soviet Nuclear-Weapon Freeze," 1980, https://livingwiththebomb .files.wordpress.com/2013/08/call-to-halt-arms-race.pdf.

11. David S. Meyer, *A Winter of Discontent: The Nuclear Freeze and American Politics* (New York: Praeger, 1990); Jonathan Schell, "The Spirit of June 12," *The Nation*, 2 July 2007, https://www.thenation.com/article/spirit-june-12.

12. See http://nevadadesertexperience.org for information.

13. See, for example, Gwen Kirk, "Our Greenham Common: Not Just a Place But a Movement," in *Rocking the Ship of State: Towards a Feminist Peace Politics*, edited by Adrienne Haris and Ynestra King (Boulder, CO: Westview Press, 1989), 263–80; and Catherine Eschle, "Beyond Greenham Women? Gender Identities and Anti-Nuclear Activism in Peace Camps," *International Feminist Journal of Politics* 19, no. 4 (2017): 471–90.

14. David Cortright, *Peace: A History of Movements* (Cambridge: Cambridge University Press, 2008).

15. Wittner, *Confronting the Bomb*.

16. Wittner, "Nuclear Disarmament Activism in Asia and the Pacific."

17. David Robie, *Eyes of Fire: The Last Voyage of the Rainbow Warrior* (Auckland: Lindon, 1986).

18. Wittner, "Nuclear Disarmament Activism in Asia and the Pacific," 7.

19. See, for example, Yoel Cohen, *The Whistleblower of Dimona: Israel, Vanunu, and the Bomb* (New York: Holmes & Meier, 2003).

20. "Kazakh Anti-Nuclear Movement Celebrates Tenth Anniversary," *BBC News*, 28 February 1999, http://news.bbc.co.uk/2/hi/asia-pacific/288008.stm.

21. Carl Kaysen, Robert S. McNamara, and George W. Rathjens, "Nuclear Weapons after the Cold War," *Foreign Affairs* 70, no. 4 (Fall 1990): 95–110.

22. Pradful Bidwai and Ackin Vanaik, *New Nukes: India, Pakistan and Global Nuclear Disarmament* (New York: Olive Branch Press, 2000), 36.

23. Wittner, *Confronting the Bomb*.

24. Meyer, *A Winter of Discontent*, 258.

25. Jacqueline Cabasso and Ray Acheson, "Dismantling Discourses: Nuclear Weapons and Human Security," in *Beyond Arms Control: Challenges and Choices*

for Nuclear Disarmament, edited by Ray Acheson (New York: Reaching Critical Will of the Women's International League for Peace and Freedom, 2010), 127–42.

26. Meyer, *A Winter of Discontent*, 262.

27. Alva Myrdal, *The Game of Disarmament: How the United States and Russia Run the Arms Race* (New York: Pantheon Books, 1976).

28. Hansard, House of Commons, Column 260, 1 February 2007.

29. Nick Ritchie, "Legitimizing and Delegitimizing Nuclear Weapons," in *Viewing Nuclear Weapons through a Humanitarian Lens*, edited by John Borrie and Tim Caughley (Geneva: United Nations Institute for Disarmament Research, 2013), 49.

30. Some countries such as Brazil and Sweden abandoned nascent nuclear weapon programs; South Africa built nuclear weapons but unilaterally disarmed at the end of the apartheid government's reign; and nuclear weapon programs have been suspected to varying degrees in Iran, Iraq, Libya, and Syria. But none of these countries acquired or developed nuclear weapons.

31. Myrdal, *The Game of Disarmament*, 174.

32. *Final Document of the Review Conference of the Parties to the Treaty on the Non-Proliferation of Nuclear Weapons*, NPT/CONF/35/I–III (Geneva, 1975).

33. For a detailed accounting of the 2000 NPT Review Conference, see Reaching Critical Will's *NPT News in Review*, as well as statements and documents from the conference at http://www.reachingcriticalwill.org/disarmament-fora/npt/2000.

34. For a detailed accounting of the negotiations during the 2005 NPT Review Conference, see Reaching Critical Will's *NPT News in Review* as well as statements and documents from the conference at http://www.reachingcritical will.org/disarmament-fora/npt/2005.

35. Paul Meyer, permanent representative of Canada to the Conference on Disarmament, statement to the 2005 Non-Proliferation Treaty Review Conference, New York, 27 May 2005, http://www.reachingcriticalwill.org/images/documents/Disarmament-fora/npt/revcon2005/GDstatements/canada27.pdf.

36. *Draft Elements of an UNGA60 First Committee Resolution "Initiating work on priority disarmament and non-proliferation issues,"* submitted by Brazil, Canada, Kenya, Mexico, New Zealand, and Sweden, October 2005, http://www.reaching criticalwill.org/images/documents/Disarmament-fora/1com/1com05/documents/draftelementsinitiating.pdf.

37. Judith Mbula Bahemuka, permanent representative of Kenya to the United Nations, statement to the First Committee on Disarmament and International Security, New York, 7 October 2005, http://www.reachingcriticalwill

.org/images/documents/Disarmament-fora/1com/1com05/statements/kenya 7oct.pdf.

38. Paul Meyer, permanent representative of Canada to the Conference on Disarmament, statement on behalf of Brazil, Canada, Kenya, Mexico, New Zealand, and Sweden to the First Committee on Disarmament and International Security, New York, 12 October 2005.

39. Jennifer Nordstrom, "Disarmament Machinery," *First Committee Monitor* 5, no. 2 (17 October 2005), http://www.reachingcriticalwill.org/images/documents/Disarmament-fora/1com/FCM05/FCM-2005-2.pdf.

40. *Discussion and Proposals on the International Campaign to Abolish Nuclear Weapons*, 28 October 2006.

41. Dimity Hawkins and Tilman Ruff, "How Melbourne Activists Launched a Campaign for Nuclear Disarmament and Won a Nobel Prize," *The Conversation*, 9 October 2017.

42. Ronald McCoy, "The International Campaign to Abolish Nuclear Weapons," presentation to ICAN Campaigners Meeting, Geneva, Switzerland, 30 April 2016, http://www.icanw.org/wp-content/uploads/2016/07/THE-CAMPAIGN-TO-BAN-NUCLEAR-WEAPONS.pdf.

43. *Discussion and Proposals on the International Campaign to Abolish Nuclear Weapons*, 28 October 2006.

44. Dimity Hawkins, "From Little Things . . . ," Lecture at the Centre for Ethical Leadership, Ormond College, Melbourne University, Melbourne, Australia, 11 April 2018, https://cel.edu.au/images/uploads/research_paper_files/Ethical-Leadership-Program-Dimity-Hawkins-ICAN.pdf.

45. Will Parrish and Darwin BondGraham, "Anti-Nuclear Nuclearism," *Foreign Policy in Focus*, 12 January 2009, http://fpif.org/anti-nuclear_nuclearism.

46. George P. Shultz, William J. Perry, Henry A. Kissinger, and Sam Nunn, "A World Free of Nuclear Weapons," *Wall Street Journal*, 4 January 2007; and George P. Shultz, William J. Perry, Henry A. Kissinger, and Sam Nunn, "Toward a Nuclear-Free World," *Wall Street Journal*, 15 January 2008.

47. Parrish and BondGraham, "Anti-Nuclear Nuclearism."

48. Darwin BondGraham, Nicholas Robinson, and Will Parrish, "California's Nuclear Nexus: A Faux Disarmament Plan Has Roots in the Golden State's Pro-Nuclear Lobby," *Z Magazine*, 20 November 2009, https://zcomm.org/zmagazine/californias-nuclear-nexus-by-darwin-bondgraham.

49. Hans Kristensen, "New START Has New Counting," Federation of American Scientists Strategic Security Blog, 29 March 2010, http://www.fas.org/blog/ssp/2010/03/newstart.php.

50. Ivan Oelrich, "Hardly a Jump START," Federation of American Scientists Strategic Security Blog, 29 March 2010, http://www.fas.org/blog/ssp/2010/03/hardly-a-jump-start.php.

51. Luiz Filipe de Macedo Soares, permanent representative of Brazil to the Conference on Disarmament, statement to the UN General Assembly First Committee on Disarmament and International Security, New York, 5 October 2010, http://www.reachingcriticalwill.org/images/documents/Disarmament-fora/1com/1com10/statements/5Oct_brazil.pdf.

52. George P. Shultz, William J. Perry, Henry A. Kissinger, and Sam Nunn, "How to Protect Our Nuclear Deterrent," *Wall Street Journal*, 19 January 2010.

53. "FY2011 Budget Request a Critical Step toward Implementing President Obama's Nuclear Security Vision," News and Information, National Nuclear Security Administration, 1 February 2010, http://nnsa.energy.gov/2816.htm.

54. Robert S. Norris and Hans M. Kristensen, "Russian Nuclear Forces, 2010," *Bulletin of the Atomic Scientists*, January/February 2010.

55. *Lifting the Nuclear Shadow: Creating the Conditions for Abolishing Nuclear Weapons*, UK Foreign and Commonwealth Office, February 2009; and *The Road to 2010: Addressing the Nuclear Question in the Twenty First Century*, UK Foreign and Commonwealth Office, July 2009.

56. John Ainslie, *The Trident Shambles* (Glasgow: Scottish CND, 2016).

57. For details of modernization programs in place by 2012, see Ray Acheson, ed., *Assuring Destruction Forever: Nuclear Weapon Modernisation around the World* (New York: Reaching Critical Will of the Women's International League for Peace and Freedom, 2012). For the most recent study of modernization programs, see Allison Pytlak, ed., *Assuring Destruction Forever: 2019 Edition* (New York: Reaching Critical Will of the Women's International League for Peace and Freedom, 2019).

58. Myrdal, *The Game of Disarmament*, 25.

59. Myrdal, *The Game of Disarmament*, 77.

60. Francisco Clementino San Tiago Dantas, representative of Brazil, statement to the Conference of the Eighteen-Nation Committee on Disarmament, ENDC/PV.3, Geneva, Switzerland, 16 March 1962.

61. Jaja Anucha Wachuku, representative of Nigeria, statement to the Conference of the Eighteen-Nation Committee on Disarmament, ENDC/PV.8, Geneva, Switzerland, 23 March 1962.

62. Luis Padilla Nervo, representative of Mexico, statement to the Conference of the Eighteen-Nation Committee on Disarmament, ENDC/PV.14, Geneva, Switzerland, 3 April 1962, p. 20.

63. *Treaty Banning Nuclear Weapon Tests in the Atmosphere, in Outer Space and under Water*, opened for signature 8 August 1963, http://www.reachingcriticalwill.org/images/documents/Resources/Treaties/PTBT.pdf.

64. *Congressional Record* 109, no. 12 (15 July 1974): 16790–1, quoted by Harold Karan Jacobson and Eric Stein, *Diplomats, Scientists, and Politicians: The United States and the Nuclear Test-Ban Negotiations* (Ann Arbor: University of Michigan Press, 1966), 462.

65. Jacobson and Stein, *Diplomats, Scientists, and Politicians*, 462.

66. Myrdal, *The Game of Disarmament*, 95.

67. Myrdal, *The Game of Disarmament*, 106–7.

68. Andrew Lichterman and Jacqueline Cabasso, *Faustian Bargain 2000: Why "Stockpile Stewardship" Is Fundamentally Incompatible with the Process of Nuclear Disarmament* (Oakland, CA: Western States Legal Foundation, May 2000), http://wslfweb.org/docs/fb2000.pdf.

69. Doug McAdam, *Political Process and the Development of Black Insurgency, 1930–1970* (Chicago: University of Chicago Press, 1982); and David Meyer, "Protest Cycles and Political Process."

70. David Meyer, "Protest and Political Opportunities," *Annual Review of Sociology* 30 (11 August 2004): 137.

71. As David Plotke has explained, the notion of what is moderate or center has been shifted away from the aspirations of the left and toward those of the right. The right-wing expanded and then divided into "traditional conservatives," a "far right," and a "militant ultraright"—and thus "redefined the political center." David Plotke, *Democracy and Boundaries: Themes in Contemporary Politics* (Uppsala: Swedish Institute for North American Studies, 2002), xxxi.

72. Sarah S. Stroup and Wendy H. Wong, *The Authority Trap: Strategic Choices of INGOs* (Ithaca, NY: Cornell University Press, 2017), 2.

73. Stroup and Wong, *The Authority Trap*, 2.

74. Scott Ludlam, "How Politics Works in Australia, and How to Fix It," *The Monthly*, March 2018, https://www.themonthly.com.au/issue/2018/march/1519822800/scott-ludlam/how-politics-works-australia-and-how-fix-it.

75. Deborah Doane, "Do International NGOs Still Have the Right to Exist?" *The Guardian*, 13 March 2016, https://www.theguardian.com/global-development-professionals-network/2016/mar/13/do-international-ngos-still-have-the-right-to-exist.

76. Meyer, *A Winter of Discontent*, 263.

77. Andrew Lichterman, "Nuclear Disarmament, Civil Society and Democracy," *Disarmament Forum* 4 (2010): 54.

78. Stroup and Wong, *The Authority Trap*, 5.

79. Statement by the People's Republic of China, France, the Russian Federation, the United Kingdom of Great Britain and Northern Ireland, and the United States of America to the 2010 Non-Proliferation Treaty Review Conference, New York, 5 May 2010, http://www.reachingcriticalwill.org/images/documents/Disarmament-fora/npt/revcon2010/statements/5May_P5-full.pdf.

80. For a detailed accounting of the 2010 NPT Review Conference, see Reaching Critical Will's *NPT News in Review* as well as statements and documents from the conference at http://www.reachingcriticalwill.org/disarmament-fora/npt/2010.

81. Steffan Kongstad, director general, Ministry of Foreign Affairs of Norway, statement to the 2010 Non-Proliferation Treaty Review Conference, Main Committee I, New York, 11 May 2010, http://www.reachingcriticalwill.org/images/documents/Disarmament-fora/npt/revcon2010/statements/11May_MCI_Norway.pdf.

82. Jürg Lauber, permanent representative of the Swiss Confederation to the Conference on Disarmament, statement to the 2010 Non-Proliferation Treaty Review Conference, New York, 7 May 2010, http://www.reaching criticalwill.org/images/documents/Disarmament-fora/npt/revcon2010/statements/7May_Switzerland.pdf.

83. Although official statements are not available for many interventions referenced below, daily reporting on these statements can be found at http://www.reachingcriticalwill.org/disarmament-fora/npt/2010/nir.

84. Ray Acheson, "We Hail Concrete, Transparent, Irreversible, Verifiable Action," *NPT News in Review* 9, no. 17 (25 May 2010): 1–2, http://www.reachingcriticalwill.org/images/documents/Disarmament-fora/npt/NIR2010/No17.pdf.

85. Vanu Gopala Menon, permanent representative of Singapore to the United Nations, statement to the 2010 Non-Proliferation Treaty Review Conference, New York, 6 May 2010, http://www.reachingcriticalwill.org/images/documents/Disarmament-fora/npt/revcon2010/statements/6May_Singapore.pdf.

86. Statement by the delegation of Ireland to the 2010 NPT Review Conference, New York, 11 May 2010.

CHAPTER 3

1. Christine Emba, "'Reclaiming My Time' Is Bigger Than Maxine Waters," *Washington Post*, 1 August 2017, https://www.washingtonpost .com/blogs/post-partisan/wp/2017/08/01/reclaiming-my-time-is-bigger-than -maxine-waters/?utm_term=.d19637107436.

2. See Hugh Gusterson, "Democracy, Hypocrisy, First Use," Virtual Round-table on Presidential First Use of Nuclear Weapons, Public Books, 26 February 2018, http://www.publicbooks.org/virtual-roundtable-on-presidential-first-use -of-nuclear-weapons/#gusterson.

3. Nick Ritchie, "Valuing and Devaluing Nuclear Weapons," *Contemporary Security Policy* 34, no. 1 (2013): 152.

4. Ritchie, "Valuing and Devaluing Nuclear Weapons." Also see Jeffrey Checkel, *Ideas and International Political Changes: Soviet/Russian Behavior and the End of the Cold War* (New Haven, CT: Yale University Press, 1997); and Albert Yee, "The Causal Effects of Ideas on Policies," *International Organization*, 50, no. 1 (1996): 69–108.

5. Seyla Benhabib, *Critique, Norm and Utopia: A Study of the Foundations of Critical Theory* (New York: Columbia University Press, 1986), 21.

6. Thomas S. Kuhn, *The Structure of Scientific Revolution* (Chicago: University of Chicago Press, 1962).

7. Kuhn, *The Structure of Scientific Revolution*, 77.

8. Alexander Kmentt, "The Development of the International Initiative on the Humanitarian Impact of Nuclear Weapons and Its Effect on the Nuclear Weapons Debate," *International Review of the Red Cross* 97 (2015): 682.

9. Nick Ritchie, "Pathways to Nuclear Disarmament: Delegitimising Nuclear Violence," working paper for the UN Open-ended Working Group on Nuclear Disarmament, Geneva, Switzerland, 11 May 2016, http:// www.reachingcriticalwill.org/images/documents/Disarmament-fora/OEWG/ statements/11May_NickRitchie-paper.pdf, 4.

10. Ritchie, "Pathways to Nuclear Disarmament," 3.

11. See, for example, Patrick Garrity, "The Depreciation of Nuclear Weapons in International Politics: Possibilities, Limits, Uncertainties," *Journal of Strategic Studies* 14, no. 4 (1991): 463–541; Jack Barkenbus, "Devaluing Nuclear Weapons," *Science, Technology & Human Values* 14, no. 4 (1989): 425–40; and Michael Quinlan, "The Future of Nuclear Weapons: Policy for Western Possessors," *International Affairs* 69, no. 3 (1993): 485–96.

12. *Report of the Canberra Commission on the Elimination of Nuclear Weapons* (Canberra: Department of Foreign Affairs and Trade, Commonwealth of Australia, 1996); *Report of the Tokyo Forum for Nuclear Non-Proliferation and*

Disarmament (Tokyo: Ministry of Foreign Affairs, Government of Japan, 1999); Hans Blix, *Weapons of Terror: Freeing the World of Nuclear, Chemical and Biological Arms* (Stockholm: WMD Commission, 2006); and *Eliminating Nuclear Threats: A Practical Agenda for Global Policymakers* (Canberra/Tokyo: International Commission on Nuclear Non-Proliferation and Disarmament, 2009).

13. Ritchie, "Valuing and Devaluing Nuclear Weapons," 149.

14. Ken Berry, Patricia Lewis, Benoît Pélopidas, Nikolai Sokov, and Ward Wilson, *Delegitimizing Nuclear Weapons: Examining the Validity of Nuclear Deterrence* (Monterey, CA: Monterey Institute of International Studies, 2010).

15. Statement by the U.S. Delegation to the UN General Assembly First Committee on Disarmament and International Security, New York, 15 October 2009, http://www.reachingcriticalwill.org/images/documents/Disarmament-fora/1com/1com09/statements/15Oct_US.pdf.

16. Ritchie, "Relinquishing Nuclear Weapons: Identities, Networks and the British Bomb," 482–83.

17. Ritchie, "Deterrence Dogma? Challenging the Relevance of British Nuclear Weapons," 84.

18. Barash, "Nuclear Deterrence Is a Myth. And a Lethal One at That."

19. Andrew Lichterman, "Deterrence, Torture, Power," *NPT News in Review* 8, no. 9 (4 May 2009), 4, http://www.reachingcriticalwill.org/images/documents/Disarmament-fora/npt/NIR2009/No1.pdf.

20. Barash, "Nuclear Deterrence Is a Myth. And a Lethal One at That."

21. Alexander Kmentt, "Nuclear Deterrence as a Belief System," *Security Index: A Russian Journal on International Security* 19, no. 2 (2013): 77.

22. Alison Kelly, delegation of Ireland, statement on behalf of the New Agenda Coalition to the UN General Assembly First Committee on Disarmament and International Security, New York, 4 October 2010, http://www.reachingcriticalwill.org/images/documents/Disarmament-fora/1com/1com10/statements/4Oct_NAC.pdf.

23. Espen Barthe Eide, deputy minister of foreign affairs for Norway, statement to the UN General Assembly First Committee on Disarmament and International Security, New York, 4 October 2010, http://www.reachingcriticalwill.org/images/documents/Disarmament-fora/1com/1com10/statements/4Oct_Norway.pdf.

24. Fazli Çorman, chargé d'affaires and interim and deputy permanent representative of Turkey to the United Nations, statement to the UN General Assembly First Committee on Disarmament and International Security, New York, 6 October 2010, http://www.reachingcriticalwill.org/images/documents/Disarmament-fora/1com/1com10/statements/6Oct_Turkey.pdf.

25. Bolivia, Chile, Colombia, Ecuador, Peru, and Suriname are associate countries; New Zealand and Mexico are observers. Venezuela is a full member but has been suspended since 2016.

26. Luiz Filipe de Macedo Soare, permanent representative of Brazil to the Conference on Disarmament, statement on behalf of MERCOSUR and Associated States to the UN General Assembly First Committee on Disarmament and International Security, New York, 13 October 2010, http://www.reaching criticalwill.org/images/documents/Disarmament-fora/1com/1com10/statements/13Oct_MERCOSUR.pdf.

27. Raymond O. Wolfe, permanent representative of Jamaica to the United Nations, statement to the UN General Assembly First Committee on Disarmament and International Security, New York, 6 October 2010, http://www.reachingcriticalwill.org/images/documents/Disarmament-fora/1com/1com10/statements/6Oct_Jamaica.pdf.

28. Ritchie, "Deterrence Dogma," 96.

29. Wilson, *Five Myths about Nuclear Weapons*.

30. Nobuo Hayashi, presentation to the Third Conference on the Humanitarian Impact of Nuclear Weapons, Vienna, 9 December 2014, http://www.reachingcriticalwill.org/images/documents/Disarmament-fora/vienna-2014/9Dec_Hayashi.pdf.

31. Hayashi, presentation to the Third Conference on the Humanitarian Impact of Nuclear Weapons.

32. Lichterman, "Deterrence, Torture, Power," 2.

33. Michel Foucault, *The Order of Things: An Archeology of the Human Sciences* (Paris: Editions Gallimard, 1966).

34. Judith Butler, *Gender Trouble: Feminism and the Subversion of Identity* (New York: Routledge, 1999).

35. Cohn, "Sex and Death in the Rational World of Defense Intellectuals."

36. Lichterman, "Deterrence, Torture, Power," 3.

37. Cohn and Ruddick, "A Feminist Ethical Perspective on Weapons of Mass Destruction," 12.

38. Cohn and Ruddick, "A Feminist Ethical Perspective on Weapons of Mass Destruction," 13.

39. Cohn and Ruddick, "A Feminist Ethical Perspective on Weapons of Mass Destruction," 15.

40. Berry et al., *Delegitimizing Nuclear Weapons*, 29.

41. Butler, *Gender Trouble*, xxiii.

42. Butler, *Gender Trouble*, xxiii.

43. Gwen Benaway, "Repair," *GUTS*, 3 May 2019, http://gutsmagazine.ca/repair.

44. Ritchie, "Legitimizing and Delegitimizing Nuclear Weapons," 44.

45. Christian Reus-Smit, "International Crises of Legitimacy," *International Politics* 44, no. 1 (2007): 157–74.

46. Steffan Kongstad, director general of the Ministry of Foreign Affairs of Norway, statement to the UN General Assembly First Committee on Disarmament and International Security, New York, 6 October 2009, http://www.reachingcriticalwill.org/images/documents/Disarmament-fora/1com/1com09/statements/6Oct_Norway.pdf.

47. Jonas Gahr Støre, "Disarmament—Reframing the Challenge," presentation to the Norwegian Atlantic Committee, 45th Annual Conference, Oslo, Norway, 1 February 2010, https://www.regjeringen.no/en/aktuelt/disarmament/id592550.

48. Jürg Lauber, permanent representative of Switzerland to the Conference on Disarmament, statement to the UN General Assembly First Committee on Disarmament and International Security, New York, 5 October 2010, http://www.reachingcriticalwill.org/images/documents/Disarmament-fora/1com/1com10/statements/5Oct_Switzerland.pdf.

49. Jakob Kellenberger, "Bringing the Era of Nuclear Weapons to an End," presentation to the Geneva Diplomatic Corps, Geneva, Switzerland, 20 April 2010, https://www.icrc.org/eng/resources/documents/statement/nuclear-weapons-statement-200410.htm.

50. See https://www.icrc.org/eng/war-and-law/treaties-customary-law/geneva-conventions/overview-geneva-conventions.htm.

51. *Nuclear Weapons and International Humanitarian Law*, International Committee of the Red Cross, May 2013, https://www.icrc.org/eng/assets/files/2013/4132-4-nuclear-weapons-ihl-2013.pdf.

52. Micheline Calmy-Rey, minister for foreign affairs of Switzerland, statement to the 2010 NPT Review Conference, New York, 3 May 2010, http://www.reachingcriticalwill.org/images/documents/Disarmament-fora/npt/revcon2010/statements/3May_Switzerland.pdf.

53. "Mankind is faced with a problem of extreme gravity . . ." International Committee of the Red Cross, 5 September 1945, https://www.icrc.org/eng/resources/documents/statement/69eezs.htm.

54. Yves Sandoz, "Advisory Opinion of the International Court of Justice on the legality of the threat or use of nuclear weapons," *International Review of the Red Cross* 37, no. 316 (February 1997): 6.

55. Myrdal, *The Game of Disarmament*, 259.

56. See Yves Sandoz, Cristophe Swinarski, and Bruno Zimmerman, eds., *Commentary on the Additional Protocols of 8 June 1977 to the Geneva Conventions of 12 August 1949* (Geneva: ICRC/Nijhoff Publishers, 1987), 592.

57. *Legality of the Threat or Use of Nuclear Weapons*, General List No. 95, Advisory Opinion of 8 July 1996.

58. *Legality of the Threat or Use of Nuclear Weapons*, para. 105(2)E.

59. "ICRC statement to the United Nations General Assembly on the Advisory Opinion of the International Court of Justice on the legality of the threat or use of nuclear weapons," *International Review of the Red Cross* 37, no. 316 (February 1997): 119.

60. John Burroughs, *The Legality of Threat or Use of Nuclear Weapons: A Guide to the Historic Opinion of the International Court of Justice* (Münster: Lit Verlag, 1997).

61. *Legality of the Threat or Use of Nuclear Weapons*, paras. 78, 79.

62. Burroughs, *The Legality of Threat or Use of Nuclear Weapons*.

63. Cohn and Ruddick, "An Ethical Feminist Perspective on Weapons of Mass Destruction."

64. Myrdal, *The Game of Disarmament*, 259.

65. Ray Acheson, "Human Security Disarmament," *First Committee Monitor* 9, no. 1 (4 October 2010): 3, http://www.reachingcriticalwill.org/images/documents/Disarmament-fora/1com/FCM10/FCM-2010-1.pdf.

66. Michael Spindelegger, minister for European and international affairs of Austria, statement to the 2010 NPT Review Conference, New York, 3 May 2010, http://www.reachingcriticalwill.org/images/documents/Disarmament-fora/npt/revcon2010/statements/3May_Austria.pdf.

67. Calmy-Rey, statement to the 2010 NPT Review Conference.

68. Eide, statement to the UN General Assembly First Committee on Disarmament and International Security.

69. Xolisa Mabhongo, permanent representative of South Africa to the United Nations in Vienna, statement to the UN General Assembly First Committee on Disarmament and International Security, New York, 13 October 2010, http://www.reachingcriticalwill.org/images/documents/Disarmament-fora/1com/1com10/statements/13Otc_SouthAfrica.pdf.

70. Ray Acheson and John Burroughs, *Revitalizing Multilateral Disarmament Negotiations: An Alternative Approach* (New York: Reaching Critical Will of the Women's International League for Peace and Freedom and the Lawyers Committee on Nuclear Policy, July 2011), http://www.reachingcriticalwill.org/images/documents/Disarmament-fora/cd/revitalizing-disarmament-negotiations.pdf.

71. Christian Strohal, permanent representative of Austria to the United Nations in Geneva, statement to the UN General Assembly First Committee on Disarmament and International Security, New York, 24 October 2011, http://www.reachingcriticalwill.org/images/documents/Disarmament-fora/1com/1com11/statements/24Oct_Austria.pdf.

72. Paul Meyer, "Disarmament: Kicking the Can down the Road," *embassymag.ca*, 9 November 2011.

73. "Working towards the Elimination of Nuclear Weapons," Resolution 1, Council of Delegates of the International Red Cross and Red Crescent Movement, Geneva, Switzerland, 26 November 2011, https://www.icrc.org/eng/resources/documents/resolution/council-delegates-resolution-1-2011.htm.

74. "Working towards the Elimination of Nuclear Weapons."

75. "Humanitarian conference on nuclear weapons to take place in 2013," Media Release, International Campaign to Abolish Nuclear Weapons, 20 April 2012, http://www.icanw.org/wp-content/uploads/2012/08/2012-20April-Oslo Conference.pdf.

76. See Beatrice Fihn, ed., *The 2010 Action Plan Monitoring Report* (New York: Reaching Critical Will of the Women's International League for Peace and Freedom, 2012), http://www.reachingcriticalwill.org/images/documents/Publications/2010-Action-Plan/RCW_Final_Report.pdf.

77. "Nuclear Weapon States Discuss Nuclear Disarmament Obligations," UK Foreign and Commonwealth Office, 6 July 2011, http://www.fco.gov.uk/en/news/latest-news/?view=PressS&id=627529382.

78. See Acheson, *Assuring Destruction Forever*.

79. Statement by the delegation of Australia to the 2012 Non-Proliferation Treaty Preparatory Committee, Vienna, 4 May 2012.

80. Mikhail I. Uliyanov, director of the department for security affairs and disarmament of the Russian Federation, statement to the 2012 Non-Proliferation Treaty Preparatory Committee, Vienna, 30 April 2012, http://www.reachingcriticalwill.org/images/documents/Disarmament-fora/npt/prepcom12/statements/30April_Russia.pdf.

81. "Russia Details Planned Nuke Updates," *Global Security Newswire*, 24 February 2011.

82. Statement on the humanitarian dimension of nuclear disarmament by Austria, Chile, Costa Rica, Denmark, Holy See, Egypt, Indonesia, Ireland, Malaysia, Mexico, New Zealand, Nigeria, Norway, Philippines, South Africa, and Switzerland to the 2012 Non-Proliferation Treaty Preparatory Committee, Vienna, 2 May 2012, http://www.reachingcriticalwill.org/images/documents/Disarmament-fora/npt/prepcom12/statements/2May_IHL.pdf.

83. Jo Adamson, ambassador for the United Kingdom to the Conference on Disarmament, statement to the 2012 Non-Proliferation Treaty Preparatory Committee, Vienna, 3 May 2012, http://www.reachingcriticalwill.org/images/documents/Disarmament-fora/npt/prepcom12/statements/3May_UK.pdf.

84. Statement by the delegation of France to the 2012 Non-Proliferation Treaty Preparatory Committee, Vienna, 3 May 2012, http://www

.reachingcriticalwill.org/images/documents/Disarmament-fora/npt/prep com12/statements/3May_France.pdf.

85. Statement by the U.S. delegation to the 2012 Non-Proliferation Treaty Preparatory Committee, Vienna, 3 May 2012, http://www.reaching criticalwill.org/images/documents/Disarmament-fora/npt/prepcom12/ statements/3May_US.pdf.

86. Geir O. Pederson, permanent representative of Norway to the United Nations, statement to the UN General Assembly First Committee on Disarmament and International Security, New York, 12 October 2012, http://www.reachingcriticalwill.org/images/documents/Disarmament-fora/ 1com/1com12/statements/12Oct_Norway.pdf.

87. See *Taking Forward Multilateral Disarmament Negotiations*, Resolution A/6.1/67/L.46, UN General Assembly First Committee on Disarmament and International Security, New York, 19 October 2012, http://www.reachingcritical will.org/images/documents/Disarmament-fora/1com/1com12/resolutions/ L46.pdf.

88. Christian Strohal, permanent representative of Austria to the United Nations in Geneva, statement to the UN General Assembly First Committee on Disarmament and International Security, New York, 10 October 2012, http://www.reachingcriticalwill.org/images/ documents/Disarmament-fora/1com/1com12/statements/10Oct_Austria.pdf.

89. Statement by civil society on disarmament machinery and the rule of consensus to the UN General Assembly First Committee on Disarmament and International Security, New York, 1 November 2012, http://www.reaching criticalwill.org/images/documents/Disarmament-fora/1com/1com12/ statements/1Nov_NGO_machinery.pdf.

90. Laura Kennedy, permanent representative of the United States to the United Nations in Geneva, statement to the UN General Assembly First Committee on Disarmament and International Security, New York, 17 October 2012, http://www.reachingcriticalwill.org/images/documents/Disarmament-fora/ 1com/1com12/statements/17Oct_USA.pdf.

91. Inga M. W. Nyhamar, deputy director general of the Ministry of Foreign Affairs of Norway, statement to the UN General Assembly First Committee on Disarmament and International Security, New York, 18 October 2012, http://www.reachingcriticalwill.org/images/documents/Disarmament-fora/ 1com/1com12/statements/18Oct_Norway.pdf.

92. See Guy Pollard, deputy permanent representative of the United Kingdom, explanation of vote by France, the United Kingdom, and the United States on L.46, "Taking Forward Multilateral Nuclear Disarmament Negotiations," to the UN General Assembly First Committee on Disarmament and

International Security, New York, 6 November 2012, http://www.reaching
criticalwill.org/images/documents/Disarmament-fora/1com/1com12/eov/
L46_France-UK-US.pdf; and Explanation of vote by the Russian Federation
on L.46, "Taking Forward Multilateral Nuclear Disarmament Negotiations," to
the UN General Assembly First Committee on Disarmament and International
Security, New York, 6 November 2012.

93. Kelly Anderson, deputy permanent representative of Canada to the Conference on Disarmament, statement to the UN General Assembly First Committee on Disarmament and International Security, New York, 2 November
2012, http://www.reachingcriticalwill.org/images/documents/Disarmament-
fora/1com/1com12/statements/2Nov_Canada.pdf.

94. Statement on the humanitarian dimension of nuclear disarmament by
Algeria, Argentina, Austria, Bangladesh, Belarus, Brazil, Chile, Colombia, Costa
Rica, Denmark, Ecuador, Egypt, Holy See, Iceland, Ireland, Kazakhstan, Liechtenstein, Malaysia, Malta, Marshall Islands, Mexico, New Zealand, Nigeria,
Norway, Peru, Philippines, Samoa, Sierra Leone, South Africa, Swaziland, and
Switzerland to the UN General Assembly First Committee on Disarmament
and International Security, New York, 22 October 2012, http://www.reaching
criticalwill.org/images/documents/Disarmament-fora/1com/1com12/
statements/22Oct_Switzerland.pdf.

CHAPTER 4

1. Algeria, Argentina, Austria, Bangladesh, Belarus, Brazil, Chile, Colombia,
Costa Rica, Denmark, Ecuador, Egypt, Holy See, Iceland, Ireland, Kazakhstan,
Liechtenstein, Malaysia, Malta, Marshall Islands, Mexico, New Zealand, Nigeria, Norway, Peru, Philippines, Samoa, Sierra Leone, South Africa, Swaziland,
and Switzerland.

2. For details, see https://humanitariandisarmament.org.

3. Felicity Ruby, "'Doing a Landmines' on Gender and Nukes," presentation to Towards Human Security: Civil Society Conference, 10th Anniversary
of the Mine Ban Treaty, Oslo, Norway, September 2007.

4. Ruby, "'Doing a Landmines' on Gender and Nukes."

5. Ray Acheson, "Time to Reframe the Debate," *First Committee Monitor* 8,
no. 1 (5 October 2009): 3, http://www.reachingcriticalwill.org/images/docu-
ments/Disarmament-fora/1com/FCM09/FCM-2009-1.pdf.

6. Participants came from diverse backgrounds and areas of work including
armed violence, the arms trade, cluster munitions, conflict prevention, human
security, humanitarian action, land mines, and small arms. Many participants had

been involved in the Oslo and Ottawa processes, as well as other disarmament-related multilateral work. A summary of the symposium and its findings is contained in John Borrie, Maya Brehm, Silvia Cattaneo, and David Atwood, "Learn, Adapt, Succeed: Potential Lessons from the Ottawa and Oslo Processes for Other Disarmament and Arms Control Challenges," in *Beyond Arms Control: Challenges and Choices for Nuclear Disarmament*, edited by Ray Acheson (New York: Women's International League for Peace and Freedom, 2010), 197–209.

7. John Borrie, *Unacceptable Harm: A History of How the Treaty to Ban Cluster Munitions Was Won* (New York and Geneva: United Nations Institute for Disarmament Research, 2009), 31–32.

8. Ray Acheson, "Crisis of Relevance," *First Committee Monitor* 7, no. 5 (3 November 2008), http://www.reachingcriticalwill.org/images/documents/ Disarmament-fora/1com/FCM08/FCM-2008-5.pdf.

9. Acheson, "Time to Reframe the Debate," 1.

10. Cohn and Ruddick, "A Feminist Ethical Perspective on Weapons of Mass Destruction," 7.

11. Cohn and Ruddick, "A Feminist Ethical Perspective on Weapons of Mass Destruction," 9.

12. Jonas Gahr Støre, "Disarmament—Reframing the Challenge," presentation to the Norwegian Atlantic Committee, 45th Annual Conference, Oslo, Norway, 1 February 2010, https://www.regjeringen.no/en/aktuelt/ disarmament/id592550.

13. At that time made up of representatives of organizations including WILPF, Acronym Institute for Disarmament Diplomacy, Article 36, International Physicians for the Prevention of Nuclear War and some of its affiliates, Norwegian People's Aid, Peace Boat, and Seguridad Humana en Latinoamérica y el Caribe, as well as a few dedicated staff members.

14. Interview with author, INT18, 15 May 2018.

15. *A Treaty Banning Nuclear Weapons: Developing a Legal Framework for the Prohibition and Elimination of Nuclear Weapons* (New York: Women's International League for Peace and Freedom and Article 36, 2014), http://www .reachingcriticalwill.org/images/documents/Publications/a-treaty-banning -nuclear-weapons.pdf.

16. "Last US Cluster Bomb Manufacturer Ends Production," *Russia Today*, 1 September 2016, https://www.rt.com/usa/357889-us-cluster-bombs -production.

17. See, for example, Mary Wareham, "Dispatches: How to Stop US Production of Banned Cluster Munitions," Human Rights Watch, 16 June 2016, https://www.hrw.org/news/2016/06/16/dispatches-how-stop-us-production -banned-cluster-munitions.

18. Adam Bower, memo on Additional Protocols I and II to the 1949 Geneva Conventions, prepared for Article 36, 20 January 2014.

19. Stein-Ivar Lothe Eide, "A Ban on Nuclear Weapons: What's in It for NATO?" *International Law and Policy Institute*, Policy Paper no. 5, January 2014.

20. Interview with author, INT2, 1 December 2017.

21. Borrie, *Unacceptable Harm*, 200.

22. Personal communication, 13 March 2013.

23. Interview with author, INT14, 20 February 2018.

24. Interview with author, INT6, 5 January 2018.

25. Interview with author, INT3, 20 December 2017.

26. Interview with author, INT1, 27 November 2017.

27. Interview with author, INT1, 27 November 2017.

28. Interview with author, INT2, 1 December 2017.

29. Interview with author, INT3, 20 December 2017.

30. Borrie, *Unacceptable Harm*, 334.

31. Interview with author, INT8, 17 January 2018.

32. Interview with author, INT8, 17 January 2018.

33. Interview with author, INT12, 2 February 2018.

34. Interview with author, INT11, 26 January 2018.

35. Interview with author, INT8, 17 January 2018.

36. Interview with author, INT3, 20 December 2017.

37. Interview with author, INT2, 1 December 2017.

38. Interview with author, INT2, 1 December 2017.

39. Interview with author, INT8, 17 January 2018.

40. See chapter 3.

41. Mona Lena Krook and Jacquie True, "Rethinking the Life Cycles of International Norms: The United Nations and the Global Promotion of Gender Equality," *European Journal of International Relations* 18, no. 1 (18 November 2010): 108.

42. Interview with author, INT18, 15 May 2018.

43. Interview with author, INT18, 15 May 2018.

44. Maritza Chan, "Non-Nuclear Weapons States Must Lead in Shaping International Norms on Nuclear Weapons: A Practitioner Commentary," *Global Policy* 7, no. 3 (September 2016): 409.

45. Chan, "Non-Nuclear Weapons States Must Lead," 408–409.

46. Nick Ritchie and Kjølv Egeland, "The Diplomacy of Resistance: Power, Hegemony and Nuclear Disarmament," *Global Change, Peace and Security* 30, no. 2 (2018): 1.

47. Ritchie and Egeland, "The Diplomacy of Resistance," 5.

48. Margaret E. Keck and Kathryn Sikkink, "Transnational Advocacy Networks in International and Regional Politics," *International Social Science Journal* 51, no. 159 (March 1999): 89–101.

49. Krook and True, "Rethinking the Life Cycles of International Norms," 107.

50. Interview with author, INT18, 15 May 2018.

51. Interview with author, INT8, 17 January 2018.

52. Interview with author, INT5, 21 December 2017.

53. Interview with author, INT1, 27 November 2017.

54. Interview with author, INT1, 27 November 2017.

55. Interview with author, INT8, 17 January 2018.

56. Interview with author, INT13, 16 February 2018.

57. Interview with author, INT11, 26 January 2018.

58. Ritchie and Egeland, "The Diplomacy of Resistance," 6.

59. Interview with author, INT8, 17 January 2018.

60. Interview with author, INT2, 1 December 2017.

61. Interview with author, INT11, 26 January 2018.

62. Interview with author, INT2, 1 December 2017.

63. Interview with author, INT5, 21 December 2017.

64. Interview with author, INT8, 17 January 2018.

65. The Non-Aligned Movement is a forum of 120 countries not formally aligned with or against any geopolitical power bloc. It was formed during the Cold War but continues to this day.

66. Interview with author, INT9, 25 January 2018.

67. Interview with author, INT6, 5 January 2018.

68. Interview with author, INT3, 20 December 2017.

69. Interview with author, INT4, 21 December 2017.

CHAPTER 5

1. See Dan Zak, *Almighty: Courage, Resistance, and Existential Peril in the Nuclear Age* (New York: Penguin, 2017); Dan Zak, "The Prophets of Oak Ridge," *Washington Post*, 30 April 2013, http://www.washingtonpost.com/sf/wp-style/2013/09/13/the-prophets-of-oak-ridge; and Eric Schlosser, "Break-In at Y-12," *New Yorker*, 9 March 2015, https://www.newyorker.com/magazine/2015/03/09/break-in-at-y-12.

2. Eric Schlosser, "A Nun Walks Free: The Government's Sabotage Case Dismissed," *New Yorker*, 18 May 2015, https://www.newyorker.com/news/news-desk/a-nun-walks-free-the-governments-sabotage-case-dismissed.

3. See *Hiroshima: Campaign Meeting Report*, International Campaign to Abolish Nuclear Weapons, August 2012, http://www.icanw.org/wp-content/uploads/2012/10/HiroshimaMeetingReport.pdf.

4. Dimity Hawkins, "From Little Things . . . ," Lecture at the Centre for Ethical Leadership, Ormond College, Melbourne University, Melbourne, Australia, 11 April 2018, https://cel.edu.au/images/uploads/research_paper_files/Ethical-Leadership-Program-Dimity-Hawkins-ICAN.pdf.

5. "Nevertheless, she persisted" became a feminist expression in the United States in 2017, when the U.S. Senate voted to silence Senator Elizabeth Warren's objections to the confirmation of Senator Jeff Sessions as U.S. attorney general. Senate Majority Leader Mitch McConnell made this remark in defense of the silencing during his comments following the vote.

6. John Borrie, Maya Brehm, Silvia Cattaneo, and David Atwood, "Learn, Adapt, Succeed: Potential Lessons from the Ottawa and Oslo Processes for Other Disarmament and Arms Control Challenges," in *Beyond Arms Control: Challenges and Choices for Nuclear Disarmament*, edited by Ray Acheson (New York: Women's International League for Peace and Freedom, 2010), 200.

7. Borrie et al., "Learn, Adapt, Succeed," 201.

8. Steffan Kongstad, director general of the Ministry of Foreign Affairs of Norway, statement to the UN General Assembly First Committee on Disarmament and International Security, 6 October 2009.

9. Borrie et al., "Learn, Adapt, Succeed," 199.

10. Interview with author, INT22, 6 June 2018.

11. See http://hibakushastories.org/students-and-teachers-respond.

12. Interview with author, INT29, 3 June 2018.

13. Interview with author, INT31, 20 February 2018.

14. Interview with author, INT31, 20 February 2018.

15. Interview with author, INT32, 21 February 2018.

16. Sally Whyte, "'Horror, Humour and Hope' Getting ICAN's Message through Nuclear Disarmament Circus," *Crikey*, 10 October 2017, https://www.crikey.com.au/2017/10/10/humour-horror-and-hope-getting-icans-message-through-nuclear-disarmament-circus.

17. Lesley J. Pruitt, "Youth Participation in the UN Human Rights Council," Australian Institute of International Affairs, 19 June 2017, http://www.international affairs.org.au/australianoutlook/youth-participation-human-rights-council.

18. Helen Berents, "Slackers or Delinquents? No, Just Politically Engaged Youth," *The Conversation*, 4 June 2014, https://theconversation.com/slackers-or-delinquents-no-just-politically-engaged-youth-27218.

19. Interview with author, INT31, 20 February 2018.

20. Interview with author, INT15, 27 February 2018.

21. Estelle Slootmaker, "Nuns Disarming the World: Two Dominicans with Grand Rapids Roots Help Win Nobel Peace Prize," *Rapid Growth*, 1 February 2018, http://www.rapidgrowthmedia.com/features/nunsnucleardisarm.aspx.

22. Interview with author, INT33, 21 February 2018.

23. Interview with author, INT22, 6 June 2018.

24. Interview with author, INT34, 20 February 2018.

25. Interview with author, INT16, 27 February 2018.

26. Interview with author, INT35, 1 March 2018.

27. Interview with author, INT29, 3 June 2018.

28. See www.twitter.com/NoNukesQueers; Jesse Boylan, "This Is Not Nowhere," *LOTL*, 14 September 2018, https://www.lotl.com/culture/political-movement/this-is-not-nowhere; and "Queers against the Nuclear Industry," *3CR Community Radio*, 17 November 2018, https://www.3cr.org.au/radioactive/episode-201811171000/queers-against-nuclear-industry.

29. Interview with author, INT33, 21 February 2018.

30. Interview with author, INT15, 27 February 2018.

31. Interview with author, INT20, 5 June 2018.

32. Interview with author, INT15, 27 February 2018.

33. Interview with author, INT29, 3 June 2018.

34. Interview with author, INT21, 6 June 2018.

35. Interview with author, INT8, 17 January 2018.

36. Interview with author, INT6, 5 January 2018.

37. Interview with author, INT16, 27 February 2018.

38. Nick Ritchie and Kjølv Egeland, "The Diplomacy of Resistance: Power, Hegemony and Nuclear Disarmament," *Global Change, Peace and Security* (27 April 2018): 11.

39. Interview with author, INT14, 20 February 2018.

40. Ritchie and Egeland, "The Diplomacy of Resistance."

41. P. Resnick, "On Consensus and Humming in the IETF," June 2014, https://tools.ietf.org/html/rfc7282.

42. Interview with author, INT15, 27 February 2018.

43. Interview with author, INT15, 27 February 2018.

44. Interview with author, INT36, 18 April 2018.

45. Interview with author, INT15, 27 February 2018.

46. Interview with author, INT29, 3 June 2018.

47. Diane Carman, "Anti-Nuke Nuns Return to Crime Scene with a Treaty and a Nobel Prize," *Denver Post*, 20 October 2017, https://www.denverpost.com/2017/10/20/anti-nuke-nuns-return-to-crime-scene-with-a-treaty-and-a-nobel-prize.

CHAPTER 6

1. Gem Romuld and Tim Wright, *(Don't Want Your) Nuclear Umbrella*, ICAN Australia, 2014. Full video, lyrics, and credits can be found at https://www.youtube.com/watch?v=reZw23A3_dw.

2. See http://www.reachingcriticalwill.org/disarmament-fora/hinw/oslo-2013.

3. Beatrice Fihn, ed., *Unspeakable Suffering: The Humanitarian Impact of Nuclear Weapons* (New York: Reaching Critical Will of the Women's International League for Peace and Freedom, February 2013), http://www.reaching criticalwill.org/images/documents/Publications/Unspeakable/Unspeakable.pdf.

4. Espen Barth Eide, former foreign minister of Norway, "Chair's Summary," Conference on the Humanitarian Impact of Nuclear Weapons, Oslo, 4–5 March 2013, https://www.regjeringen.no/en/aktuelt/nuclear_summary/id716343.

5. Alexander Kmentt, "The Development of the International Initiative on the Humanitarian Impact of Nuclear Weapons and Its Effect on the Nuclear Weapons Debate," *International Review of the Red Cross* 97 (2015): 690.

6. Kmentt, "The Development of the International Initiative," 690.

7. See the *Conference Report: Humanitarian Impact of Nuclear Weapons* (New York: Reaching Critical Will of the Women's International League for Peace and Freedom, March 2013), http://www.reachingcriticalwill.org/disarmament-fora/hinw/oslo-2013/conference-report.

8. International Campaign to Abolish Nuclear Weapons, statement to the Conference on the Humanitarian Impact of Nuclear Weapons, Oslo, 5 March 2013, http://www.icanw.org/wp-content/uploads/2013/03/ICAN-final-statement5.3.13.pdf.

9. International Campaign to Abolish Nuclear Weapons, statement to the Conference on the Humanitarian Impact of Nuclear Weapons, Oslo, 4 March 2013, http://www.icanw.org/wp-content/uploads/2013/03/ICAN1stsession statement.pdf.

10. Tim Wright, "Next Stop, a Ban on Nuclear Weapons?" *Truthout*, 26 March 2013, http://www.truth-out.org/opinion/item/15318-next-stop-a-ban-on-nuclear-weapons.

11. Wright, "Next Stop, a Ban on Nuclear Weapons?"

12. John Borrie and Tim Caughley, "After Olso: Humanitarian Perspectives and the Changing Nuclear Weapons Discourse," Humanitarian Impact of Nuclear Weapons project paper no. 3 (Geneva: United Nations Institute for Disarmament Research, 2013), 15, http://www.unidir.org/files/publications/pdfs/after-oslo-en-469.pdf.

13. Statement on the humanitarian impact of nuclear weapons by Algeria, Argentina, Austria, Belarus, Bangladesh, Bosnia and Herzegovina, Botswana, Brazil, Burkina Faso, Cambodia, Chile, Colombia, Costa Rica, Côte d'Ivoire, Cuba, Cyprus, Denmark, Djibouti, Ecuador, Egypt, El Salvador, Ethiopia, Ghana, Georgia, Grenada, Guatemala, Holy See, Honduras, Iceland, Indonesia, Iran, Ireland, Jamaica, Jordan, Kazakhstan, Kenya, Kuwait, Lebanon, Lesotho, Liechtenstein, Luxembourg, Malaysia, Maldives, Malta, Mauritius, Mexico, Morocco, Mozambique, Namibia, Nepal, New Zealand, Nicaragua, Niger, Nigeria, Norway, Palau, Panama, Papua New Guinea, Paraguay, Peru, Philippines, Qatar, Samoa, Singapore, South Africa, Swaziland, Switzerland, Tanzania, Thailand, Tonga, Trinidad and Tobago, Tunisia, Uganda, Ukraine, Uruguay, Yemen, and Zambia to the 2013 Non-Proliferation Treaty Preparatory Committee, Geneva, 24 April 2013, http://www.reachingcriticalwill.org/images/documents/Disarmament-fora/npt/prepcom13/statements/24April_SouthAfrica.pdf.

14. See Bruce G. Blair and Matthew A. Brown, "World Spending on Nuclear Weapons Surpasses $1 Trillion Per Decade, Global Zero Technical Report," Nuclear Weapons Cost Study, June 2011, https://www.globalzero.org/files/gz_nuclear_weapons_cost_study.pdf.

15. Gerard Keown, director for disarmament and nonproliferation, Department of Foreign Affairs and Trade of Ireland, statement to the 2013 NPT Preparatory Committee, Geneva, 25 April 2013, http://www.reaching criticalwill.org/images/documents/Disarmament-fora/npt/prepcom13/statements/25April_Ireland.pdf.

16. Benno Laggner, head of the Delegation of Switzerland, statement to the 2013 NPT Preparatory Committee, Geneva, 25 April 2013, http://www.reachingcriticalwill.org/images/documents/Disarmament-fora/npt/prepcom13/statements/25April_Switzerland.pdf.

17. Steffan Kongstad, head of delegation of Norway, statement to the 2013 NPT Preparatory Committee, Geneva, 23 April 2013, http://www.reaching criticalwill.org/images/documents/Disarmament-fora/npt/prepcom13/statements/23April_Norway.pdf.

18. *An exploration of some contributions that also non-nuclear weapon States could engage in to take multilateral nuclear disarmament forward*, A/AC.281/WP.5, working paper submitted by Austria to the Open-ended Working Group to develop proposals to take forward multilateral nuclear disarmament negotiations for the achievement and maintenance of a world without nuclear weapons, Geneva, 28 June 2013, http://www.reachingcriticalwill.org/images/documents/Disarmament-fora/OEWG/Documents/WP5.pdf.

19. *Identifying the essential elements for achieving and maintaining a world without nuclear weapons*, A/AC.281/WP.8, working paper submitted by Ireland and Switzerland to the Open-ended Working Group on Nuclear Disarmament, Geneva, 19 July 2013, http://www.reachingcriticalwill.org/images/documents/Disarmament-fora/OEWG/Documents/WP8.pdf.

20. Brazil, Egypt, Ireland, Mexico, New Zealand, and South Africa.

21. *Taking Forward Multilateral Nuclear Disarmament Negotiations*, A/AC.281/WP.10, working paper submitted by the New Agenda Coalition (Brazil, Egypt, Ireland, Mexico, New Zealand, and South Africa) to the Open-ended Working Group on Nuclear Disarmament, Geneva, 2013, http://www.reachingcritical will.org/images/documents/Disarmament-fora/OEWG/Documents/WP10.pdf.

22. *Achieving a Nuclear Weapon Free World*, A/AC.281/NGO/1, working paper submitted by the Reaching Critical Will program of the Women's International League for Peace and Freedom to the Open-ended Working Group on Nuclear Disarmament, Geneva, 17 July 2013, http://www.reachingcriticalwill.org/images/documents/Disarmament-fora/OEWG/Documents/NGO1.pdf.

23. Rebecca Johnson, "Perspectives on the Necessary Framework to Achieve and Maintain a Nuclear Weapons Free World," presentation to the Open-ended Working Group on Nuclear Disarmament, Geneva, 21 May 2013, http://www.reachingcriticalwill.org/images/documents/Disarmament-fora/OEWG/statements/21May_Johnson.pdf.

24. See the report on the meeting from Reaching Critical Will of the Women's International League for Peace and Freedom, 26 September 2013, http://www.reachingcriticalwill.org/disarmament-fora/others/hlm-nuclear-disarmament/report.

25. Eamon Gilmore T. D., tánaiste and minister for foreign affairs and trade of Ireland, statement to the High-level Meeting of the UN General Assembly on Nuclear Disarmament, New York, 26 September 2013, http://www.reaching criticalwill.org/images/documents/Disarmament-fora/HLM/26Sep_Ireland .pdf.

26. Liv Tørres, Madeleine Rees, Philip Jennings, Jan Gruiters, Kate Hudson, Akira Kawasaki, Michael Christ, and Hirotsugu Terasaki, "Where Is the 'Global Red Line' for Nuclear Weapons?" *Huffington Post*, 26 September 2013, https://www.huffingtonpost.com/liv-torres/nuclear-disarmament_b_3988288.html.

27. Heinz Fischer, federal president of the Republic of Austria, statement to the High-level Meeting of the UN General Assembly on Nuclear Disarmament, New York, 26 September 2013, http://www.reachingcriticalwill.org/images/documents/Disarmament-fora/HLM/26Sep_Austria.pdf.

28. Viola Onwuliri, minister of foreign affairs, Federal Republic of Nigeria, statement to the High-level Meeting of the UN General Assembly on Nuclear Disarmament, New York, 26 September 2013, http://www.reachingcriticalwill .org/images/documents/Disarmament-fora/HLM/26Sep_Nigeria.pdf.

29. Alistair Burt, parliamentary under secretary of state for the United Kingdom of Great Britain and Northern Ireland, statement on behalf of France, the United Kingdom, and the United States to the High-level Meeting of the UN General Assembly on Nuclear Disarmament, New York, 26 September 2013, http://www.reachingcriticalwill.org/images/documents/ Disarmament-fora/HLM/26Sep_UKUSFrance.pdf.

30. Ban Ki-moon, secretary-general of the United Nations, remarks to "Advancing the Disarmament and Non-proliferation Agenda: Seeking Peace in an Over-armed World," Monterey Institute of International Studies, Monterey, California, 18 January 2013, https://www.un.org/sg/ en/content/sg/statement/2013-01-18/secretary-generals-remarks-monterey -institute-international-studies.

31. Statement on the humanitarian impact of nuclear weapons by Afghanistan, Algeria, Angola, Antigua and Barbuda, Argentina, Austria, Bahamas, Bahrain, Bangladesh, Barbados, Belarus, Belize, Benin, Bolivia, Bosnia and Herzegovina, Botswana, Brazil, Burkina Faso, Cambodia, Cameroon, Cape Verde, Central African Republic, Chile, Colombia, Congo, Costa Rica, Côte d'Ivoire, Cuba, Cyprus, DR Congo, Denmark, Djibouti, Dominican Republic, Ecuador, Egypt, El Salvador, Equatorial Guinea, Eritrea, Fiji, Gabon, Georgia, Ghana, Grenada, Guatemala, Guinea, Guinea Bissau, Haiti, Holy See, Honduras, Iceland, Indonesia, Iraq, Ireland, Jamaica, Japan, Jordan, Kazakhstan, Kenya, Kiribati, Lao PDR, Lebanon, Lesotho, Liberia, Libya, Liechtenstein, Macedonia, Madagascar, Malawi, Malaysia, Maldives, Mali, Malta, Marshall Islands, Mauritius, Mexico, Mongolia, Montenegro, Morocco, Mozambique, Myanmar, Namibia, Nauru, Nepal, New Zealand, Nicaragua, Niger, Nigeria, Norway, Palau, Panama, Papua New Guinea, Paraguay, Peru, Philippines, Qatar, Rwanda, Samoa, San Marino, Senegal, Serbia, Seychelles, Sierra Leone, Singapore, Solomon Islands, South Africa, South Sudan, Suriname, Swaziland, Switzerland, Tanzania, Thailand, Timor-Leste, Togo, Tonga, Trinidad and Tobago, Tunisia, Tuvalu, Uganda, Ukraine, United Arab Emirates, Uruguay, Vanuatu, Vietnam, Yemen, and Zambia to the UN General Assembly First Committee on Disarmament and International Security, New York, 21 October 2013, http://www.reachingcriticalwill.org/images/documents/ Disarmament-fora/1com/1com13/statements/21Oct_Joint.pdf.

32. See, for example, "Japan Finally Backs U.N. Statement against Use of Nuclear Weapons," *Asahi Shimbun*, 22 October 2013.

33. Mikhail Uliyanov, director of the department for security affairs and disarmament of the Ministry of Foreign Affairs of the Russian Federation, statement to the UN General Assembly First Committee on Disarmament and International Security, New York, 8 October 2013, http://www.reachingcriticalwill.org/images/documents/Disarmament-fora/1com/1com13/statements/8Oct_Russia.pdf.

34. Uliyanov, statement to the UN General Assembly First Committee on Disarmament and International Security, 8 October 2013.

35. Statement by the United Kingdom to the UN General Assembly on Disarmament and International Security, New York, 4 November 2013, http://www.reachingcriticalwill.org/images/documents/Disarmament-fora/1com/1com13/statements/4Nov_UK.pdf.

36. Explanation of vote by Austria, Ireland, Liechtenstein, Malta, New Zealand, and San Marino on Draft Resolution L.6, "Follow-up to the 2013 high-level meeting of the General Assembly on nuclear disarmament," to the UN General Assembly First Committee on Disarmament and International Security, New York, 4 November 2013, http://www.reachingcriticalwill.org/images/documents/Disarmament-fora/1com/1com13/eov/L6_Ireland.pdf.

37. Archbishop Francis Chullikatt, apostolic nuncio and permanent observer of the Holy See, statement to the UN General Assembly First Committee on Disarmament and International Security, New York, 22 October 2013, http://www.reachingcriticalwill.org/images/documents/Disarmament-fora/1com/1com13/statements/22Oct_HolySee.pdf.

38. Matthew Rowland, head of delegation for the United Kingdom, statement to the UN General Assembly First Committee on Disarmament and International Security, New York, 17 October 2013, http://www.reachingcriticalwill.org/images/documents/Disarmament-fora/1com/1com13/statements/17Oct_UK.pdf.

39. Thomas S. Kuhn, *The Structure of Scientific Revolution* (Chicago: University of Chicago Press, 1962), 77.

40. Anthony Andanje, deputy permanent representative of the Permanent Mission of Kenya to the United Nations at Geneva, statement to the UN General Assembly First Committee on Disarmament and International Security, New York, 16 October 2013, http://www.reachingcriticalwill.org/images/documents/Disarmament-fora/1com/1com13/statements/16Oct_Kenya.pdf.

41. See http://www.reachingcriticalwill.org/disarmament-fora/hinw/nayarit-2014.

42. Kmentt, "The Development of the International Initiative," 692.

43. Juan Manuel Gómez Robledo, "Chair's Summary," Second Conference on the Humanitarian Impact of Nuclear Weapons, Nayarit, Mexico,

13–14 February 2014, http://www.reachingcriticalwill.org/images/documents/Disarmament-fora/nayarit-2014/chairs-summary.pdf.

44. Interview with author, INT2, 1 December 2017.

45. Gómez Robledo, "Chair's Summary."

46. Interview with author, INT14, 20 February 2018.

47. Kmentt, "The Development of the International Initiative," 693.

48. Julie Bishop, "We Engage, Not Enrage Nuclear Countries," *Sydney Morning Herald*, 14 February 2014, https://www.smh.com.au/opinion/we-must-engage-not-enrage-nuclear-countries-20140213-32n1s.html.

49. Bishop, "We Must Engage, Not Enrage Nuclear Countries."

50. Interview with author, INT11, 26 January 2018.

51. Interview with author, INT12, 2 February 2018.

52. "Swedish FM Attacks Signatories of Humanitarian Initiative: 'Not Serious States,'" International Campaign to Abolish Nuclear Weapons, 7 May 2013, http://www.icanw.org/campaign-news/swedish-fm-attacks-80-state-signatories-of-humanitarian-initiative-not-serious-states/#.UZCpPKJ7K85.

53. Andanje, statement to the UN General Assembly First Committee on Disarmament and International Security, 16 October 2013.

54. Julie Bishop, minister for foreign affairs and trade of Australia, statement to the Conference on Disarmament, Geneva, 26 March 2014, http://www.reachingcriticalwill.org/images/documents/Disarmament-fora/cd/2014/Statements/part1/26March_Australia.pdf.

55. Richard Lenanne, "Obstacles to Nuclear Disarmament—and How to Overcome Them: 4. The Weasels," Wildfire, May 2015, http://www.wildfire-v.org/NPT2015/Obstacles4.pdf.

56. See wildfire-v.org.

57. See https://www.youtube.com/watch?v=reZw23A3_dw.

58. See http://www.nuclearzero.org/in-the-courts.

59. Tony de Brum, minister of foreign affairs of the Marshall Islands, statement to the 2014 NPT Preparatory Committee, New York, 28 April 2014, http://www.reachingcriticalwill.org/images/documents/Disarmament-fora/npt/prepcom14/statements/28April_MarshallIslands.pdf.

60. Agence France-Presse, "Marshall Islands Nuclear Arms Lawsuit Thrown Out by UN's Top Court," *The Guardian*, 5 October 2016, https://www.theguardian.com/world/2016/oct/06/marshall-islands-nuclear-arms-lawsuit-thrown-out-by-uns-top-court.

61. Agence France-Presse, "Marshall Islands Nuclear Arms Lawsuit Thrown Out."

62. Sandy Jones, "Marshall Islands Nuclear Zero Lawsuit Appeal Dismissed by Ninth Circuit Court," Nuclear Age Peace Foundation Press Release, 31 July 2017, https://www.wagingpeace.org/marshall-islands-ninth-circuit.

63. "US and Russia Determined to Keep Nuclear Weapons Arsenal, SIPRI Says," *Moscow Times*, 16 June 2014.

64. *Article VI of the Treaty on the Non-Proliferation of Nuclear Weapons*, NPT/CONF.2015/PC.III/WP.18, working paper submitted by Ireland on behalf of the New Agenda Coalition (Brazil, Egypt, Ireland, Mexico, New Zealand, and South Africa) to the Third session of the Preparatory Committee for the 2015 Conference of the Parties to the Treaty on the Non-Proliferation of Nuclear Weapons, 2 April 2014, http://www.reachingcriticalwill.org/images/documents/Disarmament-fora/npt/prepcom14/documents/WP18.pdf.

65. Ibid.

66. Interview with author, INT9, 25 January 2018.

67. Maritza Chan, minister counselor at the Permanent Mission of Costa Rica to the United Nations, statement to the 2014 NPT Preparatory Committee, New York, 30 April 2014, http://www.reachingcriticalwill.org/images/documents/Disarmament-fora/npt/prepcom14/statements/30April_CostaRica.pdf.

68. Maritza Chan, minister counselor at the Permanent Mission of Costa Rica to the United Nations, statement to the UN General Assembly First Committee on Disarmament and International Security, New York, 20 October 2014, http://www.reachingcriticalwill.org/images/documents/Disarmament-fora/1com/1com14/statements/20Oct_CostaRica.pdf.

69. Alifeleti Soakai, Permanent Mission of Palau to the United Nations, statement to the UN General Assembly First Committee on Disarmament and International Security, New York, 21 October 2014, http://reachingcriticalwill.org/images/documents/Disarmament-fora/1com/1com14/statements/21Oct_Palau.pdf.

70. Anthony Andanje, deputy permanent representative of Kenya to the United Nations in Geneva, statement to the UN General Assembly First Committee on Disarmament and International Security, New York, 13 October 2014, http://reachingcriticalwill.org/images/documents/Disarmament-fora/1com/1com14/statements/13Oct_Kenya.pdf.

71. Korakot Parachasit, second secretary at the Permanent Mission of Thailand to the United Nations, statement to the UN General Assembly First Committee on Disarmament and International Security, New York, 23 October 2014, http://reachingcriticalwill.org/images/documents/Disarmament-fora/1com/1com14/statements/23Oct_Thailand.pdf.

336   *Notes*

72. U. Joy Ogwu, permanent presentative of Nigeria to the United Nations on behalf of the African Group, statement to the UN General Assembly First Committee on Disarmament and International Security, New York, 7 October 2014, http://reachingcriticalwill.org/images/documents/Disarmament-fora/1com/1com14/statements/7Oct_AfricanGroup.pdf.

73. Eden Charles, deputy permanent representative of the Republic of Trinidad and Tobago to the United Nations, statement on behalf of the Caribbean Community to the UN General Assembly First Committee on Disarmament and International Security, New York, 7 October 2014, http://reachingcriticalwill.org/images/documents/Disarmament-fora/1com/1com14/statements/7Oct_CARICOM.pdf.

74. Maritza Chan, minister counselor at the Permanent Mission of Costa Rica to the United Nations, statement on behalf of the Community of Latin American and Caribbean States to the UN General Assembly First Committee on Disarmament and International Security, New York, 15 October 2014, http://reachingcriticalwill.org/images/documents/Disarmament-fora/1com/1com14/statements/15Oct_CELAC.pdf.

75. Statement on the humanitarian impact of nuclear weapons by Afghanistan, Algeria, Andorra, Angola, Antigua and Barbuda, Argentina, Armenia, Austria, Azerbaijan, Bahamas, Bahrain, Bangladesh, Barbados, Belarus, Belize, Benin, Bolivia, Bosnia and Herzegovina, Botswana, Brazil, Brunei Darussalam, Burkina Faso, Burundi, Cabo Verde, Cambodia, Cameroon, Central African Republic, Chad, Chile, Colombia, Comoros, Congo, Cook Islands, Costa Rica, Côte d'Ivoire, Cuba, Cyprus, DR Congo, Denmark, Djibouti, Dominica, Dominican Republic, Ecuador, Egypt, El Salvador, Equatorial Guinea, Eritrea, Ethiopia, Fiji, Finland, Gabon, Gambia, Georgia, Ghana, Grenada, Guatemala, Guinea, Guinea Bissau, Guyana, Haiti, Holy See, Honduras, Iceland, Indonesia, Iraq, Ireland, Jamaica, Japan, Jordan, Kazakhstan, Kenya, Kiribati, Kuwait, Kyrgyzstan, Lao PDR, Lebanon, Lesotho, Liberia, Libya, Liechtenstein, Macedonia, Madagascar, Malawi, Malaysia, Maldives, Mali, Malta, Marshall Islands, Mauritania, Mauritius, Mexico, Federated States of Micronesia, Republic of Moldova, Mongolia, Montenegro, Morocco, Mozambique, Myanmar, Namibia, Nauru, Nepal, New Zealand, Nicaragua, Niger, Nigeria, Niue, Norway, Oman, Palau, Palestine, Panama, Papua New Guinea, Paraguay, Peru, Philippines, Qatar, Rwanda, Saint Kitts and Nevis, Saint Lucia, Saint Vincent and the Grenadines, Samoa, San Marino, Sao Tome and Principe, Saudi Arabia, Senegal, Serbia, Seychelles, Sierra Leone, Singapore, Solomon Islands, Somalia, South Africa, South Sudan, Sudan, Suriname, Swaziland, Sweden, Switzerland, Tanzania, Thailand, Timor-Leste, Togo, Tonga, Trinidad and Tobago, Tunisia, Tuvalu, Uganda, Ukraine, United Arab Emirates, Uruguay, Vanuatu, Venezuela, Vietnam,

Yemen, and Zambia to the UN General Assembly First Committee on Disarmament and International Security, New York, 20 October 2014, http://reachingcriticalwill.org/images/documents/Disarmament-fora/1com/1com14/statements/20Oct_NewZealand.pdf.

76. Kmentt, "The Development of the International Initiative," 688.

77. John Quinn, Australian permanent representative to the United Nations, Geneva, and ambassador for disarmament, joint statement on the humanitarian consequences of nuclear weapons by Australia, Belgium, Bulgaria, Canada, Croatia, Czech Republic, Estonia, Finland, Germany, Greece, Hungary, Italy, Japan, Lithuania, Luxembourg, the Netherlands, Poland, Portugal, Slovakia, and Spain to the UN General Assembly First Committee on Disarmament and International Security, New York, 20 October 2014, http://reachingcriticalwill.org/images/documents/Disarmament-fora/1com/1com14/statements/20Oct_Australia.pdf.

78. Kmentt, "The Development of the International Initiative," 688.

79. See http://reachingcriticalwill.org/disarmament-fora/hinw/vienna-2014.

80. Ira Helfand, *Nuclear Famine: Two Billion People at Risk? Global Impacts of Limited Nuclear War on Agriculture, Food Supplies, and Human Nutrition* (Boston: International Physicians for the Prevention of Nuclear War and Physicians for Social Responsibility, November 2013), https://www.ippnw.org/pdf/nuclear-famine-two-billion-at-risk-2013.pdf.

81. Kmentt, "The Development of the International Initiative," 686.

82. Mathias Kom, *We Don't Do That Anymore*, The Burning Hell, 2014. For the full song, see https://soundcloud.com/the-burning-hell/we-dont-do-that-anymore.

83. Kmentt, "The Development of the International Initiative," 694.

84. Kmentt, "The Development of the International Initiative," 695.

85. Kmentt, "The Development of the International Initiative," 696.

86. See "Leading Nuclear Policy Experts and Organizations Call on the United States to Participate in International Conference on Humanitarian Impacts of Nuclear Weapons," Arms Control Association, 29 October 2014, http://www.armscontrol.org/pressroom/press-release/Groups-Urge-United-States-to-participate-in-Vienna-humanitarian-impacts-conference.

87. Nobuo Hayashi, presentation to the Third Conference on the Humanitarian Impact of Nuclear Weapons.

88. Statement by the delegation of Ireland to the Third Conference on the Humanitarian Impact of Nuclear Weapons, Vienna, 9 December 2014, http://www.reachingcriticalwill.org/images/documents/Disarmament-fora/vienna-2014/9Dec_Ireland.pdf.

89. *Report and Summary of Findings of the Conference*, Vienna Conference on the Humanitarian Impact of Nuclear Weapons, 8–9 December 2014, http://www.reachingcriticalwill.org/images/documents/Disarmament-fora/ vienna-2014/ChairSummary.pdf.

90. Interview with author, INT1, 27 November 2017.

91. Statement by the Republic of Lithuania to the Third Conference on the Humanitarian Impact of Nuclear Weapons, Vienna, 9 December 2014, http:// www.reachingcriticalwill.org/images/documents/Disarmament-fora/vienna -2014/9Dec_Lithuania.pdf.

92. International Campaign to Abolish Nuclear Weapons, statement to the Third Conference on the Humanitarian Impact of Nuclear Weapons, Vienna, 9 December 2014, http://www.reachingcriticalwill.org/images/documents/ Disarmament-fora/vienna-2014/9Dec_ICAN.pdf.

93. Mia Gandenberger and Ray Acheson, "Highlights from the Vienna Conference," *Filling the Gap: Report on the Third Conference on the Humanitarian Impact of Nuclear Weapons* (New York: Reaching Critical Will of the Women's International League for Peace and Freedom, 9 December 2014), http://www .reachingcriticalwill.org/images/documents/Disarmament-fora/vienna-2014/ filling-the-gap.pdf.

94. "Austrian Pledge," paper submitted by the Federal Ministry of Europe Integration and Foreign Affairs of the Republic of Austria to the Vienna Conference on the Humanitarian Impact of Nuclear Weapons, 9 December 2014, http://www.reachingcriticalwill.org/images/documents/Disarmament-fora/ vienna-2014/Austrian_Pledge.pdf.

95. Kmentt, "The Development of the International Initiative," 701.

96. Interview with author, INT14, 20 February 2018.

97. Borrie, *Unacceptable Harm*, 313.

98. *A Treaty Banning Nuclear Weapons: Developing a Legal Framework for the Prohibition and Elimination of Nuclear Weapons* (New York: Women's International League for Peace and Freedom and Article 36, 2014), http://www .reachingcriticalwill.org/images/documents/Publications/a-treaty-banning -nuclear-weapons.pdf, 21.

99. *A Treaty Banning Nuclear Weapons*, 21.

100. See John Borrie and V. Martin Randin, eds., *Alternative Approaches in Multilateral Decision Making: Disarmament as Humanitarian Action* (Geneva: United Nations Institute for Disarmament Research, 2005), 105–106.

101. For statements and reporting from the 2015 NPT Review Conference, see http://reachingcriticalwill.org/disarmament-fora/npt/2015.

102. Ray Acheson, "¡Ya Basta! It's All about the Ban," *NPT News in Review* 13, no. 16 (22 May 2015): 1, http://www.reachingcriticalwill.org/images/documents/Disarmament-fora/npt/NIR2015/No16.pdf.

103. If you're wondering, "why Canada?," it's a great question. In earlier chapters you will have seen Canada being rather progressive on questions of nuclear disarmament, trying to push the boundaries and stand up to the nuclear-armed states. That was 2005. By 2015, the Canadian government was run by Conservative Prime Minister Stephen Harper, and he took a decidedly pro-U.S. approach to most things, including both nuclear weapons and Israel.

104. Nozipho Mxakato-Diseko, deputy director-general, Multilateral Branch, Department of International Relations and Cooperation of South Africa, statement to the 2015 NPT Review Conference, New York, 22 May 2015.

105. Statement on the humanitarian impact of nuclear weapons on behalf of Afghanistan, Algeria, Andorra, Angola, Antigua and Barbuda, Argentina, Armenia, Austria, Azerbaijan, Bahamas, Bahrain, Bangladesh, Barbados, Belarus, Belize, Benin, Bolivia, Bosnia and Herzegovina, Botswana, Brazil, Brunei Darussalam, Burkina Faso, Burundi, Cabo Verde, Cambodia, Cameroon, Central African Republic, Chad, Chile, Colombia, Comoros, Congo, Cook Islands, Costa Rica, Côte d'Ivoire, Cuba, Cyprus, DR Congo, Denmark, Djibouti, Dominica, Dominican Republic, Ecuador, Egypt, El Salvador, Equatorial Guinea, Eritrea, Ethiopia, Fiji, Finland, Former Yugoslav Republic of Macedonia, Gabon, Gambia, Georgia, Ghana, Grenada, Guatemala, Guinea, Guinea Bissau, Guyana, Haiti, Holy See, Honduras, Iceland, Indonesia, Iran, Iraq, Ireland, Jamaica, Japan, Jordan, Kazakhstan, Kenya, Kiribati, Kuwait, Kyrgyzstan, Lao PDR, Lebanon, Lesotho, Liberia, Libya, Liechtenstein, Madagascar, Malawi, Malaysia, Maldives, Mali, Malta, Marshall Islands, Mauritania, Mauritius, Mexico, Federated States of Micronesia, Republic of Moldova, Mongolia, Montenegro, Morocco, Mozambique, Myanmar, Namibia, Nauru, Nepal, New Zealand, Nicaragua, Niger, Nigeria, Niue, Norway, Oman, Palau, State of Palestine, Panama, Papua New Guinea, Paraguay, Peru, Philippines, Qatar, Rwanda, Saint Kitts and Nevis, Saint Lucia, Saint Vincent and the Grenadines, Samoa, San Marino, Sao Tome and Principe, Saudi Arabia, Senegal, Serbia, Seychelles, Sierra Leone, Singapore, Solomon Islands, Somalia, South Africa, South Sudan, Sri Lanka, Sudan, Suriname, Swaziland, Sweden, Switzerland, Tadjikistan, Tanzania, Thailand, Timor-Leste, Togo, Tonga, Trinidad and Tobago, Tunisia, Tuvalu, Uganda, Ukraine, United Arab Emirates, Uruguay, Vanuatu, Venezuela, Vietnam, Yemen, Zambia, and Zimbabwe to the 2015 NPT Review Conference, New York, 28 April 2015, http://www.reachingcriticalwill.org/images/documents/Disarmament-fora/npt/revcon2015/statements/28April_AustriaHumanitarian.pdf.

106. Dr. Caleb Otto, permanent representative of Palau to the United Nations, Statement to the 2015 NPT Review Conference, New York, 22 May 2015, http://www.reachingcriticalwill.org/images/documents/Disarmament -fora/npt/revcon2015/statements/22May_Palau.pdf.

107. Dan Zak, "U.N. Nuclear Conferences Collapses over WMD-Free Zone in Middle East," *Washington Post*, 22 May 2015, https://www.washington post.com/world/national-security/un-nuclear-conference-collapses-over-wmd -free-zone-in-the-middle-east/2015/05/22/8c568380-fe39-11e4-8c77-bf2746 85e1df_story.html?utm_term=.2e3ad68905f7.

108. Statement delivered by Austria on behalf of Afghanistan, Argentina, Austria, Brazil, Brunei Darussalam, Burundi, Chile, Colombia, Costa Rica, Cuba, Dominican Republic, Ecuador, Egypt, El Salvador, Guatemala, Indonesia, Iraq, Ireland, Jamaica, Kuwait, Lebanon, Liberia, Libya, Liechtenstein, Madagascar, Malaysia, Malta, Marshall Islands, Mexico, Morocco, Nicaragua, Nigeria, Palau, Papua New Guinea, Paraguay, Peru, Philippines, Qatar, San Marino, Saudi Arabia, Senegal, Sierra Leone, Singapore, South Africa, Swaziland, Thailand, Trinidad and Tobago, Uruguay, Venezuela, Vietnam to the 2015 NPT Review Conference, New York, 22 May 2015, http://www.reaching criticalwill.org/images/documents/Disarmament-fora/npt/revcon2015/ statements/22May_Austria.pdf.

109. Nozipho Mxakato-Diseko, statement to the 2015 NPT Review Conference.

110. Maritza Chan, minister counselor of Costa Rica, statement to the 2015 NPT Review Conference, New York, 22 May 2015, http://www.reaching criticalwill.org/images/documents/Disarmament-fora/npt/revcon2015/ statements/22May_CostaRica.pdf.

CHAPTER 7

1. Albert Camus, *The Myth of Sisyphus and Other Essays* (New York: Vintage Books, 1955), 40.

2. Albert Camus, *The Rebel: An Essay on Man in Revolt* (New York: Vintage Books, 1956).

3. Interview with author, INT1, 27 November 2017.

4. Interview with author, INT6, 5 January 2018.

5. Interview with author, INT13, 16 February 2018.

6. Interview with author, INT13, 16 February 2018.

7. Interview with author, INT9, 25 January 2018.

8. Antonio Guerreiro, permanent representative of Brazil to the Conference on Disarmament, statement to the 2012 Non-Proliferation Treaty Preparatory Committee, Vienna, 2 May 2012, http://www.reachingcriticalwill.org/images/documents/Disarmament-fora/npt/prepcom12/statements/2May_Brazil.pdf.

9. Antonio de Aguiar Patriota, permanent representative of Brazil to the United Nations, statement to the UN General Assembly First Committee on Disarmament and International Security, 15 October 2015, http://www.reaching criticalwill.org/images/documents/Disarmament-fora/1com/1com15/statements/15October_Brazil.pdf.

10. *Addressing Nuclear Disarmament: Recommendations from the Perspective of Nuclear-Weapon-Free Zones*, A/AC.286/WP.34/Rev.1, submitted by Argentina, Brazil, Costa Rica, Ecuador, Guatemala, Indonesia, Malaysia, Mexico, Philippines and Zambia to the Open-ended Working Group taking forward multilateral nuclear disarmament negotiations, 11 May 2016, http://www.reachingcriticalwill.org/images/documents/Disarmament-fora/OEWG/2016/Documents/WP34.pdf.

11. Interview with author, INT12, 2 February 2018.

12. This series of resolutions included *Humanitarian consequences of nuclear weapons*, A/C.1/70/L.37, UN General Assembly First Committee on Disarmament and International Security, 21 October 2015; *Humanitarian pledge for the prohibition and elimination of nuclear weapons*, A/C.1/70/L.38, UN General Assembly First Committee on Disarmament and International Security, 21 October 2015; *Ethical imperatives for a nuclear-weapon-free world*, A/C.1/70/L.40, UN General Assembly First Committee on Disarmament and International Security, 21 October 2015; and *Taking forward multilateral nuclear disarmament negotiations*, A/C.1/70/L.13/Rev.1, UN General Assembly First Committee on Disarmament and International Security, 29 October 2015. See http://reachingcriticalwill.org/disarmament-fora/unga/2015/resolutions for the texts.

13. Interview with author, INT13, 16 February 2018.

14. *Taking forward multilateral nuclear disarmament negotiations*, A/C.1/70/L.13/Rev.1.

15. Interview with author, INT13, 16 February 2018.

16. Interview with author, INT18, 15 May 2018.

17. Interview with author, INT12, 2 February 2018.

18. Interview with author, INT13, 16 February 2018.

19. See, for example, statement by the People's Republic of China at the Thematic Discussion on Disarmament Machinery to the UN General Assembly First Committee on Disarmament and International Security, New York, 28 October 2015, http://reachingcriticalwill.org/images/documents/Disarmament-fora/1com/1com15/statements/27October_China.pdf; and

Robert Wood, ambassador of the United States to the Conference of Disarmament, "Mexico still pursuing an unacceptable OEWG resolution. Aim is to subvert established disarmament machinery. It will not succeed." 29 October 2015, 11:06, Tweet, https://twitter.com/USAmbCD/status/659793495222276096.

20. Vladimir Yermakov, director of the Foreign Ministry Department for Non-Proliferation and Arms Control of the Russian Federation, statement to the UN General Assembly First Committee on Disarmament and International Security, New York, 21 October 2015, http://www.reachingcriticalwill.org/images/documents/Disarmament-fora/1com/1com15/statements/21October_Russia.pdf.

21. *Effective measures for nuclear disarmament*, A/C.1/70/L.28/Rev.1, UN General Assembly First Committee on Disarmament and International Security, 28 October 2015, http://www.reachingcriticalwill.org/images/documents/Disarmament-fora/1com/1com15/resolutions/L28Rev1.pdf.

22. The Joint Comprehensive Plan of Action was concluded by Iran, China, France, Germany, Russia, the United Kingdom, and United States on 14 July 2015. It was endorsed by the UN Security Council on 20 July 2015. In short, the deal places certain verifiable restrictions on Iran's nuclear program in exchange for lifting international and national sanctions. See Kelsey Davenport, "The Joint Comprehensive Plan of Action (JCPOA) at a Glance," Arms Control Association, May 2018, https://www.armscontrol.org/factsheets/JCPOA-at-a-glance.

23. Interview with author, INT13, 16 February 2018.

24. See http://www.icanw.org/wp-content/uploads/2015/10/FC-MAP-2015.pdf.

25. Alice Guitton, permanent representative of France to the Conference on Disarmament, explanation of vote on L.13/Rev.1 on behalf of People's Republic of China, the Russian Federation, the United Kingdom, the United States, and France to the UN General Assembly First Committee on Disarmament and International Security, New York, 2 November 2015, http://www.reachingcriticalwill.org/images/documents/Disarmament-fora/1com/1com15/eov/L13_N5.pdf.

26. Statement by the Islamic Republic of Iran to the UN General Assembly First Committee on Disarmament and International Security, New York, 5 November 2015, http://www.reachingcriticalwill.org/images/documents/Disarmament-fora/1com/1com15/eov/L28_Iran.pdf.

27. See http://reachingcriticalwill.org/images/documents/Disarmament-fora/1com/1com15/votes/L13Rev1.pdf.

28. Interview with author, INT13, 16 February 2018.

29. See, for example, Ian McConville, deputy permanent representative, Australian Delegation to the Conference on Disarmament, explanation of vote to the UN General Assembly First Committee on Disarmament and International Security, New York, October 2015, http://www.reachingcriticalwill.org/images/documents/Disarmament-fora/1com/1com15/eov/L13_Australia.pdf.

30. For statements, working papers, and reports from the OEWG, see http://reachingcriticalwill.org/disarmament-fora/oewg/2016.

31. Interview with author, INT12, 2 February 2018.

32. Interview with author, INT6, 5 January 2018.

33. Interview with author, INT13, 16 February 2018.

34. Interview with author, INT12, 2 February 2018.

35. Permanent Mission of Hungary to the United Nations Office at Geneva, statement to the Open-ended Working Group on Nuclear Disarmament, Geneva, 9 May 2016, http://www.reachingcriticalwill.org/images/documents/Disarmament-fora/OEWG/2016/Statements/09May_Hungary.pdf.

36. Permanent Mission of Poland to the United Nations Office at Geneva, statement to the Open-ended Working Group on Nuclear Disarmament, Geneva, 12 May 2016, http://www.reachingcriticalwill.org/images/documents/Disarmament-fora/OEWG/2016/Statements/12May_Poland.pdf.

37. Thomas S. Kuhn, *The Structure of Scientific Revolution* (Chicago: University of Chicago Press, 1962).

38. Akio Suda, ambassador extraordinary and plenipotentiary head of the Delegation of Japan to the Conference on Disarmament, statement to the UN General Assembly First Committee on Disarmament and International Security, New York, 14 October 2009, http://www.reachingcriticalwill.org/images/documents/Disarmament-fora/1com/1com09/statements/14Oct_Japan.pdf.

39. Jonas Gahr Støre, "Disarmament—Reframing the Challenge," presentation to the Norwegian Atlantic Committee, 45th Annual Conference, Oslo, Norway, 1 February 2010, https://www.regjeringen.no/en/aktuelt/disarmament/id592550.

40. Hilde Janne Skorpen, ambassador for disarmament affairs of Norway, statement to the UN General Assembly First Committee on Disarmament and International Security, New York, 14 October 2010, http://www.reachingcriticalwill.org/images/documents/Disarmament-fora/1com/1com10/statements/14Oct_Norway.pdf.

41. Permanent Mission of Norway to the United Nations, explanation of vote on Resolution A/C.1/70/L.37 at the UN General Assembly First Committee on Disarmament and International Security, New York, 3 November 2015, http://reachingcriticalwill.org/images/documents/Disarmament-fora/1com/1com15/statements/3November_Norway.pdf.

42. Permanent Mission of Norway to the United Nations, explanation of vote on Resolution A/C.1/70/L.37.

43. Permanent Mission of Poland to the United Nations Office at Geneva, statement to the Open-ended Working Group.

44. Alva Myrdal, *The Game of Disarmament: How the United States and Russia Run the Arms Race* (New York: Pantheon Books, 1976).

45. Herbert York, "The Nuclear 'Balance of Terror' in Europe," *Ambio* 4, no. 5/6 (1975): 208.

46. Interview with author, INT12, 2 February 2018.

47. Interview with author, INT9, 25 January 2018.

48. Interview with author, INT14, 20 February 2018.

49. *Zero draft of the report of the Open-ended Working group taking forward multilateral nuclear disarmament negotiations*, A/AC.286/L.1, 28 July 2016, http://www.reachingcriticalwill.org/images/documents/Disarmament-fora/OEWG/2016/Documents/A_AC.286_L.1.pdf.

50. *Elements for a treaty banning nuclear weapons*, A/AC.286/WP.14, working paper submitted by Fiji, Nauru, Palau, Samoa, and Tuvalu to the Open-ended Working Group taking forward multilateral nuclear disarmament negotiations, 3 March 2016, http://www.reachingcriticalwill.org/images/documents/Disarmament-fora/OEWG/2016/Documents/WP14.pdf; *Proposal by the Community of Latin American and Caribbean States (CELAC) on effective legal measures to attain and maintain a world without nuclear weapons*, A/AC.286/WP.15, working paper submitted by the Dominican Republic in its capacity of president *pro tempore* of CELAC to the Open-ended Working Group taking forward multilateral nuclear disarmament negotiations, 12 April 2016, http://www.reachingcriticalwill.org/images/documents/Disarmament-fora/OEWG/2016/Documents/WP15.pdf; *A legally-binding instrument that will need to be concluded to attain and maintain a world without nuclear weapons: a prohibition on nuclear weapons*, A/AC.286/WP.17, working paper submitted by Mexico to the Open-ended Working Group taking forward multilateral nuclear disarmament negotiations, 12 April 2016, http://www.reachingcriticalwill.org/images/documents/Disarmament-fora/OEWG/2016/Documents/WP17.pdf; and *Addressing nuclear disarmament: Recommendations from the perspective of nuclear-weapon-free zones*, A/AC.286/WP.34, working paper submitted by Argentina, Brazil, Costa Rica, Ecuador, Guatemala, Indonesia, Malaysia, Mexico, Philippines, and Zambia to the Open-ended Working Group taking forward multilateral nuclear disarmament negotiations, 11 May 2016, http://www.reachingcriticalwill.org/images/documents/Disarmament-fora/OEWG/2016/Documents/WP34.pdf.

51. *A treaty banning nuclear weapons*, A/AC.286/NOG/3, working paper submitted by the Women's International League for Peace and Freedom and Article

36 to the Open-ended Working Group taking forward multilateral nuclear disarmament negotiations, 24 February 2016, http://www.reachingcritical will.org/images/documents/Disarmament-fora/OEWG/2016/Documents/ NGO3.pdf.

52. This was working paper 34, cited in footnote 14. It was originally submitted by Argentina, Brazil, Costa Rica, Ecuador, Guatemala, Indonesia, Malaysia, Mexico, and Zambia, was subsequently endorsed by Austria and Jamaica, and the Philippines joined as a cosponsor.

53. Interview with author, INT1, 27 November 2017.

54. Interview with author, INT11, 26 January 2018.

55. Nick Ritchie, "Pathways to Nuclear Disarmament: Delegitimising Nuclear Violence," working paper for the UN Open-ended Working Group on Nuclear Disarmament, Geneva, Switzerland, 11 May 2016.

56. Interview with author, INT11, 26 January 2018.

57. In George Orwell's *Nineteen Eighty-Four*, doublethink is the act of simultaneously holding contradictory, opposite, or mutually exclusive concepts as correct. See George Orwell, *Nineteen Eighty-Four: A Novel* (London: Secker & Warburg, 1969).

58. "The not-so-progressive approach," International Campaign to Abolish Nuclear Weapons, 27 April 2016, http://www.icanw.org/campaign-news/ the-not-so-progressive-approach.

59. *Draft: Report of the Open-ended Working Group taking forward multilateral nuclear disarmament negotiations*, A/AC.286/CRP.2, 15 August 2016, http://www.reachingcriticalwill.org/images/documents/Disarmament-fora/ OEWG/2016/Documents/A-AC.286-CRP.2.pdf.

60. *Revised draft: Report of the Open-ended Working Group taking forward multilateral nuclear disarmament negotiations*, A/AC.286/CRP.3, 19 August 2016, 15, http://www.reachingcriticalwill.org/images/documents/Disarmament-fora/ OEWG/2016/Documents/A-AC.286-CRP.3.pdf.

61. Interview with author, INT14, 20 February 2018.

62. Interview with author, INT1, 27 November 2017.

63. Interview with author, INT1, 27 November 2017.

64. Interview with author, INT14, 20 February 2018.

65. Interview with author, INT6, 5 January 2018.

66. Interview with author, INT8, 17 January 2018.

67. Interview with author, INT1, 27 November 2017.

68. Interview with author, INT2, 1 December 2017.

69. Interview with author, INT11, 26 January 2018.

70. *Taking forward multilateral nuclear disarmament negotiations*, Resolution A/C.1/71/L.41. The voting results on L.41 can be found at http://reaching

criticalwill.org/images/documents/Disarmament-fora/1com/1com16/votes/
L41.pdf.

71. Interview with author, INT1, 27 November 2017.

72. A démarche is a diplomatic communiqué that is used by governments to protest or object to a policy of another government, and/or to persuade them to change it. Typically, it involves a phone call or a visit from representatives of the offended government.

73. Interview with author, INT12, 2 February 2018.

74. Interview with author, INT8, 17 January 2018.

75. Interview with author, INT19, 17 May 2018.

76. Interview with author, INT7, 12 January 2018.

77. Interview with author, INT5, 21 December 2017.

78. Interview with author, INT24, 12 June 2018.

79. Interview with author, INT11, 26 January 2018.

80. Interview with author, INT24, 12 June 2018; interview with author, INT11, 26 January 2018.

81. Interview with author, INT8, 17 January 2018.

82. Interview with author, INT10, 26 January 2018.

83. Interview with author, INT13, 16 February 2018.

84. Interview with author, INT10, 26 January 2018.

85. Interview with author, INT14, 20 February 2018.

86. Interview with author, INT8, 17 January 2018.

87. Interview with author, INT8, 17 January 2018.

88. *United States Non-Paper: Defense Impacts of Potential United Nations General Assembly Nuclear Weapons Ban Treaty*, North Atlantic Council, AC/333-N(2016)0029 (INV), 17 October 2016, http://www.icanw.org/wp-content/uploads/2016/10/NATO_OCT2016.pdf; Colum Lynch, "U.S. Seeks to Scupper Proposed Ban on Nuclear Arms," *Foreign Policy*, 21 October 2016, http://foreign policy.com/2016/10/21/u-s-seeks-to-scupper-proposed-ban-on-nuclear-arms.

89. "US Pressured NATO States to Vote No to a Ban," International Campaign to Abolish Nuclear Weapons, 1 November 2016, http://www.icanw.org/campaign-news/us-pressures-nato-states-to-vote-no-to-the-ban-treaty.

90. See   http://www.reachingcriticalwill.org/images/documents/Disarmament-fora/1com/1com16/votes/L41.pdf.

91. Selma van Oostward, "The Netherlands Should Actively Negotiate an International Nuclear Weapons Ban Treaty," International Campaign to Abolish Nuclear Weapons, 23 May 2016, http://www.icanw.org/campaign-news/the-netherlands-should-actively-negotiate-an-international-nuclear-weapons-ban-treaty.

92. Vladimir Yermakov, Russian Federation, statement to UN General Assembly First Committee on Disarmament and International Security, New York, 27 October 2016.

93. Helena Nolan, director of disarmament and non-proliferation, Department of Foreign Affairs and Trade of Ireland, statement to the UN General Assembly First Committee on Disarmament and International Security, New York, 17 October 2016, http://www.reachingcriticalwill.org/images/documents/Disarmament-fora/1com/1com16/statements/17Oct_Ireland.pdf.

94. Shorna-Kay Richards, deputy permanent representative of Jamaica to the United Nations, statement to the Open-ended Working Group taking forward multilateral nuclear disarmament negotiations, Geneva, 13 May 2016, 3, http://www.reachingcriticalwill.org/images/documents/Disarmament-fora/OEWG/2016/Statements/13May_Jamaica.pdf.

95. Richards, statement to the Open-ended Working Group taking forward multilateral nuclear disarmament negotiations, 4.

96. Interview with author, INT7, 12 January 2018.

CHAPTER 8

1. Zia Mian and M. V. Ramana, "Ending Nuclear Lawlessness," *The Hindu*, 13 April 2017, https://www.thehindu.com/opinion/lead/ending-nuclear-lawlessness/article17960731.ece.

2. "Ambassador Haley on Nuclear Weapons," *CSPAN*, 27 March 2017, https://www.c-span.org/video/?426068-1/un-ambassador-nikki-haley-shell-protest-debate-nuclear-weapons-ban. Emphasis added to quotation.

3. Letter to ICAN campaigners from Pacific supporter Vanessa Griffen, 28 March 2017.

4. Amr Aboutlatta, permanent representative of the Arab Republic of Egypt to the United Nations, statement to the United Nations Conference to negotiate a legally binding instrument to prohibit nuclear weapons, leading toward their elimination, New York, 27 March 2017, http://www.reaching criticalwill.org/images/documents/Disarmament-fora/nuclear-weapon-ban/statements/27March_Egypt.pdf.

5. See reporting on this meeting by Allison Pytlak and Ray Acheson, "States Discuss Rules for Nuclear Ban Negotiations," Reaching Critical Will of the Women's International League for Peace and Freedom, 16 February 2017, http://www.reachingcriticalwill.org/disarmament-fora/nuclear-weapon-ban/reports/11377-states-discuss-rules-for-nuclear-ban-negotiations.

6. *Participation of nongovernmental organizations in the conference*, A/ CONF.229/2017/4, United Nations conference to negotiate a legally binding instrument to prohibit nuclear weapons, leading toward their total elimination, 22 February 2017, http://undocs.org/A/CONF.229/2017/4.

7. *Taking forward multilateral nuclear disarmament negotiations*, A/C.1/71/L.41.

8. *Rules of procedure of the United Nations conference to negotiate a legally binding instrument to prohibit nuclear weapons, leading towards their total elimination*, A/ CONF.229/2017/5, United Nations conference to negotiate a legally binding instrument to prohibit nuclear weapons, leading toward their total elimination, 13 June 2017, 1, http://undocs.org/A/CONF.229/2017/5.

9. Pennelope Beckles, permanent representative of the Republic of Trinidad and Tobago to the United Nations, statement to the United Nations conference to negotiate a legally binding instrument to prohibit nuclear weapons, leading toward their total elimination, New York, 28 March 2017, http://www.reachingcriticalwill.org/images/documents/Disarmament-fora/ nuclear-weapon-ban/statements/28March_TT.pdf.

10. Patricia O'Brien, permanent representative of Ireland to the United Nations and other international organizations at Geneva, statement to the United Nations Conference to negotiate a legally binding instrument to prohibit nuclear weapons, leading toward their elimination, New York, 27 March 2017, http://www.reachingcriticalwill.org/images/documents/Disarmament-fora/ nuclear-weapon-ban/statements/27March_Ireland.pdf.

11. For day-to-day coverage of discussions during the negotiations, see the *Nuclear Ban Daily* published by Reaching Critical Will of the Women's International League for Peace and Freedom at http://www.reachingcriticalwill.org/ disarmament-fora/nuclear-weapon-ban/reports.

12. "United Nations Conference to negotiate a legally binding instrument to prohibit nuclear weapons, leading towards their total elimination," United Nations Web TV, 30 March 2017, http://webtv.un.org/meetings-events/ conferencessummits/watch/7th-meeting-united-nations-conference-to-negoti ate-a-legally-binding-instrument-to-prohibit-nuclear-weapons-leading-toward -their-total-elimination-27-31-march-2017/5379469891001.

13. *Draft Convention on the Prohibition of Nuclear Weapons*, A/CONF.229/2017/ CRP.1, submitted by the president of the conference, United Nations Conference to negotiate a legally binding instrument to prohibit nuclear weapons, leading toward their elimination, 22 May 2017, http://www.reachingcriticalwill .org/images/documents/Disarmament-fora/nuclear-weapon-ban/documents/ CRP1.pdf.

14. The following outlines some of the debate around key provisions for the treaty. A more comprehensive reflection of the negotiations and positions can

be found on WILPF's reporting of the conference. See the *Nuclear Ban Daily*, as well as statements and documents from the conference, at http://www.reaching criticalwill.org/disarmament-fora/nuclear-weapon-ban. Also see Ray Acheson, "Response to the First Draft Text of the Convention on the Prohibition of Nuclear Weapons," Women's International League for Peace and Freedom, 13 June 2017, http://www.reachingcriticalwill.org/images/documents/Publications/ response-to-22-May-draft-text.pdf.

15. Nozipho Mxakato-Diseko, permanent representative of South Africa to the United Nations at Geneva, statement to the United Nations Conference to negotiate a legally binding instrument to prohibit nuclear weapons, leading toward their elimination, New York, 29 March 2017, http://www.reaching criticalwill.org/images/documents/Disarmament-fora/nuclear-weapon-ban/ statements/29March_SouthAfrica-T2.pdf.

16. Nick Ritchie, "Delegitimising Nuclear Weapons in the Nuclear Weapon Ban Treaty," *Nuclear Ban Daily* 2, no. 7 (23 June 2017): 3, http://www.reaching criticalwill.org/images/documents/Disarmament-fora/nuclear-weapon-ban/ reports/NBD2.7.pdf.

17. Thomas Hajnoczi, head of the disarmament department, Ministry of Foreign Affairs of Austria, statement to the United Nations Conference to negotiate a legally binding instrument to prohibit nuclear weapons, leading toward their elimination, New York, 29 March 2017, http://www.reaching criticalwill.org/images/documents/Disarmament-fora/nuclear-weapon-ban/ statements/29March_Austria-T2.pdf.

18. See http://lcnp.org/wcourt/opinion.htm.

19. John Burroughs, "The Need for a Prohibition of Threat of Nuclear Weapons," *Nuclear Ban Daily* 2, no. 5 (21 June 2017): 4, http://www.reaching criticalwill.org/images/documents/Disarmament-fora/nuclear-weapon-ban/ reports/NBD2.5.pdf.

20. For example, the bilateral relationships between the United States and Australia, Japan, and Republic of Korea include ministerial consultations that provide political guidance for cooperation on matters related to extended deterrence in all its aspects and publicly signal the resolve of the parties to use force in the exercise of collective self-defense. Within NATO, policy planning relating to extended nuclear deterrence takes place at multiple levels, including in the Strategic Concepts that state leaders adopted and in the Nuclear Planning Group. Some states are involved in forward deployment or nuclear stationing relationships with nuclear-armed states. Training or targeting exercises, port visits, overflights, declarations and doctrines, and so forth, are all part of the planning or preparation for use of nuclear weapons that constitute these arrangements.

21. *United States Non-Paper: Defense Impacts of Potential United Nations General Assembly Nuclear Weapons Ban Treaty*, North Atlantic Council, AC/333-N(2016)0029 (INV), 17 October 2016, http://www.icanw.org/wp-content/uploads/2016/10/NATO_OCT2016.pdf; Colum Lynch, "U.S. Seeks to Scupper Proposed Ban on Nuclear Arms," *Foreign Policy*, 21 October 2016, http://foreign policy.com/2016/10/21/u-s-seeks-to-scupper-proposed-ban-on-nuclear-arms.

22. See, for example, *Nuclear Umbrella Arrangements and the Treaty on the Prohibition of Nuclear Weapons*, International Human Rights Clinic, Human Rights Program at Harvard Law School, June 2018, http://hrp.law.harvard.edu/wp-content/uploads/2018/06/Nuclear_Umbrella_Arrangements_Treaty_Prohibition.pdf.

23. *United States Non-Paper.*

24. *Text of the Convention on the Physical Protection of Nuclear Material*, INFCIRC/274, International Atomic Energy Agency, November 1979, https://www.iaea.org/sites/default/files/infcirc274.pdf.

25. *Resolution 1540 (2004)*, S/RES/1540 (2004), UN Security Council, 28 April 2014.

26. Lyndon Burford, "Addressing Transit: The New Zealand Experience," *Nuclear Ban Daily* 2, no. 9 (28 June 2017): 3, http://www.reachingcritical will.org/images/documents/Disarmament-fora/nuclear-weapon-ban/reports/NBD2.9.pdf.

27. Interview with author, INT10, 26 January 2018; interview with author, INT23, 7 June 2018.

28. Interview with author, INT10, 26 January 2018.

29. Peter Cary, Patrick Malone, and R. Jeffrey Smith, "Light Penalties and Lax Oversight Encourage Weak Safety Culture at Nuclear Weapons Labs," Center for Public Integrity, 26 June 2017, https://apps.publicintegrity.org/nuclear-negligence/light-penalties.

30. Patrick Malone, "A Near-Disaster at a Federal Nuclear Weapons Laboratory Takes a Hidden Toll on America's Arsenal," Center for Public Integrity, 18 June 2017, https://apps.publicintegrity.org/nuclear-negligence/near-disaster.

31. Cary, Malone, and Smith, "Light Penalties and Lax Oversight."

32. Frank G. Klotz, undersecretary for nuclear security, Department of Energy; and administrator, National Nuclear Security Administration, letter to the president and laboratory director of Los Alamos National Laboratory, 25 August 2015, https://energy.gov/sites/prod/files/2015/09/f26/LANS PNOV %28NEA-2015-02%29 - web.pdf.

33. See Kristen Iversen, *Full Body Burden: Growing Up in the Nuclear Shadow of Rocky Flats* (New York: Broadway Books, 2013).

34. See Patricia Calhoun, "Rocky Flats Nuclear Weapons Plant Closed Long Ago, But Is Still a Hot Topic," *Westword*, 7 August 2019, https://www.westword.com/news/rocky-flats-nuclear-plant-shut-down-thirty-years-ago-but-is-still-a-hot-topic-11437949.

35. See, for example, *Banning investment: An explicit prohibition on the financing of nuclear weapons producers*, A/CONF.229/2017/NGO/WP.5, working paper submitted by PAX to the United Nations Conference to negotiate a legally binding instrument to prohibit nuclear weapons, leading toward their elimination, 17 March 2017, http://www.reachingcriticalwill.org/images/documents/Disarmament-fora/nuclear-weapon-ban/documents/NGOWP.5.pdf.

36. See, for example, "Cluster Munitions Divestment," Don't Bank on the Bomb, 26 February 2012, https://www.dontbankonthebomb.com/cluster-munitions-divestment.

37. Helena Nolan, director of disarmament, Ministry of Foreign Affairs and Trade of Ireland, statement to the United Nations Conference to negotiate a legally binding instrument to prohibit nuclear weapons, leading toward their elimination, New York, 29 March 2017, http://www.reachingcriticalwill.org/images/documents/Disarmament-fora/nuclear-weapon-ban/statements/29March_Ireland-T2.pdf.

38. Interview with author, INT23, 7 June 2018.

39. See http://www.dontbankonthebomb.com for all the latest updates on economic divestment of nuclear weapons as well as lists of financial institutions and companies involved in the production of nuclear weapons.

40. Helena Nolan, director of disarmament, Ministry of Foreign Affairs and Trade of Ireland, statement to the United Nations Conference to negotiate a legally binding instrument to prohibit nuclear weapons, leading toward their elimination, New York, 19 June 2017.

41. *Draft Treaty on the Prohibition of Nuclear Weapons*, A/CONF.229/2017/CRP.1/Rev.1, submitted by the president of the conference, United Nations Conference to negotiate a legally binding instrument to prohibit nuclear weapons, leading toward their total elimination, New York, 27 June 2017, http://www.reachingcriticalwill.org/images/documents/Disarmament-fora/nuclear-weapon-ban/documents/CRP1-Rev1.pdf.

42. "Articles 2–4, Version as of 30 July 15:30," United Nations Conference to negotiate a legally binding instrument to prohibit nuclear weapons, leading toward their total elimination, New York, New York, 30 July 2017, http://www.reachingcriticalwill.org/images/documents/Disarmament-fora/nuclear-weapon-ban/documents/Articles-2-5-30-June.pdf.

43. *Draft treaty on the prohibition of nuclear weapons*, A/CONF.229/2017/L.X, submitted by the president of the conference, United Nations Conference

to negotiate a legally binding treaty to prohibit nuclear weapons, leading toward their total elimination, New York, 3 July 2017, http://www.reaching criticalwill.org/images/documents/Disarmament-fora/nuclear-weapon-ban/documents/L-X.pdf.

44. See, for example, John Carlson, "Nuclear Weapon Prohibition Treaty: A Safeguards Debacle," *Trust & Verify* 158, Verification Research, Training, and Information Centre (VERTIC), Autumn 2018, http://www.vertic.org/media/assets/TV/TV158.pdf.

45. Eirini Giorgou, "Safeguards Provisions in the Treaty on the Prohibition of Nuclear Weapons," *Arms Control Law*, 11 April 2018, https://armscontrollaw .com/2018/04/11/safeguards-provisions-in-the-treaty-on-the-prohibition-of -nuclear-weapons.

46. *Victim assistance in the nuclear weapon ban treaty: a comprehensive and detailed approach*, Article 36 and the International Human Rights Clinic of the Human Rights Program at Harvard Law School, June 2017, 2, http://www.article36 .org/wp-content/uploads/2017/06/VA-ban-treaty-full.pdf.

47. See, for example, Molly Doggett And Alice Osman, "Responsibility for Victim Assistance and Environmental Remediation," *Nuclear Ban Daily* 2, no. 7 (23 June 2017): 2, http://www.reachingcriticalwill.org/images/documents/Disarmament-fora/nuclear-weapon-ban/reports/NBD2.7.pdf.

48. *Environmental remediation in the nuclear weapon ban treaty: a comprehensive and detailed approach*, Article 36 and the International Human Rights Clinic of the Human Rights Program at Harvard Law School, June 2017, http://www .article36.org/wp-content/uploads/2017/06/ER-short-paper-final.pdf.

49. Lan Mei, "Recalling the Humanitarian Agenda: The Need to Strengthen Positive Obligations," *Nuclear Ban Daily* 2, no. 10 (29 June 2017): 2, http:// www.reachingcriticalwill.org/images/documents/Disarmament-fora/nuclear -weapon-ban/reports/NBD2.10.pdf.

50. *Global Fissile Material Report 2009: A Path to Nuclear Disarmament*, International Panel on Fissile Materials, 2009, 114–123, http://fissilematerials.org/library/gfmr09.pdf.

51. Ritchie, "Delegitimising Nuclear Weapons in the Nuclear Weapon Ban Treaty," 4.

52. See the Gender and Radiation Project, https://www.genderandradiation .org; and Ray Acheson, *Sex, Gender, and Nuclear Weapons*, International Campaign to Abolish Nuclear Weapons, 2016, http://www.reachingcriticalwill.org/images/documents/Publications/sex-gender-nuclear-weapons.pdf.

53. See http://www.peacewomen.org/SCR-1325.

54. *Women, disarmament, non-proliferation and arms control*, A/C.1/71/L.37, UN General Assembly First Committee on Disarmament and International

Security, New York, 14 October 2016, http://www.reachingcriticalwill.org/
images/documents/Disarmament-fora/1com/1com16/resolutions/L37.pdf.

55. *Draft Chairman's factual summary*, NPT/CONF.2020/PC.I/CRP.3,
Preparatory Committee for the 2020 Review Conference of the Parties to the
Treaty on the Non-Proliferation of Nuclear Weapons, Vienna, 11 May 2017,
http://www.reachingcriticalwill.org/images/documents/Disarmament-fora/
npt/prepcom17/documents/CRP3.pdf.

56. Sue Coleman-Haseldine, statement to the United Nations Conference to negotiate a legally binding instrument to prohibit nuclear weapons,
leading toward their total elimination, New York, 28 March 2017, http://
www.reachingcriticalwill.org/images/documents/Disarmament-fora/nuclear
-weapon-ban/statements/28March_SCH.pdf.

57. Ritchie, "Delegitimising Nuclear Weapons in the Nuclear Weapon Ban
Treaty," 3.

58. Indigenous statement to the United Nations Conference to negotiate a
legally binding instrument to prohibit nuclear weapons, leading toward their
total elimination, New York, June 2017, http://www.reachingcriticalwill.org/
images/documents/Disarmament-fora/nuclear-weapon-ban/statements/
IndigenousStatement.pdf,

59. Karina Lester, statement to the United Nations Conference to negotiate a legally binding instrument to prohibit nuclear weapons, leading toward
their total elimination, New York, 16 June 2017, http://www.reaching
criticalwill.org/images/documents/Disarmament-fora/nuclear-weapon-ban/
statements/16June_IPPNW.pdf.

60. See *Victim Rights and Victim Assistance in a Treaty Prohibiting Nuclear Weapons: A Humanitarian Perspective*, A/CONF.229/2017/NGO/WP.14, working
paper submitted by Mines Action Canada as a partner of the International Campaign to Abolish Nuclear Weapons, United Nations Conference to negotiate
a legally binding instrument to prohibit nuclear weapons, leading toward their
total elimination, 31 March 2017, http://www.reachingcriticalwill.org/images/
documents/Disarmament-fora/nuclear-weapon-ban/documents/NGOWP.14.
pdf; Ray Acheson, *Banning Nuclear Weapons: Principles and Elements for a Legally
Binding Instrument* (New York: Reaching Critical Will of the Women's International League for Peace and Freedom, March 2017), http://www.reaching
criticalwill.org/images/documents/Publications/banning-nuclear-weapons.pdf;
and Acheson, "Response to the First Draft Text of the Convention on the
Prohibition of Nuclear Weapons."

61. *Treaty on the Prohibition of Nuclear Weapons*, A/CONF.229/2017/8,
United Nations conference to negotiate a legally binding instrument to prohibit
nuclear weapons, leading toward their total elimination, New York, 7 July 2017,

http://www.reachingcriticalwill.org/images/documents/Disarmament-fora/
nuclear-weapon-ban/documents/TPNW.pdf.

CHAPTER 9

1. Simon Coveney, foreign minister of Ireland, statement to the United
Nations Conference to negotiate a legally binding instrument to prohibit nuclear
weapons, leading toward their total elimination, New York, 7 July 2017.
2. Interview with author, INT24, 12 June 2018.
3. Interview with author, INT8, 17 January 2018.
4. Interview with author, INT3, 20 December 2017.
5. Interview with author, INT14, 20 February 2018.
6. Interview with author, INT8, 17 January 2018.
7. Interview with author, INT24, 12 June 2018.
8. Interview with author, INT5, 21 December 2017.
9. Interview with author, INT19, 17 May 2018.
10. Interview with author, INT24, 12 June 2018.
11. Interview with author, INT10, 26 January 2018.
12. Interview with author, INT10, 26 January 2018.
13. Interview with author, INT8, 17 January 2018.
14. Interview with author, INT14, 20 February 2018.
15. Interview with author, INT23, 7 June 2018.
16. Interview with author, INT19, 17 May 2018.
17. Interview with author, INT23, 7 June 2018.
18. Felicity Ruby, "'Doing a Landmines' on Gender and Nukes," presentation to Towards Human Security: Civil Society Conference, 10th Anniversary
of the Mine Ban Treaty, Oslo, Norway, September 2007.
19. Interview with author, INT11, 26 January 2018.
20. Interview with author, INT7, 12 January 2018.
21. Interview with author, INT11, 26 January 2018.
22. Interview with author, INT8, 17 January 2018.
23. Interview with author, INT10, 26 January 2018.
24. Interview with author, INT7, 12 January 2018.
25. Interview with author, INT11, 26 January 2018.
26. Interview with author, INT12, 2 February 2018.
27. Interview with author, INT4, 21 December 2017.
28. Interview with author, INT3, 20 December 2017.

29. Tim Wright, "Australia's Opposition to a Nuclear Weapon Ban," International Campaign to Abolish Nuclear Weapons, 18 October 2016, http://www.icanw.org/campaign-news/australias-opposition-to-a-nuclear-weapon-ban.

30. Based on statistics compiled in John Borrie, Anne Guro Dimmen, Torbjørn Graff Hugo, Camilla Waszink, and Kjølv Egeland, *Gender, Development and Nuclear Weapons* (Geneva: International Law and Policy Institute and the United Nations Institute for Disarmament Research, October 2016), 19–20; and *List of participants*, A/CONF.229/2017/INF/4/Rev.1, United Nations Conference to negotiate a legally binding instrument to prohibit nuclear weapons, leading toward their total elimination, New York, 25 July 2017, https://www.un.org/disarmament/tpnw/participants.html.

31. Interview with author, INT24, 12 June 2018.

32. Interview with author, INT7, 12 January 2018.

33. Interview with author, INT12, 2 February 2018.

34. Interview with author, INT10, 26 January 2018.

35. Interview with author, INT24, 12 June 2018.

36. Interview with author, INT11, 26 January 2018.

37. Interview with author, INT1, 27 November 2017.

38. Interview with author, INT8, 17 January 2018.

39. Interview with author, INT12, 2 February 2018.

40. Interview with author, INT24, 12 June 2018.

41. Interview with author, INT12, 2 February 2018.

42. Interview with author, INT11, 26 January 2018.

43. Interview with author, INT10, 26 January 2018.

44. Alva Myrdal, *The Game of Disarmament: How the United States and Russia Run the Arms Race* (New York: Pantheon Books, 1976), 85.

45. Myrdal, *The Game of Disarmament*, 88.

46. Interview with author, INT12, 2 February 2018.

47. Interview with author, INT12, 2 February 2018.

48. Interview with author, INT24, 12 June 2018.

49. Interview with author, INT22, 6 June 2018.

50. Interview with author, INT23, 7 June 2018.

51. Senator Scott Ludlam, statement to the United Nations Conference to negotiate a legally binding instrument to prohibit nuclear weapons, leading toward their total elimination, New York, 6 July 2017.

52. Interview with author, INT3, 20 December 2017.

53. Interview with author, INT13, 16 February 2018.

54. Interview with author, INT5, 21 December 2017.

55. Interview with author, INT7, 12 January 2018.

56. Interview with author, INT5, 21 December 2017.

57. Interview with author, INT11, 26 January 2018.

58. Interview with author, INT10, 26 January 2018.

59. Interview with author, INT10, 26 January 2018.

60. Interview with author, INT12, 2 February 2018.

61. Interview with author, INT8, 17 January 2018.

62. Abacca Anjain Maddison, statement on behalf of the International Campaign to Abolish Nuclear Weapons (ICAN) to the United Nations Conference to negotiate a legally binding instrument to prohibit nuclear weapons, leading toward their total elimination, New York, 7 July 2017.

63. Setsuko Thurlow, statement to the United Nations Conference to negotiate a legally binding instrument to prohibit nuclear weapons, leading toward their total elimination, New York, 7 July 2017.

64. The answer to life, the universe, and everything!

65. For the current status of signatures and ratifications, see http://www.icanw.org/status-of-the-treaty-on-the-prohibition-of-nuclear-weapons.

66. See https://www.nobelpeaceprize.org/Prize-winners/Winners/2017.

CONCLUSION

1. Interview with author, INT11, 26 January 2018.

2. E. P. Thompson, "The Rituals of Enmity," in *Prospectus for a Habitable Planet*, edited by E. P. Thompson and Dan Smith (London: Penguin Books, 1986), 11.

3. Nick Ritchie, "A Hegemonic Nuclear Order: Understanding the Ban Treaty and the Power Politics of Nuclear Weapons," *Contemporary Security Policy*, 31 January 2019.

4. At the 2018 General Assembly, for example, the French ambassador said that the "emotional and divisive" approach to nuclear disarmament represented by the TPNW is "disconnected from credible work." Also see Bret Stephens, "Don't Ban the Bomb," *New York Times*, 6 October 2017, https://www.nytimes.com/2017/10/06/opinion/nobel-peace-prize-nuclear-weapons.html.

5. See www.dontbankonthebomb.com for details.

6. Alan Tovey, "BAE Ditched by Norway's $1 Trillion Investment Fund over Nuclear Weapon Concerns," *The Telegraph*, 16 January 2018, http://www.telegraph.co.uk/business/2018/01/16/bae-ditched-norways-1-trillion-investment-fund-nuclear-weapon.

7. Maaike Beenes, "Largest Dutch Pension Fund to Divest from Nuclear Weapons," Don't Bank on the Bomb, 11 January 2018, https://www.dontbankon thebomb.com/largest-dutch-pension-fund-to-divest-from-nuclear-weapons.

8. Esha Vaish, "Swedish Fund AP2 Ditches Tobacco and Nuclear Weapons Investments," *Reuters*, 4 June 2019, https://www.reuters.com/ article/us-sweden-funds-tobacco/swedish-fund-ap2-ditches-tobacco-and -nuclear-weapons-investments-idUSKCN1T50VZ; see also Tony Robinson, "Swedish Pension Fund to Abandon Nuclear Weapons Investments," *Pressenza*, 16 January 2019, https://www.pressenza.com/2019/01/swedish-pension -fund-to-abandon-nuclear-weapons-investments.

9. See ICAN's Parliamentary Pledge at www.icanw.org/projects/pledge for details. As an example of the impact this can have, the Labor Party in Australia has committed to sign and ratify the TPNW when it next forms a government. See "Australian Labor Party Commits to Joining Nuclear Ban Treaty," International Campaign to Abolish Nuclear Weapons, 18 December 2018, http://www.icanw.org/campaign-news/australian-labor -party-commits-to-joining-nuclear-ban-treaty.

10. See nuclearban.org/cities for details of ICAN's Cities Appeal.

11. See, for example, this transcript from NRK Dagsrevyen interview with Norway's prime minister Erna Solberg, 19 December 2017, https://tv.nrk.no/ serie/dagsrevyen, in which she tries to disassociate Norway's position within NATO from the possible use of nuclear weapons.

12. Nick Ritchie and Kjølv Egeland, "The Diplomacy of Resistance: Power, Hegemony and Nuclear Disarmament," *Global Change, Peace and Security* (27 April 2018): 13.

13. Such as the global day of action against BNP Paribas, a company investing in nuclear weapons (see bnp.dontbankonthebomb.com), and a bicycle journey from Melbourne to Canberra, Australia, in support of the TPNW (see www.icanw.org/au/nobelpeaceride).

14. O'Brien, statement to the United Nations Conference.

15. Matthew Bolton and Elizabeth Minor, "The Discursive Turn Arrives in Turtle Bay: The International Campaign to Abolish Nuclear Weapons' Operationalisation of Critical IR Theories," *Global Policy* 7, no. 3 (2016): 385–95.

16. Ray Acheson, "Foregrounding Justice in Nuclear Disarmament: A Practitioner Commentary," *Global Policy* 7, no. 3 (2016): 405–7.

17. What follows in the next few paragraphs is drawn from a chapter I have written for a forthcoming book: Acheson, "Feminist Solution."

18. Carol Cohn, Felicity Hill, and Sara Ruddick, "The Relevance of Gender for Eliminating Weapons of Mass Destruction," *Weapons of Mass Destruction Commission*, no. 38 (2006), 9.

19. Courtenay Rattray, permanent representative of Jamaica to the United Nations, statement to the UN General Assembly First Committee on Disarmament and International Security, New York, 3 October 2017, http://

reachingcriticalwill.org/images/documents/Disarmament-fora/1com/1com17/statements/3Oct_Jamaica.pdf.

20. Micheál Martin, Minister for Foreign Affairs of Ireland, statement to the 2010 NPT Review Conference, New York, 3 May 2010, http://www.reachingcriticalwill.org/images/documents/Disarmament-fora/npt/revcon2010/statements/3May_Ireland.pdf.

BIBLIOGRAPHY

Aboutlatta, Amr. Statement to the United Nations Conference to negotiate a legally binding instrument to prohibit nuclear weapons, leading toward their elimination, New York, 27 March 2017. http://www.reaching criticalwill.org/images/documents/Disarmament-fora/nuclear-weapon-ban/statements/27March_Egypt.pdf.

Acheson, Ray, ed. *Assuring Destruction Forever: Nuclear Weapon Modernization around the World*. New York: Reaching Critical Will of the Women's International League for Peace and Freedom, 2012. http://www.reaching criticalwill.org/images/documents/Publications/modernization/assuring-destruction-forever.pdf.

———. *Banning Nuclear Weapons: Principles and Elements for a Legally Binding Instrument*. New York: Reaching Critical Will of the Women's International League for Peace and Freedom, March 2017. http://www.reachingcritical will.org/images/documents/Publications/banning-nuclear-weapons.pdf.

———. "Creating the Environment for 'New Thinking.'" *NPT News in Review* 16, no. 3 (6 May 2019): 1–4. http://reachingcriticalwill.org/images/documents/Disarmament-fora/npt/NIR2019/NIR16.3.pdf.

———. "Crisis of Relevance." *First Committee Monitor* 7, no. 5 (3 November 2008). http://www.reachingcriticalwill.org/images/documents/Disarmament-fora/1com/FCM08/FCM-2008-5.pdf.

———. "Feminist Solution: Abolish Nuclear Weapons." In *Feminist Solutions for Ending War*, edited by Megan Mackenzie. London: Pluto Press, 2021.

———. "Foregrounding Justice in Nuclear Disarmament: A Practitioner Commentary." *Global Policy* 7, no. 3 (2016): 405–7.

———. "Human Security Disarmament." *First Committee Monitor* 9, no. 1 (4 October 2010): 3–4. http://www.reachingcriticalwill.org/images/documents/Disarmament-fora/1com/FCM10/FCM-2010-1.pdf.

———. "The Nuclear Ban and the Patriarchy: A Feminist Analysis of Opposition to Prohibiting Nuclear Weapons." *Critical Studies on Security* (30 April 2018): 1–5.

———. "Patriarchy and the Bomb: Banning Nuclear Weapons against the Opposition of Militarist Masculinities." In *The Gender Imperative: Human Security vs. State Security*, edited by Betty A. Reardon and Asha Hans, 392–409. New York: Routledge, 2019.

———. "Response to the First Draft Text of the Convention on the Prohibition of Nuclear Weapons." Women's International League for Peace and Freedom, 13 June 2017. http://www.reachingcriticalwill.org/images/documents/Publications/response-to-22-May-draft-text.pdf.

———. *Sex, Gender, and Nuclear Weapons.* International Campaign to Abolish Nuclear Weapons, 2016. http://www.reachingcriticalwill.org/images/documents/Publications/sex-gender-nuclear-weapons.pdf.

———. "Time to Reframe the Debate." *First Committee Monitor* 8, no. 1 (5 October 2009): 3. http://www.reachingcriticalwill.org/images/documents/Disarmament-fora/1com/FCM09/FCM-2009-1.pdf.

———. "We Hail Concrete, Transparent, Irreversible, Verifiable Action." *NPT News in Review* 9, no. 17 (25 May 2010): 1–2. http://www.reachingcriticalwill.org/images/documents/Disarmament-fora/npt/NIR2010/No17.pdf.

———. "¡Ya Basta! It's All about the Ban." *NPT News in Review* 13, no. 16 (22 May 2015): 1–2. http://www.reachingcriticalwill.org/images/documents/Disarmament-fora/npt/NIR2015/No16.pdf.

Acheson, Ray, and John Burroughs. *Revitalizing Multilateral Disarmament Negotiations: An Alternative Approach.* New York: Reaching Critical Will of the Women's International League for Peace and Freedom and the Lawyers Committee on Nuclear Policy, July 2011. http://www.reachingcriticalwill.org/images/documents/Disarmament-fora/cd/revitalizing-disarmament-negotiations.pdf.

Achieving a Nuclear Weapon Free World, A/AC.281/NGO/1. Working paper submitted by the Reaching Critical Will program of the Women's International League for Peace and Freedom to the Open-ended Working Group on Nuclear Disarmament, Geneva, 17 July 2013. http://www.reachingcriticalwill.org/images/documents/Disarmament-fora/OEWG/Documents/NGO1.pdf.

Adamson, Jo. Statement to the 2012 Non-Proliferation Treaty Preparatory Committee, Vienna, 3 May 2012. http://www.reachingcriticalwill.org/images/documents/Disarmament-fora/npt/prepcom12/statements/3May_UK.pdf.

Addressing Nuclear Disarmament: Recommendations from the Perspective of Nuclear-Weapon-Free Zones, A/AC.286/WP.34/Rev.1. Submitted by Argentina, Brazil, Costa Rica, Ecuador, Guatemala, Indonesia, Malaysia, Mexico, Philippines, and Zambia to the Open-ended Working Group taking forward multilateral nuclear disarmament negotiations, 11 May 2016. http://www.reachingcriticalwill.org/images/documents/Disarmament-fora/OEWG/2016/Documents/WP34.pdf.

Addressing Nuclear Disarmament: Recommendations from the Perspective of Nuclear-Weapon-Free Zones, A/AC.286/WP.34. Working paper submitted by Argentina, Brazil, Costa Rica, Ecuador, Guatemala, Indonesia, Malaysia, Mexico, Philippines, and Zambia to the Open-ended Working Group taking forward multilateral nuclear disarmament negotiations, 11 May 2016.

Agence France-Presse. "Marshall Islands Nuclear Arms Lawsuit Thrown out by UN's Top Court." *The Guardian*, 5 October 2016. https://www.theguardian.com/world/2016/oct/06/marshall-islands-nuclear-arms-lawsuit-thrown-out-by-uns-top-court.

Ainslie, John. *The Trident Shambles*. Glasgow: Scottish CND, 2016.

"Algerians Take Steps to Prosecute France for Nuclear Tests." *Middle East Monitor*, 15 February 2017. https://www.middleeastmonitor.com/20170215-algerians-take-steps-to-prosecute-france-for-nuclear-tests.

Alvarez, Robert. "Yesterday Is Tomorrow: Estimating the Full Cost of a Nuclear Buildup." *Bulletin of the Atomic Scientists*, 3 November 2017. https://thebulletin.org/yesterday-tomorrow-estimating-full-cost-nuclear-buildup11264.

"Ambassador Haley on Nuclear Weapons." *C-SPAN*, 27 March 2017. https://www.c-span.org/video/?426068-1/un-ambassador-nikki-haley-shell-protest-debate-nuclear-weapons-ban.

Andanje, Anthony. Statement to the UN General Assembly First Committee on Disarmament and International Security, New York, 16 October 2013. http://www.reachingcriticalwill.org/images/documents/Disarmament-fora/1com/1com13/statements/16Oct_Kenya.pdf.

———. Statement to the UN General Assembly First Committee on Disarmament and International Security, New York, 13 October 2014. http://reachingcriticalwill.org/images/documents/Disarmament-fora/1com/1com14/statements/13Oct_Kenya.pdf.

Anderson, Kelly. Statement to the UN General Assembly First Committee on Disarmament and International Security, New York, 2 November 2012. http://www.reachingcriticalwill.org/images/documents/Disarmament-fora/1com/1com12/statements/2Nov_Canada.pdf.

Arnold, Scot. "Does DoD Profit Policy Sufficiently Compensate Defense Contractors?" *IDA Research Notes* (Fall 2008).

Article VI of the Treaty on the Non-Proliferation of Nuclear Weapons, NPT/
CONF.2015/PC.III/WP.18. Working paper submitted by Ireland on
behalf of the New Agenda Coalition to the Third session of the Preparatory Committee for the 2015 Conference of the Parties to the Treaty on the
Non-Proliferation of Nuclear Weapons, 2 April 2014. http://www.reaching
criticalwill.org/images/documents/Disarmament-fora/npt/prepcom14/
documents/WP18.pdf.

"Articles 2–4, Version as of 30 July 15:30." United Nations Conference to negotiate a legally binding instrument to prohibit nuclear weapons, leading toward
their total elimination, New York, 30 July 2017. http://www.reaching
criticalwill.org/images/documents/Disarmament-fora/nuclear-weapon-ban/
documents/Articles-2-5-30-June.pdf.

Associated Press. "North Korean Military Parades: 70 Years of Propaganda,
Intimidation and Unity." *Los Angeles Times*, 8 September 2018. https://
www.latimes.com/world/la-fg-north-korea-military-parades-20180908
-story.html.

"Austrian Pledge." Paper submitted by the Federal Ministry of Europe Integration and Foreign Affairs of the Republic of Austria to the Vienna Conference on the Humanitarian Impact of Nuclear Weapons, 9 December 2014.
http://www.reachingcriticalwill.org/images/documents/Disarmament-fora/
vienna-2014/Austrian_Pledge.pdf.

Bahemuka, Judith Mbula. Statement to the First Committee on Disarmament
and International Security, New York, 7 October 2005. http://www.reaching
criticalwill.org/images/documents/Disarmament-fora/1com/1com05/
statements/kenya7oct.pdf.

Baker, Peter, and Choe Sang-Hun. "Trump Threatens 'Fire and Fury' against
North Korea if It Endangers U.S." *New York Times*, 8 August 2017. https://
www.nytimes.com/2017/08/08/world/asia/north-korea-un-sanctions
-nuclear-missile-united-nations.html.

Ban Ki-moon. Remarks to "Advancing the Disarmament and Non-
Proliferation Agenda: Seeking Peace in an Over-Armed World,"
Monterey Institute of International Studies, Monterey, CA, 18 January 2013. https://www.un.org/sg/en/content/sg/statement/2013-01-18/
secretary-generals-remarks-monterey-institute-international-studies.

*Banning Investment: An Explicit Prohibition on the Financing of Nuclear Weapons
Producers*, A/CONF.229/2017/NGO/WP.5. Working paper submitted
by PAX to the United Nations Conference to negotiate a legally binding
instrument to prohibit nuclear weapons, leading toward their elimination,
17 March 2017. http://www.reachingcriticalwill.org/images/documents/
Disarmament-fora/nuclear-weapon-ban/documents/NGOWP.5.pdf.

Baran, Paul, and Paul Sweezy. *Monopoly Capital: An Essay on the American Economic and Social Order.* New York: New York University Press, 1968.

Barash, David P. "Nuclear Deterrence is a Myth. And a Lethal One at That." *The Guardian,* 14 January 2018. https://www.theguardian.com/world/2018/jan/14/nuclear-deterrence-myth-lethal-david-barash.

Barkenbus, Jack. "Devaluing Nuclear Weapons." *Science, Technology & Human Values* 14, no. 4 (1989): 425–40.

Beckles, Pennelope. Statement to the United Nations conference to negotiate a legally binding instrument to prohibit nuclear weapons, leading toward their total elimination, New York, 28 March 2017. http://www.reaching criticalwill.org/images/documents/Disarmament-fora/nuclear-weapon-ban/statements/28March_TT.pdf.

Beenes, Maaike. "Largest Dutch Pension Fund to Divest from Nuclear Weapons." Don't Bank on the Bomb, 11 January 2018. https://www.dontbankon thebomb.com/largest-dutch-pension-fund-to-divest-from-nuclear-weapons.

Benaway, Gwen. "Repair." *GUTS,* 3 May 2019. http://gutsmagazine.ca/repair.

Benhabib, Seyla. *Critique, Norm and Utopia: A Study of the Foundations of Critical Theory.* New York: Columbia University Press, 1986.

Berents, Helen. "Slackers or Delinquents? No, Just Politically Engaged Youth." *The Conversation,* 4 June 2014. https://theconversation.com/slackers-or-delinquents-no-just-politically-engaged-youth-27218.

Berry, Ken, Patricia Lewis, Benoît Pélopidas, Nikolai Sokov, and Ward Wilson. *Delegitimizing Nuclear Weapons: Examining the Validity of Nuclear Deterrence.* Monterey, CA: Monterey Institute of International Studies, 2010.

Bidwai, Pradful, and Ackin Vanaik. *New Nukes: India, Pakistan and Global Nuclear Disarmament.* New York: Olive Branch Press, 2000.

Bishop, Julie. Statement to the Conference on Disarmament, Geneva, 26 March 2014. http://www.reachingcriticalwill.org/images/documents/Disarmament-fora/cd/2014/Statements/part1/26March_Australia.pdf.

———. "We Engage, Not Enrage Nuclear Countries." *Sydney Morning Herald,* 14 February 2014. https://www.smh.com.au/opinion/we-must-engage-not-enrage-nuclear-countries-20140213-32n1s.html.

Biswas, Shampa. *Nuclear Desire: Power and the Postcolonial Nuclear Order.* Minneapolis: University of Minnesota Press, 2014.

Blair, Bruce G., and Matthew A. Brown. "World Spending on Nuclear Weapons Surpasses $1 Trillion Per Decade, Global Zero Technical Report." Nuclear Weapons Cost Study, June 2011. https://www.globalzero.org/files/gz_nuclear_weapons_cost_study.pdf.

Blix, Hans. *Weapons of Terror: Freeing the World of Nuclear, Chemical and Biological Arms*. Stockholm: WMD Commission, 2006.

Bolton, Matthew, and Elizabeth Minor. "The Discursive Turn Arrives in Turtle Bay: The International Campaign to Abolish Nuclear Weapons' Operationalisation of Critical IR Theories." *Global Policy* 7, no. 3 (2016): 385–95.

BondGraham, Darwin, Jacqueline Cabasso, Nicholas Robinson, Will Parrish, and Ray Acheson. "Rhetoric vs. Reality: The Political Economy of Nuclear Weapons and Their Elimination." In *Beyond Arms Control: Challenges and Choices for Nuclear Disarmament*, edited by Ray Acheson, 9–32. New York: Women's International League for Peace and Freedom, 2010.

BondGraham, Darwin, Nicholas Robinson, and Will Parrish. "California's Nuclear Nexus: A Faux Disarmament Plan Has Roots in the Golden State's Pro-Nuclear Lobby," *Z Magazine*, 20 November 2009. https://zcomm.org/zmagazine/californias-nuclear-nexus-by-darwin-bondgraham.

Booth, Robert, and Patrick Butler. "UK Austerity Has Inflicted 'Great Misery' on Citizens, UN Says." *The Guardian*, 16 November 2018. https://www.theguardian.com/society/2018/nov/16/uk-austerity-has-inflicted-great-misery-on-citizens-un-says.

Borrie, John. *Unacceptable Harm: A History of How the Treaty to Ban Cluster Munitions Was Won*. New York and Geneva: United Nations Institute for Disarmament Research, 2009.

Borrie, John, Maya Brehm, Silvia Cattaneo, and David Atwood. "Learn, Adapt, Succeed: Potential Lessons from the Ottawa and Oslo Processes for Other Disarmament and Arms Control Challenges." In *Beyond Arms Control: Challenges and Choices for Nuclear Disarmament*, edited by Ray Acheson, 197–209. New York: Women's International League for Peace and Freedom, 2010.

Borrie, John, and Tim Caughley, "After Olso: Humanitarian Perspectives and the Changing Nuclear Weapons Discourse." Humanitarian Impact of Nuclear Weapons project paper no. 3. Geneva: United Nations Institute for Disarmament Research, 2013. http://www.unidir.org/files/publications/pdfs/after-oslo-en-469.pdf.

Borrie, John, Anne Guro Dimmen, Torbjørn Graff Hugo, Camilla Waszink, and Kjølv Egeland. *Gender, Development and Nuclear Weapons*. Geneva: International Law and Policy Institute and the United Nations Institute for Disarmament Research, October 2016.

Borrie, John, and V. Martin Randin, eds. *Alternative Approaches in Multilateral Decision Making: Disarmament as Humanitarian Action*. Geneva: United Nations Institute for Disarmament Research, 2005.

Bower, Adam. Memo on Additional Protocols I and II to the 1949 Geneva Conventions. Prepared for Article 36, 20 January 2014.

Boylan, Jesse. "This Is Not Nowhere." *LOTL*, 14 September 2018. https://www.lotl.com/culture/political-movement/this-is-not-nowhere.

Brown, David. "How Women Took over the Military-Industrial Complex." *Politico*, 2 January 2019. https://www.politico.com/story/2019/01/02/how-women-took-over-the-military-industrial-complex-1049860.

Brum, Tony de. Statement to the 2014 NPT Preparatory Committee, New York, 28 April 2014. http://www.reachingcriticalwill.org/images/documents/Disarmament-fora/npt/prepcom14/statements/28April_MarshallIslands.pdf.

Burford, Lyndon. "Addressing Transit: The New Zealand Experience." *Nuclear Ban Daily* 2, no. 9 (28 June 2017): 3. http://www.reachingcriticalwill.org/images/documents/Disarmament-fora/nuclear-weapon-ban/reports/NBD 2.9.pdf.

Burroughs, John. *The Legality of Threat or Use of Nuclear Weapons: A Guide to the Historic Opinion of the International Court of Justice.* Münster: Lit Verlag, 1997.

———. "The Need for a Prohibition of Threat of Nuclear Weapons." *Nuclear Ban Daily* 2, no, 5 (21 June 2017): 4. http://www.reachingcriticalwill.org/images/documents/Disarmament-fora/nuclear-weapon-ban/reports/NBD2.5.pdf.

Burt, Alistair. Statement on behalf of France, the United Kingdom, and the United States to the high-level meeting of the UN General Assembly on Nuclear Disarmament, New York, 26 September 2013. http://www.reachingcriticalwill.org/images/documents/Disarmament-fora/HLM/26Sep_UKUSFrance.pdf.

Butler, Judith. *Gender Trouble: Feminism and the Subversion of Identity.* New York: Routledge, 1999.

Cabasso, Jacqueline. "Putting Nuclear Weapons in Context: The Hidden Architecture of U.S. Militarism." In *The Challenge of Abolishing Nuclear Weapons*, edited by David Krieger, 119–40. New Brunswick, NJ: Transaction Publishers, 2009.

Cabasso, Jacqueline, and Ray Acheson. "Dismantling Discourses: Nuclear Weapons and Human Security." In *Beyond Arms Control: Challenges and Choices for Nuclear Disarmament*, edited by Ray Acheson, 127–42. New York: Reaching Critical Will of the Women's International League for Peace and Freedom, 2010.

Calhoun, Patricia. "Rocky Flats Nuclear Weapons Plant Closed Long Ago, but Is Still a Hot Topic." *Westword*, 7 August 2019. https://www.westword.com/news/rocky-flats-nuclear-plant-shut-down-thirty-years-ago-but-is-still-a-hot-topic-11437949.

Calmy-Rey, Micheline. Statement to the 2010 NPT Review Conference, New York, 3 May 2010. http://www.reachingcriticalwill.org/images/documents/Disarmament-fora/npt/revcon2010/statements/3May_Switzerland.pdf.

Camus, Albert. *The Myth of Sisyphus and Other Essays*. New York: Vintage Books, 1955.

———. *The Rebel: An Essay on Man in Revolt*. New York: Vintage Books, 1956.

Carlson, John. "Nuclear Weapon Prohibition Treaty: A Safeguards Debacle." *Trust & Verify* 158, Verification Research, Training, and Information Centre (VERTIC), Autumn 2018. http://www.vertic.org/media/assets/TV/TV158.pdf.

Carman, Diane. "Anti-Nuke Nuns Return to Crime Scene with a Treaty and a Nobel Prize." *Denver Post*, 20 October 2017. https://www.denverpost.com/2017/10/20/anti-nuke-nuns-return-to-crime-scene-with-a-treaty-and-a-nobel-prize.

Carpenter, R. Charli. "Recognizing Gender-Based Violence against Civilian Men and Boys in Conflict Situations." *Security Dialogue* 37, no. 1 (March 2006): 83–103.

———. "Women, Children and Other Vulnerable Groups: Gender, Strategic Frames and the Protection of Civilians as a Transnational Issue." *International Studies Quarterly* 49, no. 2 (June 2005): 295–344.

Cary, Peter, Patrick Malone, and R. Jeffrey Smith. "Light Penalties and Lax Oversight Encourage Weak Safety Culture at Nuclear Weapons Labs." Center for Public Integrity, 26 June 2017. https://apps.publicintegrity.org/nuclear-negligence/light-penalties.

Castañeda, Jorge. Statement to the Eighteen-Nation Committee on Disarmament, ENDC/PV.430. Geneva, Switzerland, 21 August 1969.

Castledine, Jacqueline. *Cold War Progressives: Women's International Organizing for Peace and Freedom*. Urbana: University of Illinois Press, 2012.

Chan, Maritza. "Non-Nuclear Weapons States Must Lead in Shaping International Norms on Nuclear Weapons: A Practitioner Commentary." *Global Policy* 7, no. 3 (September 2016): 408–10.

———. Statement on behalf of the Community of Latin American and Caribbean States to the UN General Assembly First Committee on Disarmament and International Security, New York, 15 October 2014. http://reachingcriticalwill.org/images/documents/Disarmament-fora/1com/1com14/statements/15Oct_CELAC.pdf.

———. Statement to the 2014 NPT Preparatory Committee, New York, 30 April 2014. http://www.reachingcriticalwill.org/images/documents/Disarmament-fora/npt/prepcom14/statements/30April_CostaRica.pdf.

———. Statement to the 2015 NPT Review Conference, New York, 22 May 2015. http://www.reachingcriticalwill.org/images/documents/ Disarmament-fora/npt/revcon2015/statements/22May_CostaRica.pdf.

———. Statement to the UN General Assembly First Committee on Disarmament and International Security, New York, 20 October 2014. http://www.reachingcriticalwill.org/images/documents/Disarmament-fora/ 1com/1com14/statements/20Oct_CostaRica.pdf.

Charles, Eden. Statement on behalf of the Caribbean Community to the UN General Assembly First Committee on Disarmament and International Security, New York, 7 October 2014. http://reachingcriticalwill.org/images/documents/ Disarmament-fora/1com/1com14/statements/7Oct_CARICOM.pdf.

Checkel, Jeffrey. *Ideas and International Political Changes: Soviet/Russian Behavior and the End of the Cold War.* New Haven, CT: Yale University Press, 1997.

Chullikatt, Francis. Statement to the UN General Assembly First Committee on Disarmament and International Security, New York, 22 October 2013. http://www.reachingcriticalwill.org/images/documents/Disarmament -fora/1com/1com13/statements/22Oct_HolySee.pdf.

Cohen, Yoel. *The Whistleblower of Dimona: Israel, Vanunu, and the Bomb.* New York: Holmes & Meier, 2003.

Cohn, Carol. "Sex and Death in the Rational World of Defense Intellectuals." *Signs* 12, no. 4 (Summer 1987): 687–718.

———. "Slick 'Ems, Glick 'Ems, Christmas Trees, and Cookie Cutters: Nuclear Language and How We Learned to Pat the Bomb." *Bulletin of the Atomic Scientists* (June 1987): 17–24.

———. "Wars, Wimps and Women: Talking Gender and Thinking War." In *Gender and War Talk*, edited by Miriam G. Cooke and Angela Woollacott, 226–46. Princeton, NJ: Princeton University Press, 1993.

Cohn, Carol, Felicity Hill, and Sara Ruddick. "The Relevance of Gender for Eliminating Weapons of Mass Destruction." *Weapons of Mass Destruction Commission*, no. 38 (2006).

Cohn, Carol, and Sara Ruddick. "A Feminist Ethical Perspective on Weapons of Mass Destruction." In *Ethics and Weapons of Mass Destruction: Religious and Secular Perspectives*, edited by Sohail H. Hashmi and Steven P. Lee, 405–34. Cambridge: Cambridge University Press, 2004.

Coleman-Haseldine, Sue. Statement to the United Nations Conference to negotiate a legally binding instrument to prohibit nuclear weapons, leading toward their total elimination, New York, 28 March 2017. http:// www.reachingcriticalwill.org/images/documents/Disarmament-fora/nuclear -weapon-ban/statements/28March_SCH.pdf.

Conference Report: Humanitarian Impact of Nuclear Weapons. New York: Reaching Critical Will of the Women's International League for Peace and Freedom, March 2013. http://www.reachingcriticalwill.org/disarmament-fora/hinw/oslo-2013/conference-report.

Cordier, Andrew W., and Wilder Foote, eds. *Public Papers of the Secretaries-General of the United Nations: Dag Hammarskjöld, Volume III*. New York: Columbia University Press, 1972.

Çorman, Fazli. Statement to the UN General Assembly First Committee on Disarmament and International Security, New York, 6 October 2010. http://www.reachingcriticalwill.org/images/documents/Disarmament -fora/1com/1com10/statements/6Oct_Turkey.pdf.

Cortright, David. *Peace: A History of Movements*. Cambridge: Cambridge University Press, 2008.

Coveney, Simon. Statement to the United Nations Conference to negotiate a legally binding instrument to prohibit nuclear weapons, leading toward their total elimination, New York, 7 July 2017.

Crawford, Neta C. *Pentagon Fuel Use, Climate Change, and the Costs of War*. Providence, RI: Brown University Press, 2019.

Cypher, James M. "Critical Analyses of Military Spending and Capitalism." *Eastern Economic Journal* 11, no. 3 (July–September 1985): 273–82.

Das, Runa. "Colonial Legacies, Post-Colonial (in)Securities, and Gender(ed) Representations in South Asia's Nuclear Policies." *Social Identities* 16, no. 6 (2010): 717–40.

Davenport, Kelsey. "The Joint Comprehensive Plan of Action (JCPOA) at a Glance." Arms Control Association, May 2018. https://www.armscontrol .org/factsheets/JCPOA-at-a-glance.

DeGrasse, Robert W. *Military Expansion, Economic Decline*. New York: Council on Economic Priorities, 1983.

Doane, Deborah. "Do International Ngos Still Have the Right to Exist?" *The Guardian*, 13 March 2016. https://www.theguardian.com/global -development-professionals-network/2016/mar/13/do-international-ngos -still-have-the-right-to-exist.

Doggett, Molly, and Alice Osman. "Responsibility for Victim Assistance and Environmental Remediation." *Nuclear Ban Daily* 2, no. 7 (23 June 2017): 2. http://www.reachingcriticalwill.org/images/documents/Disarmament-fora/ nuclear-weapon-ban/reports/NBD2.7.pdf.

Don't Bank on the Bomb. "Cluster Munitions Divestment." 26 February 2012. https://www.dontbankonthebomb.com/cluster-munitions-divestment.

Draft Chairman's Factual Summary, NPT/CONF.2020/PC.I/CRP.3. Preparatory Committee for the 2020 Review Conference of the Parties to the

Treaty on the Non-Proliferation of Nuclear Weapons, Vienna, 11 May 2017. http://www.reachingcriticalwill.org/images/documents/Disarmament-fora/npt/prepcom17/documents/CRP3.pdf.

Draft Convention on the Prohibition of Nuclear Weapons, A/CONF.229/2017/CRP.1. Submitted by the president of the conference, United Nations Conference to negotiate a legally binding instrument to prohibit nuclear weapons, leading toward their elimination, 22 May 2017. http://www.reachingcriticalwill.org/images/documents/Disarmament-fora/nuclear-weapon-ban/documents/CRP1.pdf.

Draft Elements of an UNGA60 First Committee Resolution "Initiating Work on Priority Disarmament and Non-Proliferation Issues." Submitted by Brazil, Canada, Kenya, Mexico, New Zealand, and Sweden, October 2005. http://www.reachingcriticalwill.org/images/documents/Disarmament-fora/1com/1com05/documents/draftelementsinitiating.pdf.

Draft: Report of the Open-Ended Working Group Taking Forward Multilateral Nuclear Disarmament Negotiations, A/AC.286/CRP.2, 15 August 2016. http://www.reachingcriticalwill.org/images/documents/Disarmament-fora/OEWG/2016/Documents/A-AC.286-CRP.2.pdf.

Draft Treaty on the Prohibition of Nuclear Weapons, A/CONF.229/2017/CRP.1/Rev.1. Submitted by the president of the conference, United Nations Conference to negotiate a legally binding instrument to prohibit nuclear weapons, leading toward their total elimination, New York, 27 June 2017. http://www.reachingcriticalwill.org/images/documents/Disarmament-fora/nuclear-weapon-ban/documents/CRP1-Rev1.pdf.

Draft Treaty on the Prohibition of Nuclear Weapons, A/CONF.229/2017/L.X. Submitted by the president of the conference, United Nations Conference to negotiate a legally binding treaty to prohibit nuclear weapons, leading toward their total elimination, New York, 3 July 2017. http://www.reachingcriticalwill.org/images/documents/Disarmament-fora/nuclear-weapon-ban/documents/L-X.pdf.

Duncanson, Clare, and Catherine Eschle. "Gender and the Nuclear Weapons State: A Feminist Critique of the UK Government's White Paper on Trident." *New Political Scientist* 30, no. 4 (2008): 545–63.

Early, Rosalind. "How to Stop a Nuclear Bomb: The St. Louis Baby Tooth Survey, 50 Years Later." *St. Louis Magazine*, 20 September 2013. https://www.stlmag.com/How-to-Stop-a-Nuclear-Bomb-The-St-Louis-Baby-Tooth-Survey-50-Years-Later.

Economic and Social Consequences of Disarmament, E/3593/Rev.1. New York: Department of Economic and Social Affairs, United Nations, 1962. http://undocs.org/E/3593/Rev.1.

Effective Measures for Nuclear Disarmament, A/C.1/70/L.28/Rev.1. UN General Assembly First Committee on Disarmament and International Security, 28 October 2015. http://www.reachingcriticalwill.org/images/documents/Disarmament-fora/1com/1com15/resolutions/L28Rev1.pdf.

Eichler, Maya. "Militarized Masculinities in International Relations." *Brown Journal of World Affairs* 21, no. 1 (2014): 81–93.

Eide, Espen Barth. "Chair's Summary." Conference on the Humanitarian Impact of Nuclear Weapons, Oslo, 4–5 March 2013. https://www.regjeringen.no/en/aktuelt/nuclear_summary/id716343.

———. Statement to the UN General Assembly First Committee on Disarmament and International Security, New York, 4 October 2010. http://www.reachingcriticalwill.org/images/documents/Disarmament-fora/1com/1com10/statements/4Oct_Norway.pdf.

Eide, Stein-Ivar Lothe. "A Ban on Nuclear Weapons: What's in It for NATO?" International Law and Policy Institute, Policy Paper no. 5, January 2014.

Elements for a Treaty Banning Nuclear Weapons, A/AC.286/WP.14. Working paper submitted by Fiji, Nauru, Palau, Samoa, and Tuvalu to the Open-ended Working Group taking forward multilateral nuclear disarmament negotiations, 3 March 2016. http://www.reachingcriticalwill.org/images/documents/Disarmament-fora/OEWG/2016/Documents/WP14.pdf.

Eliminating Nuclear Threats: A Practical Agenda for Global Policymakers. Canberra/Tokyo: International Commission on Nuclear Non-Proliferation and Disarmament, 2009.

Ellsberg, Daniel. *The Doomsday Machine: Confessions of a Nuclear War Planner.* New York: Bloomsbury, 2017.

Elson, Diane. "The Impact of Austerity on Women." Women's Budget Group, 3 December 2018. https://wbg.org.uk/resources/the-impact-of-austerity-on-women.

Emba, Christine. "'Reclaiming My Time' Is Bigger than Maxine Waters." *Washington Post,* 1 August 2017. https://www.washingtonpost.com/blogs/post-partisan/wp/2017/08/01/reclaiming-my-time-is-bigger-than-maxine-waters/?utm_term=.d19637107436.

Enloe, Cynthia. *Bananas, Beaches, and Bases: Making Feminist Sense of International Politics.* Berkeley: University of California Press, 1990.

———. "Beyond 'Rambo': Women and the Varieties of Militarized Masculinity." In *Women and the Military System,* edited by Eva Isaakson, 71–93. New York: St. Martin's, 1988.

———. *Globalization and Militarism: Feminists Make the Link.* New York: Rowman & Littlefield, 2007.

———. *Maneuvers: The International Politics of Militarizing Women's Lives*. Berkeley: University of California Press, 2000.

Eschle, Catherine. "Beyond Greenham Women? Gender Identities and Anti-Nuclear Activism in Peace Camps." *International Feminist Journal of Politics* 19, no. 4 (2017): 471–90.

———. "Gender and Valuing Nuclear Weapons." Working paper for *Devaluing Nuclear Weapons: Concepts and Challenges*, University of York, Department of Politics, 20–21 March 2012.

Estes, Nick. *Our History Is the Future*. New York: Verso, 2019.

Ethical Imperatives for a Nuclear-Weapon-Free World, A/C.1/70/L.40. UN General Assembly First Committee on Disarmament and International Security, 21 October 2015. http://reachingcriticalwill.org/images/documents/Disarmament-fora/1com/1com15/resolutions/L40.pdf.

Explanation of vote by Austria, Ireland, Liechtenstein, Malta, New Zealand, and San Marino on Draft Resolution L.6, "Follow-up to the 2013 high-level meeting of the General Assembly on nuclear disarmament." UN General Assembly First Committee on Disarmament and International Security, New York, 4 November 2013. http://www.reachingcriticalwill.org/images/documents/Disarmament-fora/1com/1com13/eov/L6_Ireland.pdf.

Explanation of vote by Norway on Resolution A/C.1/70/L.37 at the UN General Assembly First Committee on Disarmament and International Security, New York, 3 November 2015. http://reachingcriticalwill.org/images/documents/Disarmament-fora/1com/1com15/statements/3November_Norway.pdf.

Explanation of vote by the Russian Federation on Resolution A/C.1/67/L.46, "Taking forward multilateral nuclear disarmament negotiations." UN General Assembly First Committee on Disarmament and International Security, New York, 6 November 2012.

An Exploration of Some Contributions That Also Nonnuclear Weapon States Could Engage in to Take Multilateral Nuclear Disarmament Forward, A/AC.281/WP.5. Working paper submitted by Austria to the Open-ended Working Group to develop proposals to take forward multilateral nuclear disarmament negotiations for the achievement and maintenance of a world without nuclear weapons, Geneva, 28 June 2013. http://www.reachingcriticalwill.org/images/documents/Disarmament-fora/OEWG/Documents/WP5.pdf.

"Facts, Figures." Los Alamos National Laboratory, last updated July 2019. https://www.lanl.gov/about/facts-figures/index.php.

Fihn, Beatrice, ed. *The 2010 Action Plan Monitoring Report*. New York: Reaching Critical Will of the Women's International League for Peace and

Freedom, 2012. http://www.reachingcriticalwill.org/images/documents/
Publications/2010-Action-Plan/RCW_Final_Report.pdf.

———. *Unspeakable Suffering: The Humanitarian Impact of Nuclear Weapons*. New York: Reaching Critical Will of the Women's International League for Peace and Freedom, February 2013.

Final Document of the Review Conference of the Parties to the Treaty on the Non-Proliferation of Nuclear Weapons, NPT/CONF/35/I–III (Geneva, 1975).

Fischer, Heinz. Statement to the high-level meeting of the UN General Assembly on Nuclear Disarmament, New York, 26 September 2013. http://www.reachingcriticalwill.org/images/documents/Disarmament-fora/HLM/26Sep_Austria.pdf.

Ford, Zack. "Media Fawns over President Trump's Strike on Syria." *ThinkProgress*, 7 April 2017. https://thinkprogress.org/trump-media-syria-attack-cd8bee9d61d6.

Forsberg, Randall. "Call to Halt the Nuclear Arms Race: Proposal for a Mutual US-Soviet Nuclear-Weapon Freeze." (1980). https://livingwiththebomb.files.wordpress.com/2013/08/call-to-halt-arms-race.pdf.

Foster, Dawn. "Britain's Austerity Has Gone from Cradle to Grave." *Jacobin*, 9 April 2019. https://www.jacobinmag.com/2019/04/britain-life-expectancy-austerity-conservative-party-tories.

Foucault, Michel. *The Order of Things: An Archeology of the Human Sciences*. Paris: Editions Gallimard, 1966.

Fraser, Nancy, Tithi Bhattacharya, and Cinzia Arruzza. "Notes for a Feminist Manifesto." *New Left Review* 114 (November–December 2018): 113–34.

Frohmberg, Eric, Robert Goble, Virginia Sanchez, and Dianne Quigley. "The Assessment of Radiation Exposures in Native American Communities from Nuclear Weapons Testing in Nevada." *Risk Analysis* 20, no. 1 (March 2000): 101–11.

"FY2011 Budget Request a Critical Step toward Implementing President Obama's Nuclear Security Vision." News and Information, National Nuclear Security Administration, 1 February 2010. http://nnsa.energy.gov/2816.htm.

Gandenberger, Mia, and Ray Acheson. "Highlights from the Vienna Conference." *Filling the Gap: Report on the Third Conference on the Humanitarian Impact of Nuclear Weapons*. New York: Reaching Critical Will of the Women's International League for Peace and Freedom, 9 December 2014. http://www.reachingcriticalwill.org/images/documents/Disarmament-fora/vienna-2014/filling-the-gap.pdf.

Garrity, Patrick. "The Depreciation of Nuclear Weapons in International Politics: Possibilities, Limits, Uncertainties." *Journal of Strategic Studies* 14, no. 4 (1991): 463–541.

Georgescu, Calin. *Report of the Special Rapporteur on the Implications for Human Rights of the Environmentally Sound Management and Disposal of Hazardous Substances and Wastes.* Human Rights Council, Twenty-First Session, Agenda Item 3, Promotion and Protection of all Human Rights, Civil, Political, Economic, Social and Cultural Rights, Including the Right to Development, 2013. http://www.un.org/en/ga/search/view_doc.asp?symbol=%20A/HRC/21/48/Add.1.

Gerson, Joseph. *Empire and the Bomb: How the U.S. Uses Nuclear Weapons to Dominate the World.* London: Pluto Press, 2007.

Gilmore, Eamon. Statement to the high-level meeting of the UN General Assembly on Nuclear Disarmament, New York, 26 September 2013. http://www.reachingcriticalwill.org/images/documents/Disarmament-fora/HLM/26Sep_Ireland.pdf.

Giorgou, Eirini. "Safeguards Provisions in the Treaty on the Prohibition of Nuclear Weapons." *Arms Control Law*, 11 April 2018. https://armscontrollaw.com/2018/04/11/safeguards-provisions-in-the-treaty-on-the-prohibition-of-nuclear-weapons.

Gómez Robledo, Juan Manuel. "Chair's Summary." Second Conference on the Humanitarian Impact of Nuclear Weapons, Nayarit, Mexico, 13–14 February 2014. http://www.reachingcriticalwill.org/images/documents/Disarmament-fora/nayarit-2014/chairs-summary.pdf.

Graham, Whitney, and Elena I. Nicklasson. "Maternal Meltdown: From Chernobyl to Fukushima." *Inter Press Service*, 26 April 2011. http://www.ipsnews.net/2011/04/op-ed-maternal-meltdown-from-chernobyl-to-fukushima.

Guerreiro, Antonio. Statement to the 2012 Non-Proliferation Treaty Preparatory Committee, Vienna, 2 May 2012. http://www.reachingcriticalwill.org/images/documents/Disarmament-fora/npt/prepcom12/statements/2May_Brazil.pdf.

Guitton, Alice. Explanation of vote on L.13/Rev.1 on behalf of People's Republic of China, the Russian Federation, the United Kingdom, the United States, and France to the UN General Assembly First Committee on Disarmament and International Security, New York, 2 November 2015. http://www.reachingcriticalwill.org/images/documents/Disarmament-fora/1com/1com15/eov/L13_N5.pdf.

Gusterson, Hugh. "Democracy, Hypocrisy, First Use." Virtual Roundtable on Presidential First Use of Nuclear Weapons, Public Books, 26 February 2018. http://www.publicbooks.org/virtual-roundtable-on-presidential-first-use-of-nuclear-weapons/#gusterson.

———. *Nuclear Rites: A Weapons Laboratory at the End of the Cold War.* Berkeley: University of California Press, 1996.

Hajnoczi, Thomas. Statement to the United Nations Conference to negotiate a legally binding instrument to prohibit nuclear weapons, leading toward their elimination, New York, 29 March 2017. http://www.reaching criticalwill.org/images/documents/Disarmament-fora/nuclear-weapon-ban/statements/29March_Austria-T2.pdf.

Harries, Matthew. "The Real Problem with a Nuclear Ban Treaty." Carnegie Endowment for Peace, 15 March 2017. http://carnegieendowment.org/2017/03/15/real-problem-with-nuclear-ban-treaty-pub-68286.

Harrington de Santana, Anne. "Nuclear Weapons as the Currency of Power: Deconstructing the Fetishism of Force." *Nonproliferation Review* 16, no. 3 (2009): 325–45.

Hawkins, Dimity. "From Little Things . . ." Lecture at the Centre for Ethical Leadership, Ormond College, Melbourne University, Melbourne, Australia, 11 April 2018. https://cel.edu.au/images/uploads/research_paper_files/Ethical-Leadership-Program-Dimity-Hawkins-ICAN.pdf.

————. "Nuclear Weapons Testing in the Pacific: Lessons for the Treaty on the Prohibition of Nuclear Weapons." Unpublished paper in author's possession, draft as of 21 May 2018.

Hawkins, Dimity, and Tilman Ruff. "How Melbourne Activists Launched a Campaign for Nuclear Disarmament and Won a Nobel Prize." *The Conversation*, 9 October 2017.

Hayashi, Nobuo. Presentation to the Third Conference on the Humanitarian Impact of Nuclear Weapons, Vienna, 9 December 2014. http://www.reachingcriticalwill.org/images/documents/Disarmament-fora/vienna-2014/9Dec_Hayashi.pdf.

Hayda, Julian. "Women Now at Top of Military-Industrial Complex. A Feminist Reaction." *WBEZ 91.5 Chicago*, 8 January 2019. https://www.wbez.org/shows/worldview/women-now-at-top-of-militaryindustrial-complex-a-feminist-reaction/900b5028-9f25-4fe0-b778-24b04f4a6115.

Heeley, Laicie. "To Make and Maintain America's Nukes, Some Communities Pay the Price." *PRI*, 30 January 2018. https://www.pri.org/stories/2018-01-30/make-and-maintain-americas-nukes-some-communities-pay-price.

Helfand, Ira. *Nuclear Famine: Two Billion People at Risk? Global Impacts of Limited Nuclear War on Agriculture, Food Supplies, and Human Nutrition.* Boston: International Physicians for the Prevention of Nuclear War and Physicians for Social Responsibility, November 2013. https://www.ippnw.org/pdf/nuclear-famine-two-billion-at-risk-2013.pdf.

Hersey, John. "Hiroshima." *New Yorker*, 23 August 2016.

"Humanitarian Conference on Nuclear Weapons to Take Place in 2013." Media release, International Campaign to Abolish Nuclear Weapons, 20 April

2012. http://www.icanw.org/wp-content/uploads/2012/08/2012-20April
-OsloConference.pdf.

Humanitarian Consequences of Nuclear Weapons, A/C.1/70/L.37. UN General
Assembly First Committee on Disarmament and International Security, 21 October 2015. http://reachingcriticalwill.org/images/documents/Disarmament
-fora/1com/1com15/resolutions/L37.pdf.

Humanitarian Pledge for the Prohibition and Elimination of Nuclear Weapons,
A/C.1/70/L.38. UN General Assembly First Committee on Disarmament
and International Security, 21 October 2015. http://reachingcriticalwill.org/
images/documents/Disarmament-fora/1com/1com15/resolutions/L38.pdf.

Hurlburt, Heather, Elizabet Weingarten, Alexandra Stark, and Elena Souris.
The "Consensual Straitjacket": Four Decades of Women in Nuclear Security. Washington, DC: New America, 2019. https://www.newamerica.org/political
-reform/reports/the-consensual-straitjacket-four-decades-of-women-in
-nuclear-security.

Hussain, Murtaza. "War on the World: Industrialized Militaries Are a Bigger
Part of Climate Change Than You Know." *The Intercept*, 15 September 2019.
https://theintercept.com/2019/09/15/climate-change-us-military-war.

Hutchings, Kimberly. "Making Sense of Masculinities and War." *Men and Masculinities* 10, no. 4 (June 2008): 389–404.

Hymans, Jacques. *The Psychology of Nuclear Proliferation*. Cambridge: Cambridge
University Press, 2006.

"ICRC Statement to the United Nations General Assembly on the Advisory
Opinion of the International Court of Justice on the Legality of the Threat
or Use of Nuclear Weapons." *International Review of the Red Cross* 37, no. 316
(February 1997): 118–19.

*Identifying the Essential Elements for Achieving and Maintaining a World without
Nuclear Weapons*, A/AC.281/WP.8. Working paper submitted by Ireland and
Switzerland to the Open-ended Working Group on Nuclear Disarmament,
Geneva, 19 July 2013. http://www.reachingcriticalwill.org/images/docu-
ments/Disarmament-fora/OEWG/Documents/WP8.pdf.

Indigenous Statement to the UN Nuclear Weapons Ban Treaty Negotiations, June
2017. http://www.icanw.org/wp-content/uploads/2017/05/Indigenous
-Statement-June-2017.pdf.

International Atomic Energy Agency. *Text of the Convention on the Physical Protection
of Nuclear Material*, INFCIRC/274. November 1979. https://www.iaea.org/
sites/default/files/infcirc274.pdf.

International Campaign to Abolish Nuclear Weapons. "Australian Labor Party
commits to Joining Nuclear Ban Treaty." 18 December 2018. http://

www.icanw.org/campaign-news/australian-labor-party-commits-to-joining
-nuclear-ban-treaty.

———. *Discussion and Proposals on the International Campaign to Abolish Nuclear Weapons.* 28 October 2006.

———. *Hiroshima: Campaign Meeting Report.* August 2012. http://www.icanw.org/wp-content/uploads/2012/10/HiroshimaMeetingReport.pdf.

———. Statement to the Final Session of the Conference on the Humanitarian Impact of Nuclear Weapons, Oslo, 5 March 2013. http://www.icanw.org/wp-content/uploads/2013/03/ICAN-final-statement5.3.13.pdf.

———. Statement to the First Session of the Conference on the Humanitarian Impact of Nuclear Weapons, Oslo, 4 March 2013. http://www.icanw.org/wp-content/uploads/2013/03/ICAN1stsessionstatement.pdf.

———. Statement to the Third Conference on the Humanitarian Impact of Nuclear Weapons, Vienna, 9 December 2014. http://www.reachingcritical will.org/images/documents/Disarmament-fora/vienna-2014/9Dec_ICAN .pdf.

———. "Swedish FM Attacks Signatories of Humanitarian Initiative: 'Not Serious States.'" 7 May 2013. http://www.icanw.org/campaign-news/swedish-fm-attacks-80-state-signatories-of-humanitarian-initiative-not -serious-states/#.UZCpPKJ7K85.

———. "The Not-So-Progressive Approach." 27 April 2016. http://www .icanw.org/campaign-news/the-not-so-progressive-approach.

———. "US Pressured NATO States to Vote No to a Ban." 1 November 2016. http://www.icanw.org/campaign-news/us-pressures-nato-states-to -vote-no-to-the-ban-treaty.

International Commission on Radiological Protection. *Report of the Task Group on Reference Man*, no. 23. Oxford: Pergamon Press, 1975.

International Committee of the Red Cross. "Mankind Is Faced with a Problem of Extreme Gravity . . ." 5 September 1945. https://www.icrc.org/eng/resources/documents/statement/69eezs.htm.

———. *Nuclear Weapons and International Humanitarian Law.* May 2013. https://www.icrc.org/eng/assets/files/2013/4132-4-nuclear-weapons-ihl-2013.pdf.

International Human Rights Clinic of the Human Rights Program at Harvard Law School. *Nuclear Umbrella Arrangements and the Treaty on the Prohibition of Nuclear Weapons.* June 2018. http://hrp.law.harvard.edu/wp-content/uploads/2018/06/Nuclear_Umbrella_Arrangements_Treaty_Prohibition .pdf.

International Human Rights Clinic of the Human Rights Program at Harvard Law School and Article 36. *Environmental Remediation in the Nuclear Weapon*

Ban Treaty: A Comprehensive and Detailed Approach. June 2017. http://www .article36.org/wp-content/uploads/2017/06/ER-short-paper-final.pdf.

———. *Victim Assistance in the Nuclear Weapon Ban Treaty: A Comprehensive and Detailed Approach*. June 2017. http://www.article36.org/wp-content/ uploads/2017/06/VA-ban-treaty-full.pdf.

International Panel on Fissile Materials. *Global Fissile Material Report 2009: A Path to Nuclear Disarmament*. 2009. http://fissilematerials.org/library/gfmr09 .pdf.

Intondi, Vincent. *African Americans against the Bomb*. Stanford, CA: Stanford University Press, 2015.

Iversen, Kristen. *Full Body Burden: Growing Up in the Nuclear Shadow of Rocky Flats*. New York: Broadway Books, 2013.

Jacobson, Harold Karan, and Eric Stein. *Diplomats, Scientists, and Politicians: The United States and the Nuclear Test-Ban Negotiations*. Ann Arbor: University of Michigan Press, 1966.

"Japan Finally Backs U.N. Statement against Use of Nuclear Weapons." *Asahi Shimbun*, 22 October 2013.

Johnson, Rebecca. "Perspectives on the Necessary Framework to Achieve and Maintain a Nuclear Weapons Free World." Presentation to the Open-ended Working Group on Nuclear Disarmament, Geneva, 21 May 2013. http://www.reachingcriticalwill.org/images/documents/Disarmament-fora/ OEWG/statements/21May_Johnson.pdf.

Johnson, Taylor N. "'The Most Bombed Nation on Earth': Western Shoshone Resistance to the Nevada National Security Site." *Atlantic Journal of Communication* 26, no. 4 (2018): 224–39.

Jones, Sandy. "Marshall Islands Nuclear Zero Lawsuit Appeal Dismissed by Ninth Circuit Court." Nuclear Age Peace Foundation Press Release, 31 July 2017. https://www.wagingpeace.org/marshall-islands-ninth-circuit.

Kaldor, Mary. "Warfare and Capitalism." In *Exterminism and Cold War*, edited by New Left Review, 261–87. London: Verso, 1982.

Kaysen, Carl, Robert S. McNamara, and George W. Rathjens. "Nuclear Weapons after the Cold War." *Foreign Affairs* 70, no. 4 (Fall 1990): 95–110.

"Kazakh Anti-Nuclear Movement Celebrates Tenth Anniversary." *BBC News*, 28 February 1999. http://news.bbc.co.uk/2/hi/asia-pacific/288008.stm.

Keck, Margaret E., and Kathryn Sikkink. "Transnational Advocacy Networks in International and Regional Politics." *International Social Science Journal* 51, no. 159 (March 1999): 89–101.

Kellenberger, Jakob. "Bringing the Era of Nuclear Weapons to an End." Presentation to the Geneva Diplomatic Corps, Geneva, Switzerland, 20 April

2010. https://www.icrc.org/eng/resources/documents/statement/nuclear
-weapons-statement-200410.htm.

Kelly, Alison. Statement on behalf of the New Agenda Coalition to the UN
General Assembly First Committee on Disarmament and International
Security, New York, 4 October 2010. http://www.reachingcriticalwill
.org/images/documents/Disarmament-fora/1com/1com10/statements/4Oct
_NAC.pdf.

Kennedy, Laura. Statement to the UN General Assembly First Committee on Disarmament and International Security, New York, 17 October
2012. http://www.reachingcriticalwill.org/images/documents/Disarmament
-fora/1com/1com12/statements/17Oct_USA.pdf.

Keown, Gerard. Statement to the 2013 NPT Preparatory Committee, Geneva,
25 April 2013. http://www.reachingcriticalwill.org/images/documents/
Disarmament-fora/npt/prepcom13/statements/25April_Ireland.pdf.

Kirk, Gwen. "Our Greenham Common: Not Just a Place But a Movement." In
Rocking the Ship of State: Towards a Feminist Peace Politics, edited by Adrienne
Haris and Ynestra King, 263–80. Boulder, CO: Westview Press, 1989.

Klotz, Frank G. Letter to the president and laboratory director of Los Alamos National Laboratory, 25 August 2015. https://energy.gov/sites/prod/
files/2015/09/f26/LANS PNOV %28NEA-2015-02%29 - web.pdf.

Kmentt, Alexander. "The Development of the International Initiative on the
Humanitarian Impact of Nuclear Weapons and Its Effect on the Nuclear
Weapons Debate." *International Review of the Red Cross* 97 (2015): 681–709.

———. "Nuclear Deterrence as a Belief System," *Security Index: A Russian
Journal on International Security* 19, no. 2 (2013): 77–79.

Kom, Mathias. *We Don't Do That Anymore.* The Burning Hell, 2014. https://
soundcloud.com/the-burning-hell/we-dont-do-that-anymore.

Kongstad, Steffan. Statement to the 2010 Non-Proliferation Treaty Review
Conference, Main Committee I, New York, 11 May 2010. http://www
.reachingcriticalwill.org/images/documents/Disarmament-fora/npt/revcon
2010/statements/11May_MCI_Norway.pdf.

———. Statement to the 2013 NPT Preparatory Committee, Geneva,
23 April 2013. http://www.reachingcriticalwill.org/images/documents/
Disarmament-fora/npt/prepcom13/statements/23April_Norway.pdf.

———. Statement to the UN General Assembly First Committee on
Disarmament and International Security, New York, 6 October 2009.
http://www.reachingcriticalwill.org/images/documents/Disarmament
-fora/1com/1com09/statements/6Oct_Norway.pdf.

Kristensen, Hans. "New START Has New Counting." Federation of American Scientists Strategic Security Blog, 29 March 2010. http://www.fas.org/blog/ssp/2010/03/newstart.php.

Kristensen, Hans M., and Matt Korda. "Status of World Nuclear Forces." Federation of American Scientists, updated May 2019. https://fas.org/issues/nuclear-weapons/status-world-nuclear-forces.

Krook, Mona Lena, and Jacquie True. "Rethinking the Life Cycles of International Norms: The United Nations and the Global Promotion of Gender Equality." *European Journal of International Relations* 18, no. 1 (18 November 2010): 103–27.

Kuhn, Thomas S. *The Structure of Scientific Revolution.* Chicago: University of Chicago Press, 1962.

Laggner, Benno. Statement to the 2013 NPT Preparatory Committee, Geneva, 25 April 2013. http://www.reachingcriticalwill.org/images/documents/Disarmament-fora/npt/prepcom13/statements/25April_Switzerland.pdf.

"Last US Cluster Bomb Manufacturer Ends Production." *Russia Today*, 1 September 2016. https://www.rt.com/usa/357889-us-cluster-bombs-production.

Lauber, Jürg. Statement to the 2010 Non-Proliferation Treaty Review Conference, New York, 7 May 2010. http://www.reachingcriticalwill.org/images/documents/Disarmament-fora/npt/revcon2010/statements/7May_Switzerland.pdf.

———. Statement to the UN General Assembly First Committee on Disarmament and International Security, New York, 5 October 2010. http://www.reachingcriticalwill.org/images/documents/Disarmament-fora/1com/1com10/statements/5Oct_Switzerland.pdf.

Lavoy, Peter. "Nuclear Myths and the Causes of Nuclear Proliferation." *Security Studies* 2, no. 3 (1993): 192–212.

"Leading Nuclear Policy Experts and Organizations Call on the United States to Participate in International Conference on Humanitarian Impacts of Nuclear Weapons." Arms Control Association, 29 October 2014. http://www.armscontrol.org/pressroom/press-release/Groups-Urge-United-States-to-participate-in-Vienna-humanitarian-impacts-conference.

Legality of the Threat or Use of Nuclear Weapons. General List No. 95, Advisory Opinion of 8 July 1996.

A legally binding instrument that will need to be concluded to attain and maintain a world without nuclear weapons: a prohibition on nuclear weapons, A/AC.286/WP.17. Working paper submitted by Mexico to the Open-ended Working Group taking forward multilateral nuclear disarmament negotiations, 12 April 2016. http://www.reachingcriticalwill.org/images/documents/Disarmament-fora/OEWG/2016/Documents/WP17.pdf.

Lenanne, Richard. "Obstacles to Nuclear Disarmament—and How to Overcome Them: 4. The Weasels," Wildfire, May 2015, http://www.wildfire-v.org/NPT2015/Obstacles4.pdf.

Lester, Karina. Statement to the United Nations Conference to negotiate a legally binding instrument to prohibit nuclear weapons, leading toward their total elimination, New York, 16 June 2017. http://www.reaching criticalwill.org/images/documents/Disarmament-fora/nuclear-weapon-ban/statements/16June_IPPNW.pdf.

Lichterman, Andrew. "Deterrence, Torture, Power." *NPT News in Review* 8, no. 9 (4 May 2009): 2–5. http://www.reachingcriticalwill.org/images/documents/Disarmament-fora/npt/NIR2009/No1.pdf.

———. "Nuclear Disarmament, Civil Society and Democracy." *Disarmament Forum* 4 (2010): 49–60.

Lichterman, Andrew, and Jacqueline Cabasso. *Faustian Bargain 2000: Why 'Stockpile Stewardship' Is Fundamentally Incompatible with the Process of Nuclear Disarmament*. Oakland, CA: Western States Legal Foundation, May 2000. http://wslfweb.org/docs/fb2000.pdf.

Lifting the Nuclear Shadow: Creating the Conditions for Abolishing Nuclear Weapons. UK Foreign and Commonwealth Office, February 2009.

Lifton, Robert J., and Richard Falk. *Indefensible Weapons: The Political and Psychological Case against Nuclearism*. New York: Basic Books, 1982.

Lindell, Ulf. Statement to the UN General Assembly First Committee on Disarmament and International Security, New York, 20 October 2014. http://reachingcriticalwill.org/images/documents/Disarmament-fora/1com/1com14/statements/20Oct_Sweden.pdf.

List of participants, A/CONF.229/2017/INF/4/Rev.1. United Nations Conference to negotiate a legally binding instrument to prohibit nuclear weapons, leading toward their total elimination, New York, 25 July 2017. https://www.un.org/disarmament/tpnw/participants.html.

Ludlam, Scott. "How Politics Works in Australia, and How to Fix It." *The Monthly*, March 2018. https://www.themonthly.com.au/issue/2018/march/1519822800/scott-ludlam/how-politics-works-australia-and-how-fix-it.

———. Statement to the United Nations Conference to negotiate a legally binding instrument to prohibit nuclear weapons, leading toward their total elimination, New York, 6 July 2017.

Luxemburg, Rosa. *The Accumulation of Capital*. New York: Modern Reader Paperbacks, 1968.

Lynch, Colum. "U.S. Seeks to Scupper Proposed Ban on Nuclear Arms." *Foreign Policy*, 21 October 2016. http://foreignpolicy .com/2016/10/21/u-s-seeks-to-scupper-proposed-ban-on-nuclear-arms.

Mabhongo, Xolisa. Statement to the UN General Assembly First Committee on Disarmament and International Security, New York, 13 October 2010. http://www.reachingcriticalwill.org/images/documents/Disarmament -fora/1com/1com10/statements/13Otc_SouthAfrica.pdf.

Macedo Soare, Luiz Filipe de. Statement on behalf of MERCOSUR and Associated States to the UN General Assembly First Committee on Disarmament and International Security, New York, 13 October 2010. http://www.reaching criticalwill.org/images/documents/Disarmament-fora/1com/1com10/ statements/13Oct_MERCOSUR.pdf.

———. Statement to the UN General Assembly First Committee on Disarmament and International Security, New York, 5 October 2010. http://www.reachingcriticalwill.org/images/documents/Disarmament -fora/1com/1com10/statements/5Oct_brazil.pdf.

Maclellan, Nic. *Banning Nuclear Weapons: A Pacific Islands Perspective*. Melbourne: International Campaign to Abolish Nuclear Weapons, 2014.

———. *Grappling with the Bomb: Britain's Pacific H-bomb Tests*. Canberra: Australian National University, 2017.

Maddison, Abacca Anjain. Statement on behalf of the International Campaign to Abolish Nuclear Weapons to the United Nations Conference to negotiate a legally binding instrument to prohibit nuclear weapons, leading toward their total elimination, New York, 7 July 2017.

Malone, Patrick. "A Near-Disaster at a Federal Nuclear Weapons Laboratory Takes a Hidden Toll on America's Arsenal." Center for Public Integrity, 18 June 2017. https://apps.publicintegrity.org/nuclear-negligence/near-disaster.

Martin, Micheál. Statement to the 2010 NPT Review Conference, New York, 3 May 2010. http://www.reachingcriticalwill.org/images/documents/ Disarmament-fora/npt/revcon2010/statements/3May_Ireland.pdf.

Marx, Karl. *Capital: A Critique of Political Economy, Volume I*. London: Penguin Books, 1991.

———. *Capital: A Critique of Political Economy, Volume III*. London: Penguin Books, 1991.

———. *Grundrisse: Foundations of the Critique of Political Economy*. London: Penguin Books, 1993.

Masco, Joseph. *The Nuclear Borderlands: The Manhattan Project in Post-Cold War New Mexico*. Princeton, NJ: Princeton University Press, 2006.

Mason, Rowena, Anushka Asthana, and Rajeev Syal. "Theresa May Would Authorize Nuclear Strike Causing Mass Loss of Life." *The Guardian*,

18 July 2016. http://www.theguardian.com/uk-news/2016/jul/18/
theresa-may-takes-aim-at-jeremy-corbyn-over-trident-renewal.

McAdam, Doug. *Political Process and the Development of Black Insurgency, 1930–1970*. Chicago: University of Chicago Press, 1982.

McClelland, Jim. *The Report of the Royal Commission into British Nuclear Tests in Australia*. Canberra: Australian Government Publishing Service, 1985.

McConville, Ian. Explanation of vote to the UN General Assembly First Committee on Disarmament and International Security, New York, October 2015. http://www.reachingcriticalwill.org/images/documents/Disarmament-fora/1com/1com15/eov/L13_Australia.pdf.

McCoy, Ronald. "The International Campaign to Abolish Nuclear Weapons." Presentation to ICAN Campaigners Meeting, Geneva, Switzerland, 30 April 2016. http://www.icanw.org/wp-content/uploads/2016/07/THE-CAMPAIGN-TO-BAN-NUCLEAR-WEAPONS.pdf.

Mei, Lan. "Recalling the Humanitarian Agenda: The Need to Strengthen Positive Obligations." *Nuclear Ban Daily* 2, no. 10 (29 June 2017): 2. http://www.reachingcriticalwill.org/images/documents/Disarmament-fora/nuclear-weapon-ban/reports/NBD2.10.pdf.

Mello, Greg. "Does Los Alamos National Lab Help or Hurt the New Mexico Economy?" Los Alamos Study Group, 2006. http://www.lasg.org/LANLecon_impact.pdf.

Melman, Seymour. *Pentagon Capitalism: The Political Economy of War*. New York: McGraw-Hill, 1970.

Menon, Vanu Gopala. Statement to the 2010 Non-Proliferation Treaty Review Conference, New York, 6 May 2010. http://www.reachingcriticalwill.org/images/documents/Disarmament-fora/npt/revcon2010/statements/6May_Singapore.pdf.

Meyer, David. "Peace Protest and Policy: Explaining the Rise and Decline of Antinuclear Movements in Postwar America." *Policy Studies Journal* 21, no. 1 (1993): 35–51.

———. "Protest and Political Opportunities." *Annual Review of Sociology* 30 (11 August 2004): 125–45.

———. "Protest Cycles and Political Process: American Peace Movements in the Nuclear Age." *Political Research Quarterly* 46, no. 3 (1993): 451–79.

———. *A Winter of Discontent: The Nuclear Freeze and American Politics*. New York: Praeger, 1990.

Meyer, Paul. "Disarmament: Kicking the Can Down the Road." *embassymag.ca*, 9 November 2011.

————. Statement on behalf of Brazil, Canada, Kenya, Mexico, New Zealand, and Sweden to the First Committee on Disarmament and International Security, New York, 12 October 2005.

————. Statement to the 2005 Non-Proliferation Treaty Review Conference, New York, 27 May 2005. http://www.reachingcriticalwill.org/images/documents/Disarmament-fora/npt/revcon2005/GDstatements/canada27.pdf.

Meyer, Stephen. *The Dynamics of Nuclear Proliferation.* Chicago: University of Chicago Press, 1984.

Mian, Zia. "Beyond the Security Debate: The Moral and Legal Dimensions of Abolition." In *Abolishing Nuclear Weapons: A Debate*, edited by George Perkovich and James Acton, 295–305. Washington, DC: Carnegie Endowment for Peace, 2009.

Mian, Zia, and M. V. Ramana. "Ending Nuclear Lawlessness." *The Hindu*, 13 April 2017. https://www.thehindu.com/opinion/lead/ending-nuclear-lawlessness/article17960731.ece.

Mills, C. Wright. *The Power Elite.* New York: Oxford University Press, 2000.

Mizokami, Kyle. "America Has Dropped 1,032 Nuclear Weapons (on Itself)." *National Interest*, 30 August 2018. https://nationalinterest.org/blog/buzz/america-has-dropped-1032-nuclear-weapons-itself-30042.

Morgan, David H. J. "Theater of War: Combat, the Military, and Masculinities." In *Theorizing Masculinities*, edited by Harry Brod and Michael Kaufman, 165–82. Thousand Oaks, CA: Sage, 1994.

Mort, Maggie. *Building the Trident Network: A Study of the Enrollment of People, Knowledge, and Machines.* Cambridge, MA: MIT Press, 2002.

Mxakato-Diseko, Nozipho. Statement to the 2015 NPT Review Conference, New York, 22 May 2015.

————. Statement to the United Nations Conference to negotiate a legally binding instrument to prohibit nuclear weapons, leading toward their elimination, New York, 29 March 2017. http://www.reachingcriticalwill.org/images/documents/Disarmament-fora/nuclear-weapon-ban/statements/29March_SouthAfrica-T2.pdf.

Myrdal, Alva. *The Game of Disarmament: How the United States and Russia Run the Arms Race.* New York: Pantheon, 1976.

Neisius, Matthew. "Western Shoshone Nation Opposes Yucca Mountain Nuclear Repository." *Commodities, Conflict, and Cooperation* (Fall 2016 and Winter 2017). https://sites.evergreen.edu/ccc/warnuclear/shoshone-tribe-opposes-yucca-mountain-nuclear-repository.

Nervo, Luis Padilla. Statement to the Conference of the Eighteen-Nation Committee on Disarmament, ENDC/PV.14. Geneva, Switzerland, 3 April 1962.

Nolan, Helena. Statement to the UN General Assembly First Committee on Disarmament and International Security, New York, 17 October 2016. http://www.reachingcriticalwill.org/images/documents/Disarmament-fora/1com/1com16/statements/17Oct_Ireland.pdf.

———. Statement to the United Nations Conference to negotiate a legally binding instrument to prohibit nuclear weapons, leading toward their elimination, New York, 29 March 2017. http://www.reachingcriticalwill.org/images/documents/Disarmament-fora/nuclear-weapon-ban/statements/29March_Ireland-T2.pdf.

———. Statement to the United Nations Conference to negotiate a legally binding instrument to prohibit nuclear weapons, leading toward their elimination, New York, 19 June 2017.

Nordstrom, Jennifer. "Disarmament Machinery." *First Committee Monitor* 5, no. 2 (17 October 2005). http://www.reachingcriticalwill.org/images/documents/Disarmament-fora/1com/FCM05/FCM-2005-2.pdf.

Norris, Robert S., and Hans M. Kristensen. "Russian Nuclear Forces, 2010." *Bulletin of the Atomic Scientists*, January/February 2010.

"Nuclear Notebook." *Bulletin of the Atomic Scientists*. https://thebulletin.org/nuclear-risk/nuclear-weapons/nuclear-notebook.

"Nuclear War: Uranium Mining and Nuclear Tests on Indigenous Land." *Cultural Survival Quarterly Magazine*, September 1993. https://www.culturalsurvival.org/publications/cultural-survival-quarterly/nuclear-war-uranium-mining-and-nuclear-tests-indigenous.

"Nuclear Weapon States Discuss Nuclear Disarmament Obligations." UK Foreign and Commonwealth Office, 6 July 2011. http://www.fco.gov.uk/en/news/latest-news/?view=PressS&id=627529382.

Nyhamar, Inga M. W. Statement to the UN General Assembly First Committee on Disarmament and International Security, New York, 18 October 2012. http://www.reachingcriticalwill.org/images/documents/Disarmament-fora/1com/1com12/statements/18Oct_Norway.pdf.

O'Brien, Patricia. Statement to the United Nations Conference to negotiate a legally binding instrument to prohibit nuclear weapons, leading toward their elimination, New York, 27 March 2017. http://www.reachingcriticalwill.org/images/documents/Disarmament-fora/nuclear-weapon-ban/statements/27March_Ireland.pdf.

Oelrich, Ivan. "Hardly a Jump START." Federation of American Scientists Strategic Security Blog, 29 March 2010. http://www.fas.org/blog/ssp/2010/03/hardly-a-jump-start.php.

Ogwu, U. Joy. Statement to the UN General Assembly First Committee on Disarmament and International Security, New York, 7

October   2014.   http://reachingcriticalwill.org/images/documents/
Disarmament-fora/1com/1com14/statements/7Oct_AfricanGroup.pdf.

Olson, Mary. "Human Consequences of Radiation: A Gender Factor in Atomic Harm." In *Civil Society Engagement in Disarmament Processes: The Case for a Nuclear Weapon Ban*, 26–34. New York: United Nations Office for Disarmament Affairs, 2016.

Onwuliri, Viola. Statement to the high-level meeting of the UN General Assembly on Nuclear Disarmament, New York, 26 September 2013. http://www.reachingcriticalwill.org/images/documents/Disarmament-fora/HLM/26Sep_Nigeria.pdf.

Oostward, Selma van. "The Netherlands Should Actively Negotiate an International Nuclear Weapons Ban Treaty." International Campaign to Abolish Nuclear Weapons, 23 May 2016. http://www.icanw.org/campaign-news/the-netherlands-should-actively-negotiate-an-international-nuclear-weapons-ban-treaty.

O'Reilly, Breifne. Statement to the Non-Proliferation Treaty Preparatory Committee, New York, 2 May 2014. http://www.reachingcriticalwill.org/images/documents/Disarmament-fora/npt/prepcom14/statements/2May_Ireland.pdf.

Orwell, George. *Animal Farm*. New York: Harcourt Brace, 1945.

———. *Nineteen Eighty-Four: A Novel*. London: Secker & Warburg, 1969.

Otto, Caleb. Statement to the 2015 NPT Review Conference, New York, 22 May 2015. http://www.reachingcriticalwill.org/images/documents/Disarmament-fora/npt/revcon2015/statements/22May_Palau.pdf.

Parachasit, Korakot. Statement to the UN General Assembly First Committee on Disarmament and International Security, New York, 23 October 2014. http://reachingcriticalwill.org/images/documents/Disarmament-fora/1com/1com14/statements/23Oct_Thailand.pdf.

Parrish, Will, and Darwin BondGraham. "Anti-Nuclear Nuclearism." *Foreign Policy in Focus*, 12 January 2009. http://fpif.org/anti-nuclear_nuclearism.

Participation of Non-Governmental Organizations in the Conference, A/CONF.229/2017/4. United Nations conference to negotiate a legally binding instrument to prohibit nuclear weapons, leading toward their total elimination, 22 February 2017. http://undocs.org/A/CONF.229/2017/4.

Patriota, Antonio de Aguiar. Statement to the UN General Assembly First Committee on Disarmament and International Security, 15 October 2015. http://www.reachingcriticalwill.org/images/documents/Disarmament-fora/1com/1com15/statements/15October_Brazil.pdf.

Pederson, Geir O. Statement to the UN General Assembly First Committee on Disarmament and International Security, New York, 12 October 2012.

http://www.reachingcriticalwill.org/images/documents/Disarmament-fora/
1com/1com12/statements/12Oct_Norway.pdf.

Peterson, Spike V. "How (the Meaning of) Gender Matters in Political Economy." *New Political Economy* 10, no. 4 (2005): 499–521.

Pflugbei, Sebastian, Henrik Paulitz, Angelika Claussen, and Inge Schmitz-Feuerhake. *Health Effects of Chernobyl: 25 Years after the Reactor Catastrophe.* Berlin: German Affiliate of the International Physicians for the Prevention of Nuclear War, April 2011. https://ratical.org/radiation/Chernobyl/HEof C25yrsAC.html.

Pinto-Coelho, Pedro Motta. Statement to the 2014 NPT Preparatory Committee, New York, 2 May 2014. http://www.reachingcriticalwill.org/images/documents/Disarmament-fora/npt/prepcom14/statements/2May_Brazil.pdf.

Piper, Elizabeth. "UK Nuclear Deterrent to Cost $256 Billion, Far More Than Expected." *Reuters*, 25 October 2015. https://www.reuters.com/article/us-britain-defence-trident-exclusive/exclusive-uk-nuclear-deterrent-to-cost-256-billion-far-more-than-expected-idUSKCN0SJ0EP20151025.

Plotke, David. *Democracy and Boundaries: Themes in Contemporary Politics.* Uppsala: Swedish Institute for North American Studies, 2002.

Pollard, Guy. Explanation of vote by France, the United Kingdom, and the United States on L.46, "Taking forward multilateral nuclear disarmament negotiations." UN General Assembly First Committee on Disarmament and International Security, New York, 6 November 2012. http://www.reaching criticalwill.org/images/documents/Disarmament-fora/1com/1com12/eov/L46_France-UK-US.pdf.

Proposal by the Community of Latin American and Caribbean States (CELAC) on Effective Legal Measures to Attain and Maintain a World without Nuclear Weapons, A/AC.286/WP.15. Working paper submitted by the Dominican Republic in its capacity of president pro tempore of CELAC to the Open-ended Working Group taking forward multilateral nuclear disarmament negotiations, 12 April 2016. http://www.reachingcriticalwill.org/images/documents/Disarmament-fora/OEWG/2016/Documents/WP15.pdf.

"Protest, Dissent, and Witness at the Nevada Test Site." *Online Nevada Encyclopedia.* http://www.onlinenevada.org/articles/protest-dissent-and-witness-nevada-test-site.

Pruitt, Lesley J. "Youth Participation in the UN Human Rights Council." Australian Institute of International Affairs, 19 June 2017. http://www.international affairs.org.au/australianoutlook/youth-participation-human-rights-council.

Pytlak, Allison, ed. *Assuring Destruction Forever: 2019 Edition.* New York: Women's International League for Peace and Freedom, 2019. http://

reachingcriticalwill.org/images/documents/Publications/modernization/ assuring-destruction-forever-2019.pdf.

Pytlak, Allison, and Ray Acheson. "States Discuss Rules for Nuclear Ban Negotiations." Reaching Critical Will of the Women's International League for Peace and Freedom, 16 February 2017. http://www.reaching criticalwill.org/disarmament-fora/nuclear-weapon-ban/reports/11377 -states-discuss-rules-for-nuclear-ban-negotiations.

"Queers against the Nuclear Industry." *3CR Community Radio*, 17 November 2018. https://www.3cr.org.au/radioactive/episode-201811171000/queers -against-nuclear-industry.

"Quick Take: Women in Science, Technology, Engineering, and Mathematics (STEM)." Catalyst, 14 June 2019. https://www.catalyst.org/research/ women-in-science-technology-engineering-and-mathematics-stem.

Quinlan, Michael. "The Future of Nuclear Weapons: Policy for Western Possessors." *International Affairs* 69, no. 3 (1993): 485–96.

Quinn, John. Joint statement on the humanitarian consequences of nuclear weapons to the UN General Assembly First Committee on Disarmament and International Security, New York, 20 October 2014. http://reaching criticalwill.org/images/documents/Disarmament-fora/1com/1com14/ statements/20Oct_Australia.pdf.

Rasor, Dina. "Heads Up, Supercommittee: Here's How to Cut Billions from Overpriced Weapons." *Truthout*, 2 November 2011.

Rattray, Courtenay. Statement to the UN General Assembly First Committee on Disarmament and International Security, New York, 3 October 2017. http://reachingcriticalwill.org/images/documents/ Disarmament-fora/1com/1com17/statements/3Oct_Jamaica.pdf.

Report and Summary of Findings of the Conference. Vienna Conference on the Humanitarian Impact of Nuclear Weapons, 8–9 December 2014. http://www.reachingcriticalwill.org/images/documents/Disarmament-fora/ vienna-2014/ChairSummary.pdf.

Report of the Canberra Commission on the Elimination of Nuclear Weapons. Canberra: Department of Foreign Affairs and Trade, Commonwealth of Australia, 1996.

Report of the Tokyo Forum for Nuclear Non-Proliferation and Disarmament. Tokyo: Ministry of Foreign Affairs, Government of Japan, 1999.

Resolution 1540 (2004), S/RES/1540 (2004). UN Security Council, 28 April 2014.

Reus-Smit, Christian. "International Crises of Legitimacy." *International Politics* 44, no. 1 (2007): 157–74.

Revised Draft: Report of the Open-Ended Working Group Taking forward Multilateral Nuclear Disarmament Negotiations, A/AC.286/CRP.3, 19 August 2016.

http://www.reachingcriticalwill.org/images/documents/Disarmament-fora/
OEWG/2016/Documents/A-AC.286-CRP.3.pdf.

Richards, Shorna-Kay. Statement to the Open-ended Working Group taking forward multilateral nuclear disarmament negotiations, Geneva, 13 May 2016. http://www.reachingcriticalwill.org/images/documents/Disarmament-fora/
OEWG/2016/Statements/13May_Jamaica.pdf.

Ritchie, Nick. "Delegitimising Nuclear Weapons in the Nuclear Weapon Ban Treaty." *Nuclear Ban Daily* 2, no. 7 (23 June 2017): 3–4. http://www.reaching criticalwill.org/images/documents/Disarmament-fora/nuclear-weapon-ban/
reports/NBD2.7.pdf.

———. "Deterrence Dogma: Challenging the Relevance of British Nuclear Weapons," *International Affairs* 85, no. 1 (2009): 81–98.

———. "A Hegemonic Nuclear Order: Understanding the Ban Treaty and the Power Politics of Nuclear Weapons." *Contemporary Security Policy*, 31 January 2019.

———. "Legitimizing and Delegitimizing Nuclear Weapons." In *Viewing Nuclear Weapons through a Humanitarian Lens*, edited by John Borrie and Tim Caughley, 44–77. Geneva: United Nations Institute for Disarmament Research, 2013.

———. "Pathways to Nuclear Disarmament: Delegitimising Nuclear Violence," Working paper for the UN Open-ended Working Group on Nuclear Disarmament, Geneva, Switzerland, 11 May 2016. http://www.reaching criticalwill.org/images/documents/Disarmament-fora/OEWG/statements/
11May_NickRitchie-paper.pdf.

———. "Relinquishing Nuclear Weapons: Identities, Networks and the British Bomb." *International Affairs* 86, no. 2 (2010): 465–87.

———. "Valuing and Devaluing Nuclear Weapons." *Contemporary Security Policy* 34, no. 1 (2013): 155–59.

Ritchie, Nick, and Kjølv Egeland. "The Diplomacy of Resistance: Power, Hegemony and Nuclear Disarmament." *Global Change, Peace and Security* 30, no. 2 (2018): 1–21.

The Road to 2010: Addressing the Nuclear Question in the Twenty First Century. UK Foreign and Commonwealth Office, July 2009.

Robie, David. *Eyes of Fire: The Last Voyage of the Rainbow Warrior.* Auckland: Lindon, 1986.

Robinson, Tony. "Swedish Pension Fund to Abandon Nuclear Weapons Investments." *Pressenza*, 16 January 2019. https://www.pressenza.com/2019/01/
swedish-pension-fund-to-abandon-nuclear-weapons-investments.

Romuld, Gem, and Tim Wright. *(Don't Want Your) Nuclear Umbrella.* ICAN Australia, 2014. https://www.youtube.com/watch?v=reZw23A3_dw.

Rowland, Matthew. Statement to the 2014 NPT Preparatory Committee, New York, 2 May 2014. http://www.reachingcriticalwill.org/images/documents/ Disarmament-fora/npt/prepcom14/statements/2May_UK.pdf.

———. Statement to the UN General Assembly First Committee on Disarmament and International Security, New York, 17 October 2013. http://www.reaching criticalwill.org/images/documents/Disarmament-fora/1com/1com13/ statements/17Oct_UK.pdf.

———. Statement to the UN General Assembly First Committee on Disarmament and International Security, New York, 20 October 2014. http://reaching criticalwill.org/images/documents/Disarmament-fora/1com/1com14/ statements/20Oct_Uk.pdf.

Roy, Arundhati. *The Cost of Living*. New York: Modern Library, 1999.

Ruby, Felicity. "'Doing a Landmines' on Gender and Nukes." Presentation to Towards Human Security: Civil Society Conference, 10th Anniversary of the Mine Ban Treaty, Oslo, Norway, September 2007.

Rules of Procedure of the United Nations Conference to Negotiate a Legally Binding Instrument to Prohibit Nuclear Weapons, Leading toward Their Total Elimination, A/CONF.229/2017/5. United Nations conference to negotiate a legally binding instrument to prohibit nuclear weapons, leading toward their total elimination, 13 June 2017. http://undocs.org/A/CONF.229/2017/5.

"Russia Details Planned Nuke Updates." *Global Security Newswire*, 24 February 2011.

Rydell, Randy. *Explaining Hammarskjöld's 'Hardy Perennial'—The Role of the UN in Nuclear Disarmament*. London: United Nations Association—UK, February 2013. https://www.una.org.uk/sites/default/files/TZ%20Explaining %20Hammarskj%C3%B6ld's%20Hardy%20Perennial%20-%20Randy%20 Rydell_0.pdf.

Sagan, Scott. "Why Do States Build Nuclear Weapons? Three Models in Search of a Bomb." *International Security* 21, no. 3 (Winter 1996/1997): 54–86.

Sandoz, Yves. "Advisory Opinion of the International Court of Justice on the Legality of the Threat or Use of Nuclear Weapons." *International Review of the Red Cross* 37, no. 316 (February 1997): 6–8.

Sandoz, Yves, Christophe Swinarski, and Bruno Zimmerman, eds. *Commentary on the Additional Protocols of 8 June 1977 to the Geneva Conventions of 12 August 1949*. Geneva: ICRC/Nijhoff, 1987.

Sangari, Kumkum, Neeraj Malik, Sheba Chhachhi, and Tanika Sarkar, "Why Women Must Reject the Bomb." In *Out of Nuclear Darkness: The Indian Case for Disarmament*, 47–56. New Delhi: Movement in India for Nuclear Disarmament, 1998.

San Tiago Dantas, Francisco Clementino. Statement to the Conference of the Eighteen-Nation Committee on Disarmament, ENDC/PV.3, Geneva, Switzerland, 16 March 1962.

Schell, Jonathan. "The Spirit of June 12." *The Nation*, 2 July 2007. https://www.thenation.com/article/spirit-june-12.

Schelling, Thomas C. Arms and Influence. New Haven, CT: Yale University Press, 1966.

Schlosser, Eric. "Break-In at Y-12." *New Yorker*, 9 March 2015. https://www.newyorker.com/magazine/2015/03/09/break-in-at-y-12.

———. *Command and Control: Nuclear Weapons, the Damascus Accident, and the Illusion of Safety*. New York: Penguin Books, 2013.

———. "A Nun Walks Free: The Government's Sabotage Case Dismissed." *New Yorker*, 18 May 2015. https://www.newyorker.com/news/news-desk/a-nun-walks-free-the-governments-sabotage-case-dismissed.

Shultz, George P., William J. Perry, Henry A. Kissinger, and Sam Nunn. "How to Protect Our Nuclear Deterrent." *Wall Street Journal*, 19 January 2010.

———. "Toward a Nuclear-Free World." *Wall Street Journal*, 15 January 2008.

———. "A World Free of Nuclear Weapons." *Wall Street Journal*, 4 January 2007.

Simon-Michel, Jean-Hugues. Statement to the 2014 NPT Preparatory Committee, New York, 2 May 2014. http://www.reachingcriticalwill.org/images/documents/Disarmament-fora/npt/prepcom14/statements/2May_France.pdf.

Skorpen, Hilde Janne. Statement to the UN General Assembly First Committee on Disarmament and International Security, New York, 14 October 2010. http://www.reachingcriticalwill.org/images/documents/Disarmament-fora/1com/1com10/statements/14Oct_Norway.pdf.

Slootmaker, Estelle. "Nuns Disarming the World: Two Dominicans with Grand Rapids Roots Help Win Nobel Peace Prize." *Rapid Growth*, 1 February 2018. http://www.rapidgrowthmedia.com/features/nunsnucleardisarm.aspx.

Snyder, Susi. *Shorting Our Security—Financing the Companies That Make Nuclear Weapons*. Utrecht: PAX and International Campaign to Abolish Nuclear Weapons, 2019.

Soakai, Alifeleti. Statement to the UN General Assembly First Committee on Disarmament and International Security, New York, 21 October 2014. http://reachingcriticalwill.org/images/documents/Disarmament-fora/1com/1com14/statements/21Oct_Palau.pdf.

Spindelegger, Michael. Statement to the 2010 NPT Review Conference, New York, 3 May 2010. http://www.reachingcriticalwill.org/images/documents/Disarmament-fora/npt/revcon2010/statements/3May_Austria.pdf.

Statement by Australia to the 2012 Non-Proliferation Treaty Preparatory Committee, Vienna, 4 May 2012.

Statement by Austria on behalf of Afghanistan, Argentina, Austria, Brazil, Brunei Darussalam, Burundi, Chile, Colombia, Costa Rica, Cuba, Dominican Republic, Ecuador, Egypt, El Salvador, Guatemala, Indonesia, Iraq, Ireland, Jamaica, Kuwait, Lebanon, Liberia, Libya, Liechtenstein, Madagascar, Malaysia, Malta, Marshall Islands, Mexico, Morocco, Nicaragua, Nigeria, Palau, Papua New Guinea, Paraguay, Peru, Philippines, Qatar, San Marino, Saudi Arabia, Senegal, Sierra Leone, Singapore, South Africa, Swaziland, Thailand, Trinidad and Tobago, Uruguay, Venezuela, Viet Nam to the 2015 NPT Review Conference, New York, 22 May 2015. http://www.reaching criticalwill.org/images/documents/Disarmament-fora/npt/revcon2015/statements/22May_Austria.pdf.

Statement by civil society on disarmament machinery and the rule of consensus to the UN General Assembly First Committee on Disarmament and International Security, New York, 1 November 2012. http://www.reaching criticalwill.org/images/documents/Disarmament-fora/1com/1com12/statements/1Nov_NGO_machinery.pdf.

Statement by France to the 2012 Non-Proliferation Treaty Preparatory Committee, Vienna, 3 May 2012. http://www.reachingcriticalwill.org/images/documents/Disarmament-fora/npt/prepcom12/statements/3May_France.pdf.

Statement by Hungary to the Open-ended Working Group on Nuclear Disarmament, 9 May 2016. http://www.reachingcriticalwill.org/images/documents/Disarmament-fora/OEWG/2016/Statements/09May_Hungary.pdf.

Statement by Ireland to the 2010 NPT Review Conference, New York, 11 May 2010.

Statement by Ireland to the Third Conference on the Humanitarian Impact of Nuclear Weapons, Vienna, 9 December 2014. http://www.reachingcritical will.org/images/documents/Disarmament-fora/vienna-2014/9Dec_Ireland.pdf.

Statement by Poland to the Open-ended Working Group on Nuclear Disarmament, Geneva, 12 May 2016. http://www.reachingcriticalwill.org/images/documents/Disarmament-fora/OEWG/2016/Statements/12May_Poland.pdf.

Statement by the Islamic Republic of Iran to the UN General Assembly First Committee on Disarmament and International Security, New York, 5 November 2015. http://www.reachingcriticalwill.org/images/documents/Disarmament-fora/1com/1com15/eov/L28_Iran.pdf.

Statement by the People's Republic of China at the Thematic Discussion on Disarmament Machinery to the UN General Assembly First Committee on Disarmament and International Security, New York, 28 October 2015. http://reachingcriticalwill.org/images/documents/Disarmament-fora/1com/1com15/statements/27October_China.pdf.

Statement by the People's Republic of China, France, the Russian Federation, The United Kingdom of Great Britain and Northern Ireland, and the United States of America to the 2010 Non-Proliferation Treaty Review Conference, New York, 5 May 2010. http://www.reachingcriticalwill.org/images/documents/Disarmament-fora/npt/revcon2010/statements/5May_P5-full.pdf.

Statement by the Republic of Lithuania to the Third Conference on the Humanitarian Impact of Nuclear Weapons, Vienna, 9 December 2014. http://www.reachingcriticalwill.org/images/documents/Disarmament-fora/vienna-2014/9Dec_Lithuania.pdf.

Statement by the United Kingdom to the UN General Assembly on Disarmament and International Security, New York, 4 November 2013. http://www.reaching criticalwill.org/images/documents/Disarmament-fora/1com/1com13/statements/4Nov_UK.pdf.

Statement by the U.S. Delegation to the 2012 Non-Proliferation Treaty Preparatory Committee, Vienna, 3 May 2012. http://www.reaching criticalwill.org/images/documents/Disarmament-fora/npt/prepcom12/statements/3May_US.pdf.

Statement by the U.S. Delegation to the UN General Assembly First Committee on Disarmament and International Security, New York, 15 October 2009. http://www.reachingcriticalwill.org/images/documents/Disarmament-fora/1com/1com09/statements/15Oct_US.pdf.

Statement on the humanitarian dimension of nuclear disarmament to the 2012 Non-Proliferation Treaty Preparatory Committee, Vienna, 2 May 2012. http://www.reachingcriticalwill.org/images/documents/Disarmament-fora/npt/prepcom12/statements/2May_IHL.pdf.

Statement on the humanitarian dimension of nuclear disarmament to the UN General Assembly First Committee on Disarmament and International Security, New York, 22 October 2012. http://www.reachingcriticalwill.org/images/documents/Disarmament-fora/1com/1com12/statements/22Oct_Switzerland.pdf.

Statement on the humanitarian impact of nuclear weapons to the 2013 Non-Proliferation Treaty Preparatory Committee, Geneva, 24 April 2013, http://www.reachingcriticalwill.org/images/documents/Disarmament-fora/npt/prepcom13/statements/24April_SouthAfrica.pdf.

Statement on the humanitarian impact of nuclear weapons to the 2015 NPT Review Conference, New York, 28 April 2015. http://www.reaching criticalwill.org/images/documents/Disarmament-fora/npt/revcon2015/statements/28April_AustriaHumanitarian.pdf.

Statement on the humanitarian impact of nuclear weapons to the UN General Assembly First Committee on Disarmament and International Security, New York, 21 October 2013. http://www.reachingcriticalwill.org/images/documents/Disarmament-fora/1com/1com13/statements/21Oct_Joint.pdf.

Statement on the humanitarian impact of nuclear weapons to the UN General Assembly First Committee on Disarmament and International Security, New York, 20 October 2014. http://reachingcriticalwill.org/images/documents/Disarmament-fora/1com/1com14/statements/20Oct_NewZealand.pdf.

Stephens, Bret. "Don't Ban the Bomb." *New York Times*, 6 October 2017. https://www.nytimes.com/2017/10/06/opinion/nobel-peace-prize-nuclear-weapons.html.

Støre, Jonas Gahr. "Disarmament—Reframing the Challenge." Presentation to the Norwegian Atlantic Committee, 45th Annual Conference, Oslo, Norway, 1 February 2010. https://www.regjeringen.no/en/aktuelt/disarmament/id592550.

Strohal, Christian. Statement to the UN General Assembly First Committee on Disarmament and International Security, New York, 24 October 2011. http://www.reachingcriticalwill.org/images/documents/Disarmament-fora/1com/1com11/statements/24Oct_Austria.pdf.

———. Statement to the UN General Assembly First Committee on Disarmament and International Security, New York, 10 October 2012. http://www.reachingcriticalwill.org/images/documents/Disarmament-fora/1com/1com12/statements/10Oct_Austria.pdf.

Stroup, Sarah S., and Wendy H. Wong. *The Authority Trap: Strategic Choices of INGOs*. Ithaca, NY: Cornell University Press, 2017.

Suda, Akio. Statement to the UN General Assembly First Committee on Disarmament and International Security, New York, 14 October 2009. http://www.reachingcriticalwill.org/images/documents/Disarmament-fora/1com/1com09/statements/14Oct_Japan.pdf.

Swerdlow, Amy. *Women Strike for Peace: Traditional Motherhood and Radical Politics in the 1960s*. Chicago: University of Chicago Press, 1993.

Taking forward Multilateral Disarmament Negotiations, A/C.1/67/L.46. UN General Assembly First Committee on Disarmament and International Security, New York, 19 October 2012. http://www.reachingcriticalwill.org/images/documents/Disarmament-fora/1com/1com12/resolutions/L46.pdf.

Taking forward Multilateral Nuclear Disarmament Negotiations, A/C.1/70/L.13/ Rev.1. UN General Assembly First Committee on Disarmament and International Security, 29 October 2015. http://reachingcriticalwill.org/images/ documents/Disarmament-fora/1com/1com15/resolutions/L13Rev1.pdf.

Taking forward Multilateral Nuclear Disarmament Negotiations, A/AC.281/WP.10. Working paper submitted by the New Agenda Coalition (Brazil, Egypt, Ireland, Mexico, New Zealand, and South Africa) to the Open-ended Working Group on Nuclear Disarmament, Geneva, 2013. http://www.reachingcritical will.org/images/documents/Disarmament-fora/OEWG/Documents/WP10. pdf.

Taylor, Bryan C., and Judith Hendry. "Insisting on Persisting: The Nuclear Rhetoric of Stockpile Stewardship." *Rhetoric and Public Affairs* 11, no. 2 (2008): 303–34.

Thompson, E. P. "The Rituals of Enmity." In *Prospectus for a Habitable Planet*, edited by E. P. Thompson and Dan Smith, 11–43. London: Penguin Books, 1986.

Thurlow, Setsuko. Statement to the United Nations Conference to negotiate a legally binding instrument to prohibit nuclear weapons, leading toward their total elimination, New York, 7 July 2017.

Tørres, Liv, Madeleine Rees, Philip Jennings, Jan Gruiters, Kate Hudson, Akira Kawasaki, Michael Christ, and Hirotsugu Terasaki. "Where Is the 'Global Red Line' for Nuclear Weapons?" *Huffington Post*, 26 September 2013. https:// www.huffingtonpost.com/liv-torres/nuclear-disarmament_b_3988288.html.

Tovey, Alan. "BAE Ditched by Norway's $1 Trillion Investment Fund over Nuclear Weapon Concerns." *The Telegraph*, 16 January 2018. http:// www.telegraph.co.uk/business/2018/01/16/bae-ditched-norways-1-trillion -investment-fund-nuclear-weapon.

A treaty banning nuclear weapons, A/AC.286/NOG/3. Working paper submitted by the Women's International League for Peace and Freedom and Article 36 to the Open-ended Working Group taking forward multilateral nuclear disarmament negotiations, 24 February 2016. http://www.reachingcritical will.org/images/documents/Disarmament-fora/OEWG/2016/Documents/ NGO3.pdf.

A Treaty Banning Nuclear Weapons: Developing a Legal Framework for the Prohibition and Elimination of Nuclear Weapons. New York: Women's International League for Peace and Freedom and Article 36, 2014. http://www .reachingcriticalwill.org/images/documents/Publications/a-treaty-banning -nuclear-weapons.pdf.

Treaty Banning Nuclear Weapon Tests in the Atmosphere, in Outer Space and under Water. Opened for signature 8 August 1963. http://www.reachingcriticalwill .org/images/documents/Resources/Treaties/PTBT.pdf.

Treaty on the Prohibition of Nuclear Weapons, A/CONF.229/2017/8. Opened for signature 20 September 2017. http://www.reachingcriticalwill.org/images/ documents/Disarmament-fora/nuclear-weapon-ban/documents/TPNW .pdf.

Uliyanov, Mikhail I. Statement to the 2012 Non-Proliferation Treaty Preparatory Committee, Vienna, 30 April 2012. http://www.reaching criticalwill.org/images/documents/Disarmament-fora/npt/prepcom12/ statements/30April_Russia.pdf.

———. Statement to the UN General Assembly First Committee on Disarmament and International Security, New York, 8 October 2013. http://www.reachingcriticalwill.org/images/documents/Disarmament -fora/1com/1com13/statements/8Oct_Russia.pdf.

"United Nations Conference to Negotiate a Legally Binding Instrument to Prohibit Nuclear Weapons, Leading toward Their Total Elimination." United Nations Web TV, 30 March 2017. http://webtv.un.org/meetings-events/ conferencessummits/watch/7th-meeting-united-nations-conference-to -negotiate-a-legally-binding-instrument-to-prohibit-nuclear-weapons-leading -toward-their-total-elimination-27-31-march-2017/5379469891001.

United States Non-Paper: "Defense Impacts of Potential United Nations General Assembly Nuclear Weapons Ban Treaty." North Atlantic Council, AC/333 -N(2016)0029 (INV), 17 October 2016. http://www.icanw.org/wp-content/ uploads/2016/10/NATO_OCT2016.pdf.

United States Nuclear Tests: July 1945 through September 1992. Las Vegas, NV: U.S. Department of Energy, National Nuclear Security Administration Nevada Field Office, September 2015. https://www.nnss.gov/docs/docs _LibraryPublications/DOE_NV-209_Rev16.pdf.

"US and Russia Determined to Keep Nuclear Weapons Arsenal, SIPRI Says." *Moscow Times,* 16 June 2014.

"U.S. Relations with Marshall Islands." U.S. Department of State, Bureau of East Asian and Pacific Affairs, Fact Sheet, 27 December 2016. https://www .state.gov/r/pa/ei/bgn/26551.htm.

Vaish, Esha. "Swedish Fund AP2 Ditches Tobacco and Nuclear Weapons Investments." *Reuters,* 4 June 2019. https://www.reuters.com/article/ us-sweden-funds-tobacco/swedish-fund-ap2-ditches-tobacco-and-nuclear -weapons-investments-idUSKCN1T50VZ.

Victim Rights and Victim Assistance in a Treaty Prohibiting Nuclear Weapons: A Humanitarian Perspective, A/CONF.229/2017/NGO/WP.14. Working paper submitted by Mines Action Canada as a partner of the International Campaign to Abolish Nuclear Weapons, United Nations Conference to negotiate a legally binding instrument to prohibit nuclear weapons, leading toward their total elimination, 31 March 2017. http://www.reachingcriticalwill.org/images/documents/Disarmament-fora/nuclear-weapon-ban/documents/NGOWP.14.pdf.

Wachuku, Jaja Anucha. Statement to the Conference of the Eighteen-Nation Committee on Disarmament, ENDC/PV.8. Geneva, Switzerland, 23 March 1962.

———. Statement to the Eighteen-Nation Committee on Disarmament, ENDC/PV.3. Geneva, Switzerland, 16 March 1962.

Waltz, Kenneth N. "The Spread of Nuclear Weapons: More May Be Better." *Adelphi Papers* 21, no. 171 (1981).

Wareham, Mary. "Dispatches: How to Stop US Production of Banned Cluster Munitions." Human Rights Watch, 16 June 2016. https://www.hrw.org/news/2016/06/16/dispatches-how-stop-us-production-banned-cluster-munitions.

Watanuki, Reiko, Yuko Yoshida, and Kiyoko Futagami. *Radioactive Contamination and the Health of Women and Post-Chernobyl Children.* Chernobyl Health Survey and Healthcare for the Victims—Japan Women's Network, 2006.

Whitlam, Gough. *The Whitlam Government 1972–1975.* Melbourne: Penguin, 1985.

Whyte, Sally. "'Horror, Humour and Hope' Getting ICAN's Message through Nuclear Disarmament Circus." *Crikey*, 10 October 2017. https://www.crikey.com.au/2017/10/10/humour-horror-and-hope-getting-icans-message-through-nuclear-disarmament-circus.

Wilson, Ward. *Five Myths about Nuclear Weapons.* Boston: Houghton Mifflin Harcourt, 2013.

———. "The Myth of Nuclear Deterrence." *Nonproliferation Review* 15, no. 3 (2008): 421–39.

Wittner, Lawrence S. *Confronting the Bomb: A Short History of the World Nuclear Disarmament Movement.* Stanford, CA: Stanford University Press, 2009.

———. "Nuclear Disarmament Activism in Asia and the Pacific, 1971–1996." *Asia-Pacific Journal* 5:25, no. 5 (15 June 2009). https://apjjf.org/-Lawrence-S.-Wittner/3179/article.html.

Wolfe, Raymond O. Statement to the UN General Assembly First Committee on Disarmament and International Security, New York, 6 October 2010. http://www.reachingcriticalwill.org/images/documents/Disarmament-fora/1com/1com10/statements/6Oct_Jamaica.pdf.

Wolfsthal, Jon, Jeffrey Lewis, and Marc Quint. "The One Trillion-Dollar Triad—US Strategic Nuclear Modernization over the Next Thirty Years." James Martin Center for Nonproliferation Studies, January 2014. http://www.nonproliferation.org/wp-content/uploads/2016/04/140107_trillion _dollar_nuclear_triad.pdf.

Women, Disarmament, Non-Proliferation and Arms Control, A/C.1/71/L.37. UN General Assembly First Committee on Disarmament and International Security, New York, 14 October 2016. http://www.reachingcriticalwill.org/ images/documents/Disarmament-fora/1com/1com16/resolutions/L37.pdf.

Wood, Robert. Explanation of vote on A/C.1/73/L.54 to the UN General Assembly First Committee on Disarmament and International Security, New York, 1 November 2018.

———. "Mexico still pursuing an unacceptable OEWG resolution. Aim is to subvert established disarmament machinery. It will not succeed." 29 October 2015, 11:06. Tweet. https://twitter.com/USAmbCD/status/ 659793495222276096.

"Working Towards the Elimination of Nuclear Weapons." Resolution 1, Council of Delegates of the International Red Cross and Red Crescent Movement, Geneva, Switzerland, 26 November 2011. https://www.icrc.org/eng/ resources/documents/resolution/council-delegates-resolution-1-2011.htm.

"World Nuclear Forces." *Stockholm International Peace Research Institute Yearbook*. https://www.sipri.org/yearbook.

Wright, Tim. "Australia's Opposition to a Nuclear Weapon Ban." International Campaign to Abolish Nuclear Weapons, 18 October 2016. http://www .icanw.org/campaign-news/australias-opposition-to-a-nuclear-weapon-ban.

———. "Next Stop, a Ban on Nuclear Weapons?" *Truthout*, 26 March 2013. http://www.truth-out.org/opinion/item/15318-next-stop-a-ban-on -nuclear-weapons.

Yee, Albert. "The Causal Effects of Ideas on Policies." *International Organization* 50, no. 1 (1996): 69–108.

Yermakov, Vladimir. Statement to the UN General Assembly First Committee on Disarmament and International Security, New York, 22 October 2013.

———. Statement to the UN General Assembly First Committee on Disarmament and International Security, New York, 21 October 2015. http://www.reachingcriticalwill.org/images/documents/Disarmament -fora/1com/1com15/statements/21October_Russia.pdf.

———. Statement to UN General Assembly First Committee on Disarmament and International Security, New York, 27 October 2016.

York, Herbert. "The Nuclear 'Balance of Terror' in Europe." *Ambio* 4, no. 5/6 (1975): 203–8.

Zabarte, Ian. "Indigenous Peoples Condemn Nuclear Colonialism on 'Columbus' Day," *PopularResistance.org*, 10 October 2016. https://popularresistance.org/indigenous-peoples-condemn-nuclear-colonialism-on-columbus-day.

Zak, Dan. *Almighty: Courage, Resistance, and Existential Peril in the Nuclear Age.* New York: Penguin, 2017.

————. "The Prophets of Oak Ridge." *Washington Post*, 30 April 2013. http://www.washingtonpost.com/sf/wp-style/2013/09/13/the-prophets-of-oak-ridge.

————. "U.N. Nuclear Conference Collapses over WMD-Free Zone in Middle East." *Washington Post*, 22 May 2015. https://www.washingtonpost.com/world/national-security/un-nuclear-conference-collapses-over-wmd-free-zone-in-the-middle-east/2015/05/22/8c568380-fe39-11e4-8c77-bf27 4685e1df_story.html?utm_term=.2e3ad68905f7.

Zarate, Robert. "Albert and Roberta Wohlstetter on Nuclear-Age Strategy." In *Nuclear Heuristics: Selected Writings of Albert and Roberta Wohlstetter*, edited by Robert Zarate and Henry Sokolski, 1–90. Carlisle, PA: Strategic Studies Institute, U.S. Army War College, January 2009.

Zero Draft of the Report of the Open-ended Working Group Taking forward Multilateral Nuclear Disarmament Negotiations, A/AC.286/L.1, 28 July 2016. http://www.reachingcriticalwill.org/images/documents/Disarmament-fora/OEWG/2016/Documents/A_AC.286_L.1.pdf.

INDEX

 актуаль

Eisenhower, Dwight D., 208
elimination, of nuclear weapons, xxi–xxiii, 2, 9–10, 13, 25, 32, 33, 51, 54, 56–60, 81, 87, 91, 95–96, 108, 110, 133, 145, 161, 164–65, 169–70, 179, 182, 186, 189, 205, 220–21, 260 277, 282; provisions for in ban treaty, 240–44, 292; timeframe for, 51–52, 79, 93, 109
Ellsberg, Daniel, 14–17
El Salvador, 188
Emba, Christine, 75
emotion: as derogatory accusation, 16–17, 30, 32, 85, 201–2, 273–74, 289; as positive motivator, 175, 207
empire, 19, 22, 38
Emu Field, 35
Eniwetok Atoll, 34
Enloe, Cynthia, 20–21, 29
environment: activism to protect, xxiii, 6, 63, 69, 89, 286–87, 295; harm to, 2, 24, 68, 77–78, 87, 105, 154, 159, 170, 177, 187–89, 229, 237, 248; remediation of, 228, 248–50, 268–69
Eschle, Catherine, 31
Ethiopia, 46, 154
Europe, 40, 48–49, 50, 139, 141–42, 152, 176, 184, 208, 210, 216, 245, 287
explosive weapons, 106

Falk, Richard, 22–23
famine, 10, 76
Fangataufa, 35
Fat Man, 16
fear, 1, 32, 56–57, 80, 83, 182, 189, 214, 220–21, 258, 291, 295

feminist, xx, 4, 5–6, 9, 21, 84, 85, 103–4, 115, 140, 194, 280, 294–95; activism, 26, 69, 92, 94, 107, 132, 133, 293; analysis of nuclear weapons, 26–33, 37, 45, 108, 293
fetishization, of nuclear weapons, 17, 23–26
Fiji, 38, 48, 152, 210
financing nuclear weapons, xxii, 19, 51, 59, 105, 109, 111–12, 165, 230, 236–39, 266, 267, 289
First Nations. *See* Indigenous
fissile materials treaty, 181
Forsberg, Randall, 48
Foucault, Michel, 84
France, 61, 70–71, 72–74, 100, 203, 287; nuclear weapon testing, 34–35, 38, 46, 48; opposition to humanitarian initiative, 160, 167; opposition to prohibition, 30–31, 184, 217, 224; support for nuclear weapons, 11, 98
Fraser, Nancy, 28–29
French Polynesia, 34–35

gaslighting, 33, 42, 215, 224, 288–89
Georgescu, Calin, 36
Geneva Conventions, 89, 90, 173, 251–52
Geneva Forum, 106
gender, 8, 14, 18 20, 26–33, 35–36, 85–86, 107, 137, 140–41, 154, 175, 224, 254–56, 260, 273–74, 276–77, 292–93. *See also* humanitarian impacts of nuclear weapons, gendered
Germany, 152, 166, 172, 211–12, 244, 287